# Look Smarter Than You Are with Oracle Analytics Cloud Standard

## interRel Consulting

1st Edition

interRel Press, Arlington, Texas

# Look Smarter Than You Are
# with Oracle Analytics Cloud Standard

## interRel Consulting

Published by:
interRel Press
A Division of interRel Consulting Partners
1000 Ballpark Way, Suite 304
Arlington, TX 76011

Library of Congress Cataloging-in-Publication Data
interRel Consulting
Look Smarter Than You Are with Oracle Analytics Cloud Standard

interRel Consulting 1st ed.
p. 719 cm.
Includes index.
978-1-387-01145-2

**Trademarks**

Various trademarked names appear throughout this book. Rather than list all the names and the companies/individuals that own those trademarks or try to insert a trademark symbol every time a trademarked name is mentioned, the author and publisher state that they are using the names only for editorial purposes and to the benefit of the trademark owner with no intention of trademark infringement.

This book is dedicated to 20 years of excellence at interRel Consulting and its founder, Edward Roske. During the past two decades, Edward has fearlessly led his amazing team at interRel to many achievements, including Specialized EPM/BI Partner of the Year, Global EPM/BI Cloud Partner of the Year, and over 1,000 successful projects.

Edward, you are an inspiration to us all.

Thanks to you, we at interRel will always be part of a family that delivers best practice business analytics solutions while laughing and having fun along the way.

# ABOUT THE AUTHORS AND EDITORS

This book is an interRel collaboration of many, many people. Primary authors and editors are:

## Opal Alapat (interRel Oracle EPM Cloud Specialist, Cloud Oracle ACE, ODTUG Board of Directors)

Opal refuses to date herself, so all she'll say is that she's been wandering around in the EPM and BI space for almost 20 years…and something about how side ponytails need to be back in style again. Since joining interRel, Opal has been immersed in all things Oracle EPM/BI Cloud. She's been writing, speaking, and training on Oracle EPM & EPM Cloud technologies, as well as working with the Oracle Product teams on Enterprise Performance Reporting Cloud, Enterprise Planning Cloud, Financial Close & Consolidation Cloud, and Oracle Analytics Cloud (OAC). She was honored to earn Oracle ACE Associate status in 2016, then Cloud Oracle ACE status in 2017. When not evangelizing Oracle software, Opal enjoys working on her second and third (volunteer) jobs, the Oracle user groups ODTUG and NTxHUG, as well as being a complete goofball at home and eating her way through Dallas' new and exciting cuisines. Visit Opal's blog at http://womaninepm.com/ or follow her on Twitter at @opal_EPM.

## Sarah Branhagen (interRel Consultant)

Sarah's interest in computers started when she was a little girl. When not involved in soccer, tennis, basketball, or gymnastics, she could almost always be found in front of a computer. She started her career as an Administrator for a marketing firm working for various wholesaler companies. There, her love for learning (particularly learning client systems and learning them swiftly) was quickly discovered. Due to a "realignment" that left her with thirty-three clients to maintain (true story), she left and started working for a company that creates and sustains fully-integrated databases for K-12 education in her native state of Texas. It was there she discovered her fascination with complex databases, and after a couple of years moved on to become an IT consultant. She has been consulting, focusing on Enterprise Performance Management solutions with an emphasis on planning, budgeting, and forecasting applications ever since.

## Robert Gideon (Principal Consultant, Oracle ACE, OAUG EPM/Hyperion SIG Co-Coordinator)

Robert, a longtime Edward groupie, began his work in Hyperion 11 years ago as an Essbase Administrator. After a few years of looking smarter than he really was, he joined forces with interRel. Robert loves building things with his hands in his spare time whether it's an engine overhaul or remodeling his home. With certifications in Essbase, Planning, and Exalytics, he has worked with nearly all of the Oracle EPM products at some point. Follow Robert on Twitter at @rjgideon and visit his blog at http://cubistramblings.wordpress.com.

## Rich Magee (interRel Consultant Lead)

Rich started in the OLAP world in the 1980's with a product known as "System W", which provided multi-dimensional modeling on a mainframe. For you younger folks, a "mainframe" used to take up an entire room…and now the same computing power is available on a laptop. Rich caught the Essbase bug way back in the early 1990's. He has worked in the EPM space for his entire career. In 2008 he joined interRel and now enjoys working on all aspects of Oracle EPM. Rich is a certified Essbase professional and is also specialized in all of the available Cloud EPM products. He enjoys his work in the EPM world because he sees each application as a puzzle. His job is to put the puzzle pieces together. He keeps his technical skills sharp by consistently learning new products and innovative ways to help interRel's customers achieve their business needs through the use of Oracle products.

## Tracy McMullen (interRel Director of Strategic Projects, Oracle ACE Director, OAUG Planning Domain Lead)

Tracy, a.k.a. Goddess of all things Oracle EPM and now Oracle EPM Cloud, has been leading the development of EPM and Data Warehousing applications for over 15 years. She co-wrote the Oracle Essentials certification exams with Oracle for Hyperion Planning, Hyperion Financial Management, Essbase, and Data Relationship Management. As if those achievements weren't enough, she's also a certified Project Management Professional (PMP). She's a regular speaker, instructor, mentor, proponent of women in technology, and visionary leader. She currently holds the title for most Hyperion books authored by a single person. Her strong technical background is complemented by comprehensive practical experience, a skill important not only on the job but at home as well where she manages her kids on a daily basis (ok, she attempts to, but with moderate success). Tracy calls interRel "home" and has been there for 10+ years. She is currently the Director of Strategic Projects. Follow Tracy on Twitter at @TracyAMcMullen1.

## Glenn Schwartzberg (interRel Analytics Practice Lead, Oracle ACE Director)

Glenn Schwartzberg has been an IT professional for over 35 years, yet he still knows very little. He doesn't really exist, but is actually a pseudonym for George Clooney, who does not want anyone to know that he has a technical background. (Anyone believing this?) Glenn started his career in IT working on IBM mainframes writing COBOL and CICS programs. In the late '80s he entered the world of consulting and became a DBA on Teradata DBC1012 computers. In 1991, he ran into a little program from Arbor Software called Essbase. Glenn immediately saw its value, so he started learning all he could about it. In 2008, he was honored with the title of Oracle ACE in Business Intelligence. In 2010, he was privileged to be awarded Oracle ACE Director. Glenn continues to share his knowledge of Essbase and its associated products though Oracle EPM discussion forums, conference presentations, user group meetings, webcasts, and his blog (it has the longest name in history): http://glennschwartzbergs-essbase-blog.blogspot.com/. He has worked extensively with Oracle Product Development on Smart View, Oracle Analytics Cloud (OAC), and Essbase. When he's not busy serving as the Analytics Practice Lead for interRel Consulting, he spends his time as a volunteer referee officiating youth soccer matches.

## Edward Roske (interRel CEO, Oracle ACE Director)

Edward, the leader of the vast interRel empire, was hit by the Hyperion cupid waaaaaay back in 1995. When he saw his first demo of Arbor Essbase (as it was known at the time), he quit his job to become a full-time Essbase consultant. He then went on to become one of the world's first Essbase Certified consultants. He was also one of the first people in the world to become certified in Hyperion Planning. In May of 1997, Edward co-founded interRel Consulting. He has been the CEO of interRel ever since, growing the company to a multi-million dollar firm that spans coast to coast.

Edward still keeps his technical skills sharp and you can find him evangelizing Oracle EPM and BI (and now Oracle EPM and BI Cloud), as well as billing on customer projects. Edward continues to be a regular speaker at conferences, and he's known for his humorous slant on boring technical information. In the last ~20 years, Edward has spoken to over 10,000 people in 15+ countries across five continents. Visit Edward's blog at http://looksmarter.blogspot.com/ or follow him on Twitter at @ERoske.

### Wayne Van Sluys (interRel Senior Consultant, Oracle ACE)

Wayne started programming computers with an Apple II+ and thought that Computer Science would be a great major in college. But alas, that was not to be – a Bachelor of Science in Psychology was in his future, and soon after, a Master's degree in Education Policy and Leadership from Ohio State University. His professional life started in University Student Services and Residence Life, but he kept dabbling in information systems. In 1998, Wayne left higher education for corporate life and was introduced to the world of Business Intelligence. His life was inextricably changed. He often wishes his advisor in college would have introduced him to Management Information Systems. He soon started giving back to the BI Technical Community by speaking at Brio Software Conferences, then Hyperion Worldwide Solutions, and now BIWA, Kscope, and Oracle Open World conferences. In 2007, Wayne was introduced to the world of EPM, and he has been splitting his time between BI and EPM ever since. In his free time, Wayne enjoys time with his wife working in their gardens, traveling, and hiking.

# ABOUT INTERREL CONSULTING

Founded in 1997, interRel Consulting is the longest-standing Hyperion partner dedicated solely to implementing EPM/BI solutions for Fortune 500 and mid-size companies, and is the only four-time winner of Oracle's Specialized Partner of the Year for BI and EPM. interRel is the 2016 Global EPM & BI Cloud Partner of the Year.

The company is a nine-time Inc. 5000 honoree committed to education with a platform that includes 10+ books in its best-selling technical reference series, *Look Smarter Than You Are with Hyperion*; free, twice-weekly webcasts; the free-access video education platform, Play it Forward, on YouTube; and multi-track EPM/BI Solutions conferences across the U.S. and Canada. Home to three Oracle ACE Directors, two Oracle ACE's (including the world's first Cloud Oracle ACE), and one Oracle ACE Associate, interRel frequently participates in Oracle Technology Network international tours in developing markets. To learn more about interRel Consulting, please visit www.interRel.com.

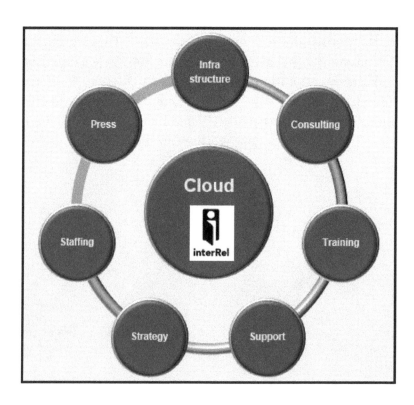

# ACKNOWLEDGEMENTS

If we were to thank all of those who assisted us in the creation of this book, we would have to not only personally mention hundreds of people but also several companies and one or two federal agencies (though we will give a special shout-out to those wacky guys over at the Internal Revenue Service: keep it real, yo!). Suffice to say, if this book stands tall, it is only by balancing on the heads of giants.

Thank you to the following individuals who provided significant contributions to this book (content, proofing, and more): Dawn Frost, Bernie Han, and Justin Haley.

We also want to thank some folks from Oracle whose help was invaluable in writing this book: Karen Imber, Pete Monteiro, Kumar Ramaiyer, Gabby Rubin, and Eric Smadja. Karen and Gabby, thanks also for helping us to set up our own OAC instance!

Finally, a big thank you to Oracle for allowing us to use some of their sample objects and data, specifically Sample.Basic, KoolKart samples, and Vision.

We give our sincerest gratitude to all the people above, and we hope that they feel that this book is partly theirs as well (just without the fame, glory, and most importantly, the royalties).

# DISCLAIMER

This book is designed to provide supporting information about the related subject matter. It is being sold to you and/or your company with the understanding that the author and the publisher are not engaged by you to provide legal, accounting, or any other professional services of any kind. If assistance is required (legal, expert, or otherwise), seek out the services of a competent professional such as a consultant.

It is not the purpose of this book to reprint all of the information that is already available on the subject at hand. The purpose of this book is to complement and supplement other texts already available to you. For more information, please see the Oracle documentation.

Great effort has been made to make this book as complete and accurate as possible. That said, there may be errors, both typographic and in content. In addition, due to the accelerated software updates provided by Oracle for BI Cloud, you might see slight differences in the screenshots and navigation steps compared to your version of Cloud. Therefore, use this book only as a general guide and not as the ultimate source for specific information on the software product. Further, this book contains information on the software that was generally available as of the publishing date. Please note that Oracle Cloud products are ever-changing and some differences are likely to be found between this book and the current versions of the Cloud products.

The purpose of this book is to entertain while educating. The authors and interRel Press shall have neither liability nor responsibility to any person, living or dead, or entity, currently or previously in existence, with respect to any loss or damage caused or alleged to be caused directly, indirectly, or otherwise by the information contained in this book.

We've included a storyline to go along with the educational Cloud content – a parody on a recent book and movie. No real clients were harmed in the making of this book

**If you do not wish to abide by all parts of the above disclaimer, please stop reading now and return this book to the publisher for a full refund.**

# FOREWORD

When the interRel team asked me to write the foreword to this book, they probably thought it would be a short recommendation for people to buy and read the book. However, since the release of Oracle Analytics Cloud, those same individuals (I'm talking to you Opal, Glenn, and Edward) have been hammering me with emails, phone calls, text messages, and tweets. As a result, while the book is great and contains a lot of information that I believe many will find useful – do not buy it. These people have no respect for personal time, holidays, and lunch breaks. By buying this book you are not only supporting such behavior, but also enticing them to write more books. If you already bought the book, the link to the Amazon return policy page will be posted at the end.

Now that we got that out of the way, let's move ahead with the foreword.

Probably the worst and the most cliché way to start a book foreword is to use an overused and unoriginal quote: "The only thing that never changes is that everything changes," attributed to Louis L'Amour (which is probably an adaptation of an earlier quote by Heraclitus). For the most part, especially in technology, this seems to be true. Nevertheless, sometimes the recipe to success is the acknowledgment that some things don't really change – we only come up new, smarter, and hopefully better ways to cater to the same needs. Social networks transformed the way that we communicate, express ourselves, and seek recognition (and attention). Smartphones changed the way that we consume information and entertainment. Uber changed the way that we use public transportation. However, the core needs that these technologies addressed pre-dated the technology. Some of the most successful and innovative products that we use today did not convince us that we needed something new, but successfully re-imagined ways to serve our existing, basic needs.

Business Analytics is no different. In the last few years we've seen an accelerated rate of innovation that has not only addressed the explosive growth of data that enterprises accumulate and access, but also empowered the business users with interactive capabilities that, just a few years ago, required long and complex IT projects. Business Analytics serves our needs to understand our business and make the right decisions for the future in a dynamic and complex marketplace. Staying true to these core needs and values is the basis of Oracle Analytics Cloud, coupled with new capabilities aimed at addressing current and future challenges, reducing complexities, and finding smarter ways to enable our users to achieve their goals. These concepts are at the heart of many of the innovations that went into the product, from learning user patterns on mobile applications to integrating machine learning capabilities into the user data discovery process, as well as the ability to automatically analyze and design Essbase cubes based on any data source.

While many of the new abilities might not be directly related to a Cloud infrastructure, the Cloud has an important role to play in removing obstacles and empowering our customers. Essbase is probably one of the best examples for that. When Essbase was first introduced, it was a business led product – the business user would push a 3.5" floppy into his desktop (or a "server" under his desk), install it, and happily start gaining immediate business value. Fast forward 20+ years (and hundreds of regulations), and now Essbase needs to comply with strict security guidelines, IT procedures, and a host of other "Enterprise Readiness" aspects. These policies are very important, but might also be obstacles for the business. This is where a Cloud solution presents us with the opportunity to go back to the original, business-led deployments of Essbase, and allows the users to focus on the business value that they get out of Essbase, not the infrastructure management and instance administration.

As many organizations chart their unique Cloud journey, having a strong and capable partner community is one of the most important assets a product ecosystem can have. Partners bring to the table not just their skill sets, but also expertise and perspectives gained from multiple implementations. In that respect, having a partner share their knowledge in a book is always an exciting event for us, as it does not only have a greater reach, but it also provides the type of information and insights that might otherwise take an individual or an organization a long time to obtain. So if you choose to keep the book, I hope you will enjoy it and find it useful. If not…well, I warned you about these people.

Gabby Rubin
Sr. Director of Product Management at Oracle
June 8, 2017

P.S. Click here for the Amazon Return Policy Page.

# TABLE OF CONTENTS

# PROLOGUE: THE BUSINESS ANALYTICS MARTIAN

**LOG ENTRY FOR MISSION SPECIALIST EDWARD ROSKE**
*SOL 10, Entry 1*

I'm pretty much screwed.

That's my considered opinion. Screwed, and not in a good way.

Nine sols into what should be the best implementation of my life, and it's turned into a complete nightmare.

For the record… the implementation didn't die on Sol 9. Certainly the rest of my team thought it did, and I can't blame them. And they'll be right eventually.

So, where do I begin?

Oracle EPM Cloud. Oracle reaching out to send customers to the Cloud and expand the horizons of companies beyond traditional servers… blah, blah, blah. First Hyperion introduced System 9, creating a common workspace for all of the EPM (that's "Enterprise Performance Management" for newbies) products. They got accolades, fame, and a lovely Solutions conference in their honor. Oracle then bought Hyperion and improved the EPM solution to its current "Business Analytics" state. They got a press release and a boxed lunch at OpenWorld. And now we are flying in the clouds with Oracle's latest direction.

We were charged with what seemed like a straightforward mission. Implementing a best practice EPM and Business Analytics solution for the globe-dominating Juggling Wolverines Enterprises (JWE). JWE got its start about ten years ago with a pioneer and a passion for juggling wolverines. (Editor's Note: For additional details, read *Look Smarter Than You Are with Essbase*.)

After dominating the juggling wolverine entertainment industry, JWE expanded its pursuit of dominance by acquiring The Beverage Company (TBC). This infamous company sold colas, root beers, and

fruit sodas to markets across the United States. TBC's
analytic design was used as the training model for
Essbase multidimensional databases everywhere!

JWE didn't stop there, next acquiring the Vision
Company which sells computer hardware and software.
The latest acquisition for JWE was KoolKart, a
retailer of books, electronics, movies, clothing, and
more. Juggling Wolverine Enterprises was just your
typical run-of-the-mill amalgamated, consolidated,
multi-national entity.

Each of JWE's companies have unique requirements
to report, analyze, and plan. TBC needs a solution for
users to perform speed of light ad hoc analysis in
Excel. And while they love Excel (I mean really love
Excel), one visionary TBC analyst wants to see if
maybe there is a better way to analyze data through
visualizations instead of spreadsheets and
spreadsheets of numbers.

JWE's recent acquisition, KoolKart, has no
reporting and business intelligence solution. They are
struggling to report and analyze information out of
their ERP system, and we all know how challenging that
can be. They need visibility into revenue trends, and
Marketing wants to understand how social media could
provide insights into the reasons behind revenue
results. They also need visibility into costs across
business lines.

Vision Company needs a planning and forecasting
solution to plan revenue with driver-based
calculations and direct inputs. They also need a
robust narrative reporting solution.

So, that is my mission: to address the business
challenges facing JWE. Okay, not mine per se. Project
Commander McMullen was in charge. I was just one of
her crew along with i.n.t.e.r.R.e.l.'s best of the
best ACE specialists: Educator Mission Specialist Opal
Alapat, Essbase Pilot Robert Gideon, Data
Visualization Pilot Wayne Van Sluys, and Flight
Engineer Glenn Schwartzberg.

Actually, I was the lowliest member of her crew,
Edward Roske. I would only be "in command" of the
mission if I were the only remaining person.

What do you know? I'm in command.

It was a ridiculous sequence of events that led to me and the project almost dying. My client, JWE, needed the solution and fast. They were on board and ready to move forward before the IT roadblocks started. The hardware was too expensive. It would be costly to upgrade in the future. IT resources were scarce. Getting consensus from the JWE subsidiaries and finding a single solution to support unique requirements across multiple companies was going nowhere. So the project was not approved and the JWE companies were left without a solution.

On top of that, I was somehow catapulted into the vast expanse which is the Cloud. How, exactly? I don't know. I just know I'm stranded, and the crew thinks I'm dead along with the project. Why couldn't I be stranded on Mars where there aren't any clouds? Hence, the "I'm screwed" complaint. Really it was JWE that was screwed.

So, that's the situation. I have no way to communicate with i.n.t.e.r.R.e.l. or Earth. Everyone thinks the project is dead. The crew of the Ranger is no doubt mourning my loss as they travel back to Earth, not knowing that they are leaving me behind in this Oracle Cloud.

Oh well. Maybe someday a good-looking, A-list actor like Matt Damon will play me in the movie version of my story…

# CHAPTER 1: INTRODUCTION TO THE CLOUD

## THE DARK DAYS OF SERVERS

This is hard to believe, but in the not too distant past when companies wanted to implement enterprise software they had to call up a computer manufacturer, describe the exact specifications of the computer they wanted, and then wait a few weeks for the machine to be assembled and shipped to the company. Now, manufacturers – in an attempt to make computers built from off-the-shelf commodity parts sound more impressive – call these computers "servers."

When I started implementing Hyperion back in the '90s, all we had was Essbase, and it really didn't require much of a server. The servers back then often had a single CPU and, frankly, were less powerful than the average modern-day smartphone. The good news about this is that a so-called server could be bought by a CFO and placed under her desk without IT ever realizing it. One of these under-the-desk servers was powerful enough to host an entire finance department's implementation of Essbase.

Essbase grew up really quickly and servers did, too. By the turn of the century when Essbase 7 came out, most companies had data centers at their corporate headquarters. These "data centers" were basically a lot of raised, air conditioned floors housing all of the company's servers. Even though it was just a room of chilled computers off in the basement, IT realized that calling them data centers would make them sound more impressive. (Notice the tendency people have of "making things sound more impressive than they really are.")

Around 2004, Hyperion released System 9. It was an enterprise-class suite of EPM (Enterprise Performance Management) and BI (Business Intelligence) tools, and it took a trained professional to install System 9 on one or more servers. By this time, most enterprise-class products couldn't be installed by mere mortals.

At about the same time, IT departments realized that having a data center in the company's headquarters wasn't the best use of corporate office space, so they started to move their data centers off-site. Users would still access the servers as before, but they were now only connected to the corporate servers by – for lack of a better way to put it – really long cables. This is also about the time users stopped knowing where the servers were actually physically located. IT wasn't pleased when they realized that no one actually cared where the servers were physically located.

In mid-2007, Oracle bought Hyperion (now rebranded to "Oracle EPM") and helped turn it into a truly enterprise-class product (Hyperion only thought they already had one, but looking back, System 9 was really pitiful compared to what exists now).

With the onslaught of the Great Recession shortly after, IT departments were being forced to cut costs. One of the ways to lower spending was to move their data centers even farther away – preferably near a waterfall (hydroelectric power is cheap) and somewhere cold (to reduce air conditioning needs).

Since most companies couldn't afford to go buy their own building in Norway (in my mind all modern data centers are in Norway, surrounded by little villages straight out of *Frozen*), they started having other companies manage their data centers. So now we had data centers attached to our users by virtual cables and it turned out that no one really cared how their computers talked to the servers as long as it worked.

Now, jump ahead several years. In the days after the Great Recession, smartphones became a standard extension of people's hands. The web became the default place to go for information. Applications installed on computers started to become a thing of the past. And flying cars finally became available.

(That last sentence actually isn't true. Despite being promised flying cars since I was a kid, there still aren't flying cars. To be honest, it really annoys me that we'll have self-driving cars before flying cars...but I digress.)

In other words, we became comfortable with storing our information remotely because we could then access it any time from any device. We no longer have any idea where our servers are, who owns them, or how the magic happens that lets us talk to the servers. For all we know, there aren't even physical servers out there, and it turns out that no one really cares.

So to make it sound more impressive, we decided to call these far away servers owned by no one in particular that house data and run applications...the Cloud.

---

**LOG ENTRY FOR FLIGHT ENGINEER GLENN SCHWARTZBERG**
*SOL 10, Entry 1*

The JWE project is dead. And Edward is gone. The rest of the crew is devastated with the loss of our crew member. I have to say I was pretty shaken up at first, but now I'm starting to envision life without my frenemy and protagonist. Maybe losing Edward isn't such a bad thing? Wait. What am I thinking? Of course, what happened to Edward is a terrible tragedy. Shocking. Awful. Painful. Come on, tears! I know you are in there somewhere. I need to at least make a good show of mourning for the rest of the crew.

As we make our way back to Earth, I open up the latest webcast recording from i.n.t.e.r.R.e.l. Maybe learning about the Oracle Cloud will take our mind off this impossible situation.

---

## THE CLOUD

Yes, that's right. The "Cloud" is just a cool way of saying servers that are really far away that we don't own. Or to put it a different way, the Cloud is software and services that run on the internet.

Pause for a moment and look down at your smartphone. (It's probably in your hand, in your pocket, or at worst, within arm's reach.) Notice the applications you use most: email, messages, weather, browser, etc. Each one of these is a Cloud application. Your email isn't really stored on your phone: it's on a far flung server somewhere. Your messages are bouncing all around people's servers that you couldn't locate even if you wanted to. The weather app is accessing data stored someplace else. The browser is pulling up information stored around the world. And so on. *Your smartphone is a Cloud-access device.*

As consumers, we're completely comfortable with the Cloud. We don't think we understand the Cloud, but that's just because people have been trying to make us think the Cloud is some complicated thing that can only be understood by rocket surgeons. (I blame the movie *Sex Tape* for this, but I tend to blame that movie for a lot of what's wrong in the world.)

The Cloud has a lot of benefits. Companies no longer have to buy servers. No one has to install (and then forever patch) software on the servers. There's no need to manage the server because *it's now someone else's problem.*

At the time I'm writing this, some IT departments who should know better are afraid of the Cloud (which is weird because those same people in IT are comfortable with their whole personal life being on the Cloud). Is our data secure in the Cloud? What if the Cloud crashes? Is the software in the Cloud any good? Will it slow things down to put them in the Cloud?

A lot of this is fear of the unknown, and, speaking from the standpoint of someone who just lost a crewmate to the Cloud, I have a lot of that fear myself. I know I shouldn't be scared: Cloud companies should be a whole lot better at security than I am. They are better at making sure things shouldn't crash than I am, and they are probably running their Cloud products on far faster servers than I could ever hope to buy… but nonetheless, I'm filled with uncertainty and doubt. Plus the idea that I'm no longer owning my software but rather renting it by the month is a little unnerving (though I do lease my car and rent my apartment).

To recap the key definitions:

- **Cloud** – software and services that run on the Internet; physical infrastructure (servers) in massive data centers all over the world
    - o   Centrally hosted, limiting additional hardware
    - o   Accessed via thin client or web browser
- **SaaS** (Software as a Service) – software licensing and delivery model
    - o   Software is licensed on a subscription basis – "pay as you grow"

- **PaaS** (Platform as a Service) – platform offering with different licensing and delivery model from SaaS; provides a platform allowing customers to develop, run, and manage applications without the complexity of building and maintaining the infrastructure
    o OAC software is a PaaS solution and is licensed based on OCPUs (Oracle CPU's); also "pay as you grow"…but different
- **IaaS** (Infrastructure as a Service) – provides virtualized computing resources over the Internet

### Cloud Benefits

The Cloud provides a number of benefits to companies including facilitating the expansion to new geographies, products, or departments. Lower software fees could be found with a SaaS or PaaS model. IT costs are absolutely reduced with fewer personnel and less equipment required. Related to business analytics, the Cloud can accelerate EPM and BI adoption within your organization. An intuitive user interface means a reduction in training costs. The Cloud allows companies to focus on analytics versus software support.

Oracle Cloud offerings are available via a monthly subscription with self-service sign-up, instant provisioning, self-service management, and self-service monitoring.

### Cloud Challenges & Considerations

The Cloud is not without some challenges, including security management, target and source integration, defining new strategies between IT and the business, what to do with existing software investments, and compliance and reliability concerns.

---

```
LOG ENTRY FOR FLIGHT ENGINEER GLENN SCHWARTZBERG
SOL 10, Entry 2

    Is the Cloud "ready" for me? Is it ready for
i.n.t.e.r.R.e.l. to implement or JWE to use? I think
that it's not a matter of if I'll be using the Cloud,
but rather when. It seems like it's coming faster than
```

anyone expected, so maybe it isn't a bad thing after
all.
    With that comforting knowledge, I took stock of
what's in the Cloud for Oracle EPM and BI and here's
the situation.

## ORACLE ENTERPRISE PLANNING CLOUD

In 2014, Oracle rolled out its first EPM Cloud product, and they
called it Planning and Budgeting Cloud Service (PBCS). In the early days
of the Cloud, companies took their on-premises (also known as "on-
premise" by contrarian grammarians or "on-prem" by people in too
much of a hurry to utter two extra syllables) products and released
limited versions of those products on the Cloud. In Oracle's case, they
took Hyperion Planning (which had been around since 2001 and had
thousands of companies using it), installed it on some Oracle Exalytics
servers, changed the front end a little, and called it PBCS.

PBCS is a Cloud solution to support planning, forecasting,
reporting, and analysis requirements for an organization. Key features
include:

- Structured user interfaces to collect and display plans and actuals
  data
- Customizable tasks and navigation flows to guide users through
  defined processes
- Secured, central repository for dimensions, data, and
  calculations
- Powerful business rules and calculations
- Fast reporting and analysis with Financial Reporting and in Excel
  with the Oracle Smart View add-in
- Approvals and process management
- Data integration capabilities using Data Management

Highlights of the benefits of PBCS include shortened planning
cycles, improved plan and forecast accuracy, flexible modeling and
"what-if" analysis, and fast and easy deployments.

The customer designs and implements the PBCS application to support their specific requirements. This means they create and import their dimensions, build calculation rules, and build end user data forms and reports. PBCS contains out of the box features and functions, but does not provide out of the box business process frameworks.

Oracle wasn't sure if companies were ready for a Cloud-based EPM solution, but in less than 2 years after the launch of PBCS, over 750 companies had bought it, making it the #1 Cloud-based budgeting product in the world.

Next, Oracle introduced the Oracle Enterprise Planning Cloud option (referred to as EPBCS). EPBCS is a world-class Cloud solution that balances built-in best practice, configurable frameworks with high flexibility. At its core, it leverages the robust Planning and Budgeting Cloud technology, which provides familiar features for powerful analytics, dashboarding, reporting, predicting, and planning. A number of pre-configured, best-in-breed frameworks are delivered with the Enterprise Planning solution and can save customers time when implementing solutions for:

- Financials planning, including income statement, balance sheet, and cash flow (with driver-based or direct input for revenue and expense planning)
- Strategic Modeling (a throwback to the Hyperion Strategic Finance technology)
- Workforce planning
- Capital assets planning
- Project planning

Customers can upgrade their Enterprise Planning Cloud framework to suit their needs as their business grows. If a customer buys PBCS, there are options directly within the tool to upgrade to EPBCS. Enterprise Planning Cloud is easy to use and easy to maintain through its wizards and intuitive interfaces. It allows customers to spend more time running the business and less time maintaining planning processes. It fits both finance and operational needs by offering scalability to evolve with the business, in addition to transparency and control. The federated architecture allows for operational independence and an aligned planning solution.

In summary, the two pricing scenarios offered today are:

- Original PBCS solution called Oracle Planning and Budgeting Cloud - contains no prebuilt frameworks:

- Enterprise Planning Cloud (also called EPBCS) - contains prebuilt frameworks to support the entire enterprise-wide planning function:

Oracle sells these Cloud services through the SaaS model: Software as a Service. As I mentioned earlier, you pay by the month to use the software instead of paying a huge amount up front to own the software (and then still having to pay a monthly amount to Oracle to support the software).

## BUSINESS INTELLIGENCE CLOUD/DATA VISUALIZATION CLOUD

In September 2014, Oracle released the next Cloud product in the Oracle Business Analytics space: BICS (Business Intelligence Cloud). Technically, it's an Oracle BI product (not EPM) but it's in the same family at Oracle and delivers analytics and reporting over the web. It's similar to PBCS in that it took an existing on-premises product, OBIEE (Oracle Business Intelligence Enterprise Edition) and ported it to the Cloud.

It is a different animal than Enterprise Planning Cloud, though, because while Enterprise Planning Cloud delivers application-ready functionality, BICS is more of a platform waiting for you to build your own solutions on top of it. As such, it is not considered to be a SaaS solution, but rather PaaS (Platform as a Service). PaaS is sometimes priced per user and for a set amount of storage. In the case of BICS, Oracle does both. They charge you a monthly fee per user, and then they also charge you a flat monthly fee for the underlying Oracle Database Schema Service (sometimes called "DBaaS" or "Database as a Schema").

Like Enterprise Planning Cloud before it, BICS quickly started adding functionality that its on-premises version (OBIEE) did not have. Later, one of these awesome features, Visual Analyzer, became available as a stand-alone product outside of BICS. In November 2015, Oracle started selling DVCS (Data Visualization Cloud), which was cheaper than BICS (since it was a subset of BICS) and didn't require a separate fee for the underlying database. Data Visualization Cloud focuses on the Visual Analyzer (VA) feature from BICS. DVCS allows users to upload and blend data files and then visualize the data in a multitude of graphical presentations. Users can then share insights and "tell a story" using the Story Teller mode. Just think… no more death by PowerPoint! Keep discussions interactive and present! DVCS is fully mobile supported and requires 50% fewer clicks to create dashboards (when compared to competitors' tools and BICS Answers and Dashboards).

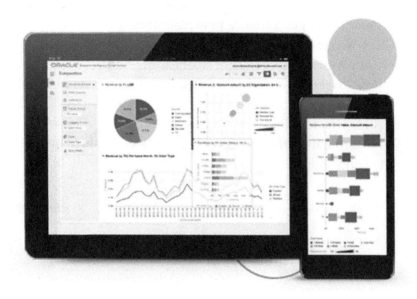

In 2017, Oracle decided to merge Essbase, BICS, and Data Visualizer into one and called it Oracle Analytics Cloud. I'll discuss this in just a moment since I'm taking a chronological approach to introducing Oracle's EPM and BI Cloud products.

LOG ENTRY FOR FLIGHT ENGINEER GLENN SCHWARTZBERG
SOL 10, Entry 3

Some BI purists will wonder why we are talking about "EPM" in a "BI" book. The divide of BI versus EPM has always irked Project Commander McMullen. Each involves solutions to help users make better decisions, and they will always go hand in hand.

## ENTERPRISE PERFORMANCE REPORTING CLOUD

Users have been asked to explain their numbers since, roughly, the beginning of time. When the first tax collector came to the first pharaoh to show him that the expected tax revenue fell short of projections, pharaoh had him beheaded before he could explain that tax revenue was down due to a series of plagues befalling the country. Sadly, the idea that narration should accompany the numbers died with him (and all subsequent tax collectors who simply showed pharaoh the numbers and never got a chance to explain them).

Yes, my knowledge of ancient times apparently is limited to the existence of pharaohs, tax collectors, beheadings, and plagues... and I'm not totally sure there were beheadings. But my point is still valid: the world needs narration, because numbers alone don't tell the whole story. In July 2015, Oracle released Enterprise Performance Reporting Cloud (EPRCS) to solve that problem (and hopefully end future metaphorical corporate beheadings).

Enterprise Performance Reporting Cloud is not only Oracle's solution for narrative reporting, it's also their first Oracle EPM product to exist only in the Cloud. Created from day one to be a Cloud solution (and not a port of an on-premises product), EPRCS lets users author report packages, review them, and collect commentary on the packages no matter where the data (or the user, for that matter) resides. Like PBCS, EPRCS is sold using a SaaS model.

## ACCOUNT RECONCILIATION CLOUD

Oracle Account Reconciliation Cloud is a purpose-built Cloud-based solution that manages, supports, and improves the global account reconciliation process. Leveraging the capabilities of the current release of on-premises Account Reconciliation Manager (ARM), it reduces risk and increases efficiency by leveraging prebuilt reconciliation formats and automating certain reconciliation tasks. Customers can also choose to create their own custom solutions. Built upon best practices for global reconciliation, this solution provides an intuitive interface, interactive and real-time dashboards, and instant visibility into the reconciliation process. Collaboration is driven by role-based tasks and work areas, signoffs, and approvals. Oracle Account Reconciliation Cloud provides flexible balance mapping rules; rule-based thresholds; workflow and audit capabilities; and reporting, monitoring, and analysis. It can integrate data from ERP (that's "Enterprise Resource Planning" for those of you not familiar) and EPM systems and supplemental data sources like spreadsheets and databases. Oracle Account Reconciliation Cloud follows the Software as a Service (SaaS) licensing model.

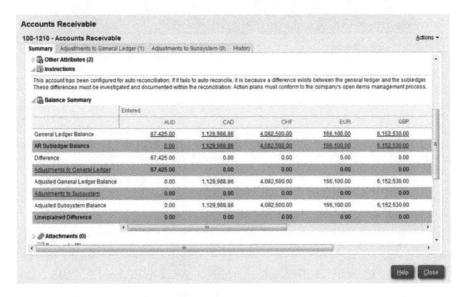

# FINANCIAL CONSOLIDATION & CLOSE CLOUD

Oracle Financial Consolidation & Close Cloud (FCCS) is a new, enterprise-wide Cloud solution that provides a consolidation solution to optimize the close cycle. Just to be clear, this is NOT "HFM on the Cloud." FCCS is a newly architected, alternative end-to-end consolidation solution built upon Essbase and delivered on the Cloud. It can be implemented quickly and with less stress and maintenance by providing out of the box functionality. It gives customers visibility into all of the close, consolidation, data collection and management, workflow, audit, monitoring, reporting, and lights out processes. In addition, it can connect to core source systems and comes prebuilt with cash flow, balance sheet, and income statement reporting. It supports IFRS, GAAP, and Multi-GAAP so that customers can feel confident and secure with their regulatory-compliant solution. Some of the common business processes included are full currency support, intercompany eliminations, equity eliminations, adjustments, and detailed data tracking. It can also integrate with Microsoft Office and Enterprise Performance Reporting Cloud (EPRCS). Oracle Financial Consolidation & Close Cloud follows the Software as a Service (SaaS) licensing model.

And Oracle didn't stop there. At OpenWorld 2015, they announced that they would be the first company in the world to have a complete EPM suite in the Cloud. Starting early in 2016, they began to roll out Cloud products faster than any company before or since.

## PROFITABILITY AND COST MANAGEMENT CLOUD

Oracle Profitability and Cost Management Cloud (PCMCS) is a nearly fully ported version of the successful Management Ledger module of its sister on-premises product, Hyperion Profitability and

Cost Management (HPCM). PCMCS answers the most important questions for your organization:

- Am I as profitable as I could be?
- What percentage of my customers, products, channels, etc., are driving most of my profitability? Which ones are unprofitable?
- What proportion of resources do my customers, products, channels, etc., consume?
- What are my true costs to provide services or complete a business process?

PCMCS is a user-driven profitability and cost management solution. Business users create, update, and maintain cost allocation logic and profitability models (no scripting required!). It supports dashboarding, profit curves, KPIs, and ad hoc analysis in Excel via Smart View. PCMCS provides full transparency of allocation logic and rules; there are no black boxes in this solution.

This product is architected on an Essbase platform and allows customers to measure their costs and profitability with complex rule sets. Built with a fierce allocation engine, this technology can scale well across an enterprise while still providing flexibility and security. PCMCS is sold using a Software as a Service (SaaS) licensing model.

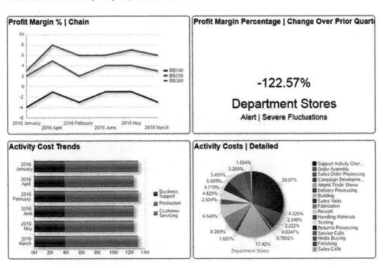

## TAX REPORTING CLOUD

Tax Reporting Cloud (TRCS) manages the collection, calculation, and distribution of tax information. This Cloud solution utilizes best practices in tax reporting, allows for tax process improvements, and provides collaboration and transparency between Finance and Tax. TRCS supports state/provincial, federal, and international tax requirements. TRCS integrates with both on-premises HFM and its sister Cloud consolidation service, FCCS. TRCS is sold using a Software as a Service (SaaS) licensing model.

## ORACLE ANALYTICS CLOUD

Essbase is finally in the Cloud! In March 2017, Oracle introduced Oracle Analytics Cloud. This Cloud offering provides a full Business Intelligence platform, combining Essbase Cloud, Data Visualization Cloud, and Business Intelligence Cloud together. Within Oracle Analytics Cloud, users can take advantage of the powerful multi-dimensional database, Essbase. Administrators can utilize web interfaces and tools (like Excel spreadsheets) to create and manage Essbase cubes. Essbase Cloud introduces new features compared to its on-premises sister, like sandboxing, scenario management, cell status visibility, and enhanced financial intelligence and aggregation. Users will be able to analyze data sets from DV, BI Cloud, or Excel via Smart View. Oracle Analytics Cloud follows the Platform as a Service (PaaS) licensing model. There are two flavors: Standard and Enterprise Edition.

In just over three years from launching their first EPM Cloud product, Oracle has a complete suite of EPM and BI Cloud solutions.

## HYBRID IMPLEMENTATION APPROACH

I was skeptical. What if a company had an on-premises solution and wasn't ready to move their entire EPM and BI suite? Would they be able to go entirely to the Cloud overnight? Luckily, Oracle EPM & Analytics Cloud was designed to work with the Oracle on-premises solutions. So let's say a company wanted to put part of their EPM/BI strategy into the Cloud and leave part of it in their data center. This is called a "hybrid" solution, and there are a number of ways it can play out:

- If your company has existing on-premises EPM tools, they can keep using those and deploy new products into the Cloud. For instance, maybe they've been using HFM for years for financial consolidation. They can still implement PBCS for forecasting and share the data with HFM using tools like FDMEE (Financial Data Quality Management Enterprise Edition).
- If your company likes the Oracle EPM/Analytic Cloud products, but is more comfortable with certain on-premises products, they can pay for servers and software up front for the on-premises solutions and pay as you go for the Cloud products.
- If your company wants production data to stay on-premises, they can still use the Cloud for developing applications. As long as you're on a fairly recent version of the equivalent on-premises product, the Cloud and on-premises applications can be migrated back and forth.
- If your corporation has divisions or departments around the world, you don't have to put all of them onto one platform. Your corporate headquarters might use on-premises Essbase while your remote offices use Essbase Cloud.

The most likely scenario is that a company with on-premises products will migrate them over time to the Cloud. As IT departments get tired of being hacked, get annoyed at users begging for newer versions, and get pressured to stop spending so much money up front, the Cloud adoption at your company will take off like a Martian rocket.

---

**LOG ENTRY FOR FLIGHT ENGINEER GLENN SCHWARTZBERG**
*SOL 10, Entry 4*

Okay. I've had the best night's sleep in years (may Edward rest in peace), and things don't seem as hopeless as they did yesterday. Watching the i.n.t.e.r.R.e.l. webcast and thinking about this Oracle Cloud revolution helped me to feel a little hopeful about JWE's situation. I'm wondering if we can bring part of the JWE project back to life using the Cloud? The Cloud addresses many of IT and Finance's concerns. No hardware required. And we get to pay for the software as we use it.

Now if we could only bring Edward back to life, too, you know, because someone out there must love him.

# CHAPTER 2: INTRODUCTION TO OAC

**Meanwhile, back on earth...**

i.n.t.e.r.R.e.l. Consultant Rich Magee stared at the ceiling, monitoring Cloud access. Implementing EPM solutions at i.n.t.e.r.R.e.l. had sounded exciting when Director Glen Chang had recruited him out of school. But it turns out that the Cloud actually monitors itself. His job turned out to involve merely sending emails.

As he scrolled through the PBCS activity log reports, he saw something that made his heart stop. A login for roske@interRel.com. But that project (and Edward WhatsHisName) was dead! Edward is dead! However, if he logged into the Cloud that could only mean one thing: the project was still alive, and Edward was trying to implement in the Cloud.

"I need Director Glen Chang's contact information now," he thought to himself. Director Chang was in charge of i.n.t.e.r.R.e.l. operations and would know what to do next.

## OAC DEFINED

These are exciting times that we're living in! This is the Essbase renaissance. Essbase hasn't been fundamentally changed for a number of years, and now we're living through the next iteration.

Oracle Analytics Cloud is a Cloud-based, full business analytics solution. Depending on the license option that I choose – Standard Edition or Enterprise Edition – the service will include:

1) Cloud version of the multi-dimensional database, Essbase (Essbase Cloud)
2) Ad hoc analysis in Excel for Essbase (Smart View)
3) Modeling, analyses, and dashboarding (BI Cloud)
4) Data visualization (DV Cloud and DVD)

I defined those terms in the previous chapter in case you missed them. (Wink, wink.) With these solutions, users have the ability to:

- Perform self-service data visualization, preparation, and smart discovery (this is the "DV" option)
- Build enterprise data models, analyses, and dashboards (this includes "OBIEE Lite" or BI Cloud features); you must have an Enterprise Edition subscription to select this option
- Conduct collaborative data collection, build scenarios, and perform what-if analysis (this is the "Essbase Cloud" option)

When I was working with the Oracle Product Management team on Essbase Cloud in the year leading up to its release, it was immediately made clear that this iteration would be more reminiscent of the Essbase that our grandmothers would have used. With its super cool and fast methods for creating cubes from spreadsheets, the addition of geeky options like Java and the REST API, and the direct integration with BI visualization technologies, it's clear that the maturity of Essbase from a standalone crunching engine to a full BI suite has come to fruition. It will be fascinating to see the new pathways this solution creates in EPM, BI, and Business Analytics.

### OAC Licensing Options

OAC is a PaaS (Platform as a Service) solution, which is important to understand when considering the licensing options. First, let's start with the two flavors of OAC that are offered: Standard Edition and Enterprise Edition.

OAC Standard Edition features include: foundational components of Essbase that users have grown to love over the years, easy to use Excel interface in Smart View, intuitive web interface, mobile capabilities, powerful calculations, cube building from Excel spreadsheets, one-click visualizations via Data Visualization Cloud, and more. You also get 50 licenses of DV Desktop per OCPU with OAC Standard.

OAC Enterprise Edition features include: all of the benefits of Standard Edition plus more robust analysis and dashboarding capabilities via Business Intelligence Cloud (BI Cloud), sandboxing and scenario management (which are Essbase features), smart insights, partitions to external sources, and more. The Day by Day feature anticipates what users need and can deliver the "right" information to make better decisions. You also get 50 licenses of DV Desktop per OCPU with OAC Enterprise.

Regardless of which licensing model I choose, I receive a variety of tools with the subscription. At a minimum, Essbase Cloud, Smart View, and DV (both DV Cloud and DVD) will come with my license. Oracle also provides a free app called Synopsis, which can take a native Excel or CSV file on a mobile device and transform the rows and columns of numbers into meaningful insights (anyone can download this, and it is a cool view into Oracle's BI capabilities).

In addition to choosing Standard or Enterprise, I need to choose whether I want to utilize a metered or a non-metered subscription. Metered options include hourly or monthly charges based on usage. Hourly metered usage makes sense if I expect to only use OAC at certain times of the month (e.g., during the close cycle). Monthly metered usage makes sense if I plan to utilize OAC throughout the month.

Because OAC is a PaaS solution, I can have many compute shapes (i.e., number of OCPUs and amount of memory). "OCPU" is short for "Oracle Compute Unit" and it represents one hyper-threaded CPU. Each OCPU comes with 15 GB of memory. For example, I can order one OCPU and 15 GB of memory, or I can order eight OCPUs and 120 GB memory. I can change the compute shape after I create the service to meet the fluctuations in business needs.

Finally, in order to support my OAC instance, I must also subscribe to additional Cloud services depending on the edition that I choose. OAC requires Oracle Compute Cloud Service, Oracle Database Cloud Service, Oracle Storage Cloud Service, and Oracle Backup Cloud Service.

Oracle Compute Cloud Service is the server management aspect of OAC.

Oracle Database Cloud Service is needed to store the underlying schemas for Essbase Cloud and BI Cloud. You can optionally have other databases in the Cloud as needed for data warehousing or data mart requirements. Oracle Database Cloud does not store the data for Essbase cubes.

Oracle Storage Cloud Service is the disk storage that is needed for OAC. I need Storage Cloud for active cubes, data stored within DV, etc.

Oracle Backup Cloud Service manages the backups for OAC services.

Quick reference of acronyms and terms related to Oracle Analytics Cloud:

- **OAC** - Oracle Analytics Cloud
- **OAC Standard** - Standard Edition of OAC (which includes Essbase Cloud, DV, and Smart View); this might not be the official Oracle term but I'm going to use it in this book
- **OAC Enterprise** - Enterprise Edition of OAC (which includes Essbase Cloud, BI Cloud features and functions, DV features and functions, and Smart View); this might not be an official Oracle term but I'm going to use it in this book
- **Essbase Cloud** - Essbase multi-dimensional database features and functionality within OAC; there are two flavors of Essbase Cloud: Essbase Standard (if you purchase OAC Standard Edition) and Essbase Enterprise (if you purchase OAC Enterprise Edition) which includes additional Essbase features for sandboxing, scenario management, partitioning, and drill through
- **DV** - Data Visualization, the general term for Oracle's data exploration and visualization capabilities that is available in both the Cloud (OAC, DVCS) and on-premises (DVD)
- **DVD** - Data Visualization Desktop, an on-premises client tool that offers additional features for data visualization
- **DVCS** - specific Data Visualization Cloud offering by Oracle
- **BICS** - specific Business Intelligence Cloud offering by Oracle

- **BI Cloud** - the enterprise modeling, analyses, and dashboarding features within OAC enabled with the Enterprise license option
- **BI** - Business Intelligence
- **EPM** - Enterprise Performance Management

### Access OAC

Depending on the roles and responsibilities within OAC and desired tasks, OAC can be accessed from a couple of different places:

- To access the Essbase Cloud web interface, I will go to the OAC URL ending in */essbase/ui*
- To access the Data Visualization web interface, I will go to the OAC URL ending in */va*
- To access the BI Cloud functionality (the traditional "OBIEE"/"BI Cloud" features like data models, analyses, and dashboards) web interface, I will go to the OAC URL ending in */analytics*
- To create and manage users for OAC, I will go to https://cloud.oracle.com and select My Services

I'll go into all of this in much more detail as we take this OAC journey.

### Explore and Report with OAC

OAC offers various reporting options, each with different capabilities and purposes. For direct reporting (where users can create highly formatted or static reports) OAC offers two options:

- Smart View
- Enterprise Performance Reporting Cloud Service (EPRCS)

Smart View is both a reporting and ad hoc analytics tool. Most users use Smart View with Excel to accomplish these types of tasks. Smart View comes out of the box with OAC at no additional licensing cost.

EPRCS is a Cloud-only comprehensive reporting solution that offers very flexible reporting options. It has a feature called Management Reporting which handles highly formatted, static reporting – similar to the web version of Oracle Hyperion Financial Reporting. It also has a collaborative narrative reporting feature which allows customers to create highly dynamic and flexible report packages, which combine data and narration. And as recently as June 2017, EPRCS includes a separate licensing feature for Disclosure Management, which supports XBRL (eXtensible Business Reporting Language) and regulatory reporting. EPRCS is a separately licensed Cloud solution.

For data visualization and exploration needs, OAC offers Data Visualization features either through DV Cloud or DVD. These DV solutions allow for one-click visualizations of data and includes a separate web interface where visualizations are created, stored, and managed. DV Cloud offers special features that do not come with the other solutions – insights, mashups, and presentation mode. DVD is a desktop client and takes DV Cloud capabilities a step further by allowing for more rich features. DVD includes up to 50 user licenses. However, it is more of a user-based tool and does not directly centralize data and data visualizations, as it is not Cloud-hosted.

For recurring analyses, reports, and dashboarding, OAC Enterprise Edition offers BI Cloud features and functions. BI Cloud includes more robust data integration options, as well as custom dashboards and a relational database backend. BI Cloud can also integrate with Cloud and on-premises relational databases.

### Migrate On-Premises Content to OAC

There are multiple ways for customers to migrate on-premises content into OAC. On-premises Essbase customers can use one of several utilities to migrate their native cubes to the Cloud. Business users can leverage prebuilt templates to build cubes quickly, copy existing cubes, port on-premises cubes to master templates to spawn other cubes, create cubes from free-form spreadsheets, etc. The possibilities are endless! On-premises OBIEE users can do a lift and shift of the RPD (the OBIEE repository) and Web Catalog to migrate their objects to BI Cloud with OAC.

### Integrate with OAC

Direct integration between on-premises and Cloud, as well as Cloud to Cloud, will also be possible with OAC. Finally, OAC will soon be able to connect directly to other EPM Cloud sources like PBCS, EPBCS, and FCCS.

## ESSBASE CLOUD CUBES DEFINED

I want to introduce "Essbase" and its cubes for any newbie readers out there. An Essbase Cloud cube is a grouping of related dimensions, data, interfaces, and calculation (or "calc") scripts to meet a specific analytic or reporting need. See Chapter 5, "Essbase Concepts Defined" for more information on what exactly is this "Essbase."

An Essbase cube (sometimes called "Essbase database") consists of many dimensions (hierarchies and groupings of data elements that models a business framework). Dimension examples include a Time dimension, Entity dimension, Account dimension, and Market dimension. The nodes within a dimension are called members. Data is loaded and then aggregated (dynamically if I want) by all intersection points of the dimensions and their members, providing a multi-dimensional cube for fast reporting and analysis.

The "compute shape", or number of OCPUs a customer decides to license, determines the boundaries of my Essbase Cloud environment. I can have as many Essbase Cloud cubes that can be supported by the number of OCPUs selected. Note that there isn't a rule of thumb on how many cubes a single OCPU can support. There are too many factors involved: design, storage, efficiency, and performance of all cubes created, etc.

I can design the cubes to meet specific reporting and analytic needs. I might create a cube that consolidates company data from multiple department cubes. I might have individual cubes that contain very specific department detail.

Each application and cube has a number of components:

- **Dimensions** - hierarchies of related master data or metadata
- **Rules files** – objects used to build dimensions and load data to Essbase cubes
- **Files** – text files that are loaded into Essbase cubes to build dimensions and populate data

- **Calculation scripts** - objects that are executed to perform pre-defined calculation logic or other operations on data; common calculation scripts include those to roll up data from base data to totals, perform allocations from upper level data to lower levels, copy data, and clear data
- **Substitution variables** - dynamic objects with changing values that are used to streamline maintenance in calculation scripts and other Essbase Cloud objects
- **Application workbooks** – Excel workbook template to create and maintain Essbase Cloud cubes

Essbase Cloud has a few rules related to its application components:

- Unlike its sister on-premises Essbase solution, Essbase Cloud application and cube names may have more than eight characters
- Member names may include some special characters, although spaces, quotations, brackets, and tabs are not allowed
- There is a list of reserved words for member names (e.g., "Count" is a reserved word)
- Dimension, member, and alias names are limited to 1024 characters
- Application and cube names are limited to 30 characters
- File names uploaded to Essbase Cloud are limited to 30 characters
- Application workbook names used in Cube Designer to create/update a cube cannot exceed 30 characters

## ESSBASE CLOUD WEB INTERFACE

The Essbase Cloud web interface, like other Oracle PaaS solutions, includes an interface that was first developed for tablets and has a minimalist look and feel and intuitive navigation.

Although the PaaS interfaces differ in general from those offered by the EPM Cloud/SaaS solutions, there is a commonality to their designs:

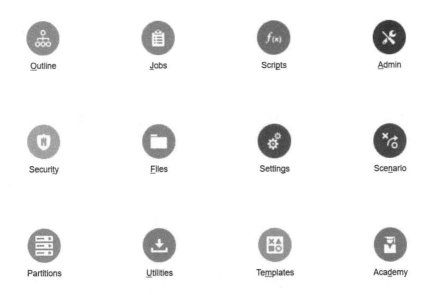

| Outline | Jobs | Scripts | Admin |
| Security | Files | Settings | Scenario |
| Partitions | Utilities | Templates | Academy |

To access the Essbase Cloud web interface, enter the OAC URL ending in /essbase/ui (sent from the Administrator) into the web browser.

**Note!**

Check out the latest documentation for supported browsers. I have found Firefox to be the most stable browser for OAC when using Windows-based machines. In this book, I am using the latest version of Firefox (v45+) for all functionality tests and screenshots.

# NAVIGATE THE ESSBASE CLOUD WEB INTERFACE

The home page displays upon logging in:

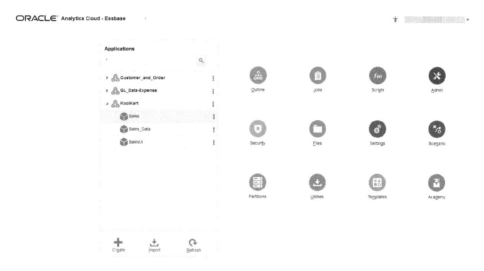

The home page includes a series of icons that users can click to navigate to various areas of the solution. In addition, a flipboard on the left hand side shows the entire list of applications and databases that the user has access to, as well as some commonly used actions. From the home page of Essbase Cloud, users can quickly access applications and cubes, create new applications and cubes, and import Excel files from the flipboard. Icons may be greyed out based on what is selected. Icons may also vary depending on where you are in the Essbase Cloud web interface.

**Note!** If you are logging in for the very first time, no Essbase applications and cubes will have been created yet.

Icons can take users to various areas of Essbase Cloud:

- **Outline** - where users can go to manually manage the Essbase application cube outlines, dimensions, and members
- **Jobs** - where jobs can be created, scheduled, and reviewed

- **Scripts** - where Essbase Cloud calculation scripts and load rules can be manually created and managed
- **Admin** - administration area focused on object unlocks, variable maintenance, and location alias maintenance
- **Security** - administration area focused on Essbase security filters for dimensions and provisioning access for users to both security filters and calculation scripts
- **Files** - where files are stored and managed; these may include rules files, xml files, and text files created by or migrated into the system, and any files that are uploaded by users
- **Settings** - administration area focused on the application, database, and dimension settings and details
- **Scenario** - where the details of the scenario management feature (workflow + sandboxing) can be set up and managed
- **Partitions** - where partitions can be created and managed
- **Utilities** - where administration utilities can be downloaded
- **Templates** - where sample "design by example" templates for creating each type of Essbase cube can be downloaded
- **Academy** - where users can learn more about Essbase Cloud through Oracle's documentation and video libraries

Upon selecting one of these icons, a list of "cards" (Oracle's fancy word for icon) appears across the top for easy navigation to each area:

### Outline

The *Outline* icon appears when an existing Essbase cube is selected within the flipboard. Here, users can maintain the outline, dimensions, and members for a particular Essbase cube.

The outline can be locked and edited. Sandboxes ("play areas") for individual users in the Enterprise Edition) can also be created:

**Block Storage Outline**

View ▼    [ ]

**All Dimensions**

| Name | | Member ID | Statistics | Formula | Two-Pass Calc |
|------|------|-----------|-----------|---------|----------------|
| Measures | [ ] | Measures | C 2 D 2 G.1 L 1 | | — |
| TimePeriod | [ ] | TimePeriod | C.2 D 191 G 1 L 4 | | — |
| Category_Dim | [ ] | Category_Dim | C.4 D 8 G.1 L 2 | | — |
| | < | | | | |
| | | Columns Frozen   1 | | | |

## Jobs

The *Jobs* icon is where users can set up jobs for common tasks, view currently running and past jobs, and edit job settings like the maximum number of jobs running in parallel. Jobs can be set up for tasks like data loads, dimension builds, calc script execution, and data clears:

## Scripts

The *Scripts* icon appears when an existing Essbase cube is selected within the flipboard. This is where users can create and maintain calculation scripts and load rules. Calculation scripts can be created manually, edited, deleted, locked, unlocked, copied, renamed, validated, and saved within this area. Load rules can be created for both dimensions and data loads:

## Admin

The *Admin* icon is where Essbase objects and blocks can be unlocked, variables can be created and maintained, and location aliases can be created and maintained:

## Security

The *Security* icon is where security filters can be set up, verified, and maintained, in addition to user provisioning for scripts and security filters:

## Files

The *Files* icon appears when an existing Essbase cube is selected within the flipboard. This is where users can upload, view, and maintain files for the server. These may include system-generated files like load rules, data files, and xml files. This may also include files that users upload to the server:

### Settings

The *Settings* icon is where properties and statistics for the application or database (depending on which is selected on the flipboard) can be viewed and set. Dimension properties can also be viewed and set here:

### Scenario

The *Scenario* icon (available in OAC Enterprise) appears when an existing Essbase cube is selected within the flipboard. This area is where sandboxes can be maintained and assigned to users via Workflow:

### Partitions

The *Partitions* icon appears when an existing Essbase cube is selected within the flipboard. Partitions are an Essbase feature that allow data sharing across Essbase Cloud cubes and this is where partitions to other Essbase cubes can be created and managed. Currently, the Essbase Cloud web interface supports transparent partitions:

## Utilities

The *Utilities* icon is where users can download various utilities to help with migrations, administration, and usage of OAC. At the time that this book was written, utilities for exporting a cube to a formatted Essbase Cloud workbook, migrating artifacts, and a command line interface were available. In addition, a link to the latest version of Smart View was included:

| Name | Provider | Description |
|------|----------|-------------|
| Export Utility | Oracle | Command-line tool for exporting the outline of a cube into a formatted Excel workbook template and, optionally, exporting the cube data to a text file |
| Smart View for Essbase | Oracle | Smart View for Essbase |
| Life Cycle Management | Oracle | Backup and restore the Essbase artifacts |
| Command Line Tool | Oracle | Command Line Tool for Essbase platform |

## Templates

The *Templates* icon is where prebuilt "design by example" templates have been created for every type of Essbase Cloud cube. Users can download these templates as a starting location for their new Essbase Cloud application and database:

| Name | Provider | Description |
|------|----------|-------------|
| Block Storage Sample (Stored) | Oracle | Block storage application workbook. |
| Block Storage Sample (Dynamic) | Oracle | Block storage application workbook. All non-leaf level members are dynamic. |
| Block Storage Sample (Scenario) | Oracle | Block storage application workbook with scenario enabled. All non-leaf level members are dynamic. |
| Demo Basic | Oracle | Basic demo application workbook |
| Aggregate Storage Sample | Oracle | Aggregate storage application workbook. |
| Aggregate Storage Sample Data | Oracle | Data for the aggregate storage application workbook. |
| Free-form Tabular Data Sample | Oracle | Tabular data Excel file. |

### Academy

The *Academy* icon is where users can go to find links to helpful resources on learning more about Essbase Cloud:

## DATA VISUALIZATIONS DEFINED

Another key component to OAC is its data visualization solution. Data visualization is the graphical display of information for data analysis and communication. Data visualization is a powerful way to review data and understand its story. Ultimately, this can help companies identify issues and their causes more quickly so that they can be addressed.

As I mentioned earlier, OAC includes "Data Visualization" or DV. Two data visualization solutions are offered with OAC Standard: DV Cloud and DVD. Users can perform data exploration and data visualization on Essbase Cloud data sets or Excel files that they upload themselves. DV provides Smart Insights to help find trends and patterns in the data. DV can portray visual stories with insights for data sets, too.

## NAVIGATE THE DATA VISUALIZATION WEB INTERFACE

The other web interface available within OAC Standard is DV Cloud web interface. The DV Cloud web interface also has a minimalist look and feel and intuitive navigation. More detailed information on this interface will be covered later in Chapter 10, "Explore Data in Data Visualization."

≡ ORACLE Analytics Cloud

Home          Data Sources          Console          Academy

A quick summary of the purpose behind these icons:

- **Home** - navigate and search for existing content, along with options to create new content
- **Data Sources** - navigate and search for existing data sources, along with options to create new data sources, connections, and data flows; for Enterprise Edition, create and manage models
- **Console** - manage DV settings
- **Academy** - learn more through Oracle's documentation and video libraries

To access the DVCS interface, enter the OAC URL ending in /va (sent from the Administrator) into the web browser. I will cover DV Cloud in more detail later in the mission.

---

**Meanwhile, back on earth...**

"Crap!" Danielle said. "You have got to be frakking kidding me! Edward Roske and the project are still alive?"

Director Chang glared across the room and said, "Not helping, Danielle."

He turned to the Operations Directorate, Jenny Hughes. "How sure are we of this?"

"Nearly a hundred percent," said Jenny in her Canadian accent.

"So what you're saying is that there's still a chance he's gone?" Danielle said. "Don't get me wrong. I am relieved, ecstatic, overjoyed that he is alive, but I've already released a press release on this loss. Now I have to go back and say, 'Oopsy, we made a mistake', and, 'by the way, he also implemented PBCS in a few short sols while being stranded in the Oracle Cloud'?"

Ignoring Danielle, Director Chang turned to face the rest of people in the room which was comprised of the i.n.t.e.r.R.e.l. shared services team, Flight Director Ali Flint, Mission Operations Directorate Jenny Hughes, and Flight Surgeon Robin Alex. Consultant Rich Magee was also discreetly sitting in the back corner of the conference room, trying to look invisible.

"We have to tell them. The crew. They need to know Edward is alive," said Flight Director Flint.

"No," replied Director Chang instantly.

"What?!" Danielle said. "How can you not tell them?"

"The crew has another 10 months on their trip home. And they're afraid of the Cloud. They need to be alert and not distracted. They are sad right now that they lost a crewmate, but they'd be devastated if they found out that they abandoned him alive."

"This is ridiculous. We should tell the crew," snarled Flight Director Flint. She turned to face Rich then looked back at Director Chang. "Who is the guy trying to look invisible?"

"Rich is the one who found out that Edward and the project are alive," replied Director Chang. "Besides, Ali, even if we tell the crew now about Edward, if my math is correct, he is doomed to starve to death before we can possibly save him."

# CHAPTER 3: LAUNCH INTO THE CLOUD

---

**LOG ENTRY FOR FLIGHT ENGINEER GLENN SCHWARTZBERG**
*SOL 11, Entry 1*

A launch of the N.A.S.A. Space Shuttle is complicated, involving hundreds of people, rocket boosters, propulsion systems, abort systems, and more.
Would launching JWE's Cloud instance prove to be as involved? As intense? Could I fail before I even started?
Thankfully I have my "Launching into the Cloud" Manual which documents how to get started, roles and responsibilities, and more. With this resource and all of the documentation at https://cloud.oracle.com, what could go wrong?
10, 9, 8, oh shoot, where was I? Um, 3, 2, 1…

---

## CLOUD.ORACLE.COM

The main place I need to go to first get started with the Cloud is https://cloud.oracle.com. This site is a one stop shop for all Oracle Cloud customer service subscription needs:

Because OAC is a Platform as a Service (PaaS) solution, I click on *Platform >> Business Analytics >> Analytics Cloud*. From the OAC product page, I can find an Overview, Features listing, Pricing options, and links to documentation under Learn More:

```
LOG ENTRY FOR FLIGHT ENGINEER GLENN SCHWARTZBERG
SOL 11, Entry 2

        This is where I will begin my journey to launch
into the Cloud! What should I do first?
```

## PREPARE FOR OAC SET UP

Before I purchase my OAC subscription, I want to make sure to plan accordingly. Work with Oracle and/or your implementation partner (e.g., i.n.t.e.r.R.e.l.) to answer these questions before purchasing and configuring the instance:

1) Which OAC edition do you want to purchase – Standard or Enterprise Edition?
2) A related question that you will be prompted for in the Create Service wizard is which type of services would you like to create?
    a. Self-Service Data Visualization, Preparation, and Smart Discovery (this is the "DV Cloud only" option)

b.  Enterprise Data Models, which includes Self-Service Data Visualization (this includes the BI Cloud option); you must have an Enterprise Edition subscription to select this option

c.  Collaborative Data Collection, Scenarios, and What-if Analysis (this is the "Essbase Cloud" option)

3)  What type of billing option would you like to use – metered or non-metered? If a metered subscription is selected, how do you want metered usage to be billed – hourly or monthly?

4)  What compute shape (and by compute shape, I mean number of OCPUs and amount of memory) will you need? The answers to question #1 and #2 will impact the answer to this question as you will need multiple OCPUs to support all of the OAC components.

5)  What do you want to name the service instances? There are a few rules about naming the service instance: it must be between 1 and 50 characters and may not contain any special characters other than a hyphen. I recommend keeping these short and sweet but easily recognizable. You could have multiple service instances within OAC: one for Essbase Cloud and one for BI Cloud and/or development and production service instances.

6)  Which Database Cloud Service option do you want to use? OAC requires a Database Cloud Service to store OAC schemas and data.

7)  Which user ID should be set up as the OAC Service Administrator?

8)  Do you want to set up your own public/private key pair for SSH access? By default, OAC is accessible through HTTP secure protocols, like SSL and SSH, and only uses specific ports. You can customize the default security configuration to support different access rules and security policies.

9)  Which storage container should be used for analytic data sets, backups, and logs? This can be created before you run the Create Service wizard, or you can ask the Create Service wizard to create the container.

10) Does your subscription plan include the other required services to support OAC (because it should)? OAC requires Oracle Compute Cloud Service, Oracle Database Cloud Service, and Oracle Storage Cloud Service.

```
LOG ENTRY FOR FLIGHT ENGINEER GLENN SCHWARTZBERG
SOL 11, Entry 2

    I sure wish I had an implementation partner to
help me answer these questions and prepare for this
OAC Cloud Launch.
    Wait a minute. That's me. Let me refer to the
i.n.t.e.r.R.e.l. internal guidelines to help me figure
out the best plan for JWE.
```

## CLOUD TERMS AND DEFINITIONS

I'll share some other helpful terminology to understand how the Oracle Cloud environment is set up.

| Term | What | Where to Manage |
|------|------|-----------------|
| Account | • Unique customer account<br>• May have a single identity domain or many identity domains with many Oracle Cloud services<br>• Manage account in My Account where you create identity domains, monitor account status, and designate other account administrators | Email to activate; My Account |
| Identity Domain | • Controls the authentication and authorization of the users who can sign into an Oracle Cloud service<br>• May have one or many Oracle Cloud Services<br>• Cannot be changed after activation | My Account |

| Service | • Software offering in Oracle Cloud<br>• A service will belong to a single identity domain<br>• Multiple services may belong to the same identity domain (called a Service Association) | My Services |
|---|---|---|
| Service Instance | • An instance of a Cloud Service<br>• Account could have one or more service instances (for example, you may have 3 different service instances for different lines of business in your organization) | My Services |
| Service Name | • Service name is the name assigned to the Service that must be unique within the identity domain<br>• Cannot be changed after activation | My Services |

Now that the terminology is clearer, let's take a look at this bad boy.

## ORDER MANAGEMENT - MY ACCOUNT

To access Oracle Cloud My Account,
1. Navigate to https://cloud.oracle.com.
2. Click *Sign in*.
3. The following screen displays:

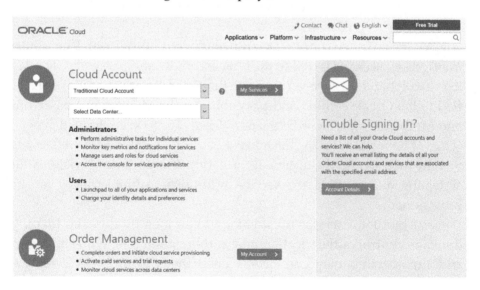

4.   At the bottom, click *My Account*.
5.   Log into your Oracle account (different than the OAC instance account).

I see a dashboard of options that is role-based. I can access details related to *Cloud Account* (linked to My Services) and *Order Management* (linked to My Account).

The *Cloud Account* section (explained in more detail in the next section) is for managing specific Cloud instances and users.

The *Order Management* section of https://cloud.oracle.com allows customers to monitor services for their entire account, across data centers and identity domains. Here, I can view information about all of my active, expired, and pending services. This is where I also activate new services, view a dashboard with the status of each of the environments that I have access to, and manage certain Administrator accounts.

To access account details within *Order Management*, the My Account URL is:

https://myaccount.cloud.oracle.com/mycloud/faces/dashboard.jspx

Username:      Use the Oracle account username
Password:      Use the Oracle account password

The My Account ID and password (used for the *Order Management* section) is tied to the Oracle.com ID and password. The My Services ID and password (used for the *Cloud Account* section) is NOT tied to the Oracle.com ID and password. So the My Account password and My Services password *could be different*. Try to keep these in sync.

I have access to the dashboard in My Account, which enables me to view metrics and the uptime information of my Cloud services. After activating and creating the service, additional Administrators can be provisioned.

The Cloud service must belong to an identity domain. Identity domains control authentication and authorization (i.e., who can log in and the services they can access once they log in). OAC Service

Administrators can create new users and define which Cloud services they can access.

> If you have different domains for each Cloud instance, you can change the domain name while logging in. I see an option to change the domain on the login screen:

**Note!**

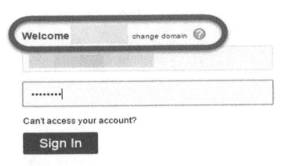

## CLOUD ACCOUNT - MY SERVICES

The *Cloud* *Account* (My Services) section of https://cloud.oracle.com allows Service Administrators to manage and monitor all services within a single identity domain. This is where I do the majority of Cloud management after the services have been activated.

> To access Oracle Cloud My Services,
> 1. Navigate to https://cloud.oracle.com.
> 2. Click *Sign in*.
> 3. Select *Traditional Cloud Account*.
> 4. Select your company's data center.
> 5. Click the *My Services* button to log in.

6.  The My Services dashboard displays (which may look a little
    different for you). You can customize the dashboard. The
    dashboard will not show any services if you haven't
    configured them yet:

I see a *Create Instance* option and a list of existing services. I can
also select *Open Analytics Cloud URL* to launch an existing service.

The Service Administrator has rights to monitor and manage the
service. After activating the service, the Service Administrator can
designate and assign other Service Administrators.

I use My Services to add and manage server Administrator access
to the service, monitor my service status, and view current and historical
usage data. Note that I do not use OAC to provision OAC users; only
OAC Service Administrators. I will assign security access for users
within Essbase Cloud or DV/BI Cloud web interfaces including Essbase
Cloud Service Administrators and BI Cloud Service Administrators.

Once the service instance is configured, I can select *Oracle
Analytics Cloud* to open the Oracle Analytics Cloud details. The Service
Details interface displays.

I can view Overview information for my OAC service, billing metrics, resource quotas, and business metrics:

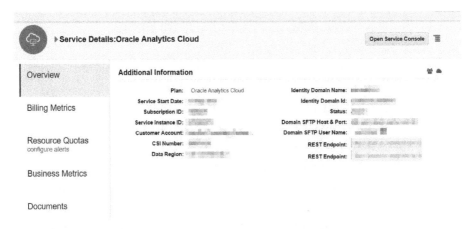

If I select *Open Service Console,* the details for Oracle Analytics Cloud display including the summary metrics for number of services, number of OCPUs, amount of memory, storage amounts, and listing of service instances:

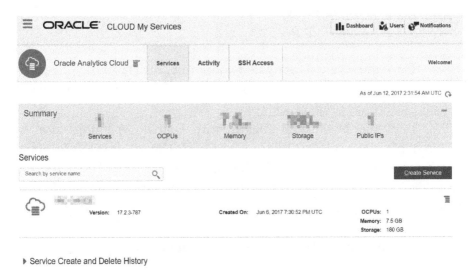

## ORDER TO SET UP

The general process from initial order to being able to actively use the system is as follows:

1) Determine how you would like to set up Oracle Analytics Cloud.
2) The buyer places an order for OAC and the other required services with the Oracle sales team.
3) In a few days, Oracle activates the account and sends a welcome email for the new Cloud instance.
4) Create and set up your Database Cloud Service and the other supporting Cloud services required for OAC.
5) Create a storage policy.
6) Create a new OAC service instance.
7) Enable network access from on-premises networks that will be associated with your OAC deployments (if needed).
8) In *Cloud Account >> My Services*, create and provision other OAC Service Administrators.
9) OAC Service Administrators manage and monitor the service instance from *Cloud Account >> My Services*.
10) In Essbase Cloud or BI Cloud web interfaces, create and provision user access.
11) Set up backup processes.

Once the service is activated and set up, the Dashboard displays the uptime and status of my instance. This dashboard is accessible at https://myaccount.cloud.oracle.com.

Both the buyer and the Identity Domain Administrator (if different people) receive a "Welcome to Oracle Cloud" email. Additional details are included within this email, including the URLs for the subscription and the Customer Support ID (CSI) number (which I'll need to log a case with Oracle Cloud Support).

**Subscription ID vs. Customer Support ID**

**Note!**

The Subscription ID is necessary if you need to make changes to your subscription. Your Customer Support ID is necessary if you need to log a support case for the Cloud.

Next, the Administrator logs into the My Services site with their email and Oracle password (or possibly a temporary password provided by Oracle via email) and sees a similar dashboard view of the service. If using a temporary password, a prompt to change the password and security questions display.

Now I'll walk through the high level steps to create a service! While I am showing you the basic steps to set up OAC, I strongly recommend that you work with your Oracle Customer Success Manager or experienced implementation partner to set up your instance. Incorrect configuration of the OAC environment could result in overage charges, so follow your ordering document.

## CREATE A SERVICE

**Note!**

Repeating this note because it's important: have your OAC Order Document on hand when configuring OAC. You want to make sure to select the options that are defined in the order document; otherwise, you might incur additional charges.

Before I create a service, I need to make sure the other supporting Cloud services (Oracle Compute Cloud Service, Oracle Database Cloud Service, and Oracle Storage Cloud Service) have been configured and set up. Once those steps are completed, I'm ready to create an OAC service instance.

To create a new service within OAC,
1. Sign into *My Services*.
2. Open the OAC dashboard.
3. Click *Create Instance.*
4. Enter a unique name for the service and a description, and any other important details required for that particular service.

5.   Click *Edit* to create or select the SSH Public Key that is used to access the service.
6.   Select the edition to deploy, either *Enterprise* or *Standard.* Ensure these details match your OAC Order Document.
7.   Select the frequency for metered billing pricing, if applicable.
8.   Click *Next*.

In the *Service Administrator* section,
9.   Enter the username and password for the Oracle Analytics Cloud Administrator.

In the *Options* section,
10.  Select the type of service to create:
     a.   *Self-Service Data Visualization, Preparation, and Smart Discovery* (DV option)
     b.   *Enterprise Data Models* (BI Cloud option which includes Self-Service Data Visualization)
     c.   *Collaborative Data Collection, Scenarios, and What-if Analysis* (Essbase Cloud option)

For a single OAC service instance, you may only choose either the Essbase Cloud option or the BI Cloud/DV Cloud option. If you want to use both features in your OAC environment, you will set up one service instance (at least) for Essbase Cloud and a different OAC service instance for BI Cloud/DV Cloud. Each service instance will likely require multiple OCPUs.

11.  Select the compute size.
12.  Enter the usable storage or accept the default.

In the *Database* section,
13.  Select the Database Cloud Service to use with this OAC service.
     a.   Enter the database name (created prior to OAC setup).

b. Enter the Database Administrator username and password.

c. Enter a schema prefix. This will be added to any OAC schema objects created. It must contain only capital letters and numbers, start with a letter, and be no longer than 11 characters in length.

In the *Cloud Storage Configuration* section,

14. Specify the container to store analytic user uploaded data sets, backups, and logs:

a. Enter the Cloud Storage Base URL, Container, and Username.

b. Select *Create a Cloud Storage Container* to create a container if one does not exist:

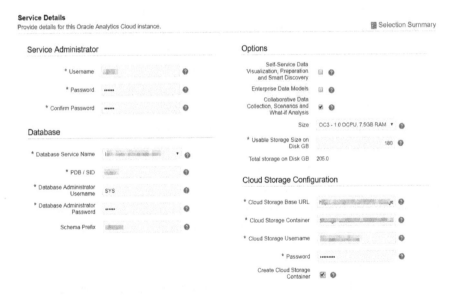

15. Click *Next*.

16. Review the setup information.

17. Click *Create* to create the service.

The OAC service instance should create, though it may take up to 45 minutes.

Now I'll walk through the different types of users within OAC.

## CLOUD ROLES, PRIVILEGES, & RESPONSIBILITIES

Users are assigned roles which will allow them to work within OAC. Roles control which tasks users can access within OAC. Within OAC, I assign roles in three main places for the available OAC options:

1) OAC Service Administrators are defined with My Services
2) Users of the BI Cloud (otherwise known as "self-service data visualization and enterprise data models and dashboards") are defined in the DV/BI web interface
3) Users of the Essbase Cloud are defined in the Essbase Cloud web interface

I identify and define the following types of users for OAC:

- **Buyer** - Subscribes to Oracle Analytics Cloud
- **OAC Administrator/Service Administrator** -
    o   Sets up the OAC and other services for use
    o   Creates the other OAC Service Administrators
    o   Adds users to the OAC instance and assigns roles
    o   Migrates existing content to OAC
    o   Monitors and manages Cloud services
    o   Patches services
    o   Performs backup of services
    o   Able to perform all of the Power User and user tasks
- **Users** - the rest of the types of users who will interact and work in OAC. User access is further defined by specific access roles. For example:
    o   Creates Essbase cubes
    o   Uploads and explores data through visualizations
    o   Creates data models
    o   Creates analyses and dashboards

The Essbase User Level Roles include the Service Administrator, Power User, and User. The Essbase Cloud Service Administrator can manage the overall Essbase Cloud environment. The Power User, who can create new applications and delete those applications that he/she created. In addition, this user can access any application assigned with the application level role. Users can access an Essbase Cloud cube based on their application level role assignment. The Essbase Application Level Roles include: Application Manager, Database Manager, Database Update (Read, Write, and Calculate access based on filter assignments), and Database Access. I'll cover the details on Essbase security later in this mission.

The DV pre-defined Application Roles are assigned in the DV web interface and include DV Content Author and DV Consumer. I'll also cover the details on DV security later in this mission.

## CREATE ADMINS FOR OAC

OAC Service Administrators can be created and provisioned by the Identity Domain Administrator in My Services. As mentioned above, users for each Cloud service instance will have its own set of roles that can be assigned in the service instance web interface.

**Note!**

The processes described below are for OAC, but they are similar across all Oracle EPM and BI Cloud tools. One obvious difference is that the pre-defined roles will differ between technologies.

To create an Administrator in My Services,
1. If not already there and assuming you have access, go to https://cloud.oracle.com/sign-in.

2.  In the Cloud Account section, select *Traditional Cloud Account* and the appropriate Data Center:

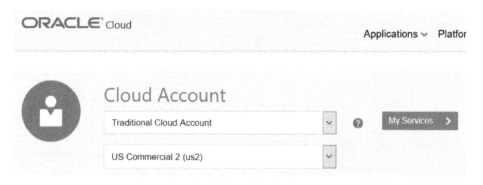

3.  Click *My Services* and then sign in with the OAC Administrator and login credentials.

4.  In the upper, right hand corner of the screen, click on *Users*:

**Note!**    If the above buttons are not available, the user who is logged in has not been granted Identity Domain Administrator rights. You must have Identity Domain Administrator rights in order to add, modify, and delete users.

5.  Click *Add*:

6.  Complete the necessary fields: *First Name, Last Name, Email,* option to *Use email as username*, and *Manager Email*.

**Note!** Optionally define a username if you do not want to use the user's email address as their login name. You can accomplish this by unchecking the *Use email as username* box and then setting a unique username.

7. In the Roles section, select the service.
8. Select the desired role(s).
9. Move the role(s) over to the *Selected Roles* window:

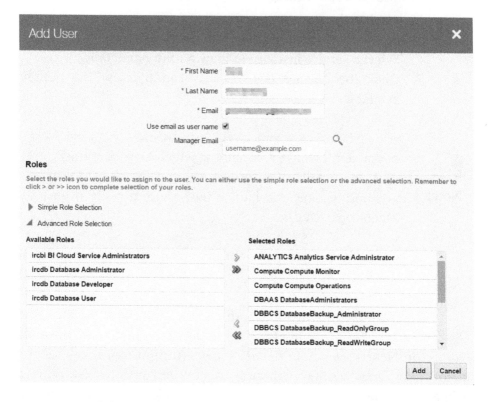

Available Administrator roles include: Analytics Service Administrator, Compute Cloud Monitor, Compute Cloud Operations, various Database Cloud Administrator roles, and various Storage Cloud roles.

After the user has been created, a confirmation email will be sent to the user's email address. This will include a temporary password which the user can log in with. They will be prompted to change their password immediately.

The Administrator can sort users by roles or by name using the drop-downs above the user list. They can also modify users, reset passwords, manage roles, and remove users in My Services.

## MANAGE & MONITOR THE CLOUD INSTANCE

### Monitor Service Status

To monitor the status of the Cloud Service,

1. Sign into *My Services*. The dashboard displays.
2. Select a service instance to view additional details.
3. Click the *Manage this instance* icon to view the options available.

**Note!** The dashboard is interactive! You can hide the service tiles you don't want to see, choose which metrics to track, launch the details of a service, expand the tiles to see charts and graphs, and launch the service directly from the icons on each tile.

4. Click the service name to open the details page for that service.

The Dashboard will show both service and activity metrics. The *Overview* page shows a variety of component, storage, and resource details for the service. Under *Administration*, Administrators can see the quantity of Cloud storage volumes, backup and restore history, and available patches. Administrators can also run Health Checks from the OAC Dashboard.

### Monitor Usage Metrics

To monitor the usage metrics in the Cloud, click on the *Business Metrics* tile. The *Business Metrics* page contains *Historical Usage* metrics which display the usage data in the form of a graph that is collected per day for the current service for the past seven days (by default).

The *Latest Usage* metric (at the bottom) shows a snapshot of the last set of metrics collected and when those metrics were collected.

### Monitor Notifications

To monitor the notifications from Oracle about the Cloud services,

1. Sign into My Services. Log directly into your specific Cloud tool.
2. Click *Notifications*:

The My Services Notifications page lists all of the notifications related to the services and displays the following information:

- Name of the Oracle data center where the services are located
- List of notifications for the logged-in domain, with the most recent at the top
- Tabs:
  - **All** - displays all notifications for each service within the domain
  - **Applications** - displays only the notifications for the Oracle Software as a Service (SaaS) applications
  - **Platform services** - displays only the notifications for the Oracle Platform as a Service (PaaS) services
  - **Notification preferences** - displays the notification preferences (I can receive notifications via email or SMS)

### Perform Operations on Services

I can access the My Services application and then drill down to the service details page to perform the following operations:

- Launch service
- Create firewall rules
- View and access related deployments

The *Manage Associations* option in the service details page allows Administrators to manage associations between certain types of services. *Service Association* allows different Cloud services to communicate with each other (e.g., BI Cloud also comes with Oracle Database Cloud Service; these two services are associated together and can share information).

### Delete a Service

From the *Manage the service* icon, I can select any services to delete.

### Start, Stop, and Restart Services

From time to time, I will need to restart my services. This might be due to slow or unexpected performance.

To start, stop, or restart a service,
1. Sign into My Services for OAC.
2. Select *Manage the service* from the OAC Dashboard for the service to start/stop/restart.
3. Select the action *Start/Stop/Restart*.

### Log a Cloud Support Case

To log a case for my Cloud instance, go to http://support.oracle.com/. Switch to the *Cloud Support* portal. I can also log a case from My Services.

To use My Oracle Support (MOS),
1. Register your company with your Customer Support ID (CSI). This was provided in the "Welcome to Oracle Cloud" email that your Account Administrator received after you activated the order.
2. Enter the names and emails of all people who need access to MOS, including partners and consultants who may log cases on your behalf.

## INSTALL SMART VIEW

While OAC has web interfaces for both administrative and end user tasks, I'll definitely want to install Smart View, which is the Microsoft add-in for OAC. I can connect to Essbase Cloud cubes in Excel (and Word and PowerPoint) for ad hoc analysis, reporting, and more. I can also install an extension to the Smart View add-in called Cube Designer. Cube Designer allows me to build and maintain cubes, all from Excel.

There are two steps for installing Cube Designer. First, install Smart View. Then, install the Cube Designer Smart View extension. Easy, right?

To install Smart View,
1. Navigate to the Essbase Cloud web interface.
2. From the home page, click the *Utilities* icon.
3. Download *Smart View for Essbase*:

4. This link will take you to the Oracle Smart View website. Select *Download Latest Version*:

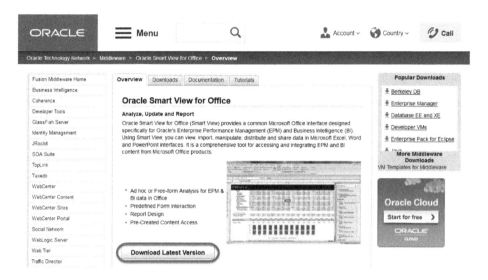

5. Accept the license agreement and choose to *Download Now*.
6. Log into Oracle with your Oracle website login credentials.
7. Save the .zip file to your local drive.
8. Close out of all Oracle websites.
9. On your local drive, find the Smart View .zip file and unzip it locally.
10. Close out of all Microsoft applications. Note that if you skip this step now, you'll get a warning during the installation and will need to close out of all Microsoft applications then.
11. Execute the *SmartView.exe* file to run the installation.

12. Select the appropriate options for the installation location:

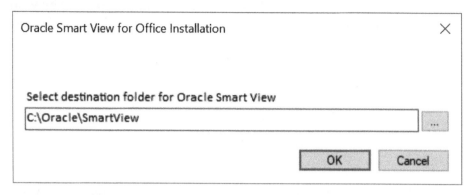

13. Once the installation completes, a message will appear:

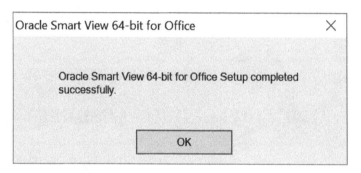

14. Open up Microsoft Excel.
15. The Smart View ribbon should appear now amongst the other Excel ribbons.

That was pretty straightforward. On to the next step!

To install Cube Designer,
16. Navigate to *Smart View >> Panel*.
17. Click on *Private Connections*.

18. Within the drop-down box under Private Connections, type in the Essbase Cloud web interface URL (can be sent by your Administrator), but stop at /essbase and then add /smartview at the end (all lowercase). Press *Enter*:

19. Log into Essbase Cloud. This connection screen requires a username and password that has been provisioned specifically to Essbase Cloud:

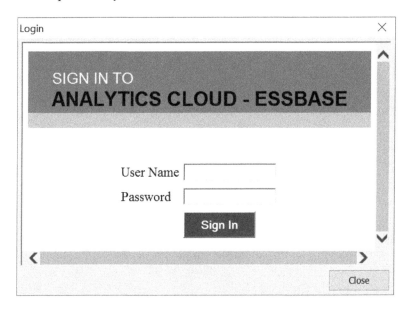

20. Expand *EssbaseCluster* to see the list of Essbase Cloud applications and databases, if you'd like to double-check the connection.

21. Back in the Smart View ribbon, click on *Options*.

22. Navigate to the *Extensions* section:

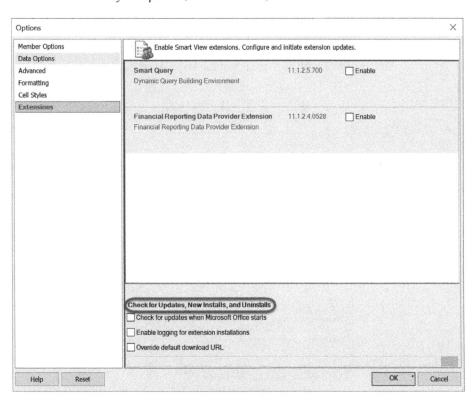

23. At the bottom of the list of extensions, click on the hyperlink *Check for Updates, New Installs, and Uninstalls*:

24. At the confirmation message, select *OK*:

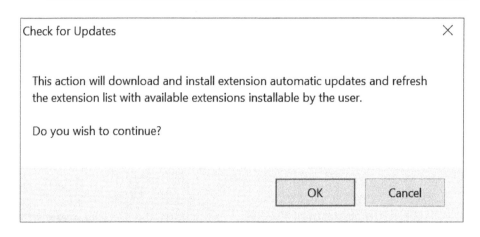

25. A list of new extensions available through the Essbase Cloud connection will display. The specific extension version will change based on what's currently available in Cloud. Notice that Cube Designer is listed as an option:

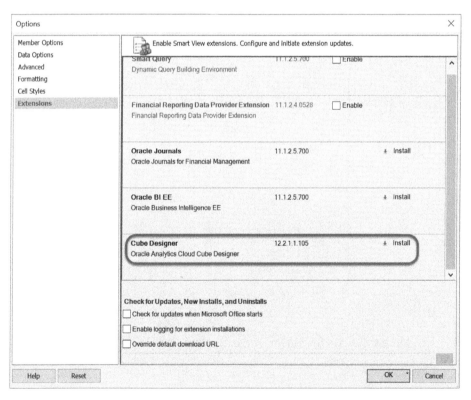

26. Click *Install* next to Cube Designer.

27. Select *Yes* to apply this extension update:

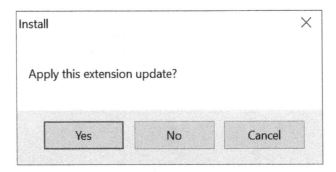

28. Select *OK* at the confirmation message:

29. Click *OK* to close out of the Smart View Options window.
30. Close down Microsoft Excel completely.
31. Reopen Microsoft Excel and a new ribbon for Cube Designer will appear:

**LOG ENTRY FOR FLIGHT ENGINEER GLENN SCHWARTZBERG**
*SOL 11, Entry 3*

Success! Launching into Oracle Cloud was a bit bumpy, but I made it. The JWE Oracle OAC environment is now in the Cloud and ready for development!

...

Now what?

# CHAPTER 4: UNSTRUCTURED SPREADSHEET TO ESSBASE CUBE

**Meanwhile, back on earth…**

Essbase Mission Specialist, Sarah "Purnell" Branhagen, sipped coffee at the table in the i.n.t.e.r.R.e.l. headquarters at the Ballpark in Arlington. From the center field offices she could see the baseball game, but wasn't really paying attention. She was thinking about the massive spreadsheet data dump from KoolKart with all their sales data.

How could she turn these thousands of rows and columns into something meaningful? Should she split the data into separate dimension files and manually build the hierarchies? It would almost be easier if…

She jumped up from her chair and turned on her laptop. OAC has the ability to build a cube from an unstructured spreadsheet! She could just upload the spreadsheet and make the artificial intelligence in OAC figure out the dimensions and hierarchies for her. If she could do this and work with the Ranger crew on their other JWE requirements, they could rescue Edward from the Cloud.

She just needed some supercomputer time from OAC.

There's no doubt that the OAC suite is powerful because of its rapid and remarkable ability to analyze and present data, but what's really fascinating is that the tool has put the power back into the hands of the average end user. Users no longer need to fully understand every aspect of Essbase: ASO vs. BSO databases, dense vs. sparse dimensions, stored vs. dynamically calculated members, and the list goes on. If you are new to Essbase, you might think I'm speaking another language. But these are all technical terms that I'll cover in the next chapter. While knowledge of these settings certainly help with the design of the Essbase cube, such as achieving faster retrieval times, they are no longer necessary to completely build a cube.

I'll repeat. I do not have to be an Essbase expert to build an Essbase cube in Essbase Cloud.

With Essbase Cloud, I have a number of options for creating an Essbase cube. I can create one from scratch within the oh-so-user-friendly web interface (if I would like to spend countless hours doing what could take minutes in Excel). I can download one of the provided structured Application Workbooks under the oh-so-cleverly-named card, Templates, manipulate the file to match my cube design, then import it into the Essbase Cloud web interface. OR... wait for it... I can simply export an unstructured flat file from my existing ERP system (or database or any other system) and upload it directly into Essbase Cloud with the click of a button! That's right, Essbase Cloud can do all the thinking for me. This means I can retire, right?

In this chapter, I'm going to jump right into working with Essbase Cloud. Why wait when it's just so easy to use? I'll demonstrate one of the coolest features – building Essbase Cloud cubes quickly from Excel spreadsheets!

## THE UNSTRUCTURED FORMAT

Essbase has become so advanced with Essbase Cloud that it has learned to transform a typical "unstructured" spreadsheet into a single Essbase cube. The days of taking a spreadsheet and puzzling together dimensionality from scratch are over. With the click of a button, Essbase Cloud can piece together which columns have dimensions, which of those text cells are hierarchies, which ones have data, and then build, load, and even calculate a corresponding cube.

Those previous tedious spreadsheets that analysts have spent hours, days, and weeks updating and referencing can be consolidated into a single cube and ready for analysis almost as soon as I desire the information. In DVCS, nice visuals such as graphs, pie charts, and more can be presented in a matter of seconds within OAC. Talk about an efficient way to gain brownie points from those upper management visual fanatics!

In addition to the unstructured format, Essbase Cloud can upload structured spreadsheets that contain more application detail and allow for easier incremental updates. An unstructured format may be used as an initial step to create a cube, but then it can be exported, edited, and imported back in a template form to create a more "controllable" application. More information on structured formats will be covered later in this book.

### Essbase Cloud Unstructured Spreadsheet Template

The primary purpose of the "unstructured" format is to utilize an existing spreadsheet of data. However, there are example templates that can be downloaded and experimented with from the Essbase Cloud web interface (and Cube Designer). I will review these in more detail in later chapters.

To download the unstructured spreadsheet template from the Essbase Cloud web interface,

1. From the Essbase Cloud home page, select *Templates*:

**Note!** Not all cards (icons) will be available until a specific cube is selected. The Templates icon will always be available.

2. Select the Download ⬇ icon next to *Free-form Tabular Data Sample*:

## Templates

| Name | Provider | Description |
|------|----------|-------------|
| Block Storage Sample (Stored) | Oracle | Block storage application workbook. |
| Block Storage Sample (Dynamic) | Oracle | Block storage application workbook. All non-leaf level m |
| Block Storage Sample (Scenario) | Oracle | Block storage application workbook with scenarios enab |
| Demo Basic | Oracle | Basic demo application workbook |
| Aggregate Storage Sample | Oracle | Aggregate storage application workbook. |
| Aggregate Storage Sample Data | Oracle | Data for the aggregate storage application workbook. |
| Free-form Tabular Data Sample | Oracle | Tabular data Excel file. |

3.  Save the spreadsheet to the local drive.

## KoolKart Spreadsheet

Below is a screenshot of the Excel file from KoolKart that will be used in this exercise:

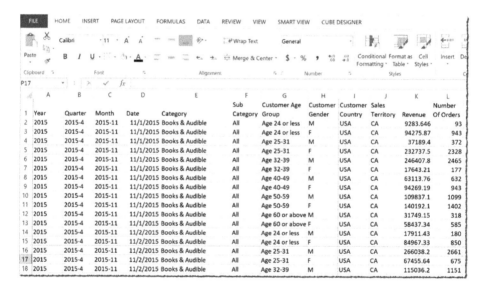

**Note!**        Email info@interrel.com for a copy of the OAC workshop files.

I see the dimensions are laid out across the columns of the spreadsheet, with the corresponding metadata beneath. This is the typical type of spreadsheet one would pull from any relational database.

In this file, row two gives us the revenue amount that came from 93 orders of the category Books & Audible on 11/1/2015 for males that are aged 24 or younger (from the USA) for the sales territory CA. That's great. Fantastic. But what if I wanted to see *total* Books & Audible revenue on 11/1/2015, regardless of gender or age? I suppose I could filter the columns accordingly, then use an Excel formula to add up the value, but where's the efficiency in that?

 It's better to be efficient vs. inefficient.

**Note!**

Imagine how I would like to analyze this data. What is the relationship between the various columns? Columns A – D are all related to time, therefore, I would like to group and subtotal the data for the dates, with dates rolling up to months, months rolling up to quarters, and quarters rolling up to years. Columns F and I – Sub Category and Customer Country, respectively – have only one value down the entire spreadsheet, which doesn't give me much information other than the Sub Category is always "All" and the Customer Country is always "USA". Column J contains Sales Territory information but, for this particular mission, I do not care about this information, so I might choose to exclude this column. Column L, Number of Orders and column K (Revenue) are the values I would like to aggregate.

## CREATE A CUBE USING THE CUBE DESIGNER

Essbase Cloud has its very own Smart View extension: the Cube Designer. While the primary function of the Cube Designer is to design cubes (go figure), it can also perform other actions, such as analyzing and calculating data. I must have at least version 11.1.2.5.620 of Smart View to utilize this feature (Smart View is backwards compatible with both Cloud and on-premises).

Using the Cube Designer, a cube can be created and imported from an unstructured file straight from Excel. The basic steps for creating a cube using the Cube Designer include:

1) Connect to the Cube Designer extension for Smart View
2) Select options
3) Define modifications
4) Review modifications
5) Build the cube

### Connect to the Cube Designer Extension for Smart View

I'm going to build KoolKart's sales application by utilizing the Cube Designer extension in Microsoft Excel.

To connect to Cube Designer,
1. Select *Panel* on the Smart View ribbon:

2. From the Smart View Panel, select *Private Connections*:

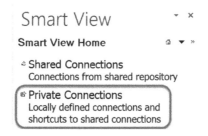

3. Create a private connection with the Cloud service instance URL, with */essbase/smartview* added to the end. For example: *http://Server:9000/essbase/smartview*

4. Navigate to the Cube Designer ribbon and select *Connections*:

5. Select the connection just created and click *Save*.
6. If prompted again, enter your *Username* and *Password* >> click *Sign In*.

## Define the Cube

To create a cube from a spreadsheet,

7. While still connected to Cube Designer, open the unstructured spreadsheet that contains the data for analysis and use it to create the cube.

**Note!**   You could have opted to open the spreadsheet before connecting.

8. Select *Transform Data*:

A wizard will now open up.

9. Enter an Application Name of *KoolKart* and Cube Name of *Sales*.

If the application already exists, the cube will be added to that application. If the application does not exist, a new application will be created.

**Note!**

Application and cube names must be 30 characters or less. Restricted characters include spaces, asterisks, brackets, colons, semicolons, commas, equal signs, greater-than signs, less-than signs, periods, plus signs, question marks, double quotation marks, single quotation marks, forward slashes, backslashes, vertical bars, and tabs: * [ ] : ; ' = > < . + ? " ' / \ |

### Define Modifications

Before data is loaded into a cube, I have the option to make definition modifications in either Tree View or Grid View. The following actions can be performed in Tree View:

- Define dimension hierarchies by dragging and dropping column headers beneath the appropriate members. Although Cube Designer could interpret how the outline should look, this ensures the hierarchy structure is just the way I want it.
- Define measures by dragging and dropping column headers beneath *Measures*. This ensures that all of the members that belong in the Measures dimension land there as expected when the cube is created.
- Define columns to leave out of the cube by dragging and dropping column headers beneath *Skipped*. Any column header moved here will be left out of the cube.

The following actions can be performed in Grid View:

- Define dimension hierarchies by entering column header parent names under the *Parent Name*. This will move the corresponding member beneath this member. If the member does not already exist in the current outline, it will be created.

**Note!** This is similar to dragging and dropping a column header beneath another while in Tree View, but gives the extra functionality of creating parent members that weren't already in the interpreted outline in Tree View.

- Update a dimension name by keying in a new name under *Name*. This allows the user to rename the dimension something different from the original column heading.
- Update the dimension type by selecting one of the following options under *Type*:

    o **Skip** - will leave the column out of the outline
    o **Generation** - will define the column as a member in the outline
    o **Measure** - will define the column as a member in the Measures dimension
    o **Alias** - will define the column as an alias
    o **Attribute** - will define the column as an attribute

To define modifications for the unstructured spreadsheet,
10. In the Transform Data Wizard, uncheck the *Modifications not required* option.

Leaving this option checked will create the cube exactly as the Cube Designer interprets it to be.

Unchecking the box will allow the user to review and update the hierarchies and member properties as outlined above:

11. Review the proposed outline structure in Tree View, which is the default view:

12. Use the drag and drop feature to better define dimension hierarchies, measures, and any columns that need to be skipped (excluded) from the cube. Make the following updates:
    a.  Drag and drop *Quarter* under *Year*
    b.  Drag and drop *Month* under *Quarter*
    c.  Drag and drop *Date* under *Month*
    d.  Drag and drop *Sub Category* under *Category*
    e.  Drag and drop *Revenue* and *Number Of Orders* under *Measures*
    f.  Drag and drop *Sales Territory* under *Skipped*

Tree View should now look like the following:

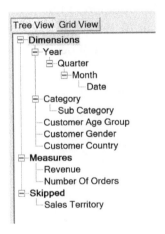

13. Select Grid View:

14. Notice that this view allows for quick, mass updates. Make the following changes:
    a.  Enter "TimePeriod" into the Year's *Parent Name* field
    b.  Set Customer Age Group, Customer Gender, and Customer Country Type to *Attribute*

Grid View should now look like the following:

| Cell | Header | Parent Name | Name | Type |
|---|---|---|---|---|
| A1 | Year | TimePeriod | Year | Generation |
| B1 | Quarter | Year | Quarter | Generation |
| C... | Month | Quarter | Month | Generation |
| D... | Date | Month | Date | Generation |
| E1 | Category | | Category | Generation |
| F1 | Sub Category | Category | Sub Category | Generation |
| G... | Customer Age Group | | Customer Age Group | Attribute |
| H... | Customer Gender | | Customer Gender | Attribute |
| I1 | Customer Country | | Customer Country | Attribute |
| J1 | Sales Territory | | | Skip |
| K1 | Revenue | Measures | Revenue | Measure |
| L1 | Number Of Orders | Measures | Number Of Orders | Measure |

⊙ To Sheet   ⊙ From Sheet   ⊙ Options

## Review Modifications

Modifications made within Grid View of the Transform Data window are automatically updated in the Tree View tab and vice-versa. Once the changes are completed, they will need to be pushed to the sheet. Then the column headers will need to be updated as well.

To review modifications,

15. Select *Tree View*:

16. Review the outline one last time:

17. Select *To Sheet*:

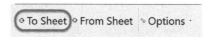

18. Review the changes in the Headers for each column.

### Build the Cube

Once I have defined the Application Name and Cube Name and created and reviewed all modifications, I am ready to build the cube.

To build the cube,
19. Select *Run* from the Transform Data Wizard and save the file.

**Note!**          The Excel workbook name must not exceed 30 characters.

20. Select *Yes* to build the cube.
21. Select *Yes* to launch the Job Viewer:

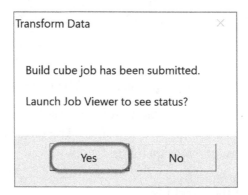

22. Review the status of the Cube Build in the Job Viewer.

If the status reads *Success*, I'm done. If the status reads *Error*, I can double-click on the word *Error* and review the Error Details section in the Job Details screen. I can also select each error's .txt file under *Server Error Files* and select *Open* to view and troubleshoot the errors.

COMMUNICATION: Director Chang and Edward Roske

[11:18] CHANG: Hi Edward. This is Director Glen Chang. We found out you are alive and on top of that, implemented PBCS for the Vision Company. All of i.n.t.e.r.R.e.l. is rooting for you! We are working on a plan to rescue you from the Cloud.

[11:29] ROSKE: Great to finally hear from you guys. Really looking forward to not dying! I want to make it clear that it wasn't the crew's fault that they left me here in the Cloud, but I still blame Glenn Schwartzberg for a lot of other things. Side question: What did they say when they found out that I'm alive?

[11:41] CHANG: Tell us about the PBCS implementation. How did you create the application, build dimensions, load and calculate data, and build the user interfaces? As to your side question: We haven't told the crew that you are alive yet. We need them to focus on getting home safely.

[11:52] ROSKE: Creating the PBCS application was simple using a guided wizard. You can easily import dimensions with the web interface and load data with Data Management. Also: Tell the crew I'm alive! What is wrong with you?

## CREATE A CUBE USING THE WEB INTERFACE

A cube can also be created and imported from an unstructured file using the Essbase Cloud web interface. The basic steps to creating a cube using the web interface include:

1) Import the Excel file
2) Define modifications
3) Build the cube

### Import the Excel File

As mentioned above, in addition to creating a cube from the Cube Designer in Excel, I can choose to upload a spreadsheet straight into the web interface.

To import an unstructured spreadsheet Excel file,
1.  From the Essbase Cloud home page, in the bottom of the flipboard, select *Import*:

2.  Select *Choose File* and browse to the appropriate local system file.
3.  Enter an Application Name of *KoolKart_UI* and Cube Name of *Sales*.

If the application already exists, the cube will be added to that application. If the application does not exist, then a new application will be created.

### Define Modifications

Like in Cube Designer, before data is transformed, I have the option to make a few modifications. At the time this was written, the Import Cube method via the web interface offered a few different options from Cube Designer and vice versa. These differences are outlined below.

**Note!**

Due to the differing functionalities at this point in time, the end result of the *KoolKart_UI.Sales* cube in the web interface workshop will differ from the *KoolKart.Sales* cube created in the Cube Designer workshop.

The following actions that are specific to the Essbase Cloud web interface Import Cube method include:

- Indication of whether the cube is ASO or BSO (read "Chapter 5: Essbase Concepts Defined" for more information on why you would choose one over the other)
- If the cube is BSO, indication if Hybrid BSO is enabled
- Indication of whether or not Sandboxing is enabled

The following actions, similar to Cube Designer options, can also be performed:

- Update dimension names by selecting *Dimensions* and keying in the new name under *New Name*
- Update dimension types by selecting one of the following options under *Type*:
    o Skip
    o Generation
    o Measure
    o Alias
    o Attribute

The ability to define dimension hierarchies, whether through the drag and drop method in the Excel Tree View or by defining Parent Names in the Excel Grid View is only available in Cube Designer (not the web interface).

To define modifications,

4.  Checkmark *Show Advanced*:

5.  Make the following updates:
    a.  Change *Sales Territory* Type to *Skip*
    b.  Change *Revenue* and *Number of Orders* Type to *Measure* (if not already set by default)

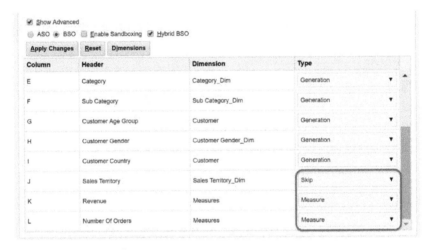

## Build the Cube

Once I have defined the Application Name and Cube Name and created and reviewed all modifications, I am ready to build the cube.

6.  Select *Apply Changes*:

7.  Select *Deploy and Close*:

The Import Cube screen will close, and the user should receive a pop-up screen window indicating that the cube was created successfully:

The application and cube can now be seen from the home page:

ORACLE' Analytics Cloud - Essbase

# REVIEW THE CUBE STRUCTURE

Once I have created the cube, it's good to review the outline and other properties. This can be done in both the Essbase web interface and Smart View.

### Review through the Web Interface

One way to review the outline is within the Essbase Cloud web interface.

To review the new cube,

1. Navigate to the Essbase Cloud web interface with the provided URL.

2. From the Essbase Cloud home page, navigate to *KoolKart >> Sales*:

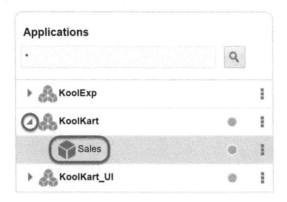

3. Now that the cube has been selected, select *Outline*.

4. Review the following properties that were defined when the cube was created:
   a. Dimension/Member Name
   b. Member ID
   c. Statistics
      i. **C.#** - the number of children the member has

ii.  **D.#** - the number of descendants the member has

iii.  **G.#** - the member's generation number

iv.  **L.#** - the member's level number

d.  Dimension Type

e.  Dimension Storage Type

f.  Data Storage Type

g.  Time Balance

h.  Skip Option

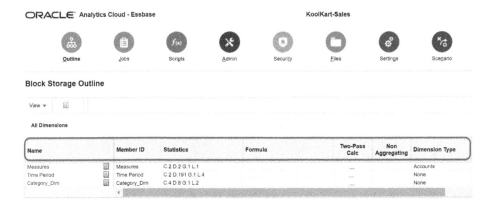

5.  Select a dimension name to drill down further to see its members. Below I have selected the *Time Period* dimension:

**All Dimensions  >  Time Period**

| Name | | Member ID | Statistics |
|---|---|---|---|
| 2015 | | Time Period.2015 | C.1 D.64 G.2 L.3 |
| 2016 | | Time Period.2016 | C.2 D.125 G.2 L.3 |

**Note!**

When drilling in, consolidation operators are now displayed between the Formula and Two-Pass Calc columns.

### Review through Smart View

I can also review the cube within Smart View. Without going into too much detail, I'm going to show the power of Essbase Cloud and its ad hoc capabilities in Smart View.

To review a cube within Smart View,

1.  From Excel, connect to Smart View by selecting *Panel* on the Smart View ribbon:

2.  From the Smart View Panel, select Private Connections:

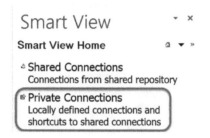

3.  Select the previously defined connection.
4.  Enter your *Username* and *Password*.
5.  Expand *EssbaseCluster*, and then the Application *KoolKart* and cube *Sales*.

6.  Select the cube and then *Ad hoc analysis* at the bottom:

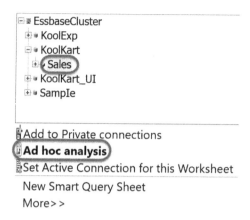

7.  You are now connected to the cube and ready to analyze data.

The Sales cube I created earlier with Cube Designer has three primary dimensions: Measures, Category_Dim, and TimePeriod:

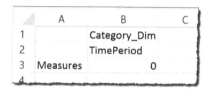

I can also select *Analyze* from the Cube Designer ribbon and it will bring up the Smart View panel, ready for analysis.

8.  Select a dimension, then select *Member Selection* from the Essbase ribbon to review the hierarchy structure of that dimension:

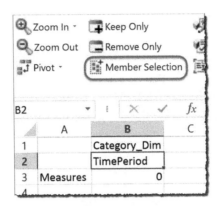

9.  Select the member or members that need to be added to the grid by placing a checkmark next them >> select the *Add* » icon >> click *OK*:

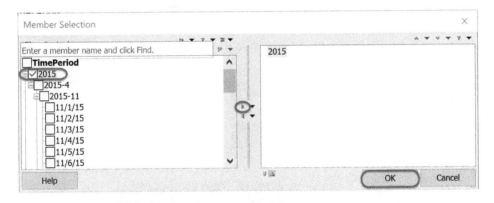

10. Repeat steps 8 & 9, selecting at least one member for the remaining dimensions:

11. Select *Refresh* from the Essbase ribbon:

The number displayed in cell B3 represents the data loaded to the intersection of each of the members represented in the ad hoc grid. In the below example, 552,710,607.84 is in the Measure *Revenue*, in the Category *Books & Audible*, for the TimePeriod *2015*:

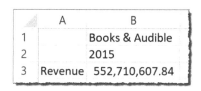

| | A | B |
|---|---|---|
| 1 | | Books & Audible |
| 2 | | 2015 |
| 3 | Revenue | 552,710,607.84 |

If you have been following along with the KoolKart Sales Data example, filter the original unstructured spreadsheet to Year: *2015*, Category: *Books & Audible*, and the *Revenue* column. Notice that the number matches 552, 710,607.8:

**Note!**

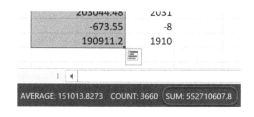

To analyze the cube from different perspectives, try moving around dimensions in the ad hoc grid, from columns to rows and rows to columns.

To pivot dimensions using the *Pivot* option,

12. Select a cell in the columns (in my example, 2015 which is my TimePeriod member). Select *Pivot* from the Essbase ribbon:

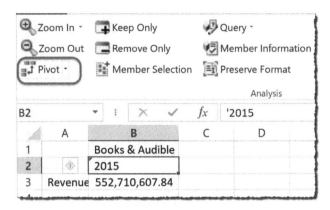

**Note!**

You must have at least one dimension in the rows and one dimension in the columns.

13. Review the new display of the grid:

|  | A | B | C |
|---|---|---|---|
| 1 |  |  | Books & Audible |
| 2 | 2015 | Revenue | 552,710,607.84 |

14. Select a dimension member in the rows (*Revenue* in this example, which is the Measures member), then select *Pivot* from the Essbase ribbon:

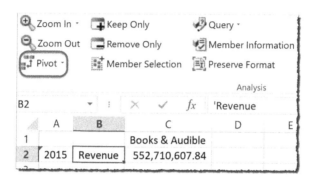

15. Review the new display of the grid:

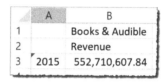

To analyze the dimensions further, try selecting multiple members or even an entire hierarchy for a dimension.

16. To zoom in on an entire hierarchy, select the dimension in the rows >> select the down arrow ▾ next to *Zoom In* >> pick *All Levels*:

17. Notice that the entire TimePeriod hierarchy appears with data for each time member and with corresponding values for *Revenue* for the category Books & Audible:

|     | A        | B              |
|-----|----------|----------------|
| 58  | 12/25/15 | 9,711,233.66   |
| 59  | 12/26/15 | 9,857,014.34   |
| 60  | 12/27/15 | 11,198,870.13  |
| 61  | 12/28/15 | 7,919,640.88   |
| 62  | 12/29/15 | 10,305,675.71  |
| 63  | 12/30/15 | 5,647,752.08   |
| 64  | 12/31/15 | 7,719,647.49   |
| 65  | 2015-12  | 274,669,273.56 |
| 66  | 2015-4   | 552,710,607.84 |
| 67  | 2015     | 552,710,607.84 |

In my example, I only had three dimensions and, therefore, did not utilize the POV (Point of View). For cubes with more than three dimensions, try moving some dimensions to the POV.

To move a dimension from the grid to the POV,

18. Select the dimension member >> select the drop-down ▼ icon next to *Pivot* >> select *Pivot to POV*:

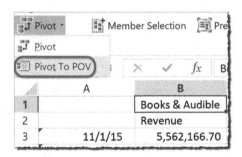

By default, the dimensions in the POV will be listed in row one with an arrow drop-down for member selection.

In my example, I only have one member in the POV (remember I must always have one dimension in a row and one in a column):

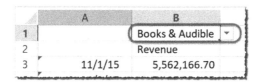

19. To remove the POV from row one and have it isolated off to the side, I can use the *POV* button on the Essbase ribbon:

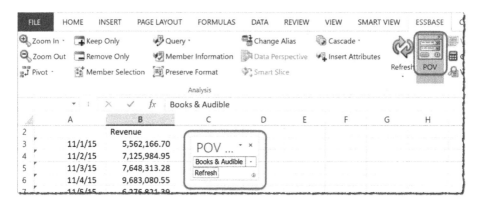

**Note!**     If you want to move the POV back to row one, select the *POV* button on the Essbase ribbon again.

20. Continue experimenting with ad hoc analysis until everything looks as expected (or until you realize you're screwed and need to start over, of course).

**Note!**     For more information on Smart View analysis, see Chapter 9, "Analyze Data in Smart View."

**Meanwhile, back on earth…**

"Uh, Director Chang?" Sarah said, peeking her head into Chang's office.

"You are?" Director Chang asked, rubbing a hand over his tired eyes.

"Sarah 'Purnell' Branhagen, from the Essbase Mission Specialist division. I know how to save the project and Edward."

"We've been trying to figure that out now for days. And you've solved it?" Doubt filled his voice (using air from his lungs).

Sarah handed Director Chang the summary of the mission plan she had created to save Edward. She'd already completed the first part of the mission by creating the KoolKart Sales cube from an unstructured Excel sheet. She'd proven that OAC could work and solve JWE's requirements. Each company can roll out an OAC solution to meet their needs, and it doesn't require a super techy Essbase resource. Now all they needed was the Ranger crew's help.

The mission was divided into six parts, or sub-missions. Sub-Mission 2 would be to upload The Beverage Company's Sample.Basic Application Workbook into OAC and build another OAC Essbase cube for the KoolKart expenses using the Cube Designer. Sub-Mission 3 would be to set up the processes and steps to manage dimensions, data loads, and calculations using TBC's Sample.Basic cube. Sub-Mission 4 would be to migrate Vision's on-premises cube to the Cloud. Sub-Mission 5 would be to perform ad hoc analysis in Excel with TBC's Sample.Basic cube. Sub-Mission 6 would be to create data visualizations for both the KoolKart and TBC data sets.

If they could do this (completing what she inexplicably called the "Sarah Purnell Maneuver"), the crew of the Ranger would be catapulted around the Earth, using the gravity assist to send them back into the Cloud where they could rescue Edward.

"It's risky," said Director Chang. The doubt was still there but now with an added sliver of hope.

"Not really," Sarah replied. "Implementing the solutions in Oracle Analytics Cloud will be simple.

Not that they need it with OAC, but with the crew's extensive experience, they can implement this in just a few sols, and we'll have the course set to rescue Edward."

# CHAPTER 5: ESSBASE CONCEPTS DEFINED

---

**Meanwhile, back on earth...**

"What the frak is 'Project Elrond'?" potty-mouthed Danielle White asked as she walked into the conference room already filled with the other i.n.t.e.r.R.e.l. members Director Glen Chang, Flight Director Ali Flint, Mission Operations Directorate Jennifer Hughes, and Flight Surgeon Robin Alex.

"I had to make up something," Director Chang said.

"So you came up with Elrond?" Danielle asked.

"Because it's a secret meeting?" Robin asked. "The email said to tell no one."

"Why does 'Elrond' mean 'secret meeting?'" Danielle asked.

"The Council of Elrond. From the Lord of the Rings. It's the meeting where they decide to destroy the One Ring."

Danielle rolled her eyes. "Geez, was Project 'I Still Live in My Parents' Basement' taken?"

In the awkward silence that followed, Director Chang passed out the "Sarah Purnell Maneuver" Mission Summary report. The group read the report and then almost all at once jumped in with questions.

"JWE and their companies don't have an Essbase Administrator. All they have are some financial analysts who love Excel," said Flight Director Flint.

"There is no way to implement the solution in time!" called Flight Surgeon Alex.

Hughes added, "Won't the front end tools be too complicated to learn?"

"With OAC, you don't have to have a super experienced Essbase Administrator. We will be able to implement this in just a few sols. The front end tools are easy to learn and very intuitive," countered Sarah.

"It can definitely work," concluded Director Chang.

"We have to let the crew of the Ranger know and weigh in," said Flight Director Flint. "They are the ones we are putting at risk and asking them to extend their journey home."

"No," Director Chang said. "It's too risky. We still haven't even told them that Edward is alive. We have to wait until we reach our final decision. Before we decide, I've asked Sarah to review some of the Essbase fundamentals that will be required for this mission."

# What is Essbase?

### History Lesson

Essbase is currently developed by a company named Oracle. Prior to the earthshaking acquisition by Oracle, Essbase was developed by a company named Hyperion Solutions Corporation. Although Hyperion was founded in 1981, the Essbase product came along in the early 1990's, compliments of a company whose only product was Essbase: Arbor Software. Up until 1998 when Hyperion and Arbor "merged," the two companies were fierce competitors who were just as likely to spit on each other in waiting rooms as work together. (I am kidding, but only slightly.)

Arbor Software was founded in 1991 by Jim Dorrian and Bob Earle. They noticed at the time that companies were beginning to use spreadsheets not just for presentation of information but as a place to store data and business logic. Often, multiple sources of data were being consolidated together in spreadsheets, and they were even seeing companies begin to release analysis to the public based on data in spreadsheets.

Jim and Bob wanted to build a database for spreadsheets. The original name for the solution was *eSSbase*, which stands for Spread Sheet database (the e was only added to help folks pronounce it correctly).

Check out the actual memo that was sent to the Arbor employees:

---

**InterOffice Memo**

**To:**        All Arbor

**From:**      Mike Florio

**Date:**      March 12, 1992

**Subject:**   Product Name

---

As you probably have heard by now, our product name is

## *eSSbase*™

It stands for "Spread Sheet Database" (the "e" is there to help people pronounce it correctly.)

Our graphic designer thinks it looks better shown as above (bold, italic, serifed typeface.)

The Lawyers have provided us with the attached guidelines for useage, please take a few minutes to review the attached. If you have any questions, just contact me

Thanks,

Mike.

---

Thanks to some creativity and venture capital (of course) from Hummer Winblad, they released the first version of Essbase in 1992. This original release of the product garnered three whole paragraphs of press coverage in Software Magazine on May 15, 1992. Here it is in all its "babe in the woods waiting to be eaten by bears" naiveté:

---

# Data server "feeds" 1-2-3 or Excel
## Arbor Software Corp.'s Essbase data server
Software Magazine; May 15, 1992

Following a three-year development effort, start-up Arbor Software Corp., Santa Clara, Calif., has built a data server that "feeds" popular desktop offerings, including 1-2-3 from Lotus Development Corp., and Excel from Microsoft Corp., on client machines.

"We conceded the front end to [widely installed] spreadsheets," said James Dorrian, president and co-founder. "We built the product with two assumptions: that people knew their spreadsheets and that people knew their jobs."

According to Marketing Vice President Michael Florio, the OS/2-based $22,000 Essbase offers users in client/server environments simultaneous access to large volumes of multidimensional spreadsheet data.

Notice that Essbase was originally developed to run on OS/2, and its claim to fame was that it fed spreadsheets. Also, notice that you could get a copy for only $22,000, which sort of goes to show you that technology doesn't always get cheaper over time.

The first version of the product wasn't nearly as user friendly as it is today. Ignoring the Herculean effort required to actually build an Essbase cube, retrieving data into Excel (or Lotus, at the time) required writing requests to Essbase in a language known as "Essbase Report Scripting":

| | A |
|---|---|
| 1 | <PAGE (Measures, Product, Market) |
| 2 | Profit |
| 3 | Product |
| 4 | Market |
| 5 | <COLUMN (Scenario) |
| 6 | <CHILD Scenario |
| 7 | <ROW (Year) |
| 8 | <ICHILD Year |
| 9 | ! |

But over time the world came to know and love the Essbase Spreadsheet add-in for Excel.

When I chose *Essbase >> Retrieve,* I saw a friendly interface:

| | A | B | C | D | E |
|---|---|---|---|---|---|
| 1 | | | Profit | Product | Market |
| 2 | | Actual | Budget | Variance | Variance % |
| 3 | Qtr1 | 24703 | 30580 | -5877 | -19.21844343 |
| 4 | Qtr2 | 27107 | 32870 | -5763 | -17.53270459 |
| 5 | Qtr3 | 27912 | 33980 | -6068 | -17.85756327 |
| 6 | Qtr4 | 25800 | 31950 | -6150 | -19.24882629 |
| 7 | Year | 105522 | 129380 | -23858 | -18.44025352 |

The Essbase add-in was everything the world thought they needed for Essbase until Smart View came along.

When Essbase was first released, no one was quite sure what it was. Was it some sort of spreadsheet on steroids? Was it a temporary employee who was really good at typing? Was it a database? If so, why didn't it have records and fields, and most importantly, why didn't it let IT geeks write SQL to access it?

Everyone was pretty sure what it wasn't: a typical relational database. The creators originally called it a "data server." Shortly after Essbase was created, they commissioned a study by the late Dr. E.F. Codd (the same Ph.D. who came up with the original rules for what constituted a true relational database) to determine what the heck Essbase was.

Dr. Codd was definitely impressed. He felt that this wasn't a relational database, yet it was definitely a database and a very important new type to boot. He called it an "OLAP" database to separate it from every other database up to that point.

To put it simply, all databases prior to Essbase were built for the purpose of storing transactions. The goal for these systems was to get individual records into the database as quickly as possible and to get those same records back out again as quickly as possible. A side goal was to store that data in as small a space as possible, because those were the days when hard drive space cost as much as a good mule. Summarization of these types of databases was possible, but definitely not the objective of the database design. Dr. Codd classified traditional relational databases "OLTP" (On-Line Transaction Processing).

He knew that Essbase was the first database designed purely to support analysis. Knowing that this was going to be The Next Big Thing, he created a term to describe these databases: OLAP (On-Line Analytical Processing). So what does that look like exactly?

### The Magic Filing Cabinet

i.n.t.e.r.R.e.l. Architect Joe Aultman best described Essbase as the magic filing cabinet. Have a look at this really simple Profit & Loss Statement:

|                  | Actual  | Budget  |
|------------------|---------|---------|
| Sales            | 400,855 | 373,080 |
| COGS             | 179,336 | 158,940 |
| **Margin**       | 221,519 | 214,140 |
| Total Expenses   | 115,997 | 84,760  |
| **Profit**       | **105,522** | **129,380** |

It only has two dimensions. The Measures dimension (often called Accounts) is shown down the rows. Across the columns is the Scenario dimension. Some people like to call this dimension Category, Ledger, or Version. It is Essbase tradition to call the dimension that contains Actual, Budget, Forecast, and the like Scenario, and I'll follow the tradition.

The only two dimensions so far are Scenario and Measures. The more detailed breakdowns of Measures (Sales, COGS, Margin, etc.) are the members of the Measures dimension. Actual and Budget are members in the Scenario dimension. A *member* identifies a particular element within a dimension.

If I pivot the Measures up to the columns and the Scenario dimension down to the rows, our report will now look like this:

|            | Sales   | COGS    | **Margin** | Total Expenses | **Profit** |
|------------|---------|---------|------------|----------------|------------|
| **Actual** | 400,855 | 179,336 | 221,519    | 115,997        | 105,522    |
| **Budget** | 373,080 | 158,940 | 214,140    | 84,760         | 129,380    |

While it doesn't look very good, it does illustrate a couple of important points. First, a dimension can be placed into the rows, columns, or the POV (as you'll see in a second). If it's really a dimension (as Scenario and Measures both are), there are no restrictions on which dimensions can be down the side or across the top. Second, notice that the values in the second report are the same as the values in the first report. Actual Sales are 400,855 in both reports. Likewise, Budgeted Profit is 129,380 in both reports. This is not magic.

**Note!**

A dimension can only exist in either the rows, columns, or POV at one time. And you must have at least one dimension in the rows and one in the columns.

A spreadsheet is inherently two dimensional (as are most printed reports). It has rows and columns. This is great if your company only produces a Profit & Loss Statement one time, but most companies will tend to have Profit (be it positive or negative) in every month. To represent this in Excel, I use the spreadsheet tabs (one for each month):

| All Products and Markets.xls | Actual | Budget |
|---|---|---|
| Sales | 31,538 | 29,480 |
| COGS | 14,160 | 12,630 |
| **Margin** | 17,378 | 16,850 |
| Total Expenses | 9,354 | 6,910 |
| **Profit** | 8,024 | 9,940 |

Jan / Feb / Mar / Apr / May / Jun / Jul / Aug / Sep / Oct / Nov / Dec

I've now introduced a third dimension. Most people call it Time, but Sample.Basic calls it Year (just to be contrary). It could be across the columns (if you wanted to see a nice trend of twelve months of data) or down the rows, but I've put it in the pages (a new tab for each "page"). That is, if I click on the Jan tab, the whole report will be for January.

If I'm looking for Actual Sales of 400,855, I won't find it now because that was the value for the whole year. I could get it by totaling the values of all twelve tabs onto a summary tab.

Right now, this spreadsheet is not broken down by product or market. Within Excel, it's problematic to represent more than three dimensions (since I've used the rows, columns, and tabs). One way is to have a separate file for each combination of product and market:

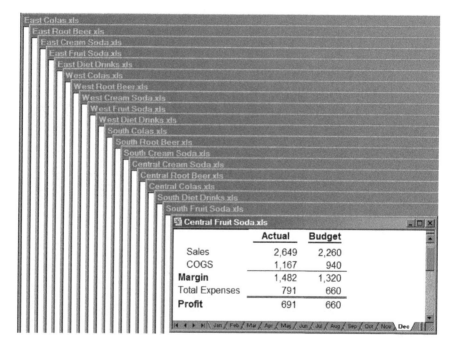

As you can see, this is getting ridiculous. What if I want to pivot our market dimension down to our columns so that I could compare profitability across different regions? To do this, I'd either have to have a series of linked spreadsheet formulas (which would break as soon as I added or deleted a new product or market) or I could hire a temporary employee to print out all the spreadsheets and type them in again with the markets now in the columns. While the latter method is obviously error-prone, the "rekeying" method is the one used by the majority of the companies in the world that do not own Essbase.

Since Market and Product are dimensions, it should be no more difficult to put them in the columns or rows than Scenario or Measures.

As I'll discuss later, producing a report with markets down the side and products across the top is no more difficult than dragging-and-dropping in the Essbase magic filing cabinet:

|  | **Actual** | **Profit** | **Year** |  |  |
|---|---|---|---|---|---|
|  | Colas | Root Beer | Cream Soda | Fruit Soda | **Product** |
| East | 12,656 | 2,534 | 2,627 | 6,344 | **24,161** |
| West | 3,549 | 9,727 | 10,731 | 5,854 | **29,861** |
| South | 4,773 | 6,115 | 2,350 | - | **13,238** |
| Central | 9,490 | 9,578 | 10,091 | 9,103 | **38,262** |
| **Market** | **30,468** | **27,954** | **25,799** | **21,301** | **105,522** |

In very basic terms, an Essbase cube is like a magic filing cabinet that stores data for fast retrievals and analysis. I can slice and dice and pivot data at the speed of light (well, maybe not that fast). It provides a very powerful aggregation and calculation engine along with security filters for end user access.

### Multi-Dimensional Databases

In reality, Essbase is not a magic filing cabinet...but *like* one. Essbase is actually a multi-dimensional database (MDDB or MDB, for short). Multi-dimensional means simply that any of the dimensions set up in a database could be put in the rows or the columns (or applied to the whole page/report).

All relational databases are two-dimensional: records and fields. While any relational database can be set up to give the appearance of having multiple dimensions, it takes a lot of upfront work by developers. Essbase and other multi-dimensional databases have dimensionality built into the cubes to support reporting and analysis.

### Optimized for Retrieval

Essbase cubes (or databases) are optimized for retrieval at any level of the hierarchy, even the very topmost number that might represent every dollar the company has ever made in its history. OLTP databases (relational databases) are nicely optimized for retrieval of detailed records but definitely not hierarchical information. By pre-saving summarized information, Essbase allows analysis to happen from the top down with no decrease in performance.

For Essbase, the hierarchy is native to the cube itself. This is far different from relational databases that store the data in one table and then have one or more other tables that can be joined in to view data in a rolled-up fashion. For Essbase, the hierarchy is the database. When I change the hierarchy logic in Essbase as to how a product is grouped or a market rolls-up, I actually change where the data is stored.

Because hierarchies are inherent to Essbase, drill-down (sometimes known as "slicing and dicing" but never known as "making julienne data") is inherent as well. Essbase is great at doing ad hoc analysis because it knows that when a user double-clicks on Qtr1, she wants to see Jan, Feb, and Mar. This is because the roll-up of months to quarters is pre-defined back on the server.

Now that I've provided a summary of Essbase and how it is different than relational databases, let's get into the more technical details of Essbase cubes. First, let's review the different types of Essbase cubes available.

## TYPES OF ESSBASE CUBES

There are three different types of Essbase Cloud cubes available. Let's review those now.

### BSO Cubes

Block storage option (BSO) cubes were the *original* Essbase cubes. Data is stored in a way that business users intuitively understand and can perform analysis on really, really quickly. BSO cubes come with a powerful calculation engine – so powerful that it can perform complex allocations and other business rules. Users can write data back to any member in the hierarchy if assigned the right access.

While our BSO cubes are awesome in many ways, there are a number of challenges. Unfortunately, the block storage architecture that allows us to create complex business models starts to have performance issues as dimensionality and outline sizes grow. BSO cubes can only get so big. They typically contain 7-10 dimensions, and as I add in thousands and thousands of members, calculation and/or retrieval performance can be negatively impacted. No matter how powerful computers have become in the past 25+ years since Essbase was created, I just can't have it all.

### ASO Cubes

Aggregate storage option cubes are designed to specifically to deal with requirements for very large, sparse data sets with a high number of dimensions and potentially millions of members (any one of these requirements would make a BSO cube hide under the bed and whimper for its mommy). ASO utilizes a different kind of storage mechanism that allows improved aggregation times from ten to one hundred times faster than BSO cubes and a different calculation method called Multi-Dimensional Expression language (MDX) for more simple calculations.

Sometimes, dear reader, when an ASO application loves a BSO application very, very much, along comes a hybrid aggregation cube.

### Hybrid Cubes

Hybrid "Advanced Analytic" (also referred to as hybrid aggregation mode) cubes were introduced in Essbase 11.1.2.3.500 as a new type of BSO cube. Hybrid aggregation cubes (as it is commonly referred to) are technically BSO cubes but they support many common functions of both BSO and ASO. It is a good candidate for most Essbase cubes unless I have a valid reason for using ASO.

Hybrid is enabled by default in Essbase Cloud. All you have to do to create a "hybrid" cube is tag upper level members of sparse dimensions as "dynamic calc" (more on this in just a bit).

Some design considerations for hybrid aggregation cubes are the same as the design considerations for a traditional BSO cube with one main difference. Unlike traditional BSO, I can tag sparse dimensions as dynamic and get faster performance because I no longer have to aggregate that dimension. Users can write back to stored dimensions at any level, and the same calculation engine in BSO is still available to hybrid aggregation cubes; however, dynamic dimensions in a hybrid aggregation cube benefit from lightning-fast aggregations like an ASO cube.

Hybrid aggregation applications truly are a blend of both ASO and BSO, which makes them perfect for cubes where there is a desire to see the latest aggregated numbers as fast as possible.

**Note!**  Essbase Cloud defaults BSO cubes into hybrid mode. To take advantage of hybrid, tag upper level sparse members as "dynamic calc." Upper level sparse members tagged as "store" will function with original BSO functionality.

## DIMENSIONS

After I create my Essbase cube, regardless of type, the next step is create dimensions and members. A "dimension" defines different categories for my data. A dimension can be located on the rows, columns, or pages of my queries. A "member" or "member name" is the short, "computery" name for the node or data element of an Essbase dimension (like 100-10). An "alias" is the longer, more descriptive name for a member (like Cola). All of the dimensions in a cube make up the Essbase "outline" for the cube.

Below is a hierarchy example of a Year dimension in an Essbase cube outline:

### Common Dimensions

While every application will be different, most applications draw from a common set of dimension templates. The details within each dimension may change, and the names of the dimensions may differ, but the same dimensions will keep appearing throughout many Essbase applications at your company. And keep in mind, while these are commonly found dimensions, I do not have to create these dimensions. The Essbase design is unique based on specific reporting and analysis needs.

### Time

All of us experience the constant effects of time and, likewise (with very few exceptions), every Essbase cube has one *or more* time dimensions. This is the dimension that contains the time periods for the cube. Sample.Basic calls this dimension Year:

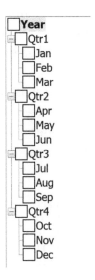

In addition to Year, other common names for this dimension include Periods, All Periods, Time (my personal favorite), Time Periods, Full Year, Year Total, and History. This dimension generally aggregates from the bottom up.

A Time dimension will usually have one or more of the following generations:

- Years
  - Seasons
    - Halves
      - Quarters
        - Months
          - Weeks
            - Days

While it is not unheard of to have an application that looks at hours or portions of hours, this is normally split off into its own dimension and called something like Hours or Time of Day. Call center analysis applications and some retail sales applications analyze data by portions of a day.

It is quite common for an Essbase application to have two time dimensions. One dimension will house the quarters, months, days, and so forth. A separate dimension, generally called Years or FY (for Fiscal Year), will contain the calendar year. Here's an example of a Years dimension:

```
☐Year
  ☐FY09
  ☐FY10
  ☐FY11
  ☐FY12
  ☐FY13
  ☐FY14
  ☐FY15
  ☐FY16
  ☐FY17
```

Unlike the Time dimensions that usually contain quarters and months, Years dimensions typically do not aggregate. Most often, the top member of a Years dimension is set to equal the data in the current year.

Some applications will combine a Time and Years dimension into one.

This is often done when the Time dimension goes all the way down to the day-level and a company wants to do analysis by day of the week:

```
⊟···Time <3> {Day of Week}
    ┊····2014 (+)
    ⊟···2015 (+) <6>
    ┊      ┊····Jan 2015 (+)
    ┊      ┊····Feb 2015 (+)
    ┊      ┊····Mar 2015 (+)
    ┊      ┊····Apr 2015 (+)
    ┊      ┊····May 2015 (+)
    ┊      ⊟···Jun 2015 (+) <11>
    ┊             ┊····Jun 1, 2015 (+) {Day of Week: Monday}
    ┊             ┊····Jun 2, 2015 (+) {Day of Week: Tuesday}
    ┊             ┊····Jun 3, 2015 (+) {Day of Week: Wednesday}
    ┊             ┊····Jun 4, 2015 (+) {Day of Week: Thursday}
    ┊             ┊····Jun 5, 2015 (+) {Day of Week: Friday}
    ┊             ┊····Jun 6, 2015 (+) {Day of Week: Saturday}
    ┊             ┊····Jun 7, 2015 (+) {Day of Week: Sunday}
    ┊             ┊····Jun 8, 2015 (+) {Day of Week: Monday}
    ┊             ┊····Jun 9, 2015 (+) {Day of Week: Tuesday}
    ┊             ┊····Jun 10, 2015 (+) {Day of Week: Wednesday}
    ┊             └····Jun 11, 2015 (+) {Day of Week: Thursday}
```

### Measures

Once I have defined the application name, cube name, and Time dimension, almost every Essbase application has a dimension that lists the metrics for the cube. While common practice is to call this dimension Measures, other frequently used names include Accounts and Metrics.

In the example below, the Measures dimension contains some profit and loss accounts, inventory metrics, and three calculated ratios:

```
☐ Measures
  ☐ Profit
    ☐ Margin
      ☐ Sales
      ☐ COGS
    ☐ Total Expenses
      ☐ Marketing
      ☐ Payroll
      ☐ Misc
  ☐ Inventory
    ☐ Opening Inventory
    ☐ Additions
    ☐ Ending Inventory
  ☐ Ratios
    ☐ Margin %
    ☐ Profit %
    ☐ Profit per Ounce
```

Notice that under Profit, there are two members: Margin and Total Expenses. Each one of these members has members below it. It's quite common for a Measures dimension to have many levels of hierarchy. A financial reporting application, for instance, might have a hierarchy all the way down to a sub-account level.

While most every application will have a Measures dimension, what constitutes the Measures dimension will differ wildly:

- A financial reporting application will have accounts for income statement, balance sheet, and sometimes cash flow
- An inventory analysis application will have measures for beginning inventory, ending inventory, additions, returns, adjustments, and so forth
- A sales analysis application will have measures for sales dollars, units sold, and average sales price
- A human capital analysis application will have metrics for payroll, FICA, FUTA, sick days, vacation days, years of employment, and so on

The Measures dimension is the most important dimension in any application since it defines what metrics are available for analysis, but I can safely expect every Measures dimension to be unique for every application.

### Scenario

This dimension is common to applications that, in addition to actual data, also have budget, forecast, and/or planning information. The Scenario dimension usually houses members such as Actual, Budget, Forecast, What-If, and several variances (differences between one scenario and another). While the most popular name for this dimension is Scenario (or Scenarios), other common names include Category, Ledger, Cases, and Versions.

As a general rule, I try to avoid calling a Scenario dimension Versions, because PBCS and Hyperion Planning also has a dimension called Versions, in addition to a Scenario dimension. In PBCS, the Versions dimension is used to differentiate between different drafts of budget and plan data. Members in a Versions dimension could be Initial, Draft 1, Draft 2, Draft 3, and Final. To avoid confusion in case you run across any lost Planning users at your company, don't name your Scenario dimension Versions when there are so many other good names from which to choose.

Here is an example Scenario dimension:

```
☐ Scenario
 ├─☐ Actual
 ├─☐ Budget
 ├─☐ Variance
 └─☐ Variance %
```

Most Scenario dimensions are non-aggregating (since it doesn't make a lot of sense to add Actual and Budget together).

### Other Dimensions

Many applications have a dimension that differentiates between different organizational entities. Commonly, this dimension is called Entities, Organization, Departments, Cost Centers, Companies, Locations, or other industry-specific names (like Stores or Branches).

Another common dimension that I might run across is Product, which houses the relationships between products and their categories and families. This is one of the few dimensions where just about everyone calls it the same thing, although the alias differs at the top of the dimension, containing something like All Products or Total Products. The greatest difference in this dimension is the depth to which different applications go. Some Product dimensions stop at different classes of products, while others will go all the way down to individual parts, items, or SKUs (Stock Keeping Units).

Other dimensions tend to be specific to different types of applications. For instance, a Customer dimension will tend to show up in sales analysis and Accounts Receivable applications.

## USER DEFINED ATTRIBUTES (UDAS)

User defined attributes are tags assigned to outline members and are used to describe members, to reference members for specific calculation purposes, and to isolate members for specialized reporting and analysis. A member can have more than one UDA associated with it.

In the example below from Sample.Basic, a UDA describing each market's category has been assigned:

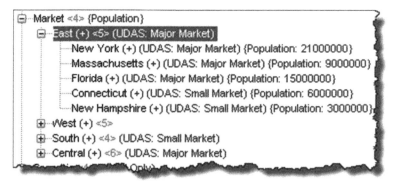

This UDA can be used in calculations. I can even create a market category-specific report, only pulling states that are considered a Major Market.

Other examples of UDA usage include reference flags like "Flip_Sign" or "Expense_Report." The reference flag type UDAs can then be used in load rules (to flip a sign for data values being loaded into the cube) or in member formulas (to help calculate valid positive/negative variances). UDAs can be used for almost anything that business requirements dictate, and do it without adding the storage requirements of extra dimensions or members.

 Data is not automatically calculated by UDA.
**Note!**

## ALTERNATE HIERARCHIES

Alternatively, another alternative is to define an alternate hierarchy that groups members by an alternate grouping. To be a bit clearer (and less funny... OK, it wasn't that funny), within a dimension, I can group the same set of members in different ways.

In an ASO cube, I have one preliminary step to do before I can create an alternate hierarchy.

Alternate hierarchy rules for ASO cubes:

- Must be composed of shared members that refer to non-shared members of a previous hierarchy
- A stored member must occur before its shared members
- The first hierarchy in a dimension should be enabled for multiple hierarchies and cannot contain a shared member
- Shared members can only reside in a dynamic hierarchy dimension or a multiple hierarchy dimension
- A stored hierarchy cannot contain multiple copies of the same shared member
- Non-shared members must be in the same dimension as the shared members
- Shared members automatically inherit any attributes associated with the non-shared member

Additional alternate hierarchy rules for BSO cubes:

- Shared members must be in the same dimension and must reside below the non-shared member
- Shared members cannot have children
- An unlimited number of shared members is allowed
- Shared members cannot have UDAs, member formulas, nor attributes
- Shared members may have aliases

One example: the alternate hierarchy would allow us to easily create a subtotal by customer rating. But what I can't do with an alternate hierarchy is create a cross tab report of Rating by Customer or Size by Customer. What's an Administrator to do?

## ATTRIBUTE DIMENSIONS

In early versions of Essbase you were limited (by practicality, if nothing else) in the number of dimensions that you could have per cube. Most cubes included 7-10 dimensions, and any more than that was seriously stretching the capabilities of Essbase Block Storage cubes. But users complained that they needed to be able to analyze data by more dimensions. For instance, if you had a product dimension, you might want to also have Product Start Date, Sales Manager, Packaging, Size, Weight, Target Group, or others as dimensions. Since all these "dimensions" were really just alternate ways of divvying up the Product dimension (in our case), attribute dimensions were born.

Attribute dimensions are dimensions that can be placed in the rows, columns, or point of view (as I discussed above) with some special considerations. Just like regular dimensions, they define characteristics about the data that is loaded to Essbase. They have hierarchies and members just like any other dimension.

One of the special qualities of attribute dimensions is that adding them to the outline does not impact the size of the Essbase cube. I can add a virtually unlimited number of attribute dimensions (I've seen cubes with over 100 attribute dimensions). Attribute dimensions work well with both ASO and BSO applications (even though ASO applications can have many more dimensions).

Another big benefit with attributes is that they can be used to develop really nice cross tab reports in ASO and hybrid cubes. For example, I can create a report with flavors across the columns and package types down the side. I can't do this with shared members from the same dimension, but attribute dimensions provide a great way to do detailed product and customer analysis that isn't possible otherwise. I can even analyze sum totals, minimums, maximums, averages, and counts of members in attribute dimensions, which certainly isn't possible with UDAs. Though, too many attributes in a report, even ASO, could slow down retrievals.

There are four types of Attribute dimensions: Text, Numeric, Boolean, and Date.

Text attributes are the default type and are used to describe text characteristics:

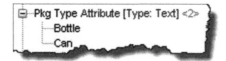

When *AND, OR NOT, <, >, =, >=, <=, <>, !=, IN,* and *NOT IN* operations are performed on text dimensions, Essbase makes logical comparisons for text attribute dimensions. Not always the most logical thing to do, but it's there all the same:

Numeric attribute dimensions contain numeric values at level-0. I can perform *AND, OR NOT, <, >, =, >=, <=, <>, !=, IN,* and *NOT IN* operations on numeric attribute dimensions. I can group numeric values into ranges (using the : symbol) and include these numeric values in calculations:

```
⊟ Ounces Attribute [Type: Numeric] <4>
    ┌─32
    ├─20
    ├─16
    └─12
```

Boolean attribute dimensions contain exactly two members: True and False, Left and Right, or Yes and No. Once the two Boolean member names are defined, I must use the same names for all Boolean attribute dimensions in the cube. When I perform *AND, OR NOT*, <, >, =, >=, <=, <>, !=, *IN*, and *NOT IN* operations on Boolean attribute dimensions, Essbase translates true to 1 and false to 0.

Date attribute members must contain date members at level-0 that are formatted properly. Valid date formats are mm-dd-yyyy or dd-mm-yyyy. All dates must be after 01-01-1970 and before 01-01-2038:

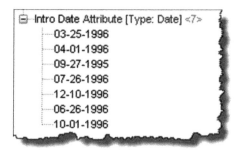

*AND, OR NOT*, <, >, =, >=, <=, <>, !=, *IN*, and *NOT IN* operations can be performed on Date attribute dimensions. Date values can be also included in calculations:

There are five ways to calculate attribute data in BSO cubes: Sum, Count, Average, Minimum, and Maximum. Sum is the default when I don't explicitly specify which one to use, but I can use the other calculations as though it was yet another dimension:

|   | A | B | C | D | E | F |
|---|---|---|---|---|---|---|
| 1 |  |  | Year | Product | Market | Actual |
| 2 |  |  | Bottle | Can | Pkg Type |  |
| 3 | Sales | Sum | $ 270,593 | $ 130,262 | $ 400,855 |  |
| 4 |  | Avg | $ 27,059 | $ 43,421 | $ 30,835 |  |
| 5 |  | Min | $ 11,750 | $ 30,469 | $ 11,750 |  |
| 6 |  | Max | $ 46,956 | $ 62,824 | $ 62,824 |  |
| 7 |  | Count | 10 | 3 | 13 |  |

Sum is the only available aggregation option for ASO and hybrid cubes.

**Note!** Attribute dimensions are always dynamically calculated, which could mean slower performance when an attribute is referenced in a retrieval.

An attribute dimension may only be associated with one "base" dimension and only one level in that dimension. In addition, only one member from an attribute dimension can be associated to a base member. When the attribute changes, all of history changes. I can't track or report that Product Manager for Colas was "Ron" last year and now "Ceca" this year. If I need to see how data varies across other dimensions, I must make the dimension a "real" dimension and store the data as an intersection.

In some cases, the design decisions are clear cut on when to use UDAs vs. alternate hierarchies vs. attribute dimensions. In other cases, the answer will be less obvious. Let's review some design decision points.

### When should you use Attribute Dimensions?

Use attribute dimensions when you need to create crosstab reports (examples include Product in the rows and Product Start Date across the columns or Product Packaging Type in rows and Product Start Date in the columns). Also use attributes when you need to hide a level of detail in most reports but still want it available upon request (e.g., showing product revenue by packaging type vs. the entire list of products).

Attributes are very helpful when performing comparisons based on certain types of data or when you're performing calculations based on characteristics. Finally, use attributes when you need to add dimensionality to the cube without increasing size of the cube. Attributes are "available on request." By default they do not show up in end user ad hoc analysis. In Smart View, attributes can be brought into the query using the Query Designer or Report Designer (as well as free form typing).

### When should you NOT use Attribute Dimensions?

Do not use attribute dimensions when you need to calculate a value by placing a formula on a member (member formulas aren't allowed on attribute members). Watch out for attributes when you need to improve retrieval performance in BSO cubes (attributes are dynamically calculated and can be slow at times for BSO).

### Comparing UDAs, Alternate Hierarchies, and Attribute Dimensions

In the instances where I can't define attributes, UDAs and/or shared members may make sense. UDAs and alternate hierarchies can be defined for dense dimensions where attributes cannot. UDAs are great ways to tag members for calculation purposes, but I don't necessarily need to report by the UDA tags.

All the alternatives I've mentioned for providing additional ways of categorizing and summarizing data (UDAs, attributes, and alternate hierarchies) can be used in Essbase without increasing the cube size like I would if I were to make the dimension a regular stored Essbase dimension.

## FAMILY TREE RELATIONSHIPS

After covering the dimension basics, let's now discuss terminology to reference members within dimensions. These terms correlate to functions within Essbase and can be used in calculations, reporting, and ad hoc analysis. The most common way to refer to members in an outline relative to each other is by using "family tree" relationships. The members directly below a member are called its children. For instance, a Product dimension has five children: Colas, Root Beer, Cream Soda, Fruit Soda, and Diet Drinks. If I ever wanted to refer to those members on a report without hard coding them, I could say "give us all the children of Product."

The advantage to this, aside from the saving in typing, is that if a new product line was to be added (say, "Water"), I wouldn't have to modify our reports. Any report designed to display the children of Product would pick up the new "Water" product and add it to the list automatically.

If Colas, Root Beer, and the other rug rats are all the children of Product, what relation is Product to its children? Assuming I didn't fail "Birds and the Bees 101," I know that Product must be the *parent* of Colas, Root Beer, and the rest. In other words, the parent of any member is the one that the member rolls up into. Qtr2 is the parent of May. Year is the parent of Qtr2.

Since Colas and Root Beer are both the children of Product, Colas and Root Beer are siblings. This is simple, but what relationship do January and May have? Well, their parents are siblings so that makes them... cousins. Correct, but "cousins," while technically correct, isn't used that often. In general, people say that January and May are at the "same level."

What if I want to refer to all the members into which May rolls (not just the one right above)? Well, those are its ancestors, which in this case would be Qtr2 and Year. Correspondingly, the descendants of Year would include all four quarters and all twelve months.

Note that there are members that don't have any children. I refer to childless members as being "level-0." If I ever want all of the bottom, child-less members of a dimension, I'll just ask for the level-0 members. For example, the level-0 members of the Year dimension are the months, and the level-0 members of the Market dimension are the states.

Level-0 members are sometimes also referred to as "leaves," because they're at the edges of the family tree. Edward sometimes refers to level-0 members as "the ones who aren't allowed to sit at the main table on Thanksgiving," but I think he is the only one.

All of the parents of the level-0 members are referred to as level-1. Since the level-0 members of the Year dimension are the months, the level-1 members are the quarters. For the Market dimension, the level-1 members are the regions: East, West, South, and Central.

Just as the parents of the level-0 members are level-1 members, the parents of level-1 members are level-2 members. Their parents are level-3 members and so on up the hierarchy. There are many places in Essbase that I can specify, for example, "All the level-2 members of the Product dimension," so remember that levels count up from the bottom of a dimension starting at 0.

If I want to count down the hierarchy, use generations instead of levels. The dimension itself is considered generation-1 (or "gen1," for short). Its children are gen2. For the Year dimension, the gen2 members are the quarters.

Yes, the quarters are both level-2 and generation-2. Why do I need both levels and generations? Well, in some dimensions with many, many levels in the hierarchy, I'll want to count up from the bottom or down from the top, depending on which I'm closer to. I've seen a dimension with 17 levels in the hierarchy, and it definitely was nice to have both options available. The children of gen2 members are gen3 and so on down the hierarchy.

**Note!** Why do generations start counting from 1 and levels from 0? It's because generation 0 is considered to be the outline itself making its children, the dimensions, generation 1.

While counting with generations is pretty straight-forward, levels can sometimes be a bit tricky. Look at this portion of a Measures (also often times called Account) dimension:

For this dimension, Gen1 is Measures. Gen2 is Profit and Inventory. Gen3 is Margin, Total Expenses, Opening Inventory, Additions, and Ending Inventory.

So far this looks pretty easy, but let's switch our focus to the levels. The level-0 members are Sales, COGS, Marketing, Payroll, Misc,

Opening Inventory, Additions, and Ending Inventory. The level-1 members are Margin, Total Expenses, and Inventory. What are the level-2 members? Profit (because it's the parent of level-1 members Margin and Total Expenses) and Measures (because it's the parent of level-1 member Inventory).

The trickiness is that Measures is *also* a level-3 member because it's the parent of Profit, a level-2 member. This means that if I ask Essbase for level-2 members, I'll get Measures, but I'll also get Measures if I ask for level-3 members. Notice that this counting oddity does not occur with generations.

 This instance of a dimension with unbalanced levels is **Note!** also known as a "ragged hierarchy."

## MEMBER PROPERTIES

Now that I'm fully fluent in Essbase dimensions, hierarchies, and members, let's discuss member properties in more detail. A member is a node or data element in an Essbase dimension, and it will have many member properties that control its behavior in Essbase.

There are some common member properties that exist across all dimensions. I've already discussed two – member name and alias. Other common member properties include consolidation, UDAs, and member formulas. Some member properties are specific to the type of Essbase cube. Some member properties like Expense Reporting and Time Balance (to be discussed shortly) are specific to a dimension type.

### Dimension Types

Dimensions can be assigned dimension types which enable specific functionality. Valid dimension types include:

- None
- Account
- Time
- Country

- Currency
- Attribute

Essbase uses these special Dimension Type tags for helpful prebuilt intelligence calculations. The "Time" dimension tag allows for special logic like time balancing in accounts and Dynamic Time Series functionality. Similarly, there is a special "Account" tag for the dimension containing metrics or measures that provides special intelligence for calculating the member across time and for calculating the proper positive and negative variances.

Currency and Country dimension types are used for the currency module (which you shouldn't really use and was removed in version 11.1.2.4). This little fact is only important to know for customers who are migrating on-premises cubes to Cloud from versions prior to 11.1.2.4.

Only one dimension may have one of these Dimension Types.

### Consolidation Operators

Consolidation operators (or sometimes referred to as unary operators) tell the outline how to consolidate the member. Yes, this is a user friendly description that accurately describes the property. Imagine that! Should the members Dallas and Houston add together to reach a total for Texas? Should units sold be multiplied by price to calculate revenue? I can use consolidation operators to define how a member rolls up in the cube.

Valid consolidation operators include:

- **Addition** (+) - the default consolidation property
- **Subtraction** (-)
- **Multiplication** (*)
- **Division** (/)
- **Percent** (%)
- **No consolidate** (~) - does not consolidate in the same dimension
- **Never consolidate** (^) - does not consolidate across all dimensions

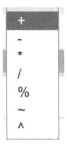

In most cases I will use the default addition consolidation tag (+).

The second most common consolidation tag is "no consolidate" (~). Use this in places where it doesn't make sense to add up members. Would I want to add Actual and Budget together for Scenario? No, so I would tag both Actual and Budget "no consolidate" or ~ in the outline.

A similar consolidation operator is "never consolidate" (^). This is similar to "no consolidate," which will not consolidate a member up its assigned dimension. The "never consolidate" option will not consolidate data across ANY dimension in the Essbase cube. Use this tag for stored members like Price or Index, where it doesn't make sense to sum up together across dimensions like Customer or Product.

Although the ^ operator is valid in ASO applications, it works exactly like the ~ operator. The best advice is to use ~ in ASO, as it still enables dimensions to be marked as "stored" dimensions. I'll cover that in more detail later.

### Data Storage Property

The Data Storage property tells Essbase how the member should be stored. Valid data storage options include:

- **Store data** - store the data value with the member
- **Never share** - do not allow members to be shared implicitly in on-premises Essbase; for Essbase Cloud, this has the same behavior as "Store data"
- **Label only** - create members for navigation and grouping. These members usually won't make sense from a logical consolidation standpoint.
- **Shared member** - share data between two or more members

- **Dynamic calc and store** - do not calculate the data value until a user requests it, but store the data value immediately after the retrieval (applicable to BSO only)
- **Dynamic calc** - do not calculate the data value until a user requests it, and then discard the data value

When should I set a member to "store?" In ASO cubes, most of my members by default will be set to "store data."

When should I use "never share?" When I have a parent that only has one child that rolls up to the parent. On-premises Essbase has a built in feature called Implicit Sharing, a mischievous function that can cause confusion in my Essbase cubes. Essbase tries to be smart for us. When a parent only has one aggregating child, the values for both the parent and the child will always be the same, right? So Essbase decides to only store one value, the child value, which reduces my cube size. But Essbase Cloud does not support implied sharing, so "never share" behaves like "store."

When should I use "dynamic calc?" Use "dynamic calc" for members that have member formulas with variance or ratio calculations. Tagging upper level members of a dimension "dynamic calc" results in dynamic aggregation of that dimension (I don't need to aggregate the dimension in a calc script). It is a common practice to tag upper level dense members as "dynamic calc" in BSO cubes. If I tag all upper level members of a sparse dimension as "dynamic calc," Essbase Cloud kicks the cube into hybrid mode automatically.

When should I use "label only?" Use "label only" for members like Scenario, Ratios, or Drivers – members whose sole purpose in life is to organize the dimension and hierarchy, members for which it never makes sense to add their children together. A member marked as "label only" will automatically pull the value of its first child when referenced. Because of this, when I make a member "label only," I will often make its first child have a plus and the other children have a tilde (~) to designate that only the first child is rolling to the parent member. This is entirely to help indicate what's going on in Essbase to a user who might not know that a "label only" member pulls the value from its first child.

In this example below, it makes no sense to add No Scenario, Forecast, Budget, Actual, Plan, and Current together, so I flag Scenario as "label only":

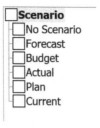

When should I use "shared member?" First, let's further define "shared member." Shared members have the same name as another member, belong to the same dimension, and point to the same data values; however, shared members belong to different parents and participate in different roll-ups for alternate views of the same data. The original member contains the value, and the shared member has a pointer to the original member. Members can be shared among many parents and can be shared with multiple generations.

Let's look at an example from Sample.Basic, where products are organized by product category. An alternate hierarchy to obtain a total for all Diet drinks is present, utilizing shared members for all of the different diet products underneath the parent:

So when should I use "shared member?" When I'd like to create alternate rollups of data in the same dimension. For example, rolling up products both by Market and by Product Category, rolling up a department both by Manager and by Organization Structure, and rolling up revenue both by standard income statement hierarchy and a custom reporting hierarchy. Shared members provide powerful analysis capabilities by aggregating and analyzing values in many different ways, without creating a burden on either the end user or the Administrator.

### Member Types

A member in the dimension tagged Accounts may be one of three types: Numeric, Text, or Date. In earlier versions, Essbase only stored numeric data ("numbers"). Later, a feature was introduced that allows the Administrator to create and display text or date values to users. What's really happening behind the scenes is that Essbase is still storing a numeric value, but a translation happens between the stored value and a look up list with the assigned text or date value.

### Member Formulas

Member formulas define specific logic for calculating that member. This logic can range from very simple to highly complex. For most variance members, I will use a member formula for the variance calculation. Member formulas are utilized to calculate averages and ratios. The syntax for the formulas will vary depending on the type of Essbase cube. ASO cubes use MDX syntax, while BSO cubes leverage specific Essbase calc script syntax.

The different elements in a member formula could include mathematical operators, conditional operators, cross-dimensional operators, and functions.

Here is a list of the available mathematical operators:

- **Add**, +
- **Subtract**, -
- **Multiply**, *
- **Divide**, /
- Evaluate a member as a **percentage** of another, %

- Control calculation order of nested equations, ()

For example, the member formula for the member Avg Units/Transaction in an ASO cube is:

```
[Units]/[Transactions]
```

Block storage option and hybrid cubes also allow member formulas, but they use calc script syntax instead of MDX. You may notice a few immediate differences between calc script syntax and MDX syntax – the use of double quotes around member names (as opposed to brackets) and the inclusion of semicolons.

Mathematical functions define and return values based on selected member expressions. These functions include most standard statistical functions. An example with a mathematical function would be the member formula in a BSO cube for the member Variance:

```
@VAR (Actual, Budget);
```

Conditional operators allow tests based on criteria. The member formula to calculate a member called Commission is:

```
IF (Sales > 1000)
     Sales * .02;
ELSE
     10;
ENDIF
```

In English-speak, if Sales is greater than 1000, then Commission is equal to Sales times 2 percent; otherwise, Commission is equal to 10.

Functions can also be used in member formulas. The member formula for the member Market Share uses an index function:

```
Sales % @PARENTVAL (Markets, Sales);
```

In other words, Market Share is equal to the Sales for the current member as a percent of the current member's parent data value for the Markets dimension.

The member formula for the member Mar YTD uses a financial function:

```
@PTD(Jan:Mar);
```

The member formula for Payroll shows how to use conditional or Boolean criteria:

```
IF (@ISIDESC (East) OR @ISIDESC (West))
     Sales * .15;
ELSEIF (@ISIDESC(Central))
     Sales * .11;
ELSE
     Sales * .10;
ENDIF
```

To put it in English, for all of the members under and including East and West, Payroll is equal to Sales times 15 percent, for all members under and including Central, Payroll is equal to Sales times 11 percent, and for all other members, Payroll is equal to Sales times 10 percent.

**Tip!**

You can use substitution variables in member formulas.

**Tip!**

The syntax for member formulas is almost identical to the syntax used in calculation scripts.

**Note!**

Member formulas must end with a semicolon in BSO and hybrid cubes. If the member name has spaces, you must enclose the member name in double quotes.

## Expense Reporting

The Expense Reporting property is a property only available for BSO cubes in the dimension tagged as an Account Dimension Type. It is a simple flag that tells downstream calculations and reports whether a positive variance is good or bad. If revenue exceeds targets, everyone is happy. Of course, the opposite is true when office supplies expense exceeds the budget. Well, not everyone will be upset, but I don't want to be making enemies in the Finance Department when it comes time for them to cut me the bonus check for those positive-variance Revenues, right?

I'll walk you through an example. If you budget $1,000,000 in revenue and you make $1,100,000, that's a favorable variance of $100,000. Expenses are quite the opposite: if you budget $1,000,000 in marketing expenses and you spend $1,100,000, that's an unfavorable variance of $100,000. In general, you want expense data to have lower actuals than budget.

To allow for this, Essbase uses a property called Expense Reporting. If I tag all of my expense accounts with Expense Reporting, Essbase will calculate the variance correctly when using the @VAR or @VARPER functions. Essbase will show a positive variance when Actual data is higher than Budget for revenue or metric accounts.

Essbase will show a negative variance for those expense accounts tagged with the "Expense Reporting" property:

| | A | B | C | D | E | F |
|---|---|---|---|---|---|---|
| 1 | | Jan | | | | |
| 2 | | Oracle\|Hyperion Happily Ever After Wedding | | | | |
| 3 | | 2015 | | | | |
| 4 | | Actual | Budget | Variance | | |
| 5 | Net_Revenue | 100 | 75 | 25 | | |
| 6 | Op_Expense | 100 | 75 | -25 | | |
| 7 | Op_Income | 0 | 0 | 0 | | |

Check the Variance Reporting Expense property for all measures where budget should be higher than actual. This sets that property to "true."

## Time Balance

Time balance is only available in the dimension tagged as Accounts, and is used to tell Essbase how a given member should be aggregated up the Time dimension. Note, Time balance will not work if there no dimension tagged with the "Time" Dimension Type. For example, should Headcount for January, February, and March be added together for Q1? This definitely wouldn't make sense:

|   | A | B | C | D | E |
|---|---|---|---|---|---|
| 1 |   | Actual | FY2015 |   |   |
| 2 |   | Jan | Feb | Mar | Q1 |
| 3 | Headcount | 100 | 125 | 122 | 347 |

In most cases I want Qtr1 to equal the March headcount, or, in other words, the last headcount in the period. To get Essbase to do this, I tag Headcount with Time Balance Last ("TB last") so that it will take the last member's value when aggregating time:

Depending on my requirements, I could also assign Time Balance First or Time Balance Average.

Here is Q1's headcount now nicely equaling its last child, Mar:

|   | A | B | C | D | E |
|---|---|---|---|---|---|
| 1 |  | Actual | FY2015 |  |  |
| 2 |  | Jan | Feb | Mar | Q1 |
| 3 | Headcount | 100 | 125 | 122 | 122 |

What if I have just closed January? In that case, showing the March headcount wouldn't be accurate because March is blank. A sub-property associated with Time Balance allows us to define how I handle missing (and, for BSO cubes, zero) data values. In this example, I would want to ignore any blanks (or #missing). So I set Headcount to TB Last, and then select Skip "Missing":

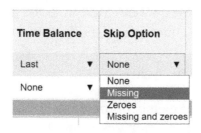

| Time Balance | | Skip Option | |
|---|---|---|---|
| Last | ▼ | None | ▼ |
| None | ▼ | None | |
|  |  | Missing | |
|  |  | Zeroes | |
|  |  | Missing and zeroes | |

Now Qtr1 will correctly show the January value:

|   | A | B | C | D | E |
|---|---|---|---|---|---|
| 1 |  | Actual | FY2015 |  |  |
| 2 |  | Jan | Feb | Mar | Q1 |
| 3 | Headcount |  | 100 #Missing | #Missing |  | 100 |

Another example of Time Balance utilization is for inventory analysis members, such as setting *TB First* for Opening Inventory and *TB Last* for Ending Inventory:

**Tip!**

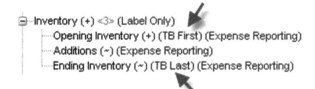

### Dynamic Time Series

Dynamic time series (DTS) allows end users to refresh 'to-date' totals from the Essbase BSO cube. To enable DTS, I must tag a dimension type as Time. I then assign a description to the generation, identifying whether year-to-date, quarter-to-date, history-to-date, etc., should be used.

### Solve Order

The solve order member property tells Essbase "here is the order to complete calculations" for ASO and hybrid cubes. Why is this important? I want to calculate the correct numbers in the correct order. Think order of operations for basic math. 4+5*2 does not equal (4+5)*2. Solve order is the way I control the order of calculations in ASO and hybrid cubes.

### ASO Hierarchy Types

You know by now that a dimension contains a hierarchy or logical grouping of members. In ASO cubes, there are two types of hierarchies: Stored and Dynamic.

Let's learn the rules of stored vs. dynamic hierarchies.

Stored hierarchies will aggregate according to the structure of the outline. In our example, months will roll up to quarters up to a year total in the Period member. This aggregation is really fast (the nature of ASO cubes). But stored hierarchies may only have the + for any member and ~ consolidation tags for members under a "label only" parent (other assigned consolidation tags are ignored). Also, stored hierarchies cannot have member formulas, and there are a few other restrictions on label only assignments.

Dynamic hierarchies are calculated by Essbase (instead of being aggregated like in stored hierarchies) so all consolidation tags and member formulas are processed. The evaluation order for the calculation of members is dictated by the solve order as mentioned above. Dynamic hierarchies, as expected, do not calculate as fast as stored hierarchies.

I can also have multiple hierarchies within a single dimension. The hierarchies within a dimension can be stored, can be all dynamic, or can have one hierarchy stored and the other hierarchy dynamic.

"Multiple hierarchies enabled" can contain alternate hierarchies with Shared Members or completely different hierarchies. The first hierarchy must be stored.

Did you fully comprehend everything I just reviewed? Quick – name the six different dimension types! Didn't think so, but don't worry.

### Dense and Sparse BSO Dimension Tags

It's time to review some key concepts related to the Essbase BSO cubes (not applicable to ASO cubes). Get ready to impress your coworkers with complicated concepts like "dense," "sparse," and "optimized block structure."

First, let's define member combinations. A member combination is the intersection of members from each dimension. See the following examples of member combinations for the Sample.Basic outline:

```
⊟┄Year Time <4> (Active Dynamic Time Series Members: H-T-D, Q-T-D) (Dynamic Calc)
  ⊞┄Qtr1 (+) <3> (Dynamic Calc)
  ⊞┄Qtr2 (+) <3> (Dynamic Calc)
  ⊞┄Qtr3 (+) <3> (Dynamic Calc)
  ⊞┄Qtr4 (+) <3> (Dynamic Calc)
⊟┄Measures Accounts <3> (Label Only)
  ⊞┄Profit (+) <2> (Dynamic Calc)
  ⊞┄Inventory (~) <3> (Label Only)
  ⊞┄Ratios (~) <3> (Label Only)
⊟┄Product <5> {Caffeinated, Intro Date, Ounces, Pkg Type}
  ⊞┄100 (+) <3> (Alias: Colas)
  ⊞┄200 (+) <4> (Alias: Root Beer)
  ⊞┄300 (+) <3> (Alias: Cream Soda)
  ⊞┄400 (+) <3> (Alias: Fruit Soda)
  ⊞┄Diet (~) <3> (Alias: Diet Drinks)
⊟┄Market <4> {Population}
  ⊞┄East (+) <5> (UDAS: Major Market)
  ⊞┄West (+) <5>
```

Example member combinations:

- Qtr1 -> Profit -> 100 -> East -> Actual
- Year -> Profit -> 100 -> East -> Actual
- Jan -> Sales -> 100-10 -> New York -> Budget
- Jan -> Sales -> 100 -> New York -> Budget

**Tip!**  The symbol "->" is known as a cross dimensional operator in Essbase. For now, when you see the "->", think of the word "at." I am referencing the data value at Qtr1 at Profit at 100 at East at Actual.

Dense data is data that occurs often or repeatedly across the intersection of all member combinations. For example, I will most likely have data for all periods for most member combinations. I will most likely have data for most of my accounts for member combinations. Time and accounts are naturally dense.

Sparse data is data that occurs only periodically or sparsely across member combinations. Product, Market, and Employee dimensions are usually sparse:

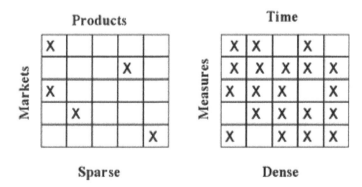

As the Administrator, I will assign a dense/sparse setting to each dimension. This will dictate how the Essbase cube is structured.

The Essbase BSO cube is composed of a number of blocks. A block is created for each intersection of the sparse dimensions. In the example below, Market and Product are sparse.

See a block for each sparse member combination in the example below:

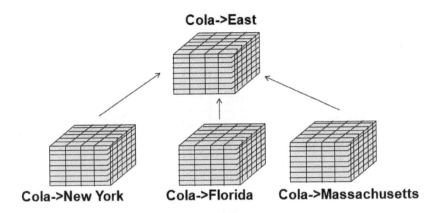

There are four types of blocks:

- **Input blocks** - blocks where data is loaded or input
- **Calculated blocks** - blocks that are created through consolidation or calculation
- **Level-0 blocks** - blocks that are created from the level-0 members of all dimensions
- **Upper-level blocks** - all blocks that contain at least one upper level member (non-level-0)

Each block is made up of cells. These cells are created for each intersection of the dense dimensions. In the example below, Time, Measures, and Scenario are dense dimensions.

See the cells for each dense member combination in the example below (I've highlighted one specific cell, Profit at Jan at Actual):

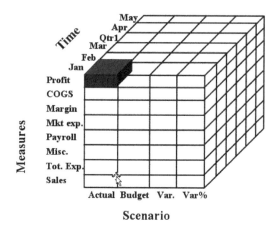

Scenario

Essbase is built to perform outline consolidations. I assign a consolidation attribute to each member that tells Essbase how to perform the consolidation, whether it should add to the total, subtract from the total, and so forth. Unary operators include +, -, *, /, %, and ~. The consolidation will use these operators and follow the path of the hierarchies for each dimension.

So what does outline consolidation and dense/sparse have to do with each other? Essbase will perform dense calculations first and then sparse calculations. The default calculation order for Essbase is the following:

1)  Accounts
2)  Time
3)  Remaining dense dimensions in outline order
4)  Remaining sparse dimensions in outline order
5)  Two Pass Calculation

Let's follow the path of an Essbase consolidation to help you better understand how this works.

In the example below, the highlighted cells indicate cells loaded with data:

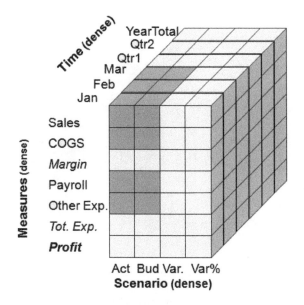

I see those cells populated with the Accounts dimension calculation (see Profit, Margin, Tot. Exp):

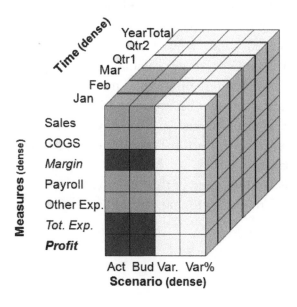

Finally, the cells in the upper portion of the block represent those cells populated with the Time dimension calculation (Qtr1, Qtr2, YearTotal):

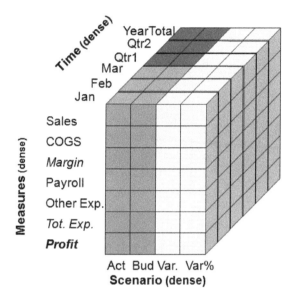

So why are dense dimensions calculated first? I can see that only one block of data is involved and numbers are just filled in, making the block denser with data. Essbase is very fast to perform this calculation.

Another question: why don't the Var. (Variance) and Var% (Variance %) members show calculated data values? Ninety-nine percent of the time I will tag these two members with the dynamic calc property so data will never be stored and in most cases, I won't need to calculate the Scenario dimension. (And in most cases, this is probably a sparse dimension instead of a dense dimension. But I'm getting a bit ahead of myself.)

Here is another view of this dense calculation. Data is loaded to Sales and COGS members for each month.

I am looking at the block for Vermont, Cola, and Actual (there's that cross dimensional symbol that means "at"):

**Vermont -> Cola -> Actual**

| Accounts | Jan | Feb | Mar | Qtr1 |
|---|---|---|---|---|
| Sales | 124.71 | 119.43 | 161.93 | |
| COGS | 42.37 | 38.77 | 47.28 | |
| Margin | | | | |

First I consolidate the Accounts dimension, calculating the Margin member:

**Vermont -> Cola -> Actual**

| Accounts | Jan | Feb | Mar | Qtr1 |
|---|---|---|---|---|
| Sales | 124.71 | 119.43 | 161.93 | |
| COGS | 42.37 | 38.77 | 47.28 | |
| Margin | 82.34 | 80.66 | 114.65 | |

Next, I consolidate the Time dimension, calculating the Qtr1 member:

**Vermont -> Cola -> Actual**

| Accounts | Jan | Feb | Mar | Qtr1 |
|---|---|---|---|---|
| Sales | 124.71 | 119.43 | 161.93 | 406.07 |
| COGS | 42.37 | 38.77 | 47.28 | 128.42 |
| Margin | 82.34 | 80.66 | 114.65 | 277.65 |

Once the Dense calculation is complete, the sparse calculation is next.

The Vermont -> Cola -> Actual block and the New York -> Cola -> Actual block are added together to create the East -> Cola -> Actual block:

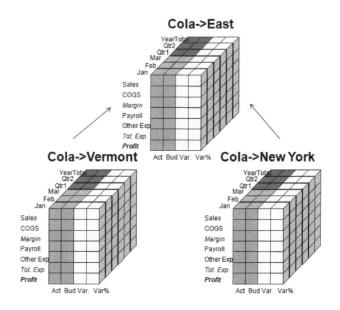

Unlike aggregate storage cubes, block storage cubes require a separate calculation step. The old school on-premises Essbase default calc is the simplest method for calculating Essbase cubes, performing outline consolidations, and calculating formulas as they appear in the outline. This default calc runs a "Calc All" calc script against the Essbase cube, but I will likely create more sophisticated calculation scripts to calculate or maybe with a fully enabled hybrid cube, I don't have to run an aggregation calc script at all.

### Essbase Cloud Rules

While this list is not comprehensive, I will highlight a few of the Essbase Cloud rules related to its artifacts:

- Unlike its sister on-premises Essbase solution, Essbase Cloud application and cube names may have more than eight characters
- Member names may include some special characters, although spaces, quotations, brackets, and tabs are not allowed

- There is a list of reserved words for member names (e.g., "Count" is a reserved word)
- Dimension, member, and alias names are limited to 1024 characters
- Application and cube names are limited to 30 characters
- File names uploaded to Essbase Cloud are limited to 30 characters
- Application workbook names used in Cube Designer to create/update a cube cannot exceed 30 characters

## COMPARE ESSBASE CUBE TYPES

Now that I understand most of the different properties for dimensions, members, ASO, and BSO cubes, let's circle back to cube type. What type of cube – ASO, BSO, or hybrid – should I use? I'll compare the different cube types and their use cases.

Let's start with the most important point – what does the user see? The beauty of ASO, BSO, and hybrid aggregation cubes is that front-end tools like Smart View and DV really don't care if the cube is BSO or ASO or a combination of both (even MaxL – that's "Multi-dimensional database A[X]ccess Language" to you Essbase newbies – sees only minor differences between the two). The three types support beloved end user actions like Zoom In, Zoom Out, Keep Only, Remove Only, and Pivot. There are some minor differences, but for the most part the cube type is pretty much transparent to the end user.

What else is the same? The three types of cubes are defined by their outline. Most dimension and member properties like dimension type, data storage (store, never share, label only), consolidation tags, and aliases are consistent for all three application types. How I build dimensions and load data is essentially the same. Certain rule files properties are cube type-specific, but the overall interface and steps are the same.

Calculating the cubes is where I really begin to see the differences between them. In ASO cubes, after data values are loaded into the level-0 cells of an outline, *the database requires no separate calculation step*. From any point in the cube, users can refresh and view values that are aggregated for only the current retrieval. ASO cubes are smaller than block storage cubes, enabling quick retrieval of data. For even faster retrieval, Administrators can pre-calculate data values and store the pre-calculated results in aggregations. I can add in calculated members with member formulas in ASO. The syntax for the formulas is MDX.

On the other side of the house, BSO and hybrid cubes also have member formulas, but they use a different syntax: Essbase calc script syntax. In most cases, I will need to aggregate the BSO cube after performing a data load. I will use the default calc script or one that I manually create to roll up all of the values for the dimensions in the cube. These BSO calculation scripts can perform complex business logic and allocations.

For hybrid aggregation applications, once data is loaded there may or may not be a need to aggregate the cube depending on the dimensions and member properties of the sparse dimensions. If not all sparse dimensions are dynamic, a more limited aggregation script may need to be run. In hybrid applications, member formulas and calculation scripts are available just like BSO apps, and hybrid aggregation uses the same syntax as the BSO Essbase calculator engine.

Write back is another differentiator. For block storage cubes, users can write back to any level in the cube if they have permissions, while aggregate storage cubes only allow write back to level-0 members. Hybrid applications allow write back to any level as long as the dimension is stored and not dynamically calculated. If most dimensions are marked as dynamic in a hybrid app, then write back at level-0 would be permitted like an ASO application.

Under the covers, the types of cubes are radically different. ASO outlines have two types of hierarchies: stored and dynamic. BSO outlines define dense and sparse dimensions. Because hybrid cubes are really BSO cubes, they also have dense and sparse dimensions (as I mentioned before, a hybrid cube is a BSO cube with one or more sparse dimensions tagged to dynamically aggregate). ASO cubes are stored in a series of tablespaces while BSO cubes are stored in a series of index and page files and hybrid applications are a combination of both. How I tune each cube is very different.

## ESSBASE CUBE EXAMPLES

To conclude our "Essbase Concepts Defined" introductory course, I'll now cover some of the examples of Essbase cubes you'll tend to see. This is by no means thorough – every day companies come up with some new way to use Essbase that no one has ever tried before. And please don't think that Essbase can only be used for financial applications. I once built an Essbase cube to track projects that families signed up for at our church Advent workshop. Okay, that's really geeky, but it goes to show you what you can do if you get out of the finance realm.

### Financial Reporting

Financial reporting (often called General Ledger, or GL analysis) cubes are by far the most common type of Essbase application. This goes back to the early days of Essbase when the Arbor Software sales team used to sell pretty much exclusively into finance and accounting departments. Even today, the first Essbase cube most companies build is to facilitate general ledger analysis.

In all fairness, Essbase is very good at doing GL analysis. Essbase has hundreds of built-in financial functions that make it a good fit for GL reporting. The Essbase outline provides a user-friendly view of how accounts, departments, and other entities roll up within hierarchies and dimensions. It is also very easy for finance-minded personnel to manage those hierarchies. The most attractive thing about Essbase to accountants, though, is that accountants love Excel, and Excel loves Essbase (or is that the other way around?).

Financial reporting applications generally receive data from one or more GL Systems (including those that are part of a larger ERP solution). Generally, this data is loaded monthly right after a financial close, but it is sometimes loaded more frequently during the close process.

Typical financial reporting dimensions include some of the dimensions discussed earlier: Time, Measures, Scenario, Organization, and Years. Measures will contain my account hierarchies for income statement, balance sheet, metrics, and cash flow. I can have alternate hierarchies to support different reporting requirements (more on that later).

In addition to the common dimensions, I will have those dimensions for which I'd like to perform analysis – by Geography, Product, Channel, or any other imaginable dimension that makes sense for my company. That's the beauty of Essbase: dimensionality is flexible and 100% customizable.

### Sales Analysis

Sales analysis applications are a natural fit for Essbase, because they require fast retrievals at detailed levels. I once built a sales analysis application (sometimes called Flash Sales) that had data by store (for over 5,000 stores) by SKU (for over 100,000 products) by day for three years. It was an obscene amount of detail, but Essbase handled it flawlessly with retrievals measured in seconds.

Typical dimensions for this class of application such as Product, Location, and Geography. I can also view sales data by demographics like age and income level of buyer, by store information like store manager, square footage, store type, or location, or by product information like promotion or introduction date:

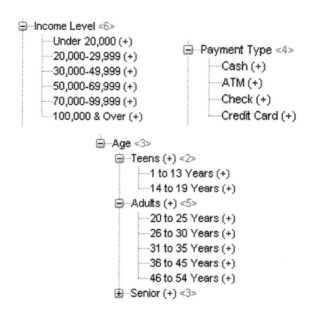

Time dimensions will often go to the day level (and be tracked across multiple years) and have attributes for day of week. Measures or Accounts will often include metrics like Units Sold, Cost of Goods Sold, Price, Revenue, and much more. Some sales applications have inventory data as well and include weeks of supply calculations.

With ASO or hybrid cubes, the level of detail that can be loaded into sales analysis applications has grown exponentially.

Unlike financial reporting applications, which are generally fed from GLs or ERPs, sales analysis applications are generally fed from data warehouses, operational data stores, and legacy systems. It is not uncommon for sales analysis cubes to be loaded every night with the prior day's sales data.

### Workforce Analysis

Workforce (or human capital) analysis applications allow companies to analyze one of their most important assets: their people. (How important are certain people in your organization? Discuss.) Sometimes these applications are called human resources analysis, employee analysis, or salary analysis. I'll go with workforce analysis because it's trendy. Human resources is *so* five minutes ago:

```
⊟···501000 <2> (Alias: Total Compensation)
   ⊟···501100 (+) <4> (Alias: Salaries and Wages)
      ⊞···501110 (+) <4> (Alias: Total Salary)
      ⊞···501120 (+) <3> (Alias: Overtime)
      ⊦····501130 (+) (Alias: Bonus Expense)
      ⌊····501150 (+) (Alias: Auto Allowance)
   ⌊····501200 (+) (Alias: Taxes and Benefits)
```

In addition to the ubiquitous Measures and Time, common dimensions for workforce applications include Employee, Employee Status, Job Grade, and Function. Detailed applications could also include title, start dates, and other employee-level information. It's also not uncommon to have Equal Employment Opportunity Commission attributes such as Race, Gender, Age, and Veteran Status.

The Measures dimension will have accounts that tend to map to the General Ledger (particularly, the payroll or compensation section of the income statement).

I can also use different drivers to budget and plan employee costs. Headcount, Start Month, Vacation Days, Sick Days, and many more can be used in calculations to complete accurate planning numbers.

These drivers can also provide invaluable insight into historical employee trends. I once knew a company that analyzed employee sick time patterns to find out which employees tended to be "sick" on Mondays more than any other day of the week. Apparently, the Monday morning flu was a big problem at their company.

### Capital Expenditure Analysis

Capital expenditure applications (often abbreviated to "CapEx" and sometimes called capital equipment or fixed asset) are another frequent type of Essbase cube. Whether it is determining the rate of return on an investment or tracking capital equipment requests from my organization, I can implement a CapEx application to suit my company's needs. Dimensions include Capital Equipment Item, Equipment Type, Asset Category, and Asset Life.

Here are some examples of capital equipment dimensions:

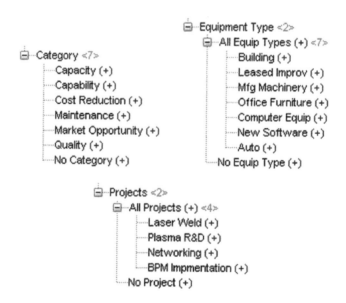

The Account dimension for these applications usually contains a portion of my Balance Sheet:

```
⊟ BalanceSheet <1> (Alias: Balance Sheet)
   ⊟ 100000 (+) <1> (Alias: Total Assets)
      ⊟ 150000 (+) <2> (Alias: Fixed Assets)
         ⊟ 151000 (+) <9> (Alias: Gross PPE)
              151100 (+) (Alias: Construction in Progress)
              151200 (+) (Alias: Land)
              151300 (+) (Alias: Buildings)
              151400 (+) (Alias: Leasehold Improvements)
              151500 (+) (Alias: Mfg Mach and Equip)
              151600 (+) (Alias: Office Furn and Fixtures)
              151700 (+) (Alias: Computer Equipment)
              151800 (+) (Alias: Computer Software)
              151900 (+) (Alias: Vehicles)
         152000 (+) (Alias: Accumulated Depreciation)
```

Other metrics that tend to show up in the Measures dimension include Quantities, Charges, Months in Service, Asset Life, and other drivers related to capital equipment. Generally, CapEx applications are loaded from the Fixed Asset module from my ERP, but it is not uncommon for plan data for capital expenditures to be entered directly into Essbase (or via the Enterprise Planning & Budgeting Cloud CapEx framework).

### Budgeting, Planning, and Forecasting

With highly sophisticated write back capabilities, Essbase provides an excellent solution for budgeting, planning, and forecasting systems. Back in 2000, Hyperion Planning was built on top of Essbase specifically to take advantage of Essbase's sublime ability to not only be used for reporting of data, but also multi-user submission of data. Then in 2014, Oracle took this one step further and provided a Cloud solution for Planning environments in the form of PBCS (which was then followed by EPBCS in 2016).

Back in the days before Hyperion Planning and PBCS were invented, many companies built Essbase cubes for budgeting purposes. They sent their data in via the Essbase add-in, and they were happy. Essbase security limited the dimensions and members for which data could be entered by users, and calculation scripts were used to calculate data if necessary.

If Essbase is perfect for budgeting, why do I need PBCS or Hyperion Planning? The answer is simply the needs of planners and budgeters expanding beyond the abilities of Essbase. Modern forecasters require things like audit trails, integrated workflow, and web-based data entry. While Essbase can meet straight-forward budget needs, it doesn't have the built-in functionality that I get when I pay for PBCS.

Budgeting and forecasting cubes written in Essbase will tend to look very similar to my reporting and analysis applications. For example, I may have a budgeting cube to capture budget for income statement items, another cube for capital equipment planning, and another cube for salary planning. Though these cubes will be similar to my reporting and analysis cubes, they often do not contain the same level of detail. In general, budget data is not as granular as actual data.

In the example below, budget is captured at the reporting line level of Marketing while actual data is captured by GL account:

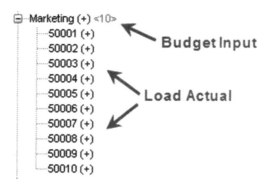

Can I just capture budget and forecast information in my reporting and analysis cubes? Yes, but there are some things to consider. First, understand the level of detail. If I am capturing budget at a higher level, I have to think carefully about how consolidations will take place in Essbase. If I enter data at an upper level and then run an aggregation, I could easily erase the data that was entered by users at the higher points in the dimension. There are ways to prevent this but the traditional work around is to use "dummy" members.

Second, I need to think about the dimensionality required for each purpose. In my reporting and analysis cubes, I may want to analyze actual data by more dimensions or slices than I would for budget data. Too many dimensions can overly complicate the budgeting and planning process.

Third, I may also want to think about splitting reporting and budgeting for backup reasons. I'll want to back up my budgeting and planning applications more often as data changes far more frequently.

### Not Just Financial

While Essbase is great at financial reporting and analysis, as I've said before, it is not limited to just the "financials." I can report and analyze on practically any subject area if it includes dimensions, hierarchies, and numbers. I can easily manage performance with reporting key metrics and drivers across the organization, delivering actionable information to change the way I do business for the better. Customer analysis is possible, providing detailed information for millions of customers. Procurement analysis cubes can track many products across many vendors. Logistics analysis delivers near real-time updates of product shipments, and market basket analysis can show important correlations between product purchases. As long as my reporting and analysis requirements don't include detailed "columns and columns" type reports (think human resources reports with the following columns: Name, Address, City, State, Zip, Position, Home Phone, Work Phone, Cell Phone, Emergency Contact), Essbase is likely a good solution.

---

**Meanwhile, back on earth…**

When the Project Elrond secret meeting finally concluded and no decision had been made, Flight Director Flint quickly pulled out her smart phone. She uploaded the "Sarah Purnell Maneuver" Mission Summary report and sent it to Project Commander McMullen. She knew she would be in big trouble for this, but she knew that this was the best way to save Edward, and the crew had the right to know and decide how they wanted to help.

# CHAPTER 6: CREATE A CUBE WITH CUBE DESIGNER

---

**LOG ENTRY FOR PROJECT COMMANDER TRACY MCMULLEN**
*SOL 19, Entry 1*

Edward is alive! I can't believe it! Well, I guess I can because he is one of those annoyingly resourceful types who can figure out anything. Maybe the hat saved him.

Not only is he alive, but he has implemented a planning and budgeting solution for the Vision Company in Oracle Planning and Budgeting Cloud. That is really annoying. This whole time we have been beating ourselves up for leaving him in the Cloud, and he took the time to build a PBCS application.

After receiving the secret email from Flight Director Flint, I met with the rest of the crew. As you can expect, there were tears and laughter and then more tears.

While this is good news, we still have one problem. Edward is still stuck in the Cloud. We left him. Actually, I left him. That was my decision.

And we now have a chance to save him.

---

**LOG ENTRY FOR PROJECT COMMANDER TRACY MCMULLEN**
*SOL 19, Entry 2*

It was unanimous (with one abstention from Schwartzberg). Despite the risk and the longer travel, the crew voted to try to save Edward. We are overriding the control systems from i.n.t.e.r.R.e.l. and launching the oddly named Sarah Purnell Maneuver.

---

**LOG ENTRY FOR ESSBASE PILOT ROBERT GIDEON**
*SOL 19, Entry 1*

So we've each been assigned a sub-mission. If we can complete our tasks, we will be catapulted around Earth with enough gravity assist to reach Edward, who is stranded in the Cloud. My mission? I have to build the TBC Sample.Basic and KoolKart expense analysis cube.

Sarah "Purnell" Branhagen proved a cube can be built in OAC with an unstructured Excel spreadsheet. But what if you wanted to have more control over the Essbase cube build process? Oracle Analytics Cloud provides a Cube Designer template that can be used to build dimensions and load data. Lucky for me, TBC's Sample.Basic cube happens to be the foundation for one of these Application Workbook templates. I'll start by uploading their cube, and then I'll use the slick Cube Designer to build KoolKart's expense cube.

That is my mission. And I'm not going to let Edward down. Plus, this step sounds fun.

## INTRODUCTION TO CUBE DESIGNER EXTENSION

Cube Designer is the new Smart View extension that offers capabilities to build Essbase Cloud cubes. The Cube Designer wizard allows me to build and maintain Essbase cubes by reading metadata from an Excel workbook or by inserting data into an Excel workbook, creating a template file called the Application Workbook with all of the build information for the Essbase cube:

| | A | B | C | D | E | F | G | H | I |
|---|---|---|---|---|---|---|---|---|---|
| 1 | Application Name | KoolExp | | | | | | | |
| 2 | Database Name | Expense | | | | | | | |
| 3 | Version | 1.0 | | | | | | | |
| 4 | | | | | | | | | |
| 5 | **Dimension Definitions** | | | | | | | | |
| 6 | | | | | | | | | |
| 7 | | Dimension Type | Storage Type | Outline Order | Base Dimension | | | | |
| 8 | Account | Accounts | Dense | 1 | | | | | |
| 9 | Period | Time | Dense | 2 | | | | | |
| 10 | Account Group | Regular | Sparse | 3 | | | | | |
| 11 | Business Line | Regular | Sparse | 4 | | | | | |
| 12 | Year | Regular | Sparse | 5 | | | | | |
| 13 | Scenario | Regular | Sparse | 6 | | | | | |
| 14 | | | | | | | | | |

Essbase.Cube | Cube.Settings | Dim.Account | Dim.Period | Dim.Account Group | Dim.Business Line | Dim.Year

In addition, with just a few clicks, I can copy the structure of one cube and apply it to a new Excel workbook for modifications.

There are five worksheet tabs in the Cube Designer wizard:

1) Cube
2) Settings
3) Dimensions
4) Data
5) Calc

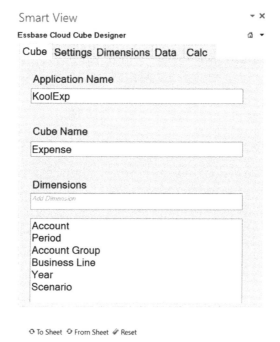

I define an application and database (cube) name on the Cube tab, as well as the dimensions that are in the application. This tab allows me to change the name of the cube and add or delete dimensions.

The Settings tab contains additional details about the cube, such as alias tables, cube properties, Dynamic Time Series setup, and attribute settings. The selections on the Settings tab populate the Cube.Settings worksheet.

Each dimension from the Cube tab is represented on the Dimensions tab. The Dimensions tab is where I can set the dimension type (Regular, Accounts, Time, or Attribute), the dense/sparse setting, the dimension build method, and which fields are shown on the Dim.*Dimension* worksheets for each dimension.

The Data tab of the wizard allows for creation of a data worksheet. The wizard allows me to choose the name of the data sheet. If there is no data sheet, the cube is created but will be empty. If a data sheet is present, the cube can be created and loaded with data during the cube build process.

A calculation worksheet(s) can be created on the Calc tab of the wizard. A calculation worksheet is basically a blank canvas to write a calculation script and upload it at the time of the cube build process.

Under the covers, Essbase Cloud will take the definition information and create dimension and data load rules that I can view and update through the Essbase Cloud web interface. It also takes the data and uploads each worksheet as a text file that is accessible from the Essbase Cloud web interface.

The ability to save and archive the Cube Designer worksheets is one of the main benefits of Cube Designer. Iterative development of cubes can be done by simply opening up an older Cube Designer workbook and copying the contents to the wizard using the *From Sheet* button. Any changes can then be made in the wizard and applied to the workbook using the *To Sheet* button. By saving copies of Cube Designer workbooks, I can build an inventory of work-in-process and finalized applications. The Private menu allows opening, saving, and exporting Essbase Cloud cubes to Application Workbooks for offline archiving.

## CUBE DESIGNER RIBBON

Before I build an Essbase cube with Cube Designer, I'll explore the other options on the Cube Designer ribbon:

The Cube Designer ribbon provides capabilities for the following tasks:

- **Connections** - toggles between different Essbase Cloud connections (when multiple instances/pods are licensed)
- **Gallery** - provides links to prebuilt Application Workbook templates that I can use for learning purposes or as a starting point for my own cube build
- **Private** - opens Application Workbooks, save Application Workbooks, or export an existing Essbase Cloud cube into an Application Workbook
- **Cube Designer** - launches the Cube Designer wizard where I can create cubes, set cube settings, define dimensions, and load data
- **Formula Editor** - provides an editor to define member formulas with a list of supported Essbase functions
- **View Hierarchy** - previews what the hierarchy will look like in Essbase for a selected dimension worksheet
- **Build Cube** - creates or updates an Essbase cube based on structured workbooks
- **Load Data** - loads data for an existing Essbase cube based on the data worksheet
- **Calculate** - runs an Essbase calc script
- **Analyze** - jumps into ad hoc analysis mode
- **View Jobs** - views current and previous jobs and their status and details
- **Transform Data** - creates or updates an Essbase cube specifically from an unstructured spreadsheet

**Note!**

One of the important distinctions between the *Build Cube* option and the *Transform Data* option is that the Build Cube option is for building cubes from structured workbooks. Transform Data is for building cubes from unstructured spreadsheets. Another distinction is that the Build Cube option, because it relies on a structured workbook, gives you additional options: incremental data loads, execution of calculation scripts, and Essbase application deletion.

### Connections

I can toggle between Essbase Cloud connections using the Connections option from the Cube Designer ribbon (I cannot connect to on-premises Essbase cubes here.

I can use the downloadable DBXtool to create application worksheets for on-premises cubes for migration to Essbase Cloud):

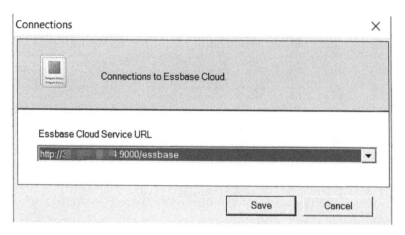

### Gallery

I can open prebuilt Application Workbook templates to help jumpstart my cube building process or learn how to set up my own template:

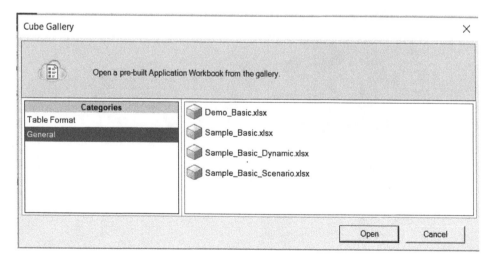

*Table Format* contains, as the title suggests, unstructured table-like formats (described in more detail in Chapter 4, "Unstructured Spreadsheet to Essbase Cube"). Below is a screenshot from the "Sample_Table" template:

| | A | B | C | D | E | F | G | H | I | J |
|---|---|---|---|---|---|---|---|---|---|---|
| 1 | Units | Discounts | Fixed Costs | Variable Costs | Revenue | Time.Month | Time.Quarter | Years | Regions.Region | Regions.Area |
| 2 | 9 | 23.94 | 72.74 | 368.58 | 375.43 | February | Qtr 1 | CY2015 | EMEA | North Africa |
| 3 | 10 | 0 | 367.44 | 372.47 | 1895.98 | May | Qtr 2 | CY2015 | EMEA | Northern |
| 4 | 9 | 1.41 | 7.53 | 36.1 | 37.52 | March | Qtr 1 | CY2015 | AMERICAS | Central |
| 5 | 13 | 26.29 | 111.06 | 484.11 | 1401.83 | December | Qtr 4 | CY2014 | AMERICAS | Central |
| 6 | 12 | 20.83 | 195.45 | 818.08 | 2218.72 | July | Qtr 3 | CY2015 | AMERICAS | South America |
| 7 | 8 | 17.03 | 55.86 | 205.73 | 697.57 | November | Qtr 4 | CY2015 | APAC | North |
| 8 | 10 | 31.45 | 108.32 | 329.57 | 1117.81 | June | Qtr 2 | CY2015 | AMERICAS | Central |
| 9 | 5 | 14.74 | 207.26 | 650.77 | 523.22 | April | Qtr 2 | CY2014 | AMERICAS | South America |
| 10 | 10 | 20 | 168.83 | 1104.13 | 1065.57 | June | Qtr 2 | CY2014 | AMERICAS | South America |
| 11 | 9 | 1.86 | 9.14 | 28.7 | 45.56 | February | Qtr 1 | CY2015 | EMEA | Northern |
| 12 | 19 | 0 | 354.48 | 33.84 | 232.03 | January | Qtr 1 | CY2016 | APAC | West |
| 13 | 12 | 83.24 | 266.75 | 20055.8 | 3223.08 | September | Qtr 3 | CY2015 | APAC | West |
| 14 | 10 | 60.09 | 413.4 | 2096.37 | 2133.1 | May | Qtr 2 | CY2015 | APAC | North |
| 15 | 4 | 0.53 | 24.97 | 1.93 | 16.58 | February | Qtr 1 | CY2014 | EMEA | Africa |
| 16 | 4 | 0.49 | 2.73 | 17.49 | 17.22 | November | Qtr 4 | CY2014 | AMERICAS | North America |
| 17 | 10 | 0 | 243.55 | 1235.4 | 1256.71 | October | Qtr 4 | CY2015 | EMEA | Europe |
| 18 | 12 | 24.5 | 114.9 | 452.43 | 1304.17 | July | Qtr 3 | CY2015 | EMEA | Middle East |
| 19 | 9 | 29.48 | 46.75 | 220.71 | 626.17 | February | Qtr 1 | CY2016 | AMERICAS | Central |
| 20 | 9 | 27.37 | 132.75 | 126.83 | 661.58 | March | Qtr 1 | CY2015 | EMEA | Eastern |
| 21 | 9 | 28.93 | 114.66 | 465.1 | 591.58 | February | Qtr 1 | CY2015 | AMERICAS | Central |
| 22 | 21 | 8.38 | 446.99 | 42.67 | 337.61 | April | Qtr 2 | CY2016 | AMERICAS | South America |

Sales ⊕

The *General* category contains structured formats that can be used for creating and updating the types of cubes emphasized in this chapter. Below is an example of the Sample_Basic template:

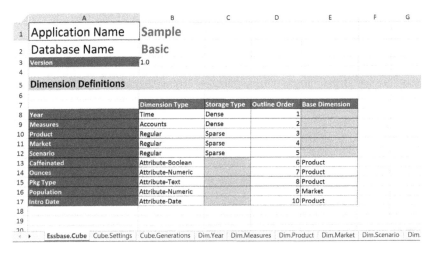

| | A | B | C | D | E | F | G |
|---|---|---|---|---|---|---|---|
| 1 | Application Name | Sample | | | | | |
| 2 | Database Name | Basic | | | | | |
| 3 | Version | 1.0 | | | | | |
| 4 | | | | | | | |
| 5 | Dimension Definitions | | | | | | |
| 6 | | | | | | | |
| 7 | | Dimension Type | Storage Type | Outline Order | Base Dimension | | |
| 8 | Year | Time | Dense | 1 | | | |
| 9 | Measures | Accounts | Dense | 2 | | | |
| 10 | Product | Regular | Sparse | 3 | | | |
| 11 | Market | Regular | Sparse | 4 | | | |
| 12 | Scenario | Regular | Sparse | 5 | | | |
| 13 | Caffeinated | Attribute-Boolean | | 6 | Product | | |
| 14 | Ounces | Attribute-Numeric | | 7 | Product | | |
| 15 | Pkg Type | Attribute-Text | | 8 | Product | | |
| 16 | Population | Attribute-Numeric | | 9 | Market | | |
| 17 | Intro Date | Attribute-Date | | 10 | Product | | |
| 18 | | | | | | | |
| 19 | | | | | | | |
| 20 | | | | | | | |

Essbase.Cube | Cube.Settings | Cube.Generations | Dim.Year | Dim.Measures | Dim.Product | Dim.Market | Dim.Scenario | Dim.

**Private**

From the Private option, I can open Application Workbooks, save Application Workbooks, or export an existing Essbase Cloud cube into an Application Workbook:

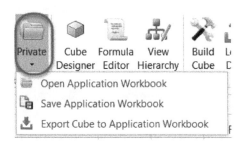

When I select *Export Cube to Application Workbook*, I'm then prompted to select the desired application and cube:

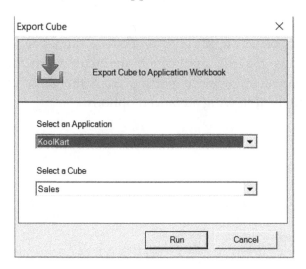

There are slightly different options when doing an export from the Essbase Cloud web interface versus doing an export from Cube Designer.

For instance, when I look at the Cube Designer export, I see only the following options:

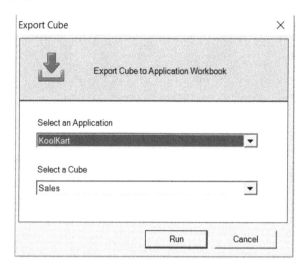

I can choose my application and cube…only. The resultant Excel workbook gives me the application and cube structure and each dimension. However, when exporting from the Essbase Cloud web interface, I see the following advanced options:

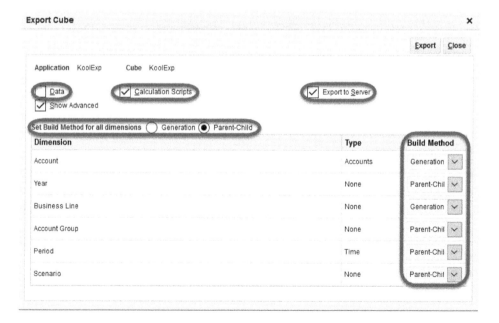

These additional options include:

- Data
- Calculation scripts
- *Export to server* option, which generates a backup file on the server instead of opening it directly within Excel
- Selection of a default build method for all dimensions (parent-child or generation)
- Option to override the individual build method by dimension (parent-child or generation)

The differences between each type of export is important, as it may drive where I choose to perform this task.

**Note!** Data exports of less than 100MB in size will be exported to an Application Workbook. Data exports larger than 100MB will export to a file instead.

### Cube Designer

The Cube Designer option launches the Cube Designer wizard.

The wizard helps me build the Application Workbook template, which I will ultimately upload to Essbase Cloud:

Smart View ▾ ✕

**Essbase Cloud Cube Designer** ⌂ ▾ »

Cube Settings Dimensions Data Calc

Application Name

KoolExp

Cube Name

Expense

Dimensions

*Add Dimension*

↻ To Sheet ↻ From Sheet ✐ Reset

**Formula Editor**

Calculated members in Essbase use a specific syntax (and that syntax is different for BSO cubes vs. ASO cubes). The Formula Editor helps me to create member formulas for BSO and hybrid cubes.

A list of supported Essbase BSO functions are available to insert into the canvas area with the correct syntax:

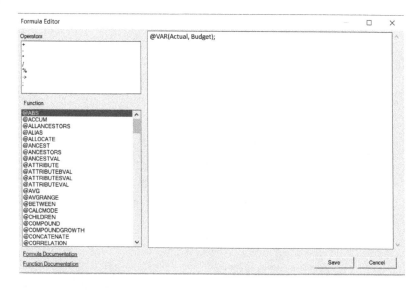

## View Hierarchy

The View Hierarchy option is a super helpful feature to preview what the hierarchy will look like in Essbase for a selected dimension worksheet:

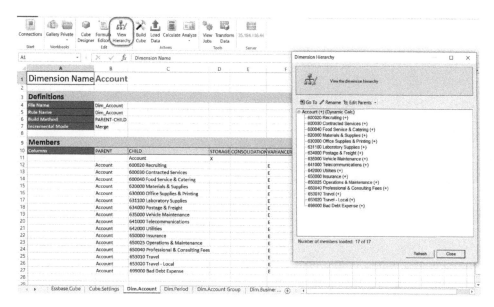

Note, the *Edit Parents* option can tag all parents "dynamic" in a single-click. This helps if I am converting a cube to hybrid.

### Build Cube

I can create or update an Essbase cube based on the active Application Workbook:

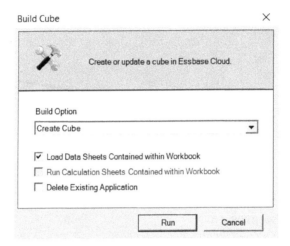

### Load Data

I can load data for an existing Essbase cube based via the Load Data option:

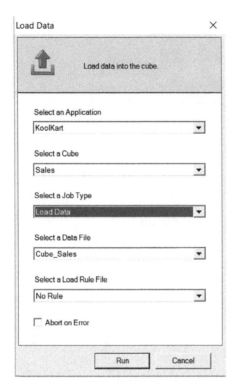

### Calculate

I can run an Essbase calc script via the Calculate option, which will take me to a list of calculation scripts:

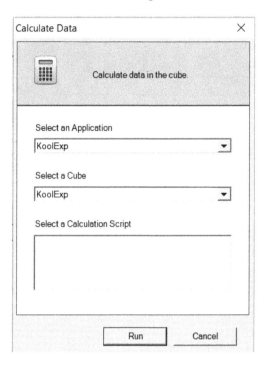

Note, calculation scripts can be created in the Essbase Cloud web interface.

### Analyze

Analyze – I can create a Smart View ad hoc grid or connect to query sheets via the Analyze option:

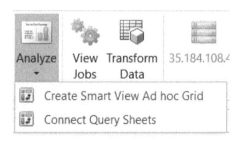

### View Jobs

I can view my current and previous jobs and their status and details via the View Jobs option. Administrators can view all job statuses:

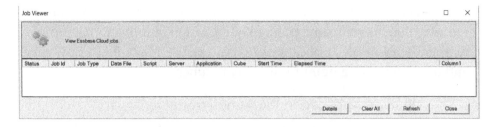

### Transform Data

As I learned in Chapter 4, "Unstructured Spreadsheet to Essbase Cube," I can create or update an Essbase cube from an unstructured spreadsheet via the Transform Data option:

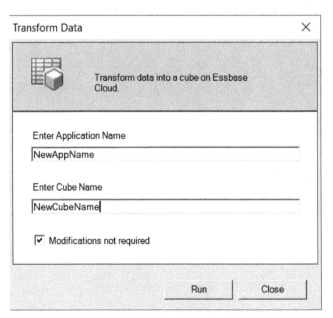

## APPLICATION WORKBOOKS DEFINED

Application Workbooks are one of the main vehicles to creating and maintaining Essbase Cloud cubes. An entire Essbase cube can be built with one Excel file (no technical programming required!).

The easiest way to understand the Application Workbook is to see one that has already been filled out. Thankfully, OAC provides templates of Sample applications that can be used to build sample cubes and use as a starting point for my "real" cubes.

### Open an Application Workbook from the Gallery

To open an Application Workbook from a Gallery template,
1. Open Excel and connect to the OAC Essbase Cloud instance.
2. Select *Gallery* from the Cube Designer ribbon.

I can choose from a General format or a Table format of sample Application Workbooks:

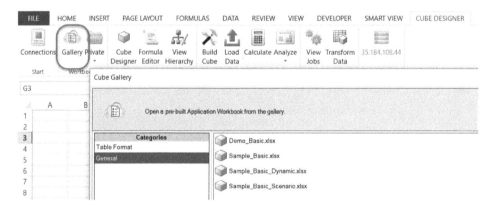

3. Select *Sample_Basic.xlsx*.
4. Click *OK*.

The fully populated Application Workbook for Sample Basic is all ready to go!

**Note!** The Essbase properties mentioned in the following section are fully defined in the previous chapter. Please reference Chapter 5, "Essbase Concepts Defined," for more details.

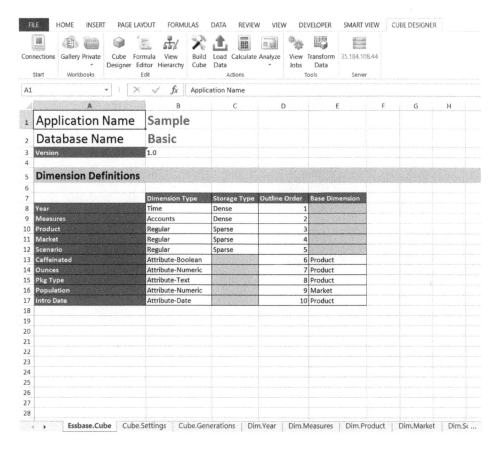

### Review Application Workbook Worksheets

Note the Application Workbook contains several worksheets that are important to the Essbase cube build process. I'll provide a high level review now and jump into more details when I build the KoolKart expense cube.

The Application Workbook contains the following worksheets:

- **Essbase.Cube** - this worksheet defines the Application Name, Database Name, dimensions and their Dimension Type, Storage Type, Outline Order (important for BSO cubes), and Base dimension association for attribute dimensions
- **Cube.Settings** - this worksheet defines the Essbase cube settings like Application Type, enabled for duplicate members (Outline Type), alias tables, Dynamic Time Series, attribute settings, and substitution variables:

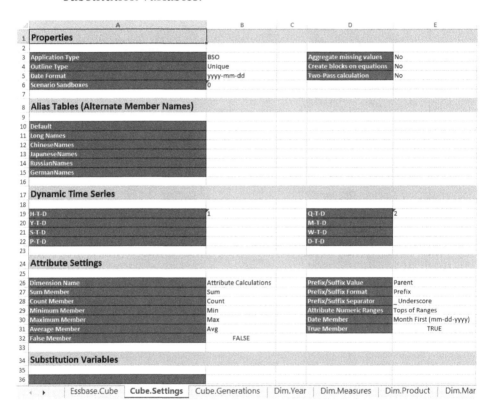

- **Cube.Generations** - this worksheet defines any generation names for dimensions in the Essbase cube (helpful when using BI Cloud or DV against an Essbase Cloud cube source):

| | A | B | C |
|---|---|---|---|
| 1 | **Generation Properties** | | |
| 2 | | | |
| 3 | **Dimension Name  Year** | | |
| 4 | | | |
| 5 | Generation Number | Generation Name | Unique |
| 6 | 1 | History | Yes |
| 7 | 2 | Quarter | Yes |
| 8 | 3 | Months | Yes |
| 9 | | | |
| 10 | **Dimension Name  Product** | | |
| 11 | | | |
| 12 | Generation Number | Generation Name | Unique |
| 13 | 1 | | Yes |
| 14 | 2 | Category | Yes |
| 15 | 3 | Product SKU | Yes |
| 16 | | | |
| 17 | **Dimension Name  Market** | | |
| 18 | | | |
| 19 | Generation Number | Generation Name | Unique |
| 20 | 1 | | Yes |
| 21 | 2 | Region | Yes |
| 22 | 3 | State | Yes |

- **Dim.***DimensionName* - this worksheet defines the hierarchy and members for the *DimensionName*; Essbase Cloud creates one worksheet for each dimension

For each Dim.*DimensionName* worksheet, I can define the following information for the specified dimension:

- Name of the filename that will be created in Essbase Cloud
- Name of the rules file that will be created in Essbase Cloud
- Build method (Parent-Child, Generation, Level)

- Incremental Mode, which determines how members in the spreadsheet will be built into an existing cube (Should members in the file merge with existing members? Should members in the file replace existing members?)
- Delimiter
- Header Rows to Skip
- Allow Moves, which determines if members are allowed to change parents during the dimension import
- Members and hierarchy structure itself along with all of the member properties like Storage property and Alias property:

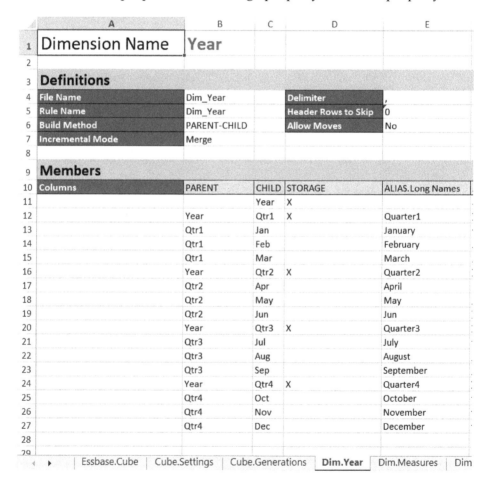

| | A | B | C | D | E |
|---|---|---|---|---|---|
| 1 | **Dimension Name** | **Year** | | | |
| 2 | | | | | |
| 3 | **Definitions** | | | | |
| 4 | File Name | Dim_Year | | Delimiter | , |
| 5 | Rule Name | Dim_Year | | Header Rows to Skip | 0 |
| 6 | Build Method | PARENT-CHILD | | Allow Moves | No |
| 7 | Incremental Mode | Merge | | | |
| 8 | | | | | |
| 9 | **Members** | | | | |
| 10 | Columns | PARENT | CHILD | STORAGE | ALIAS.Long Names |
| 11 | | | Year | X | |
| 12 | | Year | Qtr1 | X | Quarter1 |
| 13 | | Qtr1 | Jan | | January |
| 14 | | Qtr1 | Feb | | February |
| 15 | | Qtr1 | Mar | | March |
| 16 | | Year | Qtr2 | X | Quarter2 |
| 17 | | Qtr2 | Apr | | April |
| 18 | | Qtr2 | May | | May |
| 19 | | Qtr2 | Jun | | Jun |
| 20 | | Year | Qtr3 | X | Quarter3 |
| 21 | | Qtr3 | Jul | | July |
| 22 | | Qtr3 | Aug | | August |
| 23 | | Qtr3 | Sep | | September |
| 24 | | Year | Qtr4 | X | Quarter4 |
| 25 | | Qtr4 | Oct | | October |
| 26 | | Qtr4 | Nov | | November |
| 27 | | Qtr4 | Dec | | December |
| 28 | | | | | |
| 29 | | | | | |

Essbase.Cube | Cube.Settings | Cube.Generations | **Dim.Year** | Dim.Measures | Dim

**Note!**

A dimension build rules file will be created automatically in Essbase Cloud for the dimension defined in the Dim.*DimensionName* worksheet and is available under *Scripts* in the Essbase Cloud web interface.

A text file containing the dimension members will be uploaded to Essbase Cloud and available under *Files* in the Essbase Cloud web interface.

- **Data.***CubeName* - this worksheet contains the data that should be loaded to the cube along with the settings to control the data load, including: File Name, (data load) Rule Name, Data Load Option, Delimiter, and Header Rows to Skip:

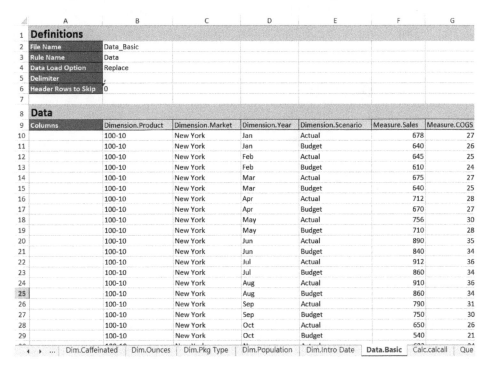

| | A | B | C | D | E | F | G |
|---|---|---|---|---|---|---|---|
| 1 | **Definitions** | | | | | | |
| 2 | File Name | Data_Basic | | | | | |
| 3 | Rule Name | Data | | | | | |
| 4 | Data Load Option | Replace | | | | | |
| 5 | Delimiter | , | | | | | |
| 6 | Header Rows to Skip | 0 | | | | | |
| 7 | | | | | | | |
| 8 | **Data** | | | | | | |
| 9 | Columns | Dimension.Product | Dimension.Market | Dimension.Year | Dimension.Scenario | Measure.Sales | Measure.COGS |
| 10 | | 100-10 | New York | Jan | Actual | 678 | 27 |
| 11 | | 100-10 | New York | Jan | Budget | 640 | 26 |
| 12 | | 100-10 | New York | Feb | Actual | 645 | 25 |
| 13 | | 100-10 | New York | Feb | Budget | 610 | 24 |
| 14 | | 100-10 | New York | Mar | Actual | 675 | 27 |
| 15 | | 100-10 | New York | Mar | Budget | 640 | 25 |
| 16 | | 100-10 | New York | Apr | Actual | 712 | 28 |
| 17 | | 100-10 | New York | Apr | Budget | 670 | 27 |
| 18 | | 100-10 | New York | May | Actual | 756 | 30 |
| 19 | | 100-10 | New York | May | Budget | 710 | 28 |
| 20 | | 100-10 | New York | Jun | Actual | 890 | 35 |
| 21 | | 100-10 | New York | Jun | Budget | 840 | 34 |
| 22 | | 100-10 | New York | Jul | Actual | 912 | 36 |
| 23 | | 100-10 | New York | Jul | Budget | 860 | 34 |
| 24 | | 100-10 | New York | Aug | Actual | 910 | 36 |
| 25 | | 100-10 | New York | Aug | Budget | 860 | 34 |
| 26 | | 100-10 | New York | Sep | Actual | 790 | 31 |
| 27 | | 100-10 | New York | Sep | Budget | 750 | 30 |
| 28 | | 100-10 | New York | Oct | Actual | 650 | 26 |
| 29 | | 100-10 | New York | Oct | Budget | 540 | 21 |

... | Dim.Caffeinated | Dim.Ounces | Dim.Pkg Type | Dim.Population | Dim.Intro Date | **Data.Basic** | Calc.calcall | Que

Even if I don't have data to load at this time, I can still use this tab to generate the rules file format for future use.

I can have one or more data file worksheets within an Application Workbook. Make sure to name the data and rules file uniquely in the Application Workbook so they will build properly in Essbase Cloud.

A data load rules file will be created automatically in Essbase Cloud for the dimension defined in the Data.*CubeName* worksheet and is available under *Scripts* in the Essbase Cloud web interface.

**Note!**

A text file containing the data will be uploaded to Essbase Cloud and will be available under *Files* in the Essbase Cloud web interface.

- **Calc.*CalcscriptName*** - this worksheet contains the calc script definition that will be imported to the Essbase cube; I can have one or more calc script worksheets in an Application Workbook:

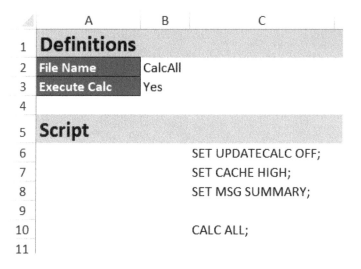

The steps to import the Application Workbook and create an Essbase cube are as easy as 1-2-3.

## Build a Cube

To build the Essbase cube from the Application Workbook,

5.   Click *Build Cube* from the Cube Designer ribbon:

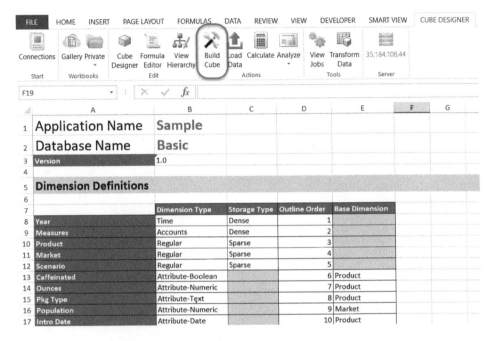

6.   Select the *Create Cube* option.
7.   Check the *Load Data Sheets Contained within Workbook* box.
8.   Check the *Run Calculation Sheets Contained within Workbook* box.

9.  Click *Run*:

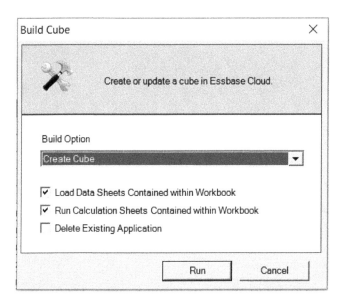

I can choose to view the job status or not. Once the Essbase cube build is successful, it is ready for analysis and reporting.

I can connect to the new Essbase cube using Smart View ad hoc functionality and slice and dice until my heart's content:

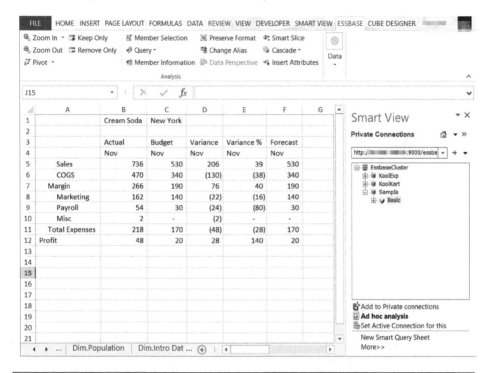

LOG ENTRY FOR ESSBASE PILOT ROBERT GIDEON
SOL 19, Entry 2

Part 1 one of my mission is complete. TBC's Sample.Basic cube has been created in Essbase Cloud.
That was easy (since Oracle had the Application Workbook in the gallery of templates). Now the pressure is on! I have to create the KoolKart Expense cube Application Workbook and build the cube.

## CREATE A CUBE USING CUBE DESIGNER

Now that I've built my first cube, I'm ready for the next. One cool thing about Cube Designer is that the majority of the Cube Designer process can be done offline. The buttons available in the Cube Designer panel run code to build the Application Workbook in the proper format for Essbase Cloud. After definitions are set and the Application

Workbook is complete, I can then connect and click *Build Cube* to build the cube in Essbase Cloud.

To create a new cube offline in the Cube Designer wizard,
1. Open a new, blank workbook in Excel.
2. On the Cube Designer ribbon, click the *Cube Designer* button:

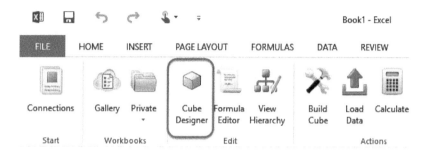

In the Smart View panel, a Cube Designer dialog box is displayed.

3. Begin by giving the new application and cube a name; I'll type "KoolExp" for the application name and "Expense" for the cube name:

4.  Click the *To Sheet* button to begin the cube building process.

This pushes the options defined in Cube Designer into various worksheets in our workbook. The tab names and the column headings are case sensitive. There are now Essbase.Cube and Cube.Settings worksheets in my workbook:

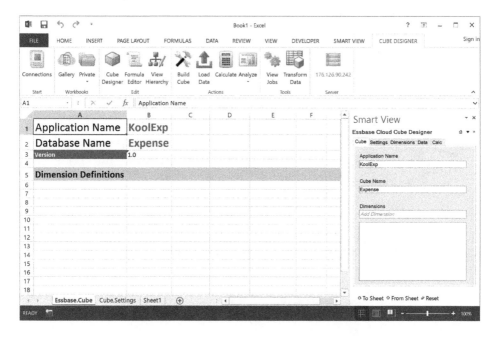

5.  Save the workbook as *KoolExp_CubeDesigner.xlsx*.

## Add Dimensions

Luckily, I have an expense data file ready to go for this cube:

| | A | B | C | D | E | F | G | H |
|---|---|---|---|---|---|---|---|---|
| 1 | Account Group | Account | Business Lines | Ye | Month | Budget | Actual | Variance |
| 2 | Contract Services | 600030 Contracted Services | Capital Leasing | 2015 | Jan-15 | 420493.3 | 441535.04 | -21041.74 |
| 3 | Contract Services | 600030 Contracted Services | Capital Leasing | 2015 | Feb-15 | 331581.34 | 306221.42 | 25359.92 |
| 4 | Contract Services | 600030 Contracted Services | Capital Leasing | 2015 | Mar-15 | 391137.88 | 429219.41 | -38081.53 |
| 5 | Contract Services | 600030 Contracted Services | Capital Leasing | 2015 | Apr-15 | 368940.28 | 336260.47 | 32679.81 |
| 6 | Contract Services | 600030 Contracted Services | Capital Leasing | 2015 | May-15 | 459186.53 | 513842.98 | -54656.45 |
| 7 | Contract Services | 600030 Contracted Services | Capital Leasing | 2015 | Jul-15 | 385485.75 | 415440.46 | -29954.71 |
| 8 | Contract Services | 600030 Contracted Services | Capital Leasing | 2015 | Aug-15 | 469642.65 | 497432.67 | -27790.02 |
| 9 | Contract Services | 600030 Contracted Services | Capital Leasing | 2015 | Sep-15 | 373486.71 | 342460.94 | 31025.77 |
| 10 | Contract Services | 600030 Contracted Services | Capital Leasing | 2015 | Oct-15 | 370091.7 | 349533.65 | 20558.05 |
| 11 | Contract Services | 600030 Contracted Services | Capital Leasing | 2015 | Nov-15 | 335391.68 | 364729.03 | -29337.35 |
| 12 | Contract Services | 600030 Contracted Services | Capital Leasing | 2015 | Dec-15 | 399802.74 | 434712.27 | -34909.53 |
| 13 | Contract Services | 600030 Contracted Services | Technology Equipment | 2015 | Jan-15 | 211546.18 | 169412.49 | 42133.69 |
| 14 | Contract Services | 600030 Contracted Services | Technology Equipment | 2015 | Feb-15 | 198449.87 | 180589.36 | 17860.51 |
| 15 | Contract Services | 600030 Contracted Services | Technology Equipment | 2015 | Mar-15 | 195994.32 | 178669.08 | 17325.24 |
| 16 | Contract Services | 600030 Contracted Services | Technology Equipment | 2015 | Apr-15 | 214085.39 | 200948.53 | 13136.86 |

I'll need to review the dimensionality represented in this data file in order to build the cube dimensions. Based on the data file, the following dimensions needed in the KoolExp.Expense cube are:

- Account
- Period
- Account Group
- Business Line
- Year
- Scenario

**Note!** The same Excel workbook will be used throughout this entire chapter. To get a copy of the workbook, please send an email to info@interrel.com and request the book workshop sample files.

6. In the Cube Designer panel, type in the list of dimensions above, pressing *Enter* after each one:

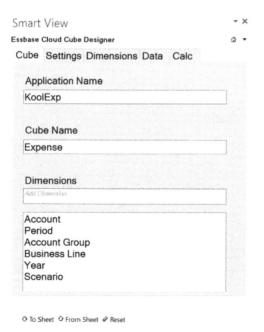

7. Click the *To Sheet* button to populate the workbook.

Note that the dimensions are populated in the workbook, and there is now a Dim.*Dimension* worksheet for each dimension:

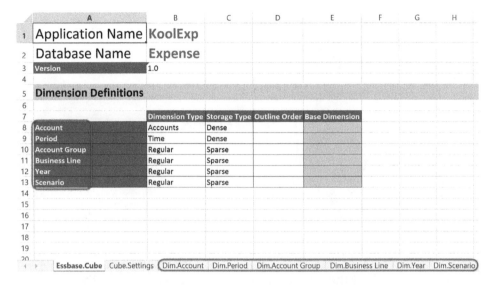

| | A | B | C | D | E | F | G | H |
|---|---|---|---|---|---|---|---|---|
| 1 | Application Name | KoolExp | | | | | | |
| 2 | Database Name | Expense | | | | | | |
| 3 | Version | 1.0 | | | | | | |
| 4 | | | | | | | | |
| 5 | **Dimension Definitions** | | | | | | | |
| 6 | | | | | | | | |
| 7 | | | Dimension Type | Storage Type | Outline Order | Base Dimension | | |
| 8 | Account | | Accounts | Dense | | | | |
| 9 | Period | | Time | Dense | | | | |
| 10 | Account Group | | Regular | Sparse | | | | |
| 11 | Business Line | | Regular | Sparse | | | | |
| 12 | Year | | Regular | Sparse | | | | |
| 13 | Scenario | | Regular | Sparse | | | | |
| 14 | | | | | | | | |
| 15 | | | | | | | | |
| 16 | | | | | | | | |
| 17 | | | | | | | | |
| 18 | | | | | | | | |
| 19 | | | | | | | | |
| 20 | | | | | | | | |

Essbase.Cube   Cube.Settings   Dim.Account   Dim.Period   Dim.Account Group   Dim.Business Line   Dim.Year   Dim.Scenario

### Dimension Settings

On the Dimensions tab in the Cube Designer panel, I can specify different options for each of the dimensions.

8. Change the Account dimension type to *Accounts* and the storage type to *Dense*.
9. Change the Period dimension type to *Time* and the storage type to *Dense*.
10. Modify the Scenario dimension to include the *Formula* dimension build field.
11. Click the *To Sheet* button to populate the worksheets.

12. On the Essbase.Cube worksheet, manually add an outline order number, 1 through 6, to each dimension, and save the workbook:

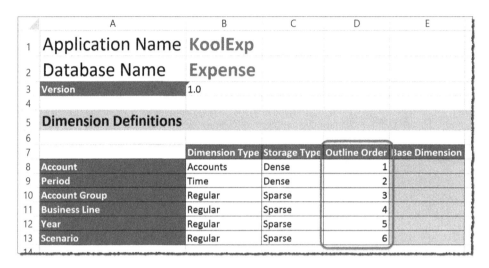

| | A | B | C | D | E |
|---|---|---|---|---|---|
| 1 | **Application Name** | **KoolExp** | | | |
| 2 | **Database Name** | **Expense** | | | |
| 3 | Version | 1.0 | | | |
| 4 | | | | | |
| 5 | **Dimension Definitions** | | | | |
| 6 | | | | | |
| 7 | | Dimension Type | Storage Type | Outline Order | Base Dimension |
| 8 | Account | Accounts | Dense | 1 | |
| 9 | Period | Time | Dense | 2 | |
| 10 | Account Group | Regular | Sparse | 3 | |
| 11 | Business Line | Regular | Sparse | 4 | |
| 12 | Year | Regular | Sparse | 5 | |
| 13 | Scenario | Regular | Sparse | 6 | |

### Build Year Members

On each of the Dim.*Dimension* workbooks, I define the members that will be in the corresponding dimension. The most basic method for building hierarchies is Parent-Child. All of the dimensions added to the KoolExp.Expense cube are set to use the Parent-Child build method by default:

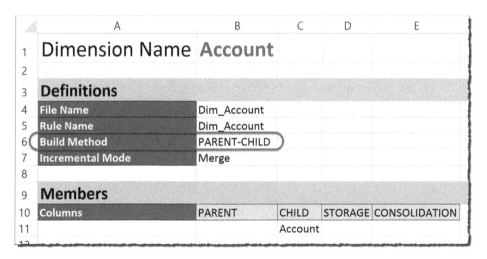

| | A | B | C | D | E |
|---|---|---|---|---|---|
| 1 | **Dimension Name** | **Account** | | | |
| 2 | | | | | |
| 3 | **Definitions** | | | | |
| 4 | File Name | Dim_Account | | | |
| 5 | Rule Name | Dim_Account | | | |
| 6 | Build Method | PARENT-CHILD | | | |
| 7 | Incremental Mode | Merge | | | |
| 8 | | | | | |
| 9 | **Members** | | | | |
| 10 | Columns | PARENT | CHILD | STORAGE | CONSOLIDATION |
| 11 | | | Account | | |

I'll start with the easiest dimension, Year.

13. Select the *Dim.Year* worksheet.

Each dimension workbook must begin with the dimension name in the CHILD column as I can see on row 11:

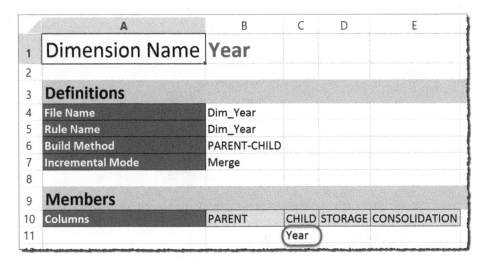

| | A | B | C | D | E |
|---|---|---|---|---|---|
| 1 | **Dimension Name** | **Year** | | | |
| 2 | | | | | |
| 3 | **Definitions** | | | | |
| 4 | File Name | Dim_Year | | | |
| 5 | Rule Name | Dim_Year | | | |
| 6 | Build Method | PARENT-CHILD | | | |
| 7 | Incremental Mode | Merge | | | |
| 8 | | | | | |
| 9 | **Members** | | | | |
| 10 | Columns | PARENT | CHILD | STORAGE | CONSOLIDATION |
| 11 | | | Year | | |

14. Add an *O* (for label only) storage setting to the Year member.

**Note!**

Mentioning again because the information is contextually relevant: just like on-premises Essbase, there are a variety of codes that correspond to different storage properties. The following basic letter codes apply to the storage property for block storage cubes:

- O = label only
- X = dynamic calc
- V = dynamic calc and store
- N = never share
- S = stored

15. On row 12, type "Year" into the PARENT column and "2015" into the CHILD column:

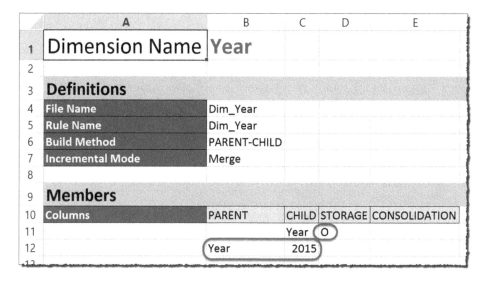

### Build Scenario Members

To build members for the Scenario dimension,

16. Select the *Dim.Scenario* worksheet.
17. Add an *O* for label only storage to the Scenario member.
18. Add the Actual child with a parent of Scenario.
19. Add the Budget child with a parent of Scenario and an ignore consolidation operator (~).

20. Add the Variance child with a parent of Scenario. Variance should have a storage property of dynamic calculation (X), an ignore consolidation operator (~), and a formula of `@VAR(Actual, Budget);`

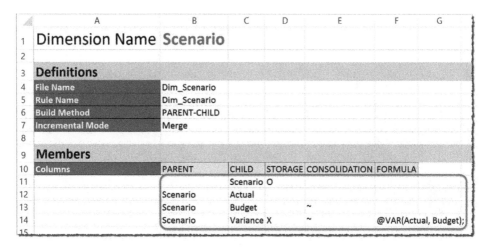

| | A | B | C | D | E | F | G |
|---|---|---|---|---|---|---|---|
| 1 | **Dimension Name** | **Scenario** | | | | | |
| 2 | | | | | | | |
| 3 | **Definitions** | | | | | | |
| 4 | File Name | Dim_Scenario | | | | | |
| 5 | Rule Name | Dim_Scenario | | | | | |
| 6 | Build Method | PARENT-CHILD | | | | | |
| 7 | Incremental Mode | Merge | | | | | |
| 8 | | | | | | | |
| 9 | **Members** | | | | | | |
| 10 | Columns | PARENT | CHILD | STORAGE | CONSOLIDATION | FORMULA | |
| 11 | | | Scenario O | | | | |
| 12 | | Scenario | Actual | | | | |
| 13 | | Scenario | Budget | | ~ | | |
| 14 | | Scenario | Variance X | | ~ | @VAR(Actual, Budget); | |
| 15 | | | | | | | |

**Note!** When the contents of a cell in Excel starts with a special character (usually one that can be used in an Excel formula) or a number, it's best to prefix the contents of the cell with an apostrophe. This lets Excel know that you are entering text and not a function or number.

### Build Business Line Members

To build in members for the Business Line dimension,

21. Select the *Dim.Business Line* worksheet.
22. Add the following children to Business Line:
    a. Leasing
    b. Services
    c. Equipment
23. Under the Leasing parent, add a child called *Capital Leasing*.
24. Under the Services parent, add the following children:
    a. Managed Services
    b. Research Services
    c. Technical Services
25. Under the Equipment parent, add the following children:

    a. Capital Equipment

    b. Medical Equipment

    c. Technology Equipment

26. Click *Save* to retain the changes.

The *Dim.Business Line* worksheet should look similar to this:

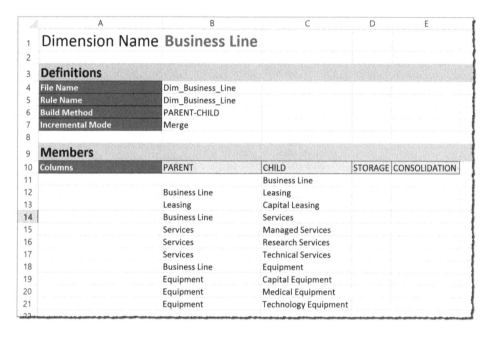

### Build Account Group Members

To build in members for the Account Group dimension,

27. Select the *Dim.Account Group* worksheet.

28. Add a storage property of dynamic calculation (*X*) to the member Account Group.

29. Add the following children to Account Group:

    a. Contract Services

    b. Operations and Maintenance

    c. Supplies

    d. Travel

    e. Other Operating Expenses

The *Dim.Account Group* worksheet should look similar to this:

| | A | B | C | D | E |
|---|---|---|---|---|---|
| 1 | **Dimension Name** | **Account Group** | | | |
| 2 | | | | | |
| 3 | **Definitions** | | | | |
| 4 | File Name | Dim_Account_Group | | | |
| 5 | Rule Name | Dim_Account_Group | | | |
| 6 | Build Method | PARENT-CHILD | | | |
| 7 | Incremental Mode | Merge | | | |
| 8 | | | | | |
| 9 | **Members** | | | | |
| 10 | Columns | PARENT | CHILD | STORAGE | CONSOLIDATION |
| 11 | | | Account Group | X | |
| 12 | | Account Group | Contract Services | | |
| 13 | | Account Group | Operations and Maintenance | | |
| 14 | | Account Group | Supplies | | |
| 15 | | Account Group | Travel | | |
| 16 | | Account Group | Other Operating Expenses | | |

### Build Period Members

To build members for the Period dimension,

30. Select the *Dim.Period* worksheet.
31. Add a storage property of dynamic calculation (X) to Period.
32. Add the following children to Period with an "X" in the STORAGE column of the each member:
    a. Q1
    b. Q2
    c. Q3
    d. Q4
33. Under the Q1 parent, add the following children:
    a. Jan
    b. Feb
    c. Mar
34. Under the Q2 parent, add the following children:
    a. Apr
    b. May
    c. Jun
35. Under the Q3 parent, add the following children:
    a. Jul
    b. Aug
    c. Sep

36. Under the Q4 parent, add the following children:
    a. Oct
    b. Nov
    c. Dec
37. Click *Save* to retain the changes.

The *Dim.Period* worksheet should look similar to this:

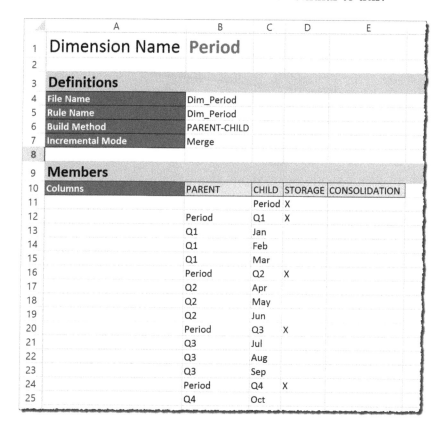

| | A | B | C | D | E |
|---|---|---|---|---|---|
| 1 | **Dimension Name Period** | | | | |
| 2 | | | | | |
| 3 | **Definitions** | | | | |
| 4 | File Name | Dim_Period | | | |
| 5 | Rule Name | Dim_Period | | | |
| 6 | Build Method | PARENT-CHILD | | | |
| 7 | Incremental Mode | Merge | | | |
| 8 | | | | | |
| 9 | **Members** | | | | |
| 10 | Columns | PARENT | CHILD | STORAGE | CONSOLIDATION |
| 11 | | | Period | X | |
| 12 | | Period | Q1 | X | |
| 13 | | Q1 | Jan | | |
| 14 | | Q1 | Feb | | |
| 15 | | Q1 | Mar | | |
| 16 | | Period | Q2 | X | |
| 17 | | Q2 | Apr | | |
| 18 | | Q2 | May | | |
| 19 | | Q2 | Jun | | |
| 20 | | Period | Q3 | X | |
| 21 | | Q3 | Jul | | |
| 22 | | Q3 | Aug | | |
| 23 | | Q3 | Sep | | |
| 24 | | Period | Q4 | X | |
| 25 | | Q4 | Oct | | |

**Build Account Members**

To build in members for the Account dimension,

38. Select the *Dim.Account* worksheet.
39. Add a storage property of dynamic calculation (*X*) to Account.
40. Add a new member property to the sheet for variance reporting by copying the contents of cell E10 into F10 and

typing over the CONSOLIDATION property name with "VARIANCEREPORT".

Note that only some of the member properties display across the columns by default. If I know the correct syntax of the property, I can type it into the column for the member build, then send it "from sheet." Cube Designer sets it correctly so that it doesn't overwrite in the next "to sheet." Remember these names are case sensitive. Use the Cube Designer to add in the columns if you are not sure.

41. Add the following children to Account. Each account should have an expense flag (E) in the VARIANCEREPORT column so the variance scenario is able to calculate properly:
    a.  600020 Recruiting
    b.  600030 Contracted Services
    c.  600040 Food Service & Catering
    d.  620000 Materials & Supplies
    e.  630000 Office Supplies & Printing
    f.  631100 Laboratory Supplies
    g.  634000 Postage & Freight
    h.  635000 Vehicle Maintenance
    i.  641000 Telecommunications
    j.  642000 Utilities
    k.  650000 Insurance
    l.  650025 Operations & Maintenance
    m.  650040 Professional & Consulting Fees
    n.  653010 Travel
    o.  653020 Travel - Local
    p.  699000 Bad Debt Expense
42. Save the workbook.

The *Dim.Account* worksheet should look similar to this:

| | A | B | C | D | E | F |
|---|---|---|---|---|---|---|
| 1 | **Dimension Name** | **Account** | | | | |
| 2 | | | | | | |
| 3 | **Definitions** | | | | | |
| 4 | File Name | Dim_Account | | | | |
| 5 | Rule Name | Dim_Account | | | | |
| 6 | Build Method | PARENT-CHILD | | | | |
| 7 | Incremental Mode | Merge | | | | |
| 8 | | | | | | |
| 9 | **Members** | | | | | |
| 10 | Columns | PARENT | CHILD | STORAGE | CONSOLIDATION | VARIANCEREPORT |
| 11 | | | Account | X | | |
| 12 | | Account | 600020 Recruiting | | | E |
| 13 | | Account | 600030 Contracted Services | | | E |
| 14 | | Account | 600040 Food Service & Catering | | | E |
| 15 | | Account | 620000 Materials & Supplies | | | E |
| 16 | | Account | 630000 Office Supplies & Printing | | | E |
| 17 | | Account | 631100 Laboratory Supplies | | | E |
| 18 | | Account | 634000 Postage & Freight | | | E |
| 19 | | Account | 635000 Vehicle Maintenance | | | E |
| 20 | | Account | 641000 Telecommunications | | | E |
| 21 | | Account | 642000 Utilities | | | E |
| 22 | | Account | 650000 Insurance | | | E |
| 23 | | Account | 650025 Operations & Maintenance | | | E |
| 24 | | Account | 650040 Professional & Consulting Fees | | | E |
| 25 | | Account | 653010 Travel | | | E |

**Note!** Another design practice for these member names that is used often with Essbase users is to have the account number as the member name and the longer description as an alias. Aliases are very easy to change without having to impact members and data loaded to them.

### Add a Data Sheet

I need to add data to the cube once it has been created. Since I have the Expense file from KoolKart, I can build a data sheet to accept the same file format and paste in the data. The Application Workbook allows one or more data sheets within the workbook; just make sure to specify different file and rule names for each data sheet. When I submit the job to build the cube, I can select an option to load the data as well.

43. In the Cube Designer wizard, click on the *Data* tab.
44. Type "KoolExp" in the Data Sheets text field and press *Enter*:

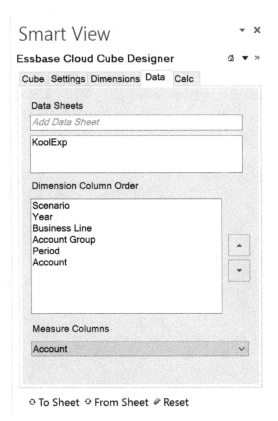

45. In the Measure Columns drop-down, select the *Scenario* dimension. This locks Scenario in the last spot in the column order, making it a column dimension for the data sheet.

46. Edit the dimension column order using the up and down arrows to match the KoolKart expense file:

- Account Group
- Account
- Business Line
- Year
- Period
- Scenario

The wizard should look similar to this:

47. Click the *To Sheet* button to create the Data sheet.
48. Click the Data.KoolExp tab.
49. Change the Measure.Scenario cell to *Measure.Actual* by replacing "Scenario" with "Actual".
50. Copy the Measure.Actual cell to the next cell and rename it to *Measure.Budget*.

The *Data.KoolExp* sheet should look similar to this:

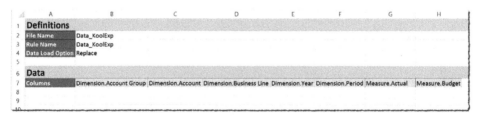

51. Copy the data from the KoolKart expense file, excluding the headers and the Variance column, and paste it into the data sheet starting at cell B8.
52. Save the workbook.

The *Data.KoolExp* sheet should look similar to this:

| | A | B | C | D | E | F | G | H |
|---|---|---|---|---|---|---|---|---|
| 1 | **Definitions** | | | | | | | |
| 2 | File Name | Data_KoolExp | | | | | | |
| 3 | Rule Name | Data_KoolExp | | | | | | |
| 4 | Data Load Option | Replace | | | | | | |
| 5 | | | | | | | | |
| 6 | **Data** | | | | | | | |
| 7 | Columns | Dimension.Account Group | Dimension.Account | Dimension.Business Line | Dimension.Year | Dimension.Period | Measure.Actual | Measure.Budget |
| 8 | | Contract Services | 600030 Contracted | Capital Leasing | 2015 | Jan | 420493.3 | 441535.04 |
| 9 | | Contract Services | 600030 Contracted | Capital Leasing | 2015 | Feb | 331581.34 | 306221.42 |
| 10 | | Contract Services | 600030 Contracted | Capital Leasing | 2015 | Mar | 391137.88 | 429219.41 |
| 11 | | Contract Services | 600030 Contracted | Capital Leasing | 2015 | Apr | 368940.28 | 336260.47 |
| 12 | | Contract Services | 600030 Contracted | Capital Leasing | 2015 | May | 459186.53 | 513842.98 |
| 13 | | Contract Services | 600030 Contracted | Capital Leasing | 2015 | Jul | 385485.75 | 415440.46 |
| 14 | | Contract Services | 600030 Contracted | Capital Leasing | 2015 | Aug | 459543.55 | 407433.63 |

## Build Cube

Just like the steps before, I use the *Build Cube* option in the Cube Designer ribbon.

53. Click the *Build Cube* icon to create the application in Essbase Cloud:

Because I am offline, I need to log into Essbase Cloud to submit the job.

54. If prompted, enter the login and password information.

55. Select the *Create Cube* build option, check the box next to *Load Data Sheets Contained within Workbook*, and click *Run*:

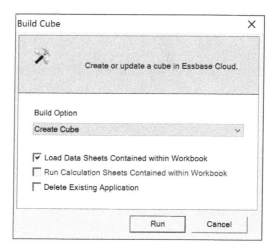

56. Select *Yes* when asked to build the cube, which will launch the job viewer so you can see the status of your create cube job.

Just like magic, Essbase Cloud reads the Cube Designer worksheets, creates the cube, and loads the data!

### Validate the Cube and Data

After the create cube job has completed, I can validate that the application has been created and the dimensions are populated with my members from the Cube Designer workbook. This can be done through two interfaces:

- In the Essbase Cloud web interface, I can verify that the dimensions have been built and contain all of the correct members and properties

- In Smart View, I can connect to the cube and do an ad hoc analysis to verify that the data is loaded:

|  | A | B | C | D | E |
|---|---|---|---|---|---|
| 1 | | Account Group | Business Line | Year | |
| 2 | | Actual | Budget | Variance | Scenario |
| 3 | | Period | Period | Period | Period |
| 4 | 600020 Recruiting | 5,425,128.57 | 5,436,478.07 | 11,349.50 | 5,425,128.57 |
| 5 | 600030 Contracted Services | 33,094,879.89 | 33,088,885.08 | (5,994.81) | 33,094,879.89 |
| 6 | 600040 Food Service & Catering | 2,975,070.17 | 3,032,315.23 | 57,245.06 | 2,975,070.17 |
| 7 | 620000 Materials & Supplies | 24,410,192.01 | 24,889,458.45 | 479,266.44 | 24,410,192.01 |
| 8 | 630000 Office Supplies & Printing | 4,469,463.56 | 4,195,453.04 | (274,010.52) | 4,469,463.56 |
| 9 | 631100 Laboratory Supplies | 5,673,972.03 | 5,255,098.96 | (418,873.07) | 5,673,972.03 |
| 10 | 634000 Postage & Freight | 677,104.17 | 629,517.08 | (47,587.09) | 677,104.17 |
| 11 | 635000 Vehicle Maintenance | 3,763,317.44 | 3,364,656.10 | (398,661.34) | 3,763,317.44 |
| 12 | 641000 Telecommunications | 1,150,544.87 | 1,001,289.75 | (149,255.12) | 1,150,544.87 |
| 13 | 642000 Utilities | 1,682,950.65 | 1,514,335.87 | (168,614.78) | 1,682,950.65 |
| 14 | 650000 Insurance | 379,514.56 | 360,391.66 | (19,122.90) | 379,514.56 |
| 15 | 650025 Operations & Maintenance | 12,045,757.10 | 10,706,206.47 | (1,339,550.63) | 12,045,757.10 |
| 16 | 650040 Professional & Consulting Fees | 707,253.68 | 609,630.95 | (97,622.73) | 707,253.68 |
| 17 | 653010 Travel | 1,103,454.54 | 990,354.72 | (113,099.82) | 1,103,454.54 |
| 18 | 653020 Travel - Local | 5,156,707.34 | 4,621,501.24 | (535,206.10) | 5,156,707.34 |
| 19 | 699000 Bad Debt Expense | 768,503.42 | 686,215.41 | (82,288.01) | 768,503.42 |
| 20 | Account | 103,483,814.00 | 100,381,788.08 | (3,102,025.92) | 103,483,814.00 |

**LOG ENTRY FOR ESSBASE PILOT ROBERT GIDEON**
*SOL 19, Entry 3*

Mission TBC Sample.Basic and KoolKart Expense Cube complete.

**LOG ENTRY FOR STRANDED EPM MARTIAN EDWARD ROSKE**
*SOL 20, Entry 1*

They are finally letting us communicate… the crew of the Ranger and myself. I might as well have some fun while I'm stuck here in the Cloud.

# CHAPTER 7: MAINTAIN DIMENSIONS, LOAD DATA, & CALCULATE

---

**LOG ENTRY FOR FLIGHT ENGINEER GLENN SCHWARTZBERG**
*SOL 20, Entry 1*

The TBC Sample.Basic and KoolKart Sales and Expense cubes are now built in OAC. So how will JWE maintain the cubes? Updating dimensions, loading new data sets, and running calculations. My mission is to show how to do just that in OAC.

If Edward can build a PBCS application in just a few sols, I should be able to do this in half that time. Suck Ionospheric particles, stranded Edward!

---

Once cubes are built, one might think they can relax. They would be right, but only when one sets up dimension maintenance processes (adding/moving/deleting new products, new accounts), data load processes (loading new data as it becomes available), and running calculations (if needed).

Surely OAC has an easy way to maintain dimensions, load data, and perform calculations? Of course it does.

## Dimension Maintenance Overview

Let's start by discussing what will happen once that bookkeeper arrives with his new account to add to the system. There are a couple of ways that I can handle this situation. With a single member, I could simply go in and add the account manually...but what happens when there are fifty accounts? Or even one hundred accounts?

The good news is that Essbase Cloud provides a few ways to maintain dimension hierarchies, and I've already worked with one of them (Application Workbooks).

Dimension data may be loaded to Essbase cubes via:

- Manual updates through the Essbase Cloud web interface
- Import Application Workbook (using one or more worksheets containing data) via the Essbase Cloud web interface. Note that Application Workbook files can be used to maintain several changes at once.
- Import Application Workbook (using one or more worksheets containing data) via Cube Designer in Excel. Note that Application Workbook files can be used to maintain several changes at once.
- Run a job using a rules file and an uploaded text file in the Essbase Cloud web interface
- Execute the Load Data option from Cube Designer in Excel and selecting the desired rules file and uploaded text file
- Dimension flat files can be imported via MaxL and used in conjunction with rules files (but more on this last bit later, when I cover MaxL)

One word of caution: It is possible for multiple Administrators (or one Administrator with multiple versions of the workbook) to inadvertently overwrite changes that have been made to a cube. There is no version control. The last change in wins, so be aware.

## UPDATE DIMENSIONS MANUALLY THROUGH THE WEB INTERFACE

One way to maintain the dimension hierarchies within a cube is to update them manually in the Essbase Cloud web interface. While this method may not be the most efficient way to handle bulk updates of many members, it is very handy for a handful of changes.

The high level steps to manually update a dimension hierarchy within the Essbase Cloud web interface are:

1) Navigate to the applicable cube outline
2) Lock and edit the outline
3) Select a dimension

4) Drill down on that dimension's hierarchy to the desired location
5) Update the appropriate field(s)
6) Save and unlock the outline

When arriving to the Outline screen, the screen defaults to view mode. In view mode the user can review member properties by scrolling from left to right:

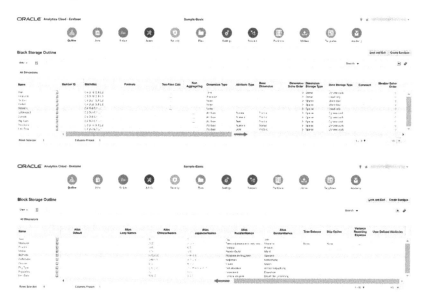

On this screen, member property order can be shifted by selecting the column heading and dragging and dropping it to its new position. For example, if I wanted the Dimension Type property to be directly next to the Name field, I place my cursor on Dimension Type, left-click, drag the column next to the Name field, and then release my mouse.

Another way to review the properties of an individual member is to select the *properties* icon ▦ next to the member.

This will display a window defaulting to four tabs: Information, Aliases, UDAs, and Formulas:

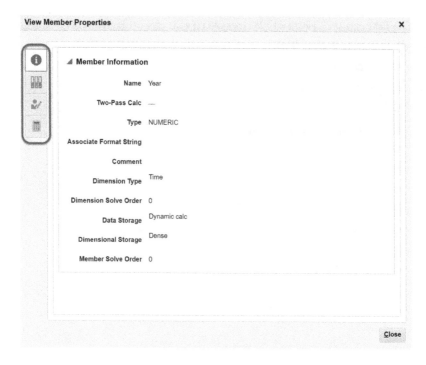

To navigate to other members within a hierarchy, the dimension and member names can be selected, drilling down to the lowest level within each:

The path that a user has drilled to is displayed above the member names:

**All Dimensions  >  Scenario**

To go back, I can click on any of the previous member selections. In the below example, I have selected the Measures dimension, then the Inventory member. This takes me to the level-0 members beneath Inventory (Opening Inventory, Additions, and Ending Inventory):

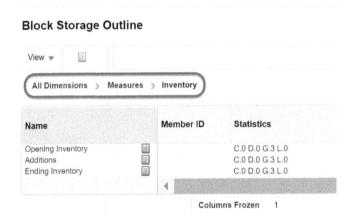

 **Note!**  You can tell that Opening Inventory, Additions, and Ending Inventory are level-0 members because they are not active links that can be drilled into any further.

Let's go through an example of how to manually add a member to a cube outline. In this exercise, I will be adding a new product to the Sample.Basic application, 200-50 - Root Beer Squared (a hilarious name to give me a brief break from all of the more realistic accounts I will be adding in the future).

To add a new member through the Essbase Cloud web interface,
1. From the Essbase Cloud home page, select the *Sample* application.

2.  Expand the *Sample* application and *Basic* cube, then select *Outline*:

3.  Select *Lock and Edit*:

4.  Select the *Product* dimension and then drill down to member *200* (from the default alias it can be discerned that this is Root Beer). The children under member 200 are displayed:

5. Select member *200-40* and then select *Add Sibling*, the icon that looks like :

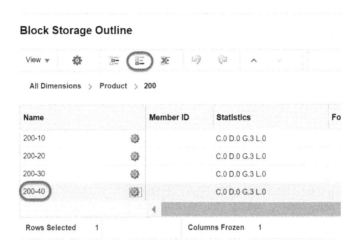

6. Enter a member name of 200-50 and then press the *Tab* key. The new member displays beneath member *200-40*:

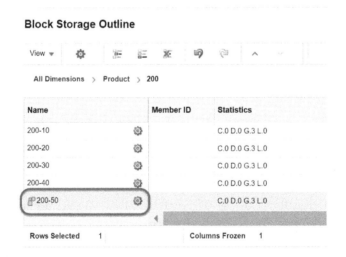

7. To the right, type "Root Beer Squared" into the *Alias Default* column for the new member:

8. Scroll to the right (unless your screen is the width of the Titanic) and update the following fields:
   a. Attribute Caffeinated to "True"
   b. Attribute Ounces to "12"
   c. Attribute Pkg Type to "Bottle"

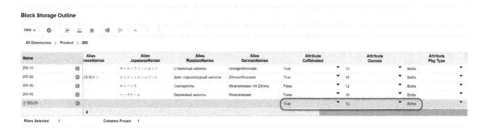

9. Select *Save and unlock*:

10. The dimensions list will reappear, as well as a pop-up notification that the member properties were successfully saved:

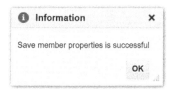

**Note!**

You might want to consider adding a "21 and over" attribute for this product.

While reviewing the outline, I notice that the Year and Measures dimensions have a dimension storage type of Dense. It is common practice for BSO cubes to set upper level members of Dense dimensions to a data storage type of Dynamic Calc. For more information on design best practices and tuning tips for Essbase Cloud cubes, see our Cloud Play it Forward series at http://epm.bi/videos.

Next, I'll go through an example of how to manually edit a member within a cube outline. I will ensure that all of the upper level members for the Measures dimension are set to dynamic calc.

To edit a member property,
1. From the Essbase Cloud home page, expand the *Sample* application and *Basic* cube, then select *Outline*.
2. Select *Lock and Edit*.

I notice the top member in the Measures dimension is set to the *Label Only* Data Storage Type. In this case, I will leave Measures set to label only because I am not looking to add Profit + Inventory + Ratios. The top level member is used for organization purposes only:

3. Select *Measures* to drill to the immediate children and review the Data Storage Type field:

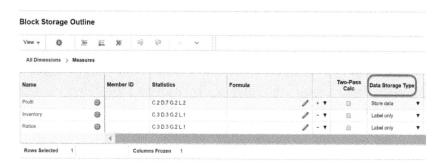

Since these children members are drillable links, I know that they are not level-0 members. Based on my best practice cube design (dense upper level members of a Block Storage cube should be dynamically calculated), the Data Storage Type property should be set to Dynamic Calc.

4. Select the drop-down below the Data Storage Type column for the members *Profit* and *Inventory* and change them to *Dynamic Calc*:

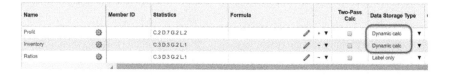

**Note!** The parent member Ratios does not make sense to roll up since it's a grouping of metrics that don't naturally aggregate. Therefore, this member will be left with Data Storage Type *Label Only*.

5.  Continue drilling into the *Profit* and *Inventory* members and update any non-level-0 member storage types to *Dynamic Calc*.

6.  Click *Save and Unlock* to save the changes and then *OK*.

## ACCESS PRE-DEFINED APPLICATION WORKBOOKS

Essbase Cloud provides pre-defined template Application Workbooks that can be downloaded and used as a starting point of how the file should look. These can be accessed and downloaded from Smart View as I learned in Chapter 6, "Create a Cube with Cube Designer," or from the Essbase Cloud web interface by utilizing the *Templates* icon on the Essbase Cloud home page:

Once within the Template screen, use the *Download* icon ⬆ to download a desired template:

**Templates**

| Name | Provider | Description |
|---|---|---|
| ⬇ Block Storage Sample (Stored) | Oracle | Block storage application workbook. |
| ⬇ Block Storage Sample (Dynamic) | Oracle | Block storage application workbook. All non-leaf level members are dynamic. |
| ⬇ Block Storage Sample (Scenario) | Oracle | Block storage application workbook with scenarios enabled. All non-leaf level members are dynamic. |
| ⬇ Demo Basic | Oracle | Basic demo application workbook |
| ⬇ Aggregate Storage Sample | Oracle | Aggregate storage application workbook. |
| ⬇ Aggregate Storage Sample Data | Oracle | Data for the aggregate storage application workbook. |
| ⬇ Free-form Tabular Data Sample | Oracle | Tabular data Excel file. |

Templates can also be accessed through Excel by utilizing the *Gallery* icon on the Cube Designer ribbon:

Once Gallery has been selected, there are Table Format and General categories listed to the left of the Cube Gallery screen:

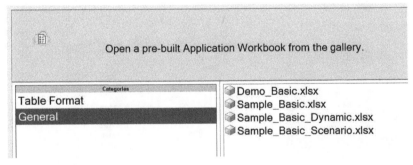

Notice that the Essbase Cloud web interface doesn't categorize the import templates in this manner. This is because the web interface contains the standard set of downloadable templates. Cube Designer will eventually contain more templates - maybe even those created by the community for sharing!

*Table Format* contains, as the title suggests, unstructured table-like formats (described in more detail in Chapter 4, "Unstructured Spreadsheet to Essbase Cube"). Below is a screenshot from the "Sample_Table" template:

| | A | B | C | D | E | F | G | H | I | J |
|---|---|---|---|---|---|---|---|---|---|---|
| 1 | Units | Discounts | Fixed Costs | Variable Costs | Revenue | Time.Month | Time.Quarter | Years | Regions.Region | Regions.Area |
| 2 | 9 | 23.94 | 72.74 | 368.58 | 375.43 February | | Qtr 1 | CY2015 | EMEA | North Africa |
| 3 | 10 | 0 | 367.44 | 372.47 | 1895.98 May | | Qtr 2 | CY2015 | EMEA | Northern |
| 4 | 9 | 1.41 | 7.53 | 36.1 | 37.52 March | | Qtr 1 | CY2015 | AMERICAS | Central |
| 5 | 13 | 26.29 | 111.06 | 484.11 | 1401.83 December | | Qtr 4 | CY2014 | AMERICAS | Central |
| 6 | 12 | 20.83 | 195.45 | 818.08 | 2218.72 July | | Qtr 3 | CY2015 | AMERICAS | South America |
| 7 | 8 | 17.03 | 55.86 | 205.73 | 697.57 November | | Qtr 4 | CY2015 | APAC | North |
| 8 | 10 | 31.45 | 108.32 | 329.57 | 1117.81 June | | Qtr 2 | CY2015 | AMERICAS | Central |
| 9 | 5 | 14.74 | 207.26 | 650.77 | 523.22 April | | Qtr 2 | CY2014 | AMERICAS | South America |
| 10 | 10 | 20 | 168.83 | 1104.13 | 1065.57 June | | Qtr 2 | CY2014 | AMERICAS | South America |
| 11 | 9 | 1.86 | 9.14 | 28.7 | 45.56 February | | Qtr 1 | CY2015 | EMEA | Northern |
| 12 | 19 | 0 | 354.48 | 33.84 | 232.03 January | | Qtr 1 | CY2016 | APAC | West |
| 13 | 12 | 83.24 | 266.75 | 20055.8 | 3223.08 September | | Qtr 3 | CY2015 | APAC | West |
| 14 | 10 | 60.09 | 413.4 | 2096.37 | 2133.1 May | | Qtr 2 | CY2015 | APAC | North |
| 15 | 4 | 0.53 | 24.97 | 1.93 | 16.58 February | | Qtr 1 | CY2014 | EMEA | Africa |
| 16 | 4 | 0.49 | 2.73 | 17.49 | 17.22 November | | Qtr 4 | CY2014 | AMERICAS | North America |
| 17 | 10 | 0 | 243.55 | 1235.4 | 1256.71 October | | Qtr 4 | CY2015 | EMEA | Europe |
| 18 | 12 | 24.5 | 114.9 | 452.43 | 1304.17 July | | Qtr 3 | CY2015 | EMEA | Middle East |
| 19 | 9 | 29.48 | 46.75 | 220.71 | 626.17 February | | Qtr 1 | CY2016 | AMERICAS | Central |
| 20 | 9 | 27.37 | 132.75 | 126.83 | 661.58 March | | Qtr 1 | CY2015 | EMEA | Eastern |
| 21 | 9 | 28.93 | 114.66 | 465.1 | 591.58 February | | Qtr 1 | CY2015 | AMERICAS | Central |
| 22 | 21 | 8.38 | 448.99 | 42.87 | 337.61 April | | Qtr 2 | CY2016 | AMERICAS | South America |

Sales

The *General* category contains structured formats that can be used for creating and updating the types of cubes emphasized in this chapter. Below is an example of the Sample_Basic template:

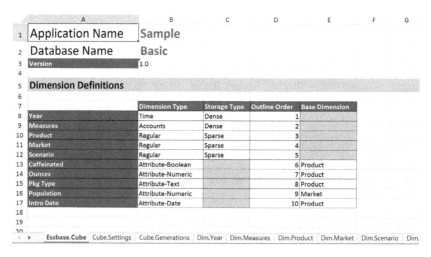

| | A | B | C | D | E | F | G |
|---|---|---|---|---|---|---|---|
| 1 | Application Name | Sample | | | | | |
| 2 | Database Name | Basic | | | | | |
| 3 | Version | 1.0 | | | | | |
| 4 | | | | | | | |
| 5 | **Dimension Definitions** | | | | | | |
| 6 | | | | | | | |
| 7 | | Dimension Type | Storage Type | Outline Order | Base Dimension | | |
| 8 | Year | Time | Dense | 1 | | | |
| 9 | Measures | Accounts | Dense | 2 | | | |
| 10 | Product | Regular | Sparse | 3 | | | |
| 11 | Market | Regular | Sparse | 4 | | | |
| 12 | Scenario | Regular | Sparse | 5 | | | |
| 13 | Caffeinated | Attribute-Boolean | | 6 | Product | | |
| 14 | Ounces | Attribute-Numeric | | 7 | Product | | |
| 15 | Pkg Type | Attribute-Text | | 8 | Product | | |
| 16 | Population | Attribute-Numeric | | 9 | Market | | |
| 17 | Intro Date | Attribute-Date | | 10 | Product | | |
| 18 | | | | | | | |
| 19 | | | | | | | |
| 20 | | | | | | | |

Essbase.Cube   Cube.Settings   Cube.Generations   Dim.Year   Dim.Measures   Dim.Product   Dim.Market   Dim.Scenario   Dim.

# EXPORT CUBES

### Export Cube Definition with Cube Designer

Probably the most efficient way to maintain hierarchies in Essbase Cloud is by using an Application Workbook file. Any time updates need to be made, simply update the Application Workbook and import it back in through either the Essbase Cloud web interface or Cube Designer (importing will be discussed in the next two sections).

However, remember that any updates made outside of the Application Workbook file (i.e., through the Essbase Cloud web interface) must also be captured by the file itself. If not, once the file is imported, it could wipe out or override prior updates, if the rules file is set to allow property changes (rules files will also be discussed later). If a local saved copy of the workbook doesn't exist or is out of date, the best way to ensure that I have the latest set of metadata before updating it is to re-export the cube to a fresh Application Workbook.

To export a cube using Cube Designer,
1. Open Excel.
2. Open the Cube Designer Smart View extension.
3. Export the Essbase cube file via *Private >> Export Cube to Application Workbook*:

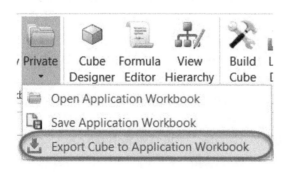

4.  Select the *Sample* application and *Basic* cube:

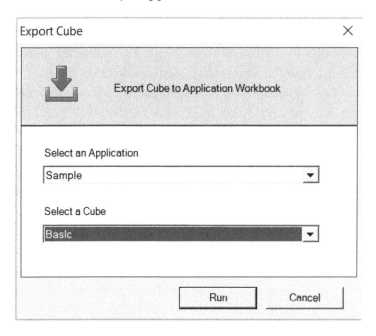

5.  Click *Run*.

The Application Workbook opens up and is ready for updates!

### Export Cube Definition with Web Interface

I can also export a cube definition using the Essbase Cloud web interface. One benefit of the web interface is that I have more control over the output and format of the Application Workbook. I can specify the dimension build method for each dimension (more on this in just a bit) and I can specify whether to include data and calculation scripts in the export.

When I export data, if the size is 100 MB or less, it will export the data into a worksheet within the Application Workbook. If the exported data is over 100 MB, it will export the data to a compressed file that is saved in the cube directory on Essbase Cloud (accessible through the web interface via Files or through the Essbase Command Line Interface, a.k.a. EssCLI).

To export a cube with the Essbase Cloud web interface,

1. Navigate to the Essbase Cloud web interface.
2. From the home page, expand the *Sample* application.
3. Select the *Basic* cube.
4. From the ⋮ menu, choose *Export:*

The Export Cube dialogue displays.

5. Check the option for *Show Advanced:*

The Advanced Export Cube dialogue displays. Now that all export options are showing, I can choose:

- To export data
- To export calculation scripts
- To export the cube definition to the server; if this is not checked, the cube definition is exported to a local file
- The build method for each dimension - as either Parent-Child or Generation:

6.  Check the options to export *Data* and *Calculation scripts*.

7. Change the Build Method for Market to *Generation:*

8. Click *Export.*

The Application Workbook is exported, and ready for review and updates! I also can see the Market and Product dimension worksheets use the generational build format (more on this in just a moment):

**Members**

| Columns | GENERATIONREFID | GENERATION.Region | UDA.UDA1 | GENERATION.State | UDA.UDA1 | UDA.UDA2 | ATTRIBUTE.Population |
|---|---|---|---|---|---|---|---|
| Reference Column | Gen1 | Gen2 | Gen2 | Gen3 | Gen3 | Gen3 | Gen3 |
| | Market | East | Major Mark | New York | Major Market | | 21000000 |
| | Market | East | | Massachusetts | Major Market | | 9000000 |
| | Market | East | | Florida | Major Market | | 15000000 |
| | Market | East | | Connecticut | Small Market | | 6000000 |
| | Market | East | | New Hampshire | Small Market | | 3000000 |
| | Market | West | | California | Major Market | | 33000000 |
| | Market | West | | Oregon | Small Market | | 6000000 |
| | Market | West | | Washington | Small Market | | 6000000 |
| | Market | West | | Utah | Small Market | | 3000000 |
| | Market | West | | Nevada | Small Marke | New Marke | 3000000 |
| | Market | South | Small Marke | Texas | Major Market | | 21000000 |
| | Market | South | | Oklahoma | Small Market | | 6000000 |
| | Market | South | | Louisiana | Small Marke | New Marke | 6000000 |
| | Market | South | | New Mexico | Small Market | | 3000000 |

## Update Application Workbook

Now that I have a current Application Workbook, I can update the hierarchies and members in Excel. Once my updates are complete, I can load the updated dimensions to the cube.

1. Open the Application Workbook for Sample.Basic.
2. Navigate to the tab or tabs you want to update. For this example, navigate to the Dim.Product tab for Sample.Basic:

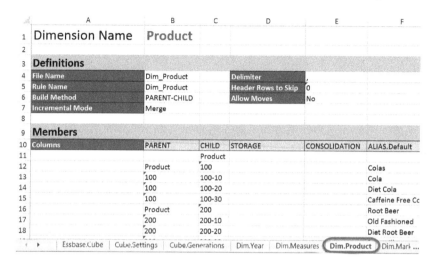

| | A | B | C | D | E | F |
|---|---|---|---|---|---|---|
| 1 | **Dimension Name** | **Product** | | | | |
| 2 | | | | | | |
| 3 | **Definitions** | | | | | |
| 4 | File Name | Dim_Product | | Delimiter | | |
| 5 | Rule Name | Dim_Product | | Header Rows to Skip | 0 | |
| 6 | Build Method | PARENT-CHILD | | Allow Moves | No | |
| 7 | Incremental Mode | Merge | | | | |
| 8 | | | | | | |
| 9 | **Members** | | | | | |
| 10 | Columns | PARENT | CHILD | STORAGE | CONSOLIDATION | ALIAS.Default |
| 11 | | | Product | | | |
| 12 | | Product | 100 | | | Colas |
| 13 | | 100 | 100-10 | | | Cola |
| 14 | | 100 | 100-20 | | | Diet Cola |
| 15 | | 100 | 100-30 | | | Caffeine Free Cc |
| 16 | | Product | 200 | | | Root Beer |
| 17 | | 200 | 200-10 | | | Old Fashioned |
| 18 | | 200 | 200-20 | | | Diet Root Beer |

Essbase.Cube | Cube.Settings | Cube.Generations | Dim.Year | Dim.Measures | Dim.Product | Dim.Mark ...

3. Insert a row above 300 and key in the following member names (for some of these, the prefixed apostrophe helps Excel understand that a member name is being entered versus a number):
   a. PARENT: '200
   b. CHILD: 200-60
   c. ALIAS.Default: Diet Root Beer Squared
   d. ATTRIBUTE.Caffeinated: True
   e. Attribute Ounces: '12
   f. Attribute Pkg Type: Bottle
4. Insert a row above "300" and key in the following member names:
   a. PARENT: '200
   b. CHILD: 200-70
   c. ALIAS.Default: Birch Beer Squared
   d. ATTRIBUTE.Caffeinated: True
   e. Attribute Ounces: '12
   f. Attribute Pkg Type: Bottle

| | A | B | C | D | E | F |
|---|---|---|---|---|---|---|
| 1 | **Dimension Name** | **Product** | | | | |
| 2 | | | | | | |
| 3 | **Definitions** | | | | | |
| 4 | File Name | Dim_Product | | Delimiter | , | |
| 5 | Rule Name | Dim_Product | | Header Rows to Skip | 0 | |
| 6 | Build Method | PARENT-CHILD | | Allow Moves | No | |
| 7 | Incremental Mode | Merge | | | | |
| 8 | | | | | | |
| 9 | **Members** | | | | | |
| 10 | Columns | PARENT | CHILD | STORAGE | CONSOLIDATION | ALIAS.Default |
| 11 | | | Product | | | |
| 12 | | Product | 100 | | | Colas |
| 13 | | 100 | 100-10 | | | Cola |
| 14 | | 100 | 100-20 | | | Diet Cola |
| 15 | | 100 | 100-30 | | | Caffeine Free Cola |
| 16 | | Product | 200 | | | Root Beer |
| 17 | | 200 | 200-10 | | | Old Fashioned |
| 18 | | 200 | 200-20 | | | Diet Root Beer |
| 19 | | 200 | 200-30 | | | Sasparilla |
| 20 | | 200 | 200-40 | | | Birch Beer |
| 21 | | 200 | 200-50 | | | Root Beer Squared |
| 22 | | 200 | 200-60 | | | Diet Root Beer Squared |
| 23 | | 200 | 200-70 | | | Birch Beer Squared |
| 24 | | Product | 300 | | | Cream Soda |

5. *Save* the file.

**Note!** The application and cube name are denoted on the Essbase.Cube tab. The actual name of the workbook has no effect on cube name, so name the file as you please.

I now have two options. I can import the entire Application Workbook or I can import just the updated Product dimension using the rules file.

## CREATE A CUBE WITH APPLICATION WORKBOOKS

### Import Application Workbook with Web Interface

Once properties have been updated in the file used to maintain the cube, I can import the Application Workbook into Essbase Cloud via the web interface or in Excel with Cube Designer. This section will focus on importing the file through the web interface.

**Note!**

These steps import the entire Application Workbook and all of its worksheets. To update a single dimension, jump down a few sections to the one titled "Dimension Build Rules."

To import a file in the Essbase Cloud web interface,

1. From the Essbase Cloud home page, select *Import*:

2. Select *Browse* and then choose the saved file.

3.  Ensure that the Application and Cube names are correct. A message should appear, indicating that the application/cube combination already exists:

4.  Leave the Build Option to the default *Update Cube - Retain All Data*.

Build Options for BSO and Hybrid cubes include:

*   **Create Cube** - initial cube build (only use this option when first creating the cube)
*   **Update Cube - Retain All Data** - all data values will be retained
*   **Update Cube - Retain Input Data** - all "input" data (upper-level and lower-level blocks containing loaded data) are retained
*   **Update Cube - Retain Leaf Data** - only level-0 data values are conserved
*   **Update Cube - Remove All Data** - all data values will be deleted

**Note!**    If all data used in calculations in a BSO cube are in level-0 members, choose the *Update Cube - Retain Leaf Data* option in order to optimize disk space. The upper-level blocks will be populated again the next time the cube is recalculated.

Build Options for ASO cubes include:

- **Create Cube** - initial cube build (only use this option when first creating the cube)
- **Update Cube - Retain All Data** - all data values will be retained
- **Update Cube - Remove All Data** - all data values will be deleted

5. Check *Show Advanced*. This will reveal the mapping of the column headings in the file to the dimensions, along with their Type and Storage options (very similar to the *Export* dialogue that I just worked with):

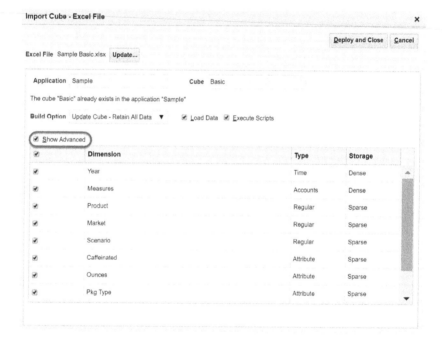

6. Leave the *Load Data* and *Execute Scripts* options checked:

**Note!** Uncheck *Load Data* if you only want the metadata imported. Uncheck *Execute Scripts* if you do not want any calculation scripts to execute upon deployment.

7. Select *Deploy and Close*:

8. A notification that the cube was updated successfully should display. Click *OK*:

My cube is updated with the new products!

### Import Application Workbook with Cube Designer

In addition to importing Application Workbooks through the Essbase Cloud web interface, they can be imported through Excel via the Cube Designer Smart View extension. This might be a little redundant but I'll still cover the steps for any readers who might have skipped the earlier chapter.

**Note!**

These steps import the entire Application Workbook and all if its worksheets. To update a single dimension, jump down to the section titled "Dimension Build Rules."

To import an Application Workbook with Cube Designer,
1. With the saved cube workbook still open, connect to Essbase Cloud via Smart View.
2. Navigate to the *Cube Designer* ribbon.
3. Select *Build Cube*:

4. Leave the Build Option to the default *Update Cube - Retain All Data*.

5. Leave the options *Load Data Sheets Contained within Workbook* and *Run Calculation Sheets Contained within Workbook* checked:

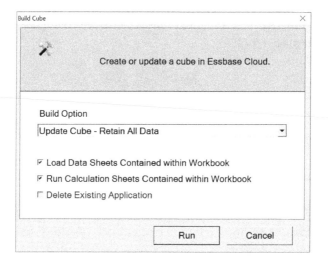

**Note!**

The *Delete Existing Application* option is only available with the *Create Cube* option. This option will be pre-selected if an application already exists with the same name.

**Note!**

Uncheck *Load Data Sheets Contained within Workbook* if you only want the metadata imported. Uncheck *Run Calculation Sheets Contained within Workbook* if you do not want any calculation scripts kicked off upon deployment.

6. Select *Run* and then *Yes*:

7. A pop-up notification should appear, indicating that the process has been submitted as a job. Select *Yes* to launch the job viewer status:

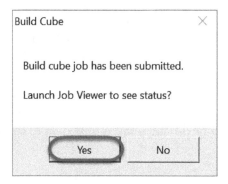

**Note!**  The Jobs console can also be viewed through the Essbase Cloud web interface via the Jobs icon.

## DIMENSION BUILD RULES

### Dimension Build Rule Fundamentals

I may not have realized it, but Essbase Cloud automatically builds rules files based on the information I define in the Application

Workbook. Rules files are used to map the data into the dimensions, as well as hierarchies into cubes. Under the Essbase Cloud covers, dimension build rules contain the instructions to build dimensions dynamically in Essbase cubes. With these dimension build rules files, I can add new dimensions and members, remove or change existing dimensions and members, or modify attributes and calculations automatically.

There are three different primary build methods for dimension rules files: generation builds, level builds, and parent/child builds. The build method I choose depends upon the format of my source system and determines the algorithm that Essbase uses to modify the outline. These are automatically generated by the system when a workbook is imported, but can be updated through the Essbase Cloud web interface.

A generation build metadata file looks like this:

```
Gen2      Gen3       Gen4
500       500-10     500-10-10
500       500-10     500-10-20
500       500-20     500-20-12
500       500-20     500-20-15
500       500-20     500-20-20
```

A generation build rules file will translate the file above into this hierarchy:

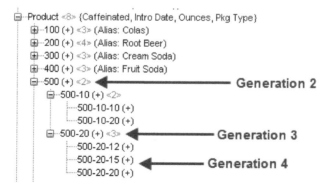

A file suitable for a level build looks like this:

```
Level0            Level1    Level2
600-10-11         600-10    600
600-20-10         600-20    600
600-20-18         600-20    600
```

A level build rules file will translate the file above into this hierarchy:

```
⊟ Product <8> {Caffeinated, Intro Date, Ounces, Pkg Type}
   ⊞ 100 (+) <3> (Alias: Colas)
   ⊞ 200 (+) <4> (Alias: Root Beer)
   ⊞ 300 (+) <3> (Alias: Cream Soda)
   ⊞ 400 (+) <3> (Alias: Fruit Soda)
   ⊞ 500 (+) <2>
   ⊟ 600 (+) <2>           ◄───── Level 2
      ⊟ 600-10 (+) <1>     ◄───── Level 1
         └ 600-10-11 (+)
      ⊟ 600-20 (+) <2>
         ├ 600-20-10 (+)   ◄───── Level 0
         └ 600-20-18 (+)
```

A parent/child build metadata file looks like this:

```
Parent    Child     Alias
200       200-10    Old Fashioned
200       200-20    Diet Root Beer
200       200-30    Sasparilla
200       200-40    Birch Beer
200       200-50    with Caffeine
```

A parent/child rules file will translate the file above into this hierarchy:

```
⊟ Product <8> {Caffeinated, Intro Date, Ounces, Pkg Type}
   ⊞ 100 (+) <3> (Alias: Colas)
   ⊟ 200 (+) <4> (Alias: Root Beer)   ◄───── Parent
      ├ 200-10 (+) (Alias: Old Fashioned)
      ├ 200-20 (+) (Alias: Diet Root Beer)   ◄─┐
      ├ 200-30 (+) (Alias: Sasparilla)         ├ Child
      └ 200-40 (+) (Alias: Birch Beer)   ◄─────┘
   ⊞ 300 (+) <3> (Alias: Cream Soda)
   ⊞ 400 (+) <3> (Alias: Fruit Soda)
   ⊞ 500 (+) <2>
```

Here are the basic steps for building an Essbase Cloud dimension build rules file:

1) Create rules file
2) Set file delimiters for the data source
3) If creating a new dimension, name it (optional)
4) Select build method
5) Define Dimensions settings (optional)
6) Set Field settings (optional)
7) Validate and save the rules file

While it seems simple enough, for now I recommend letting the Application Workbook build the dimension build rules files (versus building a dimension build rule from scratch) and then edit as needed.

So now that you have that basic understanding under your belt, let's take a look under the covers! I can manually edit rules files through the Essbase Cloud web interface.

To view an existing rules file, I expand the application and appropriate cube, then select *Scripts*:

The Scripts screen defaults to the Rules tab. I select the *Rules Editor* tab:

The Rules screen displays all of the rules for the selected cube. It also displays a few other properties, such as whether or not the rule is locked (and which user holds the lock), the rule size, and last but certainly not least, the *Actions* ⋮ icon, which will allow me to edit or delete the rule. If *Edit* is selected, all of the details of the rule are displayed within four tabs:

1) Properties
2) Dimensions
3) Fields
4) Data Source

**Note!**     Remember rules files are automatically created behind the scenes by Essbase Cloud when an Essbase cube workbook is imported. Therefore, there isn't a strong need to create them from scratch in the Essbase Cloud cube building process. However, rules files can be manually edited or created from scratch from the Essbase Cloud web interface, if necessary.

Since I am editing an existing rule, notice that it's already properly set up for dimension building. There are two formal modes for rules files: "dimension build" and "data load" (I'll talk about data loading soon enough).

When working on a dimension build rules file, the *Dimension Build* mode on the right hand side of the screen should be selected, and this mode actually changes the settings seen within each of the four tabs:

The Properties tab is where general settings, dimension build properties, and smart lists need to be defined. General settings include the rule name, locale, type of data source, and whether or not the source is of Unicode type. In addition, the Dimension Build Properties section designates the alias table being updated, whether or not I want Essbase Cloud to arrange the outline order of dimensions, and whether or not I want Essbase to auto configure the dimension storage types. Finally, the Smart lists section is where any new smart lists being added to the Essbase cube are listed:

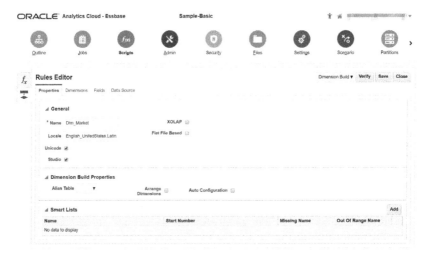

**Note!**

The screenshots in these sections are for the Sample.Basic BSO Essbase cube. The rules file settings do not change based on cube type, so proceed with caution. Some of the rules files settings do not apply to ASO and vice versa.

The *Dimensions* tab designates the dimension build properties when the *Dimension Build* option is selected for the rule. New dimensions can also be defined here. The properties of an existing dimension can be updated here as well.

When a dimension row is selected, the dimension properties are displayed in the bottom pane for that dimension. I select the dimension that will be updated in the rules file to see additional properties for that dimension:

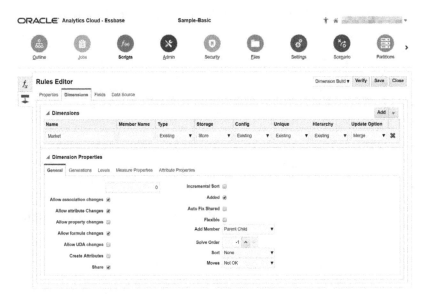

There are quite a few dimension properties that can be set here. While the settings might look different, they are the same settings that exist in on-premises load rules that you love (or hate). I can define how existing members in that dimension should be handled: *Allow association changes, Allow attribute changes, Allow property changes, Allow formula changes, Allow UDA changes, Create Attributes, Share, Sort,* and *Moves.* There are other properties, some of which do not apply to BSO.

The *Moves* option enables children to be moved from one parent to another. I select *OK* in order to enable this behavior.

I might use this, for example, if I want to reorganize the Market dimension via a dimension build rules file, splitting Southwest into South and West.

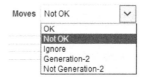

This is what the dimension looks like before I do this:

```
⊟--Southwest <9> {Population}
    ----Texas (+) (UDAS: Major Market) {Population: 21000000}
    ----Oklahoma (+) (UDAS: Small Market) {Population: 6000000}
    ----Louisiana (+) (UDAS: Small Market, New Market) {Population: 6000000}
    ----New Mexico (+) (UDAS: Small Market) {Population: 3000000}
    ----California (+) (UDAS: Major Market) {Population: 33000000}
    ----Oregon (+) (UDAS: Small Market) {Population: 6000000}
    ----Washington (+) (UDAS: Small Market) {Population: 6000000}
    ----Utah (+) (UDAS: Small Market) {Population: 3000000}
    ----Nevada (+) (UDAS: Small Market, New Market) {Population: 3000000}
```

After the dimension build rule (with the Moves option set to *OK):*

```
⊟--West (+) <5>
    ----California (+) (UDAS: Major Market) {Population: 33000000}
    ----Oregon (+) (UDAS: Small Market) {Population: 6000000}
    ----Washington (+) (UDAS: Small Market) {Population: 6000000}
    ----Utah (+) (UDAS: Small Market) {Population: 3000000}
    ----Nevada (+) (UDAS: Small Market, New Market) {Population: 3000000}
⊟--South (+) <4> (UDAS: Small Market)
    ----Texas (+) (UDAS: Major Market) {Population: 21000000}
    ----Oklahoma (+) (UDAS: Small Market) {Population: 6000000}
    ----Louisiana (+) (UDAS: Small Market, New Market) {Population: 6000000}
    ----New Mexico (+) (UDAS: Small Market) {Population: 3000000}
⊞--Central (+) <6> (UDAS: Major Market)
```

The *Allow property changes* option enables Essbase to update member properties based on the source file. For example, if I build the Measures dimension from the GL and an account description changes, I want to make sure that the alias is updated so that it is consistent with the description in the GL. Without this option selected, Essbase does not allow any alias changes.

Selecting the build method is a critical item – don't forget to do this. I must specify the appropriate build method for the dimension selected that matches the source data file. This is set through a combination of the drop-down within the General tab and options that need to be set in the Generations or Levels tab, depending on which one applies:

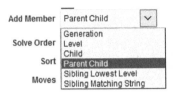

The three core build methods (generation, level, and parent/child) were discussed earlier, but there is also the flexibility to add a list of members as:

- A sibling of a member with a matching string
- A sibling of the lowest level
- A child of a specific member that I choose

For example, I have a list of new markets that have not yet been mapped to a correct parent. I can add these markets to a specific parent called New Markets so my aggregated data will be up-to-date even though the outline may not be.

The Fields tab determines the field properties for the dimension build. For instance, it can help map the column headings in the dimension file to the appropriate property.

There are other properties as well, such as the field type, selection/rejection criteria, column creation, trimming, and ignores, etc.:

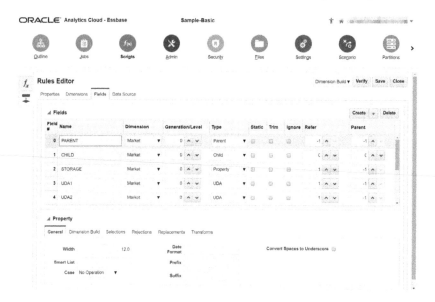

Every column in the source file must either be explicitly ignored by the rules file or assigned a specific dimension, generation, level, parent, and member property.

Selecting a field row reveals additional properties in the bottom of the window. In the General properties, I can set the field width, translate text to upper or lower or initial case, add prefixes and suffixes, convert spaces to underscores, and set a date format. In the other tabs I can also set selection or rejection criteria, perform a find and replace, and transform the source data.

For example, let's say my account number structure and Product number structure could have the exact same number. Unless I enable duplicate member names, Essbase won't allow a second member with the same name or alias. I can add the prefix "Product_" to the Product dimension build so that the members will be unique.

**Note!** I can choose to "Ignore" a field during dimension building. This setting can be found under the Fields section and is a checkbox.

The Data Source tab is similar to the old on-premises Data Source Properties section, except represented in a single screen and combined with the old SQL Interface. This section is focused around defining the parameters for the data source.

In the future, the SQL Properties feature will be fully functional and Essbase Cloud will be able to pull data dynamically from a relational cube. I will be able to load data from a DBaaS Cloud instance or from an on-premises database if I have IaaS to create a "VPN" type connection to the on-premises database.

The Properties section is the area that requires the most attention. This is where I can specify how many lines to skip or define any records that may have header information and field information. This section also tells Essbase what the delimiter is for the source file, if there is a header record already in the file, how many rows to skip, and the width of the file.

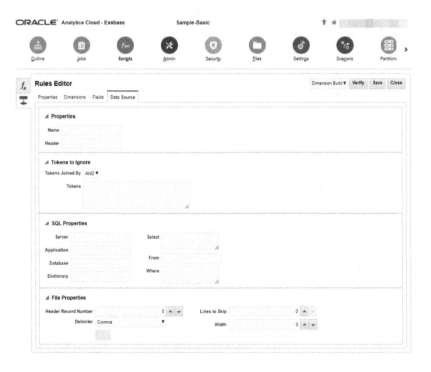

When the edit/create rules file process is complete, the final steps are to validate and save the rules file. Rules files are validated to ensure member and dimension mappings line up to the outline. Validation also does things like checking to make sure the build method is appropriate for the field properties. I can validate the rules file by selecting *Verify* in the upper right hand corner:

Then I can *Save* and *Close* the rule.

### My Rules File won't Validate – What Should I Check?

**Tip!**

- Is every field name valid?
- Are the reference numbers sequential?
- Are there repeated generations?
- Is the field type valid for the build method?
- Are the fields in correct order?
- Does the child field have a parent field?
- Do all dimension names exist in the outline?
- Are all dimensions referenced in the rules file?
- Have I remembered to set fields with no dimension to ignore?

### Upload Dimension Text File

Remember that when I first created the cube with the Application Workbook, it created dimension build rules files for each of the dimensions in the worksheets and also uploaded a text file with the dimension data.

To view the rules files and text files built from my Sample.Basic Application Workbook,

1. From the Essbase Cloud home page, navigate to *Sample >> Basic*.
2. Select the *Files* card.

The rules files and text files for Sample.Basic both display and are available for review and editing. I see the dimension build and data load rules files along with dimension and data text files:

Under the Files card, I can also upload any new or updated text files and use them in the build and load process (assuming the rows and columns are defined to match the rules file):

These files are the text files that that can be selected when running a dimension update process.

To download, update, and upload a dimension text file,

3.  Select the *Dim_Market.txt* file.

4. Under Actions, click *Download:*

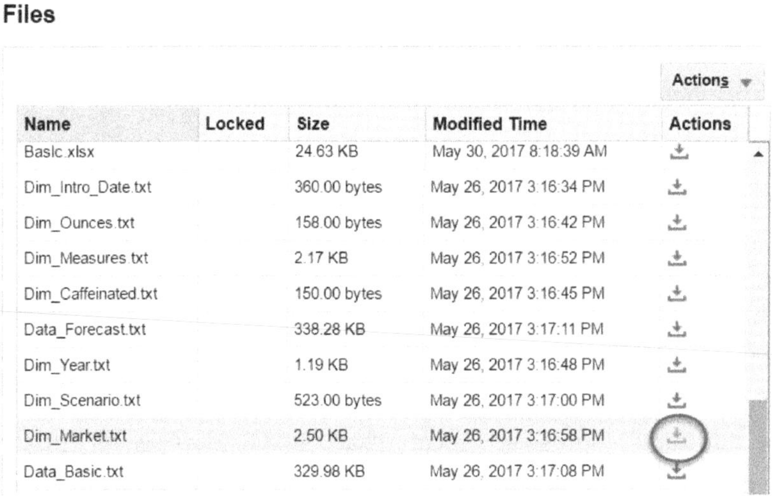

Files
Actions
Name
Locked
Size
Modified Time
Actions
Basic.xlsx
24.63 KB
May 30, 2017 8:18:39 AM
Dim_Intro_Date.txt
360.00 bytes
May 26, 2017 3:16:34 PM
Dim_Ounces.txt
158.00 bytes
May 26, 2017 3:16:42 PM
Dim_Measures.txt
2.17 KB
May 26, 2017 3:16:52 PM
Dim_Caffeinated.txt
150.00 bytes
May 26, 2017 3:16:45 PM
Data_Forecast.txt
338.28 KB
May 26, 2017 3:17:11 PM
Dim_Year.txt
1.19 KB
May 26, 2017 3:16:48 PM
Dim_Scenario.txt
523.00 bytes
May 26, 2017 3:17:00 PM
Dim_Market.txt
2.50 KB
May 26, 2017 3:16:58 PM
Data_Basic.txt
329.98 KB
May 26, 2017 3:17:08 PM

5. In a text editor, open the file and add a row at the bottom to add a new member Maine to the East region:

new 1
Dim_Market (1).txt
"","Market","","","","市場","市場","Рынок сбыта","Mark
"Market","East","","Major Market","","東部","東部","Bo
"East","New York","","Major Market","","紐約州","ニュー
"East","Massachusetts","","Major Market","","麻省","
"East","Florida","","Major Market","","佛州","フロリダ州"
"East","Connecticut","","Small Market","","康州","コネ
"East","New Hampshire","","Small
Market","","新罕布夏州","ニューハンプシャー州","Нью-Гемпшир","
"Market","West","","","","西部","西部","Запад","",""
"West","California","","Major
Market","","加州","カリフォルニア州","Калифорния","Kaliforni
"West","Oregon","","Small Market","","奥勒岡州","オレゴン
"West","Washington","","Small Market","","華盛頓州","
"West","Utah","","Small Market","","猶他州","ユタ州","Ю
"West","Nevada","","Small Market","New Market","內華達
"Market","South","","Small Market","","南部","南部","
"South","Texas","","Major Market","","德州","テキサス州"
"South","Oklahoma","","Small Market","","奥克拉荷馬州",
"South","Louisiana","","Small Market","New
Market","路易斯安那州","ルイジアナ州","Луизиана","","600000
"South","New Mexico","","Small Market","","新墨西哥州"
"Market","Central","","Major Market","","中部","中部",
"Central","Illinois","","Major Market","","伊利諾州","
"Central","Ohio","","Major Market","","俄亥俄州","オハイ
"Central","Wisconsin","","Small Market","","威斯康州",
"Central","Missouri","","Small Market","","密蘇里州","
"Central","Iowa","","Small Market","","愛荷華州","アイオ
"Central","Colorado","","Major Market","New
Market","科羅拉多州","コロラド州","Колорадо","","6000000"
"East","Maine","","Small

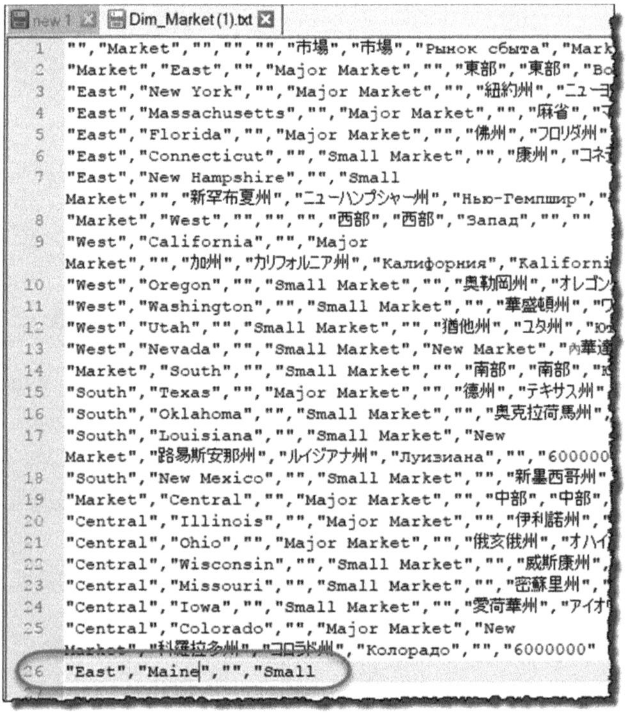

No, that is not the wingdings font. Some of the aliases are various foreign languages.

6. Save the file as "Dim_MarketwMaine.txt".
7. Navigate back to the Essbase Cloud web interface.
8. Under Files, click *Choose Files*.
9. Browse to the file "Dim_MarketwMain.txt" and select the file.
10. Click *Upload*:

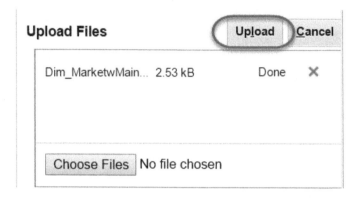

11. The file is uploaded to Essbase Cloud (but has not been loaded into the cube) and is now available for import into the cube:

**Files**

|  |  |  |  | Actions ▾ |
| --- | --- | --- | --- | --- |
| **Name** | **Locked** | **Size** | **Modified Time** | **Actions** |
| Data_Forecast.rul |  | 931.00 bytes | May 26, 2017 3:16:27 PM | ↧ |
| Dim_Product.txt |  | 2.92 KB | May 26, 2017 3:16:55 PM | ↧ |
| Dim_Population.txt |  | 863.00 bytes | May 26, 2017 3:16:37 PM | ↧ |
| Dim_MarketwMaine.txt |  | 2.53 KB | May 30, 2017 2:38:39 PM | ↧ |

## Update Dimensions using Rules Files with Web Interface

A dimension build process using rules files can be executed from the Essbase Cloud web interface or Cube Designer. The advantage of this approach is that I can update a single dimension (versus uploading the entire Application Workbook). I'll tackle the Essbase Cloud web interface first.

With this file uploaded, I can run the process to build the Market dimension using a rules file,

1. From the Essbase Cloud home page, navigate to *Sample >> Basic.*
2. Select the *Jobs* card:

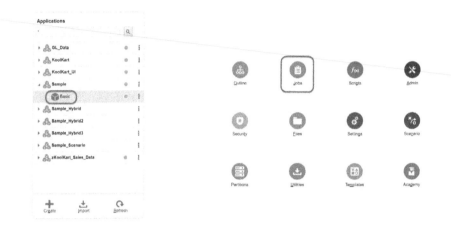

3. Select *New Job*:

4. Set the following properties in the Execute Job box:
   a. Job Type: *Dimension Build*
   b. Scripts: *Dim_Market* (this is the rules file that is created behind the scenes, based on the last imported Application Workbook)
   c. Load Type: *File*
   d. Data File: *Dim_MarketwMaine.txt*
   e. Restructure Option: *Preserve All Data*

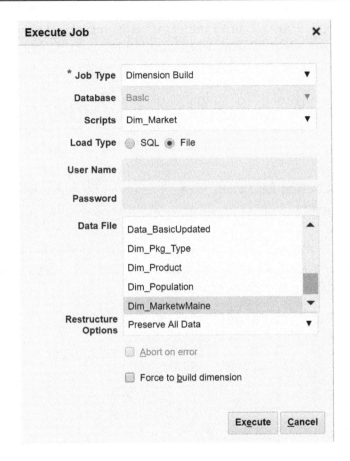

5.  Select *Execute*.

A pop-up window should indicate that the process has started.

6.  Click *OK*.

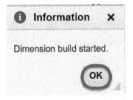

The job is displayed at the top of the list with a Running  status icon.

7.  Click *Refresh* until the status is Complete or select the *Auto Refresh* option to have the system auto refresh every few seconds:

8.  Use the *Job Details* icon ⚙ to review the details of the data load.

This option is especially helpful for troubleshooting any issues with the data load, as error messages (if there are any) will be listed beneath the Output Details section:

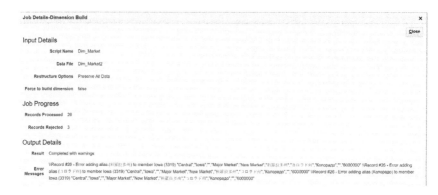

## Update Dimensions using Rules Files with Cube Designer

I can also run this same build process for a single dimension using the Cube Designer. I do not have to have an Application Workbook open to do this step. In fact, it could be sort of confusing because the steps that I am about to walk through will update the dimension using a file on the Essbase Cloud server (and not anything that I have updated locally in my Application Workbook). If I have dimension changes, I'll need to update the Dim_Market.txt file and upload it to Essbase Cloud (like I did in our Dim_MarketwithMaine.txt file earlier).

To update a dimension using a rules file with Cube Designer,

1. Open Excel and navigate to the *Cube Designer* ribbon.
2. Select *Load Data*.
3. Select the *Sample* application and *Basic* cube.
4. Select Job Type as *Load Data*.

**Note!** It might seem counterintuitive that the correct option is *Load Data*, since I am just updating a dimension. However, in Cube Designer, this is currently how it works.

5. Select Data File as *Dim_Market*.
6. Select a Load Rule File as *Dim_Market*.
7. Click *Run:*

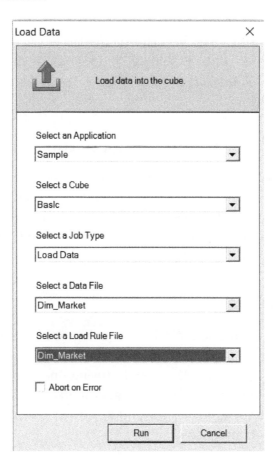

The Market dimension build process will run and update using the Dim_Market.txt file with the Dim_Market.rul file. I can view the details of the load by clicking on *View Jobs:*

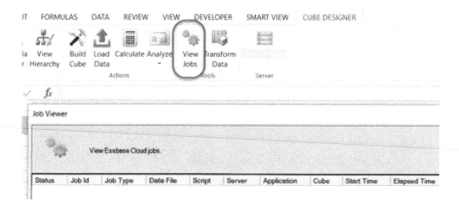

**Note!**   Remember, when you choose the *Load Data* option and select a data file, Essbase Cloud references the data file on its Cloud server (and not any local files or Excel worksheets).

## DATA LOAD OVERVIEW

At this point I've covered how to deal with the pesky bookkeeper that keeps bringing us new dimension updates. Now I'll review how to load new and updated data sets to an Essbase cube. The good news is that many of the steps and concepts that I've discussed in the dimension build section also apply for loading data.

Data may be loaded to Essbase cubes via:

- Import Application Workbook (using one or more worksheets containing data) via the Essbase Cloud web interface
- Import Application Workbook (using one or more worksheets containing data) via Cube Designer in Excel
- Run a job using a rules file and uploaded text file in the Essbase Cloud web interface

- Execute the Load Data option from Cube Designer in Excel and select the desired rules file and uploaded text file
- Dimension flat files can be imported via MaxL and used in conjunction with the rules files (but more on this last bit later, when I cover MaxL)
- Submit data via the Smart View add-in (I'll discuss this in Chapter 9, "Analyze Data in Smart View")

## IMPORT DATA VIA APPLICATION WORKBOOKS

I can update the data worksheet(s) within Application Workbooks and run the steps to import. The header definition of the data sheets will contain the *File Name* of the text file that will be uploaded to Essbase Cloud containing the data records, the *Rule Name* that will be used to load the text file (the same rule name can be used across multiple data sheets if the column definitions are the same), the *Data Load Option* (to either replace existing values with the latest record or to be additive), *Delimiter*, and the number of *Header Rows to Skip*:

| | A | B | C | D | E | F | G |
|---|---|---|---|---|---|---|---|
| 1 | **Definitions** | | | | | | |
| 2 | File Name | Basic_Actual | | | | | |
| 3 | Rule Name | Basic | | | | | |
| 4 | Data Load Option | Replace | | | | | |
| 5 | Delimiter | , | | | | | |
| 6 | Header Rows to Skip | 0 | | | | | |
| 7 | | | | | | | |
| 8 | **Data** | | | | | | |
| 9 | Columns | Dimension.Produc | Dimension.Marke | Dimension.Scenar | Dimension.Year | Measure.Sales | Measure.COGS | M |
| 10 | | 100-10 | New York | Actual | Jan | 678 | 271 | 40 |
| 11 | | 100-10 | New York | Actual | Feb | 645 | 258 | 38 |
| 12 | | 100-10 | New York | Actual | Mar | 675 | 270 | 40 |
| 13 | | 100-10 | New York | Actual | Apr | 712 | 284 | 42 |
| 14 | | 100-10 | New York | Actual | May | 756 | 302 | 45 |
| 15 | | 100-10 | New York | Actual | Jun | 890 | 356 | 53 |
| 16 | | 100-10 | New York | Actual | Jul | 912 | 364 | 54 |
| 17 | | 100-10 | New York | Actual | Aug | 910 | 364 | 54 |
| 18 | | 100-10 | New York | Actual | Sep | 790 | 316 | 47 |
| 19 | | 100-10 | New York | Actual | Oct | 650 | 260 | 39 |
| 20 | | 100-10 | New York | Actual | Nov | 623 | 249 | 37 |
| 21 | | 100-10 | New York | Actual | Dec | 699 | 279 | 42 |
| 22 | | 200-10 | New York | Actual | Jan | 61 | 105 | -4 |
| 23 | | 200-10 | New York | Actual | Feb | 61 | 121 | -6 |
| 24 | | 200-10 | New York | Actual | Mar | 63 | 125 | -6 |
| 25 | | 200-10 | New York | Actual | Apr | 66 | 125 | -5 |
| 26 | | 200-10 | New York | Actual | May | 69 | 121 | -5 |
| 27 | | 200-10 | New York | Actual | Jun | 72 | 144 | -7 |
| 28 | | 200-10 | New York | Actual | Jul | 77 | 162 | -8 |
| 29 | | 200-10 | New York | Actual | Aug | 78 | 173 | -9 |

Dim.Ounces | Dim.Pkg Type | Dim.Population | Dim.Intro Date | **Data.Actual** | Data.Budget | **Data.Forecast**

Under the covers, Essbase Cloud creates the rules file (or updates the rules file if it already exists) and uploads the data records for a single worksheet as a text file. These rules files and text files can be reused later as needed.

Once the data worksheets are updated, I can import the Application Workbook using the same steps discussed in the dimension maintenance section.

## DATA LOAD RULES

### Data Load Rule Fundamentals

The last section covered dimension build rules files. Thankfully, the concepts and processes for creating data load rules files and executing jobs for the data load are very similar.

So when should I use a data load rule?

- When I need to ignore fields or strings in data file
- When I need to change the order of fields by moving, joining, splitting or creating
- When I need to map the data in the data source to the cube by changing strings
- When I need to change the data values in the data source by scaling data values or adding them to existing values in the data source
- When I need to set header records for missing values
- When I need to reject an invalid record and continue loading data
- When I want to add new dimensions and members in the cube along with the data load
- When I want to change existing dimensions and members in the cube along with the data load

There will be times when the import workbook will not make sense, since it assumes that everything I need to load is bundled up in a nice data load sheet. Load rules offer choices and very light ETL (extract, transform, load) choices, should the need arise.

Here are the basic steps in building an Essbase Cloud data loading rules file:

1) Create rules file
2) Set file delimiters for the data source
3) Define Field settings and map fields to data source
4) Select build method
5) Define data transformation options (optional)
6) Validate and save the rules file

Remember that there are two formal modes for rules files: "dimension build" and "data load." When working on a data load rules file, the *Data Load* mode in the right hand side of the screen should be selected, and this mode actually changes the settings seen within each of the four tabs:

I can perform a dimension build only, a data load only, or both build and load together in Essbase with a single rules file. One handy tip with rules files is to build in any new members that come through from the data source but may not exist in the outline. This way data is always fully loaded with no "fallout." New members can be added to a Needs To Be Mapped or Unknown parent member.

Oftentimes Essbase Administrators like to create separate rules for dimension building and data loading. While the number of objects to manage increases, the process and components may be more easily understood. This option is also dependent on whether the source file contains both dimension build elements and data.

The Properties tab is where General settings need to be defined. General settings include the rule name, locale, type of data source, and whether or not the source is of Unicode type.

In addition, the Data Load Properties section give options for adding, subtracting, or overwriting the data, adding sign flip options based on a specified UDA, and a field to enter combinations of data that should be cleared prior to the data load:

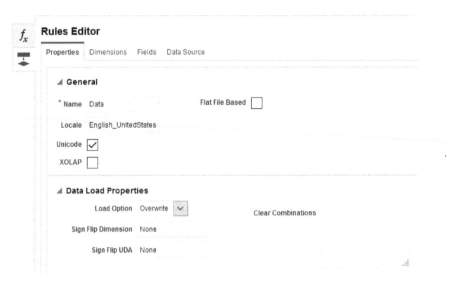

On the *Load Option* drop-down, I define whether this rules file should overwrite, add to, or subtract from existing values. In most cases, I want to overwrite, but there are some exceptions.

Here's one: the source file I load to Essbase contains daily transaction data, but my Essbase cube contains aggregated monthly data. I would want to specify *Add* for the following text file to get Essbase to calculate the total for the month (and make sure not to load the same file twice). If the data load rule is set to *Overwrite*, then only the final value in the file will be stored:

```
01/01/2007, Jan, California,Caffeine Free Cola, Sales, 145
01/02/2007, Jan, California,Caffeine Free Cola, Sales, 123
01/03/2007, Jan, California,Caffeine Free Cola, Sales, 132
01/04/2007, Jan, California,Caffeine Free Cola, Sales, 145
01/05/2007, Jan, California,Caffeine Free Cola, Sales, 102
01/06/2007, Jan, California,Caffeine Free Cola, Sales, 116|
```

I can also specify whether to flip a sign based on an assigned UDA. If my source file contains debits and credits, I want to load only positive values because I will be handling the sign flipping in Essbase using unary operators. To do this, I can assign a UDA of Flip Input (or something else descriptive of the task) to all of my accounts that will be arriving as negative values. Tag the dimension that contains the UDA in the *Sign Flip Dimension* field and then type in the UDA (e.g., Flip Input) in the *Sign Flip UDA* field. The sign will be flipped for all records in the data file for the accounts tagged with that UDA.

To clear data for a specific intersection before loading the data file, utilize the Clear Combinations field. This is helpful if I load actual data on a daily basis and want to automatically clear out the month being loaded before loading the daily data.

The Dimensions tab designates the dimensions represented by the source data set:

 A data load rules file must reference every dimension.
**Note!**

The Fields tab determines the field properties for the data load. For instance, it can help map the column headings in the data file to the appropriate dimension or data column. There are other properties as well, such as column creation, joins, splits, moves, trims, and ignores.

Selecting a field row reveals additional properties in the bottom of the window:

**Note!** You can choose to ignore a field during dimension building. This setting can be found under the Fields section and is a checkbox.

The property settings allows me to scale data, set selection/rejection criteria, translate text to upper, lower, or initial case, add prefixes and suffixes, convert spaces to underscores, and perform find and replaces. These property settings are used to make sure that the values specified in the data load match what is in the outline, especially if I've used a dimension build file to add prefixes or suffixes to member names.

Members in the data file must match the members in your outline exactly!

**Tip!** In almost every case, you want your rules file to trim (leading and trailing spaces). If you don't, you might get errors which are hard to figure out.

Data source properties will tell Essbase the data source delimiters, what field edits have been made in the rules file, and what header rows may exist:

The Properties section has the Header field, which allows me to define any dimension not represented in the data file. For instance, let's say that the entire data file represents Actual data. However, there isn't a column in the file that identifies that scenario. Essbase needs to know exactly where I want to load data for every dimension. Should it load data to Actual, or Budget, or both? Therefore, this field can be used to specify that missing dimension and member.

The File Properties section is the area that requires the most attention. Within the File Properties section, in the Delimiter field drop-down, specify Comma, Tab, Whitespace, or Custom delimiter for the data file (if someone with a perverse sense of humor gave you a data file with ! or ~ as the delimiter, Essbase can handle this with the custom option). The *Custom* option allows the user to type in the special delimiter character into the empty box below that field. Also specify how many lines to skip, the width of the field, define any records that may have header information, or define the data load record number.

When the edit/create rules file process is complete, the final steps are to validate and save the rules file. Rules files are validated to ensure member and dimension mappings line up to the outline. Validation also does things like check to make sure the build method is appropriate for the field properties. I can validate the rules file by selecting *Verify* in the upper right hand corner:

Then *Save* and *Close* the rule.

**Tip!**

### My Data Load Rules File won't Validate – What Should You Check?

- Is the field name valid?
- Are the file delimiters correctly placed?
- Is there a member in the field name?
- Is the dimension name used in another field name or the header?
- Are you using a member as member combination in one place and a single member in another?
- Is more than one field defined as the data field?
- Is the dimension used for sign flipping in the associated outline?
- Is the rules file associated with the correct outline?

As with dimension rules files, data rules files are automatically generated by the system when a workbook is imported, but can be updated in the Essbase web interface.

**Note!** Rules files can be created for data loads or dimension builds, or they can be built to accommodate both at the same time.

Data load rules are located in the same spot as dimension load rules, by navigating to a specific application and cube, then selecting *Scripts* and the *Rules Editor* tab:

Also like dimension rules, the *Actions* ⋮ icon allows me to edit or delete the rule. If *Edit* is selected, all of the details of the rule are displayed within four tabs (warning: these might look familiar):

1) Properties
2) Dimensions
3) Fields
4) Data Source

One final recommendation: Since we are no longer limited to 8 characters, I recommend making the names descriptive, for example, prefixing dimension builds with "Dim_" and Data load with "Data_".

### Upload Data Text File

Remember that when I first created the cube with the Application Workbook, it created data load rules files as defined in the worksheets and also uploaded a text file with the data. Note, large files may not be able to be downloaded or uploaded this way. I might need to FTP them to the server. Also file names must be 30 characters or less.

To view the rules files and text files built from my Sample.Basic Application Workbook,

1. From the Essbase Cloud home page, navigate to *Sample >> Basic*.
2. Select the *Files* card.

The rules files and text files for Sample.Basic both display and are available for review and editing. I see the dimension build and data load rules files along with dimension and data text files.

Under the Files card, I can also upload any new or updated text files and use them in the load process (assuming the rows and columns are defined to match the rules file):

These files are the text files that that can be selected when running a dimension update process.

To download, update, and upload a data text file,

3. Select the *Data_Basic.txt* file.
4. Under Actions, click *Download*:

## Files

| Name | | Locked | Size | Modified Time | Actions |
|------|---|--------|------|---------------|---------|
| | | | | | Actions ▾ |
| Baslc.otl | ▲ ▾ | | 16.05 KB | May 26, 2017 3:17:03 PM | ⬇ |
| Baslc.xlsx | | | 24.63 KB | May 30, 2017 8:18:39 AM | ⬇ |
| CalcAll.csc | | | 64.00 bytes | May 26, 2017 3:17:13 PM | ⬇ |
| CDSSampl.xml | | | 33.91 KB | May 26, 2017 3:16:27 PM | ⬇ |
| Data.rul | | | 931.00 bytes | May 26, 2017 3:16:27 PM | ⬇ |
| Data_Basic.txt | | | 329.98 KB | May 26, 2017 3:17:08 PM | ⬇ |
| Data_Forecast.rul | | | 931.00 bytes | May 26, 2017 3:16:27 PM | ⬇ |

5. In a text editor, open the file and notice the row and column dimensions:

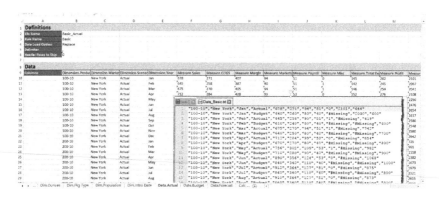

I'm going to pretend like I've received a new file from my source system. Really I am just going to *Save As* the current file but I know we are all good at using our imaginations. Because the rules file uses the *Replace* load option, Essbase Cloud will just overwrite the current data values.

6. Save the file as "Data_BasicUpdated.txt".
7. Navigate back to the Essbase Cloud web interface.
8. Under Files, click *Choose Files*.
9. Browse to the file "Data_BasicUpdated.txt" and select the file.
10. Click *Upload*:

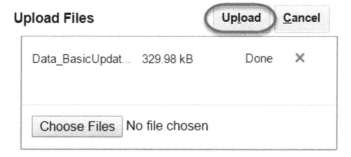

11. The file is uploaded to Essbase Cloud (but has not been loaded into the cube) and is now available for import into the cube.

### Load Data using Rules File with Web Interface

Data can be loaded using a load rule through the Essbase Cloud web interface. I run a data load job with a rules file from the same place I build a dimension with one, under *Jobs >> New Job*.

To load data using a rules file,
1. From the Essbase Cloud home page, navigate to the *Sample.Basic* cube and select *Jobs*.
2. Select *New Job*.
3. Set the following properties in the Execute Job box:
    a. Job Type: *Data Load*
    b. Scripts: *Year*
    c. Load Type: *File*
    d. Data File: *Data_BasicUpdated*
    e. Check the option: *Abort on error*

**Note!**

*Abort on error* will stop the data load process if an error is found with the data file. If this is not selected, Essbase will load the valid records and send the invalid records to the error file.

4. Select *Execute*.

A pop-up should indicate that the data load has started.

5. Click *OK*.

The job is displayed at the top of the list with a Running ⧖ status icon.

6. Click *Refresh* until the job completes.

7. Use the Job Details icon ⚙ to review the details of the data load. This option is especially helpful for troubleshooting any issues with the data load:

## Load Data using Rules Files with Cube Designer

I can also run this same data load process using Cube Designer. I do not have to have an Application Workbook open to do this step. In fact, this is kind of confusing because the steps that I'm going to walk through will load data using a file on the Essbase Cloud server (and not anything that I have updated locally in my Application Workbook). If I have data changes and want to use this process, I'll need to update the data text file and upload it to Essbase Cloud (like I did in our Data_BasicUpdated.txt file earlier).

To load data using a rules file with Cube Designer,
1. Open Excel and navigate to the *Cube Designer* ribbon.
2. Select *Load Data*.
3. Select the *Sample* application and *Basic* cube.
4. Select *Load Data* as the Job Type.
5. Select *Data_BasicUpdated.txt* as the Data File.
6. Select *Data* as the Load Rule File.

7. Click *Run:*

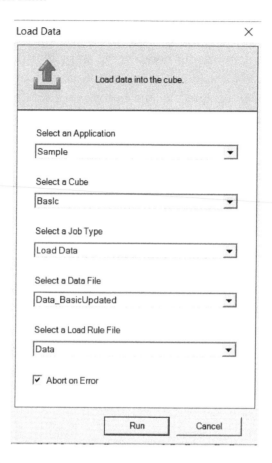

The data load process will run and update using the Data_BasicUpdated.txt file with the Data.rul file. I can view the details of the load by clicking on *View Jobs:*

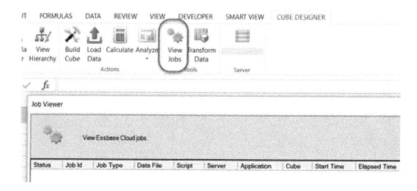

**Note!** Remember, if you choose the *Load Data* option when selecting a data file, it is the data file on Essbase Cloud that is referenced (not any local files or Excel worksheets).

## UPLOAD DATA WITH ESSCLI

Another option for uploading data is to use the Essbase Command Line Interface (CLI). This tool is used to automate a number of processes, including migrating Lifecycle Management (LCM) .zip files to the Cloud. Once the command line tool has been downloaded from the Essbase Cloud web interface and installed (see Chapter 8, "Essbase Cloud Administration" for more information), the user can use different commands to accomplish various Administrator tasks. The command and syntax used to load data to a cube is below:

```
dataload -application appname -db cubename -file
filename -abortOnError true|false
```

## LOAD DATA VIA SMART VIEW

One last super easy way to load data into Essbase Cloud is using the Smart View add-in. If I have been assigned the appropriate write security access, I can set up a spreadsheet with the desired data to submit:

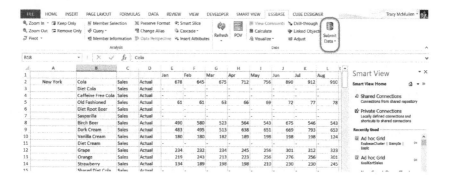

I click *Submit* on the ribbon to send data immediately back to the Essbase cube. Pretty easy, right? More on Smart View in just a bit.

**Note!**

For ASO cubes, data can only be input or loaded to level-0 members (members at the bottom of every dimension).

---

**COMMUNICATION: ROSKE TO SCHWARTZBERG**

[1:12] ROSKE: Schwartzberg, Flight Surgeon Alex says I need to write personal messages to each of the crew. She says it will keep me tethered to humanity while stranded in the Cloud. I think it is a load of crap but who would give up the chance to communicate with you? With you, I can be blunt. If I die, I'll need you to take care of the folks at i.n.t.e.r.R.e.l. They are like family. Also, I'd tell you that you're my best friend and stuff but that would be lame.

---

**COMMUNICATION: SCHWARTZBERG TO ROSKE**

[1:55] SCHWARTZBERG: Of all the things that have you have lost, do you miss your mind the most?

---

## CALCULATION OVERVIEW

Now that I have conquered dimension building and data loading, it's time to calculate. If my Essbase cube only needs to "aggregate" or roll up and it is an ASO or hybrid cube with upper level sparse dimensions set to dynamic, I don't have any further steps! Essbase ASO and hybrid cubes with the correct settings require no further calculation and will automatically roll up.

As an Essbase Cloud guru, I know that there are outline consolidations and member formulas that could possibly be utilized for calculating data, but are these options always going to resolve everything that will be requested of you?

Quite often, outline consolidations and member formulas provide all the calculation power an application will need. However, as member formulas start to reference other levels or other dimensions, they can get very complex, very quickly. While all Essbase cubes support member formulas and outline consolidations, BSO and hybrid cubes provide more powerful calculation capabilities. For BSO cubes, it's a different story and for a good reason.

Let's say I'm in charge of setting goals for the remainder of the year. I don't want our goals to be reasonable or obtainable (or else everyone would reach them), so I want to set every Budget member for Sales to be exactly ten percent greater than the Actual number from last year. I could build this into a member formula, but I might only want to run this once at the beginning of a budget cycle to seed the starting point budget and not every time the cube calculates. What to do, what to do?

For more complex calculation requirements and more control in BSO and hybrid cubes, I have Essbase calculation scripts as an option. Calculation scripts to the rescue!

## CALCULATION SCRIPTS FUNDAMENTALS

A calc script is short for "calculation script" and it allows the overriding of the standard outline calculations and takes complete control of how the cube derives its numbers. While most of the time calculation scripts are run at regular intervals to do simple things like aggregate subsets of my cube, they can also be run sporadically, such as at the start of budgeting season when I want to run my allocation processes with each what-if iteration.

A calc script is really just a sequential series of commands, equations, and formulas. It is stored in a standard text file with a .csc extension, so I can even open them in Notepad if I want to. Here's the calc script that will set all of my budget values to 10% above my actuals (I'll decode the details of this syntax shortly):

```
/* Creates Initial Starting Point Budget */
SET UPDATECALC OFF;

Fix ("Sales",  @RELATIVE ("Market", 0), @RELATIVE
("Product", 0), @RELATIVE ("Year", 0))
CLEARDATA "Budget";
 "Budget" =  "Actual" * 1.1;
ENDFIX
CALC DIM ("Market", "Product");
```

This calc script actually does a few things beyond just creating the budget, but I'll get to those in due time.

There are a lot of reasons to use a calc script. If I'm not happy with the order that Essbase uses to calculate the members and dimensions, a calc script can easily override the default order. If I don't want to calculate the entire cube, a calc script can be written to only calculate the current month. If I want to clear data or copy data from one place to another, calculation scripts can do the job. Want to create formulas that aren't in the outline? Calculation scripts are there for me. Calculation scripts will even let me perform allocations and multi-pass calculations. When one of the end users passes you a multi-stage allocation calculation that would make most Excel gurus go mad, you can just tie on my cape and write an Essbase calc script to save the day.

> Calculation scripts only apply to BSO and Hybrid Essbase cube types.

**Note!**

You can create a calc script for ASO cubes but you will use MaxL and MDX to define the logic; it is completely different than the BSO language. I'll cover more on Essbase ASO calculation scripts in my next journey.

### Simplest Calc Script

"CALC ALL;" – while it's small in stature, it's powerful in nature. This single line will aggregate all of the dimensional hierarchies in my outline, calculate all of the formulas attached to members, perform time balancing on time balanced members, and do it all quickly using "intelligent calculation." I'll be covering more sophisticated calculation scripts in the remaining sections, but you should always remember that no matter what you create, you'll always have the power of CALC ALL.

```
CALC ALL;
```

### Calc Script Syntax

There are a few simple rules to follow when writing a calc script:

1) End every statement with a semicolon
2) You do not talk about fight club
3) You can break a statement onto multiple lines, but the end of the statement must have a semicolon
4) If a member name contains spaces or starts with a number, surround it with "double quotes"
5) Start comments with /*
6) End comments with */
7) Calc script syntax is not case sensitive
8) Spaces between member names, commands, and functions do not matter

There are many more rules, but these are the important ones that people tend to forget about, and then are left wondering for hours about why their calculation scripts aren't working. Here's a calc script that demonstrates several of those syntax rules:

```
/* Increase Opening Inventory */

"Opening Inventory" =
 "Opening InVeNtOrY" * 1.1;
```

Notice that the first line is a comment and it has the appropriate start and end characters. *Opening Inventory* has a space in the member name, so it's surrounded by double quotes. At the end of the entire statement (although not at the end of the comment), there's a semicolon. (You can tell the calc script language was written by a programmer, because only programmers end sentences with semicolons;) Finally, observe that the second instance of Opening Inventory uses wacky cases just to show you that calculation scripts are indeed *not* case sensitive (unless you have explicitly told Essbase to behave otherwise).

### Calculate Single Members

One of the simplest calculations I can perform is to tell Essbase to do the calculation for a single member. In a production system, this is the leanest, meanest calc script I can write, and is used when I want the script to finish in the quickest possible time.

Imagine for a moment that the Variance member in Sample.Basic was stored and not dynamically calculated. I've just loaded data and I want to tell Essbase to calculate the formula on Variance and leave the rest of the outline alone. All I have to do is spell the member name and add a semicolon:

```
Variance;
```

How do you think you'd modify the calc script to calculate both Variance and Variance %? Hopefully it's something like this:

```
Variance;
"Variance %";
```

Notice that I have to use double quotes around Variance % due to the space in the name.

**Tip!** If you want to be safe about it, put double quotes around all member names (even Variance). It doesn't hurt anything, and it does help you identify your member names quickly during troubleshooting exercises.

The technique of specifying a member name on a line by itself can be applied to members that do not have formulas but do have members aggregating into them. Imagine that I have just loaded data to Sample.Basic into the great state of Texas. Now I want to roll up the Texas numbers to the top of the Market dimension:

```
South;
Market;
```

The nice thing about this script is that it doesn't bother rolling up totals that haven't changed. There's no Texas in the North (thankfully) so I know I don't need to modify the totals for North.

It's also possible to temporarily override the formula in the outline for a member. To do this in a calc script, I just set up an equation with Budget on the left side of the equal sign:

```
Budget = Actual * 1.1;
```

This script will set the Budget to be 10% greater (notice that I'm multiplying times 1.1) than Actual. If you're really in need of a raise, you could set the Profit of my company to double what it should be:

```
Profit = Profit * 2;
```

Forgetting that the above calc script is probably illegal (thanks, Senator Sarbanes, wherever you are), it is interesting in that it puts the member Profit on both sides of the equation. It's also useful to understand that every time you run it, Profit will double. So make sure you only run scripts like this once.

**Tip!**

There are better ways to increase your company's profitability than writing an illegal calc script.

### Intelligent Calculation

Before I go any further, I must share the command to turn off intelligent calculation for BSO cubes. Intelligent calculation allows Essbase to remember which blocks in the cube need to be calculated based on new data coming in, and which haven't been impacted (and don't need calculation). Intelligent calculation is wonderful when I'm running CALC ALL.

But (there is always a "but") intelligent calculation is the devil's work when I'm running other calculation scripts. Think about the budget calc script from earlier:

```
Budget = Actual * 1.1;
```

Do I want this calc script to only operate on so called "dirty blocks" or do I want all budgets throughout the entire system to be set 10% above actuals? If I leave intelligent calculation turned on during the running of our calc, Essbase will only calculate our new budgets for blocks that have recently been loaded with data. That's definitely not what I want, as some business units will escape with a sensible quota. I definitely can't have that!

The good news is that I don't have to turn off intelligent calculation for the entire cube. I can just tell Essbase to ignore it during the calc script with this command:

```
SET UPDATECALC Off;
```

If I want to turn Intelligent Calc on again later in the script (maybe I want a "CALC ALL" command at the end of my script to calculate just the dirty blocks), include the command **SET UPDATECALC ON;** and everything past that point will work "intelligently." I recommend that you include the command to turn intelligent calculation off at the top of every calc script. If there's a case where you actually want to use it, go ahead and remove the line on a case-by-case basis. Leaving it out is courting disaster (and take it from a guy who dated Disaster back in high school; you don't want to be courting her).

### Calculate Entire Dimensions

As I've already mentioned, there's a simple command that I can include in a calc script that tells Essbase to evaluate all my member formulas and do all of my outline aggregation. While "CALC ALL" is great and powerful, there are times when I only want to calculate specific dimensions. For instance, what would I do if I just wanted to calculate

Sample.Basic's Product dimension? I have a new command for this called "CALC DIM" (short for calculate dimension):

```
CALC DIM (Product);
```

This line calculates the Product dimension, doing both outline aggregation (such as rolling all the Colas up into the parent value) and member formulas, if they exist for members in that dimension. If I want to calculate multiple dimensions using this command (say, Market and Product), just separate them with commas:

```
CALC DIM (Market, Product);
```

Remember how I said that "CALC DIM" not only does aggregation but also member formulas? Well, how many member formulas are there in the Market and Product dimensions? That's right – *none*, so "CALC DIM" is wasting time looking for formulas that I know aren't there. For dimensions that don't have formulas, there's a faster command that only does aggregation:

```
AGG (Market, Product);
```

**Note!** "AGG" can only be used on sparse dimensions. If you have a dense dimension with no formulas that you only want to aggregate, you cannot use "AGG." You must use the "CALC DIM" command.

### Calculate a Subset of Data

While calculating entire dimensions makes me feel very powerful, sometimes I just want to calculate a portion of the cube. For instance, let's say I just updated my budgets but I didn't touch actuals. How could I ignore the Actual member? Well it turns out that there's an optional argument to the "CALC ALL" command called "EXCEPT." I use it to calculate everything except specific dimensions (DIM) or members (MBR). If I didn't want to calculate actuals, I'd say:

```
CALC ALL EXCEPT MBR (Actual);
```

It's also possible to list multiple members. Say that I didn't want to calculate Texas and New York (no offense to either state). I'd list the members separated by commas:

```
CALC ALL EXCEPT MBR (Texas, "New York");
```

If there's an entire dimension I don't want to calculate, replace "MBR" with "DIM":

```
CALC ALL EXCEPT DIM (Measures);
```

While this method may be fun at first, it's not nearly the most powerful method for limiting a calculation to a small portion of the cube. Remembering JWE, let's say I just loaded our budgets for next year for Texas. Now I just want to calculate our accounts dimension for that one member, ignoring the rest of the cube. The "CALC ALL EXCEPT..." method from above is really used to do the majority of a cube and not just a smidgen, so I need a new command: "FIX" and its sister command "ENDFIX."

If I just want to calculate Sales, I put this in double quotes after the "FIX" as such:

```
FIX ("Texas")
     CALC DIM (Account);
ENDFIX
```

**Tip!**
While the indentation is not necessary, it helps make it easier to see which commands the FIX affects.

"FIX" and "ENDFIX" are called sandwich commands because one command is like the top layer of bread and the other is the bottom with lots of things thrown in between. For instance, I could choose to calculate a few specific accounts:

```
FIX ("Texas")
     Op_Income;
     Margin;
ENDFIX
```

It's also possible to list multiple members in a FIX as long as I separate them with commas:

```
FIX ("Texas", "Colorado")
     Op_Income;
     Margin;
ENDFIX
```

Let's say I only loaded budgets to next year (which for our purposes, I will call "NextYear") for both the customers above. Here's one way to accomplish that by nesting one "FIX" within another:

```
FIX ("Texas", "Colorado")
     FIX ("NextYear")
          Op_Income;
          Margin;
     ENDFIX
ENDFIX
```

**Note!** Each "FIX" must conclude with an "ENDFIX." It is not necessary to end a "FIX" or "ENDFIX" statement with a semicolon, but it doesn't hurt anything to use one either.

While this is a valid method, two "FIX"es are not necessary. I can list members from multiple dimensions within one "FIX" command, and this is the traditional way to do it:

```
FIX ("Texas", "Colorado", "NextYear")
      Op_Income;
      Margin;
ENDFIX
```

**Tip!**
Using "FIX" commands on sparse dimensions will speed up the performance of your calculations, because it limits the number of blocks pulled into memory to just what's listed in the "FIX" statement.

Let's discuss two other commands: EXCLUDE/ENDEXCLUDE (you may see these referred to as "unchanged cells"). These commands will calculate everything except what is defined in the EXCLUDE statement. Think opposite of a FIX/ENDFIX. The following calculation will calculate everything except Texas:

```
EXCLUDE ("Texas")
      Calc Dim (Accounts, Product);
ENDEXCLUDE
```

### Point to Another Member

While I'm inside a "FIX" command, blocks outside are ignored. What if you want to refer to values from blocks that aren't being retrieved into memory? Surely there must be a way, I cry out of quiet desperation. I need to stop my incessant bawling, because there is indeed a way. It's called the cross-dimensional operator. Its job is to point to another member in the cube and it looks like this: **->**

**Note!**
There is no "cross-dimensional operator" symbol on your keyboard. You type this in by pressing the dash key followed by the greater than symbol.

If I wanted to set sales for Texas equal to sales for Colorado, I could write a calc script that looks like this:

```
FIX ("Texas")
     "Sales" = "Sales" -> "Colorado";
ENDFIX
```

What exactly is this doing? On the right side of the equation, I told Essbase to get the value from sales for the Colorado. The left side of the equation told it to put the result in sales, but which sales? Well, as you see from the "FIX", I told Essbase to only calculate Texas, so it will put the value into sales for Texas.

Whenever possible, try to avoid cross-dimensional operators. They're unseemly and slow. For instance, if I had to add another account, I would have to include it within the "FIX":

```
FIX ("Texas")
  "Sales" = "Sales" -> "Colorado";
  "Op_Expense" = "Op_Expense" -> "Colorado";
ENDFIX
```

I could remove the need for the cross-dimensional operator (called "cross-dim" for short) by pivoting the customer and account dimensions. That is, I'll put the account dimension in the "FIX" and the customer dimension inside the "FIX":

```
FIX ("Sales", "Op_Expense")
  "Texas" = "Colorado";
ENDFIX
```

This is much easier to read, and more flexible as well. It's obvious now that I'm focusing on two specific accounts and setting one state to be equal to another.

**Tip!**

If you find yourself repeating a cross-dim to the same member, it might be possible to pivot a dimension as above to remove the need for the cross-dim.

It is also possible to string cross-dims together to point to more and more specific intersections in the cube:

```
FIX ("Texas", NextYear)
   "Sales" = "Sales" -> "Colorado" -> "CurrentYear";
ENDFIX
```

`Sales -> Colorado -> CurrentYear` is called a "member combination." This is how the online documentation refers to the intersections of members via cross-dimensional operators.

### Clear Data

Have you ever had one of those days when everything was going wrong and you just wanted to wipe out the entire day and start over? Fortunately, it's much easier to do this in Essbase than it is in reality. If I wanted to clear all of the data in our cube, I'd need the following little calc script:

```
SET UpdateCalc Off;
CLEARBLOCK All;
```

The first line (as no doubt you'll recall from a few pages ago) tells Essbase to operate on all blocks in the cube and not just the dirty blocks. The second line tells Essbase to clear all the blocks in the cube.

This script will run extremely quickly and when it's finished it will certainly appear that my cube is empty, but it's not. The reason that "CLEARBLOCK" runs like a paparazzi after Angelina Jolie in that all it does is blank out the index entries (the pointers to the corresponding blocks in the page file). Since it can no longer find the blocks, they might as well be blank.

**Tip!**    "CLEARBLOCK" will leave your cube fragmented. Remember to defragment your cube periodically to improve performance.

A powerful way to use "CLEARBLOCK" is within a "FIX" statement. I want to blank out our Sample.Basic budget so that I can try again (our last attempt at the budget was horrendous, let's be honest), so I write this script:

```
FIX (Budget)
     CLEARBLOCK All;
ENDFIX
```

Remember that "CLEARBLOCK" will clear out entire blocks by removing the pointers, but in Sample.Basic, Budget is in the Scenario dimension and Scenario is a dense dimension. Since Budget is in every block in the cube, does it remove all the blocks? No, "CLEARBLOCK" is smart enough to only clear out index entries when the entire block is not being "FIX"ed on. In cases where just a portion of a block needs to be cleared, "CLEARBLOCK" will read the blocks into memory, clear out the necessary slices, and write the blocks back out to the page file. As such, "CLEARBLOCK" when used inside a "FIX" on a dense dimension is noticeably slower.

If I want to blank out a specific dense member, there's a simpler way than including a "CLEARBLOCK" inside a "FIX" on that dense member:

```
CLEARDATA Budget;
```

The "CLEARDATA" command allows me to specify a single member (in our case, Budget). Do not use this on a sparse member, because the "CLEARBLOCK" command will always be faster. It is also possible to use a cross-dim operator on the right side of a "CLEARDATA" command. If I wanted to clear out only our sales budget, I could write:

```
CLEARDATA Budget -> Sales;
```

If I need to clear out multiple dense members, do not write my script like this:

```
CLEARDATA Actual;
CLEARDATA Budget;
```

This will result in multiple passes through my cube (which equates to more time and effort) since Essbase will not know to clear my data from actual and budget during a single pass. In this case, go back to using the "CLEARBLOCK" command within a "FIX":

```
FIX (Actual, Budget)
     CLEARBLOCK All;
ENDFIX
```

At various times, I'll want to make sure that all of the aggregated blocks in my cube are cleared. For instance, if I'm about to recalculate all of the totals in my cube, it's faster if Essbase doesn't have to read the old totals into memory before writing out the new ones. There is an argument I can use in place of "All" called "Upper":

```
CLEARBLOCK Upper;
```

This command will clear all of the upper-level blocks in my cube. As before with the "All" argument, "CLEARBLOCK Upper" can be used within a "FIX" statement. A related argument is "NonInput":

```
CLEARBLOCK NonInput;
```

This will clear out all the blocks that haven't had data directly input to them. Assuming I'm following best practices and only entering data into level-0 blocks, this command will only clear out the upper-level blocks like "CLEARBLOCK Upper."

Another argument: "CLEARBLOCK Empty" removes #Missing blocks from the cube. The CLEARBLOCK Empty command sets values to #MISSING and if the entire block is empty, Essbase will remove the block. This is helpful if I've run the CREATEBLOCKONEQ command, which creates blocks on equations, but may have unnecessarily created blocks with no data.

```
CLEARBLOCK Empty;
```

There's one other way to clear data. I can set a member equal to #Missing:

```
Budget = #Missing;
```

While this is valid syntax (and I've even seen a few sub-par consultants use it), it's just weird. Stick to "CLEARBLOCK" or "CLEARDATA."

### Copying Data

There are two common ways to copy data. The first is with a simple equation:

```
"Budget" = "Actual";
```

This equation copies the Actual data over to the Budget data. Depending on the settings in my cube, this method may or may not create blocks. The way to be sure I create all necessary blocks is by using the "DATACOPY" command. It takes two arguments: a member to copy the data from and a member to copy the data to. This command accomplishes the same thing as the line of code above, but with added comfort that there will be no block creation shenanigans:

```
DATACOPY "Actual" TO "Budget";
```

Both of these methods can be used within a FIX command. Do not use multiple "DATACOPY" commands on dense members:

```
DATACOPY Jan TO Feb;
DATACOPY Feb TO Mar;
```

In the case of Sample.Basic, this calc script will actually cause two passes through the cube since Time is a dense dimension. In this case, the first method of setting one member equal to another would be better.

**Tip!**

To oversimplify, use the equation method on dense members and the "DATACOPY" method on sparse members.

**Tip!**

To create blocks use "CREATEBLOCK" for an optimized block creation routine instead of DATACOPY.

### IF and Its Other Brother, ENDIF

My favorite example of "IF" syntax is back from JWE's juggling wolverine days when they wanted to see if their number of dropped wolverines exceeded the number of juggled wolverines. If so, they wanted to fire everybody (i.e., set headcount equal to zero). Here's what this would look like if I made it the member formula for "Headcount" in the outline:

```
IF (Avg_Wolverines_Juggled < Avg_Dropped_Wolverines)
     Headcount = 0;
ENDIF
```

Now since this is attached to a member called Headcount, it's technically not necessary to specify "Headcount =" on the third line. As a matter of policy, I don't tend to include it, because if the "Headcount" member gets renamed, the member formula reference to it will *not* rename. As such, I'd write the formula like this:

```
IF (Avg_Wolverines_Juggled < Avg_Dropped_Wolverines)
     0;
ENDIF
```

Now, if I just type this into a calc script and verify it, I'll get the following message:

"Error: 1012061 The CALC command [IF] can only be used within a CALC Member Block"

First of all, note that the error message calls "IF" a command, so I was right all along about it not being a real function, online documentation be damned. To translate the error message into semi-English, "IF" can only be used in a member formula.

"Uh, oh," you say, "but I want to do IFs in a calc script. Is now the time for ritual suicide?"

While it may indeed be, don't do it over this, because there's a simple work-around: create a temporary member formula within my calc script that contains the needed "IF." I do this by specifying the member that I want to assign the temporary formula and then include the formula in parentheses. For example:

```
Headcount
    (
    IF (Avg_Wolverines_Juggled <
            Avg_Dropped_Wolverines)
        0;
    ENDIF
    )
```

Notice "Headcount" at the top and the parentheses surrounding the "IF...ENDIF." Voila! The calc script will now validate and run successfully.

### Calc Script Functions

Everything I've done up to this point has been focused around using the calculation commands. There are also at least 100+ functions that let me do most of the interesting things that Microsoft Excel functions can do (like absolute values, statistical deviations, and internal rate of return calculations) and many things that Excel functions cannot (like return the parent value of the current member in a hierarchy and allocate values down across a hierarchy).

 **Note!** These are the very same functions that you used when creating member formulas. With very few exceptions, all of the functions can be used both in member formulas and calculation scripts.

To make it easier to find the functions in the online help, Hyperion segmented the functions into several nebulous categories. Some of the categories are easily understood (like Boolean). Some, like the mysterious Miscellaneous category, are not.

Boolean functions return True or False (actually, they return a 1 for True and a 0 for False). Boolean functions are generally used inside an "IF" or an "ELSEIF." One of the common Boolean functions is "@ISMBR" and it's used to tell if a specific member is being calculated.

Let's say that I want to set budgeted sales equal to 123.45:

```
IF (@ISMBR (Budget))
    Sales = 123.45;
ENDIF
```

It's possible to put a cross-dim operator inside the "@ISMBR." All parts of the cross-dim must be true for the entire statement to be true. In this example, the current intersection being calculated must be New York and Budget:

```
IF (@ISMBR (Budget->"New York"))
    Sales = 123.45;
ENDIF
```

It's even possible to list several members in a "@ISMBR" separated by commas. For instance, if I only want to set New York and California sales, our script would look like this:

```
IF (@ISMBR ("New York", California))
    Sales = 123.45;
ENDIF
```

At times, I might want to check to see if the current member is in a range of members. For instance, say I want COGS to be set to 500 if the month being calculated is between January and June. To do this, separate the two members (in this case Jan and Jun) with a colon:

```
IF (@ISMBR (Jan:Jun))
    COGS = 500;
ENDIF
```

I might sometimes see "Jan::Jun" with a double colon between the two members. The single colon method returns all members from Jan to Jun that are at the same level. The double colon method returns all the members from Jan to Jun that are at the same *generation*. Unless my outline contains ragged hierarchies, the single and double colon methods will return the same list. For simplicity's sake, I tend to use a single colon.

There are at least fifteen other Boolean functions, some of which are actually helpful (@ISCHILD, @ISGEN, and @ISLEV, among others).

Relationship functions are used to look up values at intersections elsewhere in Essbase. Generally, the value being looked up is in the same cube, but it doesn't have to be (the extremely helpful but slightly slow "@XREF" functions looks to other cubes).

One of the common needs is to look at the value of a parent member. For instance, say Sample.Basic had a stored member named Product Share that needed to show each level-0 product's sales as a percentage of its parent's sales:

```
"Product Share" =
  Sales / @PARENTVAL (Product, Sales);
```

The first argument to the "@PARENTVAL" function is the dimension for which you want to take the value at the parent. If I had a Market Share member, I could calculate it like this:

```
"Market Share" =
  Sales / @PARENTVAL (Market, Sales);
```

Mathematical functions perform standard arithmetic calculations such as absolute value, integer, and factorial. The "@VAR" function used in Sample.Basic to calculate variances is, for no apparent reason, a mathematical function.

While simple statistical functions like maximum and minimum are found in the Mathematical category, advanced statistical functions get their own category: Statistical.

There are also some statistical type functions that have to do with moving sums, averages, minimums, and so on. These functions are found in the Forecasting category along with "@SPLINE" which finds a curve most closely fitting a range of data and "@TREND" which predicts the future (well, kinda). If you're ever curious how "@TREND" comes up with its trend calculations, the programmers at Oracle were kind enough to put the formulas in technical reference documentation.

Here's a snippet of the "Algorithm for Triple Exponential Smoothing (TES)." Sing along if you know the melody:

**Algorithm for Triple Exponential Smoothing (TES)**

*Ylist*          $y_1, y_2, \ldots, y_K$

*Xlist*          $x_1, x_2, \ldots, x_K$

TES with period $T$ (if $T$ is not given, it is assumed to be $T = 1$)

$x_1, x_2, ..., x_K,$        $y_1, y_2 ..., y_K$    are input to TES, $x$ is forecast value.

$$a_i = (1-c)^{x_{i+1} - x_i}    \qquad d_i = (1-d)^{x_{i+1} - x_i}    \qquad e_i = (1-e)^{x_{i+1} - x_i}$$

**Note:** When *Xlist* is missing, the exponents disappear.

Default          $c = .2$
                 $d = .05$
                 $e = .1$

Step 1,

$$S_1 = y_1$$
$$b_1 = \frac{y_2 - y_1}{x_2 - x_1}$$
$$I_1 = 1$$

I'll bet you're wishing you hadn't slept through your statistics class in college right about now.

Member Set functions simply return lists of members. These are commonly used in "FIX" commands. Say that I wanted to focus on just aggregating products in the East region. Rather than hard-code all the members in East, I could use a member set function called "@CHILDREN":

```
FIX (@CHILDREN (East))
     AGG (Product);
ENDFIX
```

Essentially, the "@CHILDREN (East)" portion of the "FIX" is replaced by a series of members before the calc script runs. The calculation actually performed is this (once the "@CHILDREN" is evaluated):

```
FIX ("New York":"New Hampshire")
     AGG (Product);
ENDFIX
```

Or to put it another way (not using the single colon range indicator):

```
FIX ("New York", "Massachusetts", "Florida",
  "Connecticut", "New Hampshire")
     AGG (Product);
ENDFIX
```

A common request is to calculate all of the members from a certain member on upwards to the top of the dimension. For instance, let's say I just loaded a value to the great state of Utah (thought I was going to say "the great state of Texas," didn't you?). I want to aggregate this value up through the Market dimension, but I don't want to aggregate the entire dimension (since nothing else has changed). Use the "@ANCESTORS" function on a line by itself:

```
@ANCESTORS (Utah);
```

Remembering that member set functions essentially return lists of members, the script is exactly the same as this request:

```
Utah;
West;
Market;
```

**Note!** If a member set function returns any dynamic calc or dynamic calc and store members, they will not be evaluated.

What if I wanted to calculate just the regions in the Market dimension? I could use the "@CHILDREN" function on a line by itself:

```
@CHILDREN (Market);
```

Range functions (sometimes called "Financial" functions just to be contrary) operate on a range of members. The most commonly used range function is "@PRIOR" which looks to earlier members in the outline and "@NEXT" which looks to later members in the outline. Both of these functions assume that I want to look forward and backward through the dimension marked as the Time dimension if I do not otherwise specify a range. As a result, many people think of them as time-specific, but they don't have to be.

The member Opening Inventory in Sample.Basic uses the "@PRIOR" function to refer to the prior month's Ending Inventory:

```
IF (NOT @ISMBR(Jan))
    "Opening Inventory" =
              @PRIOR ("Ending Inventory");
ENDIF;
```

The "IF (NOT ..." is used to make sure that I don't try to look back to the prior period if I am in the month of January (because Sample.Basic only contains one year of data, this wouldn't make any sense).

Allocation functions allocate summarized higher level values down to detailed members. This is often used for top-down budgeting or targeted forecasting (when values are often loaded to parent members and then spread downward). There are only two functions. "@ALLOCATE" allocates values down a single dimension and its more impressive counterpart "@MDALLOCATE" allocates values down multiple dimensions simultaneously. While the allocation functions are powerful, they're not very efficient at complex allocations so I might decide to write my own logic.

Date & Time functions change dates in the form of strings to numeric dates. This category only has one function in it at the moment, "@TODATE," which makes me wonder why they didn't just put this function in the Miscellaneous category. Somehow, I think the marketing department is involved.

Miscellaneous is the category for functions that don't have a place elsewhere. The "@TODATE" function should be here, but it's not. Instead, I get the bizarre "@CALCMODE" function which changes the way Essbase calculates a member and three string manipulation functions (@CONCATENATE, @NAME, and @SUBSTRING).

Custom-defined functions are whatever I want them to be. It is possible to write my own functions in Java, register them with Essbase using the MaxL "create function" command, and call them from a calc script as if they were part of the native language.

One of the best uses of CDFs (custom-defined functions) is for iterative type calculations (such as the common retail metric Weeks of Supply) that would take up pages in a calc script but are just a few lines of custom Java code. Other CDFs I've seen include a better implementation of internal rate of return than the "@IRR" function that comes with Essbase and a function that checks a weather database to pull back high and low temperatures.

### Where Do I Go From Here?

Learning everything there is to know about calculation scripts would take several years, I'm fairly certain. I am sure I could fill at least 700 pages with non-stop, wall-to-wall, hot, steamy calc action. Perhaps I should start a book with a working title of "Fifty Shades of Calculation scripts?" I am also sure that a book on just calculation scripts would sell no more than 100 copies worldwide, including the fifty copies I bought just to prove to my family that I had another book in me.

Rather than drag this section on any further, I'll point you in the right place for further information: the Essbase Technical Reference:

The "Calculation Functions" section contains details on all of the @Functions. The "Calculation Commands" section is where you go to find information on all of the commands that can be used in a calc script that don't start with the @ symbol. Several of the calculation functions contain examples showing you how to use them. While they're not in depth, they're plentiful, so maybe that makes up for it.

If you'd like to pre-reserve an advance copy of *Look Smarter than You Are with Calculation scripts: Essbase Goes Hardcore*, please e-mail info@interrel.com. If I get 100 advance orders, I'll start writing. Don't hold your breath.

## CREATE A CALCULATION SCRIPT

Calculation scripts are text files and, therefore, I can create these in any text editor then simply copy and paste into the Essbase Cloud web interface when ready, or I can also save my calc script as a text file in the appropriate cube directory (when you do this, remember to save the file with a .csc extension). There are a few advantages to using my own text editor:

- Visualization of more lines at once

- Better find and replace functionality
- Better line numbering
- Greater printing options

The other option is to navigate to Scripts within the Essbase Cloud web interface and create my calc script from scratch there.

### Upload Calculation Script Files

As mentioned above, I can upload a calc script as a .csc file. Once the file is uploaded, I can then view, edit, and run the calculation within the Essbase Cloud web interface as I would with any script. If I have multiple scripts as .csc files, I can choose all of those I want added then upload all at one time.

To upload a calculation script,
1. From the Essbase Cloud home page navigate to *Sample.Basic*, then select the *Files* card:

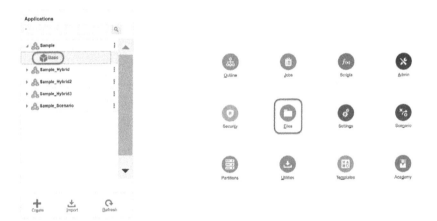

2. In a text file, create the following calc script:

```
/* Creates Initial Starting Point Budget */
SET UPDATECALC OFF;

Fix ("Sales", @RELATIVE ("Market", 0), @RELATIVE ("Product", 0), @RELATIVE ("Year", 0))
CLEARDATA "Budget";
"Budget" = "Actual" * 1.1;
ENDFIX
CALC DIM ("Market", "Product"); |
```

3. Save it locally as "BudgetStartPoint.csc" (and make sure that there is no .txt extension automatically added to it!).
4. On the right hand side of the screen beneath Upload Files, select *Choose Files*:

5.   Browse to the saved local script then select *Open*:

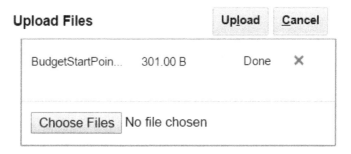

6.   Select *Upload*.
7.   A success message should appear, with the successfully uploaded file listed. Click *OK*.
8.   Verify the file or files are listed on the *Files* screen.

**Review a Calc Script with the Web Interface**

To navigate to calculation scripts in Essbase Cloud,

1.   From the Essbase Cloud home page navigate to *Sample.Basic*, then select the *Scripts* card:

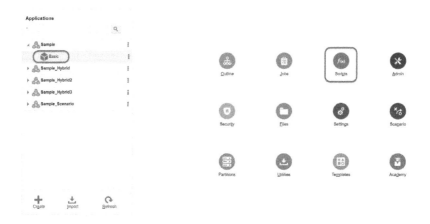

The Scripts page is displayed.

2.  The first tab with the $f_x$ icon will show calculation scripts for the selected cube.

3.  Select the BudgetStartPoint calc script and from the Actions menu, choose *Edit*:

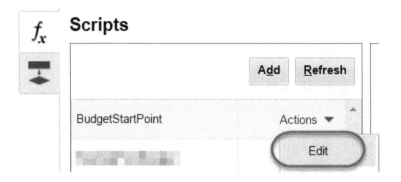

The calc script logic displays and I can make updates here in this screen if I wanted to. This looks pretty good so I'll leave as is.

4.  Click *Validate* to validate the calc script logic:

5.  Click *OK*.

6.  Click *Close* to close the calc script (since I didn't make any changes, no need to click *Save*).

### Create a Calc Script

Now I'm going to create a new script that updates the Forecast member with Actuals data through the current month. In my example below, I'm hard coding the months in the logic; an even better design would be to use a substitution variable.

To create a new script,

1.  Navigate to the Scripts page for the Sample.Basic cube as described above.
2.  Enter the script name *UpdateForecast*.
3.  Next to the *Script* field, key in the following syntax:

```
/* Update forecast with actuals */
SET UPDATECALC OFF;

Fix ("Sales", @RELATIVE ("Market", 0), @RELATIVE
("Product", 0), "Jan":"Jun")
CLEARDATA "Forecast";
 "Forecast" = "Actual";
ENDFIX
CALC DIM ("Market", "Product");
```

Which should look like the following in the Essbase Cloud web interface:

**New Script**

  * **Name**  UpdateForecast

  * **Script**  /* Update forecast with actuals data */
SET UPDATECALC OFF;

Fix ("Sales", @RELATIVE ("Market", 0), @RELATIVE ("Product", 0), "Jan":"Jun")
CLEARDATA "Forecast";
 "Forecast" = "Actual";
ENDFIX
CALC DIM ("Market", "Product");

It's helpful to include a description of what the script will actually do. It's also typical to see a section of housekeeping items at the top of the script to set certain settings. The above script first comments that it is meant to create the initial budget, then turns off intelligent calculation.

Normal design practice is to have upper level dense members set to dynamic calc. This means I don't have to include these members within the Calc Dim statement. The above syntax is fixing on members for the budget to calculate at level-0 for the Sales account, then rolling up those values. Also, note I have the members Budget and Actual in quotation marks. Although this is unnecessary, it's good practice while learning, as it will not interfere with the script and keeps the syntax on the safe side.

One other note on the two calculation scripts that I have created. If I had created Sample.Basic as a hybrid cube and set the Market and Product members to dynamic calc, I would not need to include the **CALC DIM** statement at the end.

4.  Select *Validate*:

5. The user should receive a pop-up indicating the script is valid. Click *OK*:

6. Select *Save*:

7. You should receive a message that the script save successfully. Click *OK*:

## EXECUTE A CALCULATION SCRIPT

Calculation scripts can be run from the Essbase Cloud web interface or the Smart View add-in.

### Calculate With the Web Interface

To execute a calculation within the Essbase Cloud web interface,

1.  From the Essbase Cloud home page select Sample.Basic, then select the *Jobs* card:

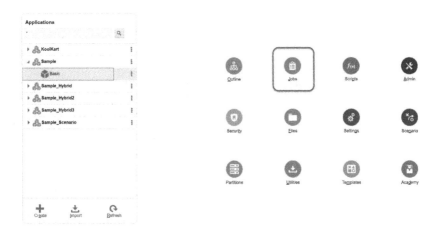

**Note!**  You don't actually have to select the cube here. This can be defined later when creating the job. It would have worked if you just selected the application (e.g., Sample instead of Basic).

2.  In the upper right hand corner, select *New Job*:

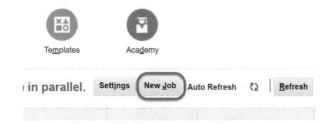

3.  Set the *Job Type* to *Calc Execution*, then select the script. Since I selected the cube already on the home page, this is already defined.

4.  Select the *BudgetStartPoint* calc script:

5.  Select *Execute*.
6.  A message pops up, indicating that the calculation has started. Click *OK*:

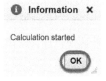

7. Use the *Refresh* button until the status shows a green check mark:

Job Details can be further reviewed using the Job Details icon 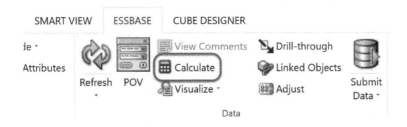. If there were any status errors, the error message(s) can be reviewed here.

### Calculate With Smart View

I can execute a calculation in Smart View in two ways:

1) With the Essbase ad hoc ribbon
2) With the Cube Designer extension

To execute a calc script through Smart View Essbase ribbon,

1. Connect to Essbase Cloud (refer to Chapter 9, "Analyze Data in Smart View", in this book for a refresher).
2. On the Essbase ribbon, select *Calculate*:

3.  Select the appropriate script then click *Launch*:

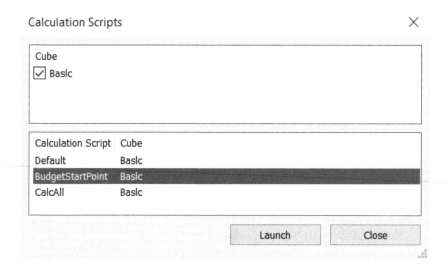

A pop-up that the calculation script has been processed should appear.

4.  Click *OK*:
5.  The Calculation Scripts box should also show that the launch was successful. Select *Close*.

To launch a calc with Cube Designer,
1.  Navigate to the Cube Designer ribbon.
2.  Click *Calculate*.

3. Select the desired calc script and click *Run:*

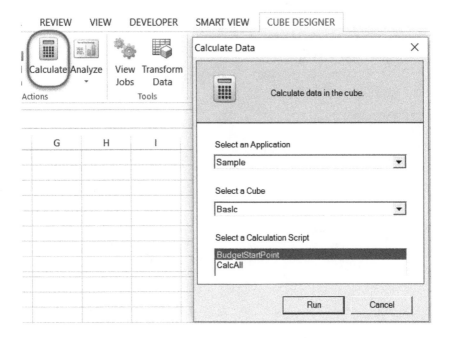

Before I conclude this calc script journey, I want to make sure I understand how to manage existing calculation scripts.

## MANAGE EXISTING CALCULATION SCRIPTS

I already covered how to upload an existing calc script.

Through the Essbase Cloud web interface I can Edit, Copy, Rename, Lock, Unlock, and Delete existing calculation scripts:

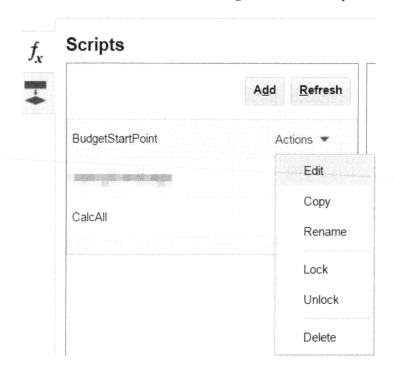

LOG ENTRY FOR ESSBASE PILOT GLENN SCHWARTZBERG
*SOL 23, Entry 1*

    Mission Essbase Build, Load, and Calculate complete. KoolKart and TBC analysts are ready to tackle the user portion of Essbase.

# CHAPTER 8: ESSBASE CLOUD ADMINISTRATION

> **LOG ENTRY FOR FLIGHT ENGINEER ROBERT GIDEON**
> *SOL 23, Entry 1*
>
> While Glenn is wrapping up his mission, I'm ready to tackle my next assignment. This one could be extremely dangerous. Seriously. I'm talking administration.
> I need to show how to run jobs, import on-premises Essbase cubes, and run automated scripts all in one sol. Time is ticking and I can't bend under the pressure now. Edward is counting on me.

## ESSBASE SECURITY

### Essbase Security Overview

I've built my cube, loaded data, and, in the case of BSO cubes, calculated them. The anticipation is killing me. Finally JWE and its subsidiaries, TBC and KoolKart, are ready for analysis. But users aren't able to see anything or they might see #NoAccess. Oh, that's right. I haven't covered one of the most important parts of Essbase Cloud – security. I'll discuss that now.

Essbase Cloud provides flexible security that can be implemented from a high level down to the individual cell level. Cell level? I can control which cells in my body I want to grant access to and even to whom to grant access? This could get interesting...

No, not those cells, dreamer. By cell level, I mean down to a single intersection in the cube. For example, I can define write access for product 100 for January for Gross Revenue for Actual for FY17 for the West region. Do I recommend this level of security? No, that would be a nightmare to maintain, but if my requirements dictate that kind of madness, I can do it.

Though security can be still defined at a very granular level, the security in Essbase Cloud is a bit more simplified (in my opinion) than using native Shared Services against on-premises Essbase.

Security is assigned to users and/or groups in Essbase Cloud. Best practice is to create groups and assign users to those groups. Security is defined by assigning these users and groups to roles. The first set of roles, referred to as "User Roles," contains three options: Service Administrator, Power User, or User. The Service Administrator role is pretty self-explanatory – this user is assigned to the Essbase Admin. Power Users can create and maintain their own applications. Users are at the mercy of the Power Users (or Service Administrator) to grant them read, write, or calculate access to Essbase cubes through Application Level Roles.

Speaking of...the second set of roles are defined at the application level and are referred to as "Application Level Roles" (follow me on that one)? These options are: Application Manager, Database Manager, User Update, and User Access. The Application Manager is the application creator, or anyone he or she (or the Service Administrator) has assigned the Application Manager role. Database Manager can do similar tasks but only at the cube level. The User Update role is similar to giving a user "write" access and the User Access role is similar to giving a user "read" access (if you are unfamiliar with native Essbase terms, they will be discussed later in the filter section).

Like in on-premises Essbase, user and application level roles are hierarchical, and contain all of the powers of each of the levels beneath them.

### User Level Roles

First, let us discuss the different types of user roles for Essbase Cloud. There are three different kinds of users:

1) Service Administrators (Essbase Cloud)
2) Power Users
3) Users

Essbase Cloud Service Administrators (a.k.a. god-like supreme beings) have full access to all of the Essbase components and applications. In addition to administering users, they can create, modify, and delete any application or cube as they please. These folks also determine user roles, so be nice to them.

If the Service Administrator is Satan, Power Users are demons who run some of the circles of hell. Power Users can create and manage applications. Within these applications, they can assign user access privileges.

**Note!** When I said above "if the Administrator is Satan," that was what I in the literary biz call "an analogy." Despite what you may think, demons are probably not administering my applications.

Users (a.k.a. the Average Joes) simply have access to any applications or cubes to which they have been granted access. The User role is the minimum amount of user level security necessary to access a cube in Essbase Cloud. Unlike Power Users (and the god-like, supreme Service Administrators, of course), they cannot create their own applications and are at the mercy of others with superior roles to grant them access.

### Application Level Roles

Now let's discuss the type of roles that are assigned at the application level:

1) Application Manager
2) Database Manager
3) Database Update
4) Database Access

The Application Manager role is the god-like role specific to an assigned application. A user assigned the Application Manager role can create, delete, and modify the cubes within the given application. The Application Manager can also update the application settings and provision users to the application. The creator of the application is assigned the Application Manager role by default.

The Database Manager role allows a user to manage the assigned cube, its artifacts, locks, and sessions. Database Managers cannot assign application roles, but they can define and provision filters and calculations, as these are defined at the cube level.

Database Update access allows a user to view and update data values. This is also the lowest level of application security allowed to create and delete scenarios in scenario-based analysis (an Enterprise edition only feature). Database Update access is similar to assigning a user "write" access to the entire cube.

Database Access gives a user the ability to access scenarios and view the data, but not update any values. This is similar to assigning "read" access to the entire cube.

Security can be further defined using filters. Let's review database (cube) filters and filter access, because they're just cool.

### Essbase Filters

Essbase filters grant access to a slice of the cube (even down to the cell level) to an end user. Filters can grant four types of access to specific dimensions and members: None, Read, Write, or MetaRead. None, read, and write access rights are pretty straightforward and specify an end user's access to the data. Though it's mostly obvious, I'll explain anyways (can you guess who gets paid by the word?). Read access within a filter allows read-only access to data in specific cells of the cube. Write access allows writable access. None access removes access to data.

MetaRead is more complicated because it doesn't grant access to the data itself. MetaRead controls access to metadata so that an end user can view only part of the dimensionality. Setting filter access to metaread restricts the end user's view to specific members or sections of an Essbase outline hierarchy. This applies when users are viewing the dimensions through the member selection feature and other dimension-viewing features of the tool.

In the example below, the user has access only to the West Region. Because their filter is set to MetaRead on the West region in the

Market dimension, they can view only the West portion of the hierarchy within member selection:

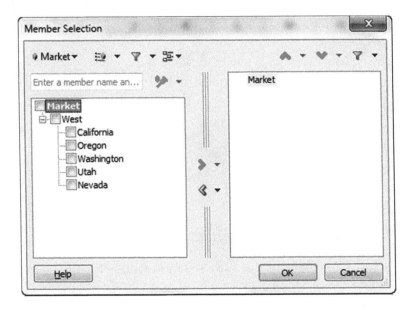

If the user had read access to the West region instead of metaread access, they would be able to view the entire Market hierarchy yet would still only have access to West region data. They would receive the message "#NoAccess" for markets outside the West region.

Once I switch the user's access from metaread to read, the user can see the full hierarchy:

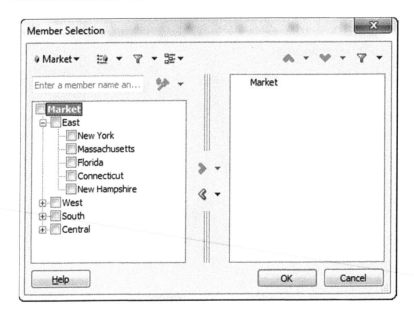

However, the user can only see data values for the descendants of West:

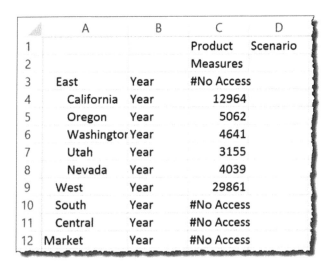

|    | A | B | C | D |
|----|----|----|----|----|
| 1 |  |  | Product | Scenario |
| 2 |  |  | Measures |  |
| 3 | East | Year | #No Access |  |
| 4 | California | Year | 12964 |  |
| 5 | Oregon | Year | 5062 |  |
| 6 | Washingtor | Year | 4641 |  |
| 7 | Utah | Year | 3155 |  |
| 8 | Nevada | Year | 4039 |  |
| 9 | West | Year | 29861 |  |
| 10 | South | Year | #No Access |  |
| 11 | Central | Year | #No Access |  |
| 12 | Market | Year | #No Access |  |

MetaRead security offers the following benefits:

- Improves the ease of use when users can only see a small number of the members

- Provides privacy so that users of sensitive applications (e.g., Payroll) can't see the existence or *non-existence* of specific members (like a company reorganization where a department may be eliminated)

### Create an Essbase Filter

Let's create the Essbase filter for the West group of users. This filter should only allow access to the West region of the Market dimension. I do not want the West users to be able to see the other members of the Market dimension. What type of filter access should be assigned? That's right – metaread.

To create an Essbase filter,

1. From the Essbase Cloud home page, select the application and cube where I am creating the filter, then select the *Security* card:

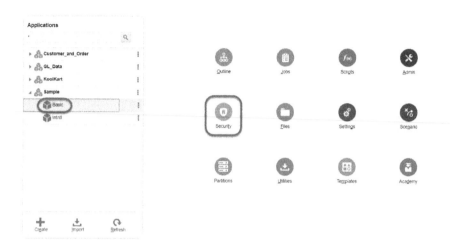

2. The screen defaults to the Filters 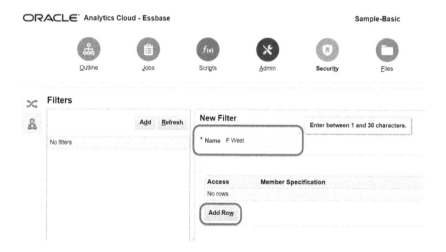 tab. Name the filter *F West*.

3. Click *Add Row*:

4.  In the new row under *Access*, select *MetaRead*:

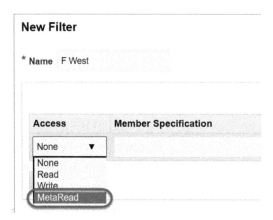

5.  Type *@DESCENDANTS ("West")* under *Member Specification*:

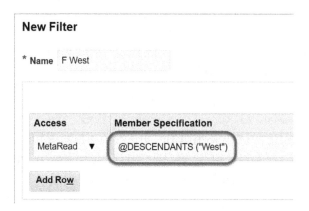

6.  Select the *Verify* button to validate the filter syntax:

7.  Click *OK* to close the Information (verification) message.

8. Select *Save*.

**Note!** Only Service Administrators, Power Users (for their applications), or any user granted an Application Manager or Database Manager role for the respective application can create cube filters.

In the above example, I used the @DESCENDANTS function, a Member Set function. This is a function that uses relationships to define what part of the dimension hierarchy to use. I can also define the filter using other methods, such as member combinations or substitution variables (indicated by a preceding ampersand sign, "&"). Multiple entries should be separated with a comma.

For more information on the various Member Set functions, please refer to the online *Technical Reference for Oracle Analytics Cloud - Essbase* guide.

I will choose descendants in this case because I want this filter to allow metaread access to West's descendants.

**Tip!** If I wanted to give access to both West *and* West's descendants, I would put the letter "I" right after the @ sign: "@IDESCENDANTS." "I" before the function name means the member specified is also included.

In our example, I only defined access to one dimension, but most companies need to define access on multiple dimensions. I could have also chosen to lock down Accounts, giving read access to Net Income accounts but not balance sheet accounts. I could have also granted write access to the Budget scenario and read access to Actual.

If a filter has overlapping member specifications, access is set by two rules. First, a filter that defines a more detailed dimension combination list takes precedence over a filter with less detail. Second, if the preceding rule does not resolve the overlap conflict, the highest access level among overlapping filter rows is applied.

### Inheritance Rules

As I discussed earlier, users can be assigned to groups, and security settings can be applied to groups. Users inherit all privileges granted to any groups to which they are assigned. Sometimes group security assignments may conflict with each other, though. How does Essbase handle conflicting security group and user assignments?

Let's use the following scenario to explain. The minimum access for the cube is Database Access, allowing the user to read data values for all levels unless supplementary restrictions are applied via a filter. The Budget group has write access to the Budget scenario and all regions via the filter F_Budget. Shaq is a member of the Budget group. Shaq is a user assigned with write access to the West Region. So here are the rules of inheritance:

If a user has more detailed access privileges than the default (via a filter), those assignments will take precedence. Shaq is a user with Database Access, so he has read access to the entire cube. However, he is a member of the Budget group which has a higher level of security – filter access to write to the Budget scenario. The Budget group's write access will take precedence over the default read access.

The Budget group has write access to all Regions, but Shaq only has write access to West. User access overrides group access, so Shaq's individual security takes precedence and he will be able to write only to the West region.

Now that I have the security basics, the next section has more information on security management.

### Access Essbase Cloud Security

All levels of Essbase Cloud security are accessed through the Security card on the Essbase home page. User Level Roles are accessed by selecting the Security card without a specific application or cube selected. Application Level Roles are accessed by selecting the appropriate application, then selecting the Security card.

To access User Level Roles,
1.  Log into the Essbase Cloud web interface.

2. Without specifying an application or cube, select the *Security* card:

The Users provisioning screen is displayed:

The left hand side of the screen contains the Users and Groups tabs (along with a Virus Scanner tab). The right hand side of the screen is used to create, import, or export users or groups.

**Note!**    Only the Essbase Cloud Service Administrator has full access to administer users and assign user level roles.

To access Application Level Roles,
1. Log into the Essbase Cloud instance.

2.  Select an application and then select the *Security* card:

The Application Role provisioning screen is displayed:

The left side of the screen is used to search for a user or group. The right hand side of the screen is used to provision the selected user or group.

**Note!**

Only Service Administrators, Power Users (for their applications), or any user granted an Application Manager role for the respective application can provision application level roles.

In SaaS applications like PBCS, when a user is provisioned, they receive an email with login information. This is not true for OAC. Users do not get notified of it automatically. It is the responsibility of the Administrator to notify the user of their credentials and URL to log into OAC.

### Create a Group and Assign Role Security

In general, I want to use group security assignments as much as possible. Groups reduce the overall maintenance for security. I define security once and, as users come and go, they can be added to and removed from groups. If security requirements change, I update the group security once instead of having to do it many times for individual users.

I'll walk through an example. End users of the Sample.Basic application will only have access to their market. I will create a native group for the West market.

1. Log into Essbase Cloud web interface.
2. From the home page (without selecting an application or cube), select *Security*.
3. On the left hand side of the screen, select the Groups tab:

4. On the right hand side of the screen, select *Create*:

**Tip!**

This is also where I could Import/Export groups with a .csv format. To generate a template of the .csv layout, create a group manually and export a file. Once exported, I can manipulate the file (adding in the new groups and appropriate properties) and import several groups at once. Shortcut!

5. Type in the group name and description.
6. Select the *User* role for the group:

7. Click Create. There should be a notification that the group was created successfully:

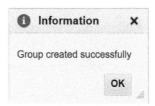

8.  To assign a group to another parent group, under the Groups
    tab 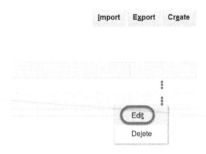, select the group you want to assign to a parent
    group, then the Actions ⋮ icon to the right of the group. Select
    *Edit*:

9.  Within the Edit Group screen, select the *Parent Groups* tab,
    select the appropriate parent group under the *Available*
    section, and move it to the *Selected* section. Click *Submit*:

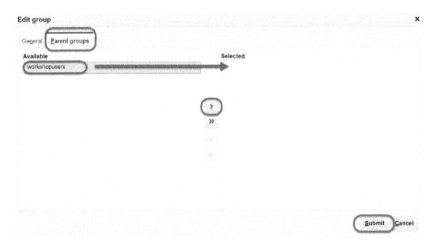

10. To assign a user to a group, under the Users tab 👤 , select the user you want to assign to a group. Click the Actions ⋮ icon to the right of the user and select *Edit*:

11. Within the Edit User screen, click the *Groups* tab. Select the appropriate group under the *Available* section and move it to the *Selected* section. Click *Submit*:

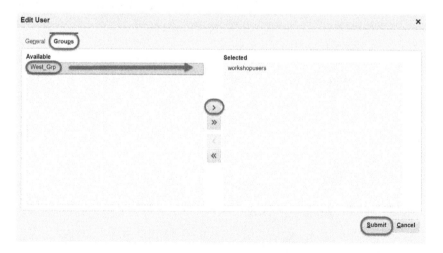

### Create a User and Assign Role Security

Shaquille O'Neal has decided to give up his lucrative endorsements for The General Car Insurance® and pursue a career in business performance management (go with me on this one; it could happen). This is good news for us, because the wildly successful Beverage Company business has recruited Shaq to be the manager for the West region. Let's create a new user, 'Shaq,' and assign him to the West Region group.

1. From the Essbase Cloud home page (without selecting an application or cube), select *Security*.
2. The screen defaults to the Users tab. On the right hand side of the screen, select *Create*:

**Note!**     This is where I can Import/Export users.

3. Type in the user ID, name, email, and password. Select the *User* role.
4. Click *Create*:

5.  A message will pop up that the user was created successfully. Click *OK*:

6.  Add Shaq to the West group by following steps in the previous section, "Create a Group."

**Note!**  Use the *Action* icon ⋮ on the right hand side of the screen to edit or delete users or groups in role security.

### Provision Users and Groups to Application Security

So far I've created users and groups and assigned user roles, but I haven't assigned any application roles. Next, I'll go through the steps to provision a user at the cube level.

**Note!**  The steps to provision a user and group are the same. If I need to provision a group, follow the steps provided below but first select *Group* in the List drop-down.

To provision a user to a cube,
1.  From the Essbase Cloud home page, select the application in which the application role will be assigned.
2.  Then select the *Security* icon.

3. From the Provisioning screen, type "Shaq" into the search field and click the *Search* button:

4. Select *Shaq*, then under the *Provision* drop-down menu on the right hand side of the screen select *Roles*:

5. In the Provision Roles selection box, select the appropriate role under *Available Roles* and move it to the right under *Selected Roles*:

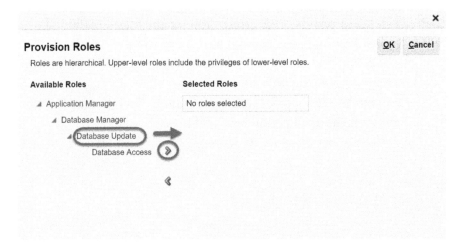

6.  Select *OK*:

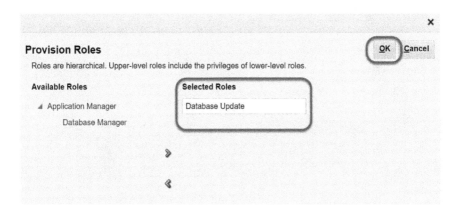

**Note!**

Notice that only Database Update is displayed under selected roles (Database Access does not display). This is because the roles have a hierarchical structure, and a role will automatically have all the access of any roles beneath it. In this example, Shaq, by default, receives Database Access with his Database Update provisioning.

If I want to assign filter or calculation access, I still need to assign the filter and/or calculations.

To assign a filter to a user,
7.  Select the user you want to provision, then select *Filters* from the *Provision* drop-down menu on the right hand side of the screen:

8.  In the Provision Filters selection box, select the cube to provision against.

9. Select the appropriate filter under *Available* and move it to the right under *Selected*:

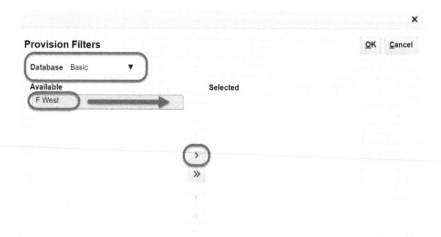

10. Select *OK*.

To assign calculation access to a user,

11. Select the user you want to provision, then select *Scripts* from the Provision menu on the right hand side of the screen:

12. In the Provision Scripts selection box, select the Cube and the appropriate script on the left hand *Available* side and move it to the right under *Selected*:

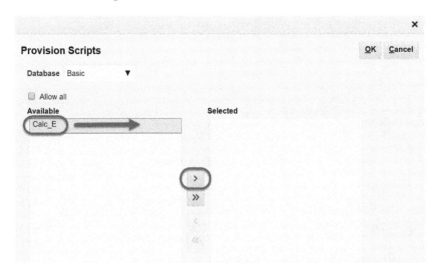

13. Select *OK*.

**Note!**
The user or group must have a minimum application level role of Database Update in order to be granted the ability to run a calculation script. Users with Application Manager or Database Manager roles have access to all of the calculations in their assigned cube by default.

In some cases I may need to remove a user's or group's application access. I can remove user or group application access, including roles, filters, and scripts by accessing Application level security (described above), selecting the appropriate user or group, and then selecting *Deprovision All*.

The Deprovision All box will display:

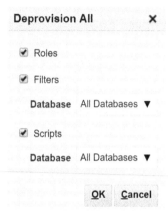

To deprovision the user or group, select the appropriate options for the type of object you would like to deprovision and click *OK*.

### Running Security Reports

I can run predefined reports to understand role assignments for users.

To run a security report,

1. From the Essbase Cloud home page, select the application for which the report should be run, and then select the *Security* icon:

2.  Leave the default List selection as *User*. Type name of the user you are searching for in the search field and click *Search*:

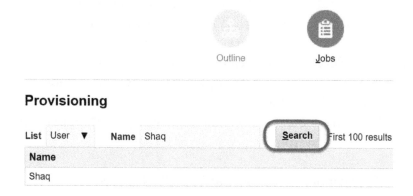

3.  Select the user (or multiple users by holding Ctrl and selecting more than one) for which you want to run a provision report and select *Provision Report*:

4.  The Provision Report is displayed, and you have the ability to see details for Roles, Filters, and Scripts:

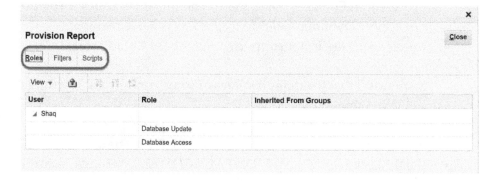

# LCM UTILITY

### LCM Utility Overview

The Essbase LCM (Life Cycle Management) Utility provides a method of migrating artifacts from on-premises Essbase to an Essbase Cloud instance or migrating artifacts between Essbase Cloud service instances. The LCM utility is executed from the command line on a local computer or Server. LCM creates a .zip file of all of the artifacts that belong to an Essbase cube. I can optionally choose to include cube data as part of the LCM.zip file.

There are some items to consider when preparing to move an Essbase application from on-premises to the Cloud:

- Applications and associated artifacts must be converted to Unicode mode before you export
- Application level artifacts are recommended to be converted to cube level artifacts before running the LCM export. The Essbase Cloud web interface only provides access to these artifacts at a cube level (not an application level). These artifacts include the following:
  - o  Calculation scripts (.csc)
  - o  Rule files (.rul)
  - o  Text files (.txt)
- Additionally, substitution variables must be at the application or cube level. Global level variables are not supported.
- Hybrid Aggregation Mode is the default calculation and query processor in Essbase Cloud; there is no impact to cubes if you do not apply "Dynamic Calc" to upper level sparse members
- Implied sharing is not supported in Essbase Cloud

Be mindful that the default values of some configuration settings change when moving to the Cloud:

- IGNORECONSTANTS is now set to TRUE by default
- INDEXCACHESIZE and DATACACHESIZE settings control cache sizes for cubes on the Cloud service (except ASO cubes)

- GRIDSUPPRESSINVALID is now set to TRUE by default
- QRYGOVEXECTIME is now set to 300 seconds

**Note!** Important documentation note: "Oracle strongly recommends managing all configuration settings at the application level. Application-level configuration is preserved during the LCM utility export and import processes."

There are a few rules about partitions and migrating them to the Cloud. Transparent and replicated partitions are the only types of partitions that are migrated using LCM (though replicated partitions must be created and maintained using MaxL for now; the Essbase Cloud web interface does not support replicated partitions yet). Linked partitions are not supported. Source partitions should be migrated prior to the migration of the target partitions. Migrating a target partition prior to migrating a source partition will cause the partition to break. This can be remedied by using MaxL to recreate the partition. If the credentials are different on the Cloud versus on-premises, I will need to edit the partition information in the .zip file.

To edit the partition information in the .zip file,
1. Unzip the .zip file so it can be edited.
2. Open the application/cube folder.
3. Edit the partition file (user, password, host).
4. The password field in the partitions file is encrypted. Search for the string "{enc}." Replace both the password and the string "{enc}" with the new password.

**Create LCM of On-Premises Cube**

The export is quite simple but requires some setup.

To set up the LCM export,
1. Navigate to the Essbase Cloud web interface.

2.  Click on *Utilities*:

3.  Download the *Life Cycle Management* (LCM) utility:

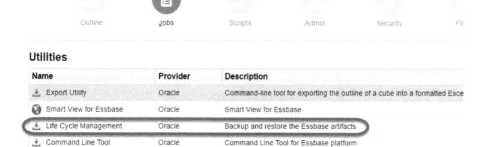

4. Unzip the file to a location on the server or the local machine:

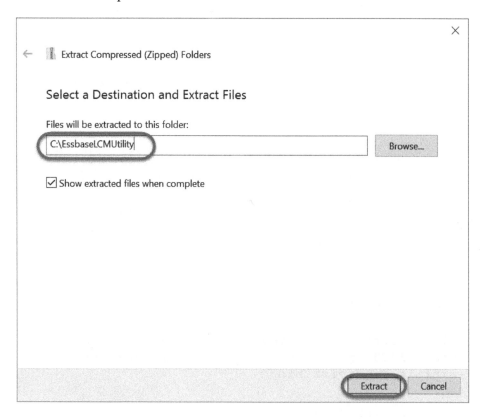

Two scripts are provided: EssbaseLCM.bat for Windows machines and EssbaseLCM.sh for Linux machines. Use the script that is appropriate for the on-premises Essbase operating system. I need to know several parameters for running the LCM utility:

- -server (Essbase Host:Port)
- -user
- -password (optional)
- -application
- -zipfile (path and name of zip file)
- -nodata (optional)

The –password parameter is optional. Omitting the password parameter will cause a prompt for the password.

The –nodata parameter should be used if I do not want LCM to export data. If the –nodata parameter is omitted, then the cube's data will be exported.

**Note!**    You must have at least JAVA 8 installed on your client to use the LCM Utility.

Here is an example of the command line entry in Windows to export an on-premises application called "Vision":

```
C:\EssbaseLCM\EssbaseLCM.bat export -server
myhost:1423 -password mypassword -application Vision
-zipfile C:\Vision.zip
```

If running the command from a batch file, the LCM the syntax would look more like:

```
CALL C:\EssbaseLCM\EssbaseLCM.bat export -server
myhost:1423 -password mypassword -application Vision
-zipfile C:\Vision.zip
```

To execute the LCM export,
5.  Open a command window.
6.  Navigate to the location that the zip file was extracted to:

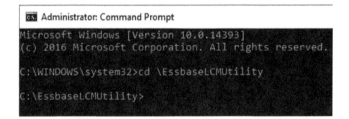

7.  Type in the appropriate command to execute the LCM utility:

```
Administrator: Command Prompt
Exporting /Vision/Databases/Plan2/Calc scripts/Default Calc...Success
Exporting /Vision/Databases/Plan2/Plan2 outline...Success
Exporting /Vision/Databases/Plan2/Location Aliases/_BsCube_...Success
Exporting /Vision/Databases/Plan2/Location Aliases/_RevCube_...Success
Exporting /Vision/Databases/Plan3/Data...Success
Exporting /Vision/Databases/Plan3/Database Properties...Success
Exporting /Vision/Databases/Plan3/Calc scripts/Default Calc...Success
Exporting /Vision/Databases/Plan3/Plan3 outline...Success
Exporting /Vision/Databases/Plan3/Location Aliases/_PnlCube_...Success
Exporting /Vision/Databases/Plan3/Location Aliases/_RevCube_...Success
Adding directory [Vision] to [C:\Vision.zip]
Export Complete: Application [Vision] exported to [C:\Vision.zip]

C:\EssbaseLCMUtility>
```

The .zip file is now ready to be used to create and/or update the Essbase application in the Cloud. I could then import the zip file into the OAC Cloud service instance using the LCM Utility and the **IMPORT** command.

I can also import the zip file using the Command Line Interface for Essbase Cloud. Let's learn about that option now!

## COMMAND LINE INTERFACE

The Command Line Interface (CLI) can be used to migrate the LCM .zip file to Essbase Cloud. The CLI can be executed from a command line or can be called from a .bat or .sh file. In order to execute commands from the interface, a download from Cloud is required.

To prepare for and download the CLI,

1. If it's not already installed, install JDK 1.8 to the computer/server that will run the CLI. (Google "jdk 1.8 download" and be sure to download it only from the "Java SE Development Kit 8 - Downloads - Oracle" website.) If possible, use the default install location.

2. Create/set the JAVA_HOME environment variable. This can be accomplished from a command window. Point the variable to the folder where JDK 1.8 is installed. For example:

**SET JAVA_HOME=C:\Program Files\Java\jdk1.8.0_nn**
(where "nn" refers to the specific version installed)

**Note!**    To check the value of an environment variable from a command line, use the syntax **SET VariableName** and the value will appear, as shown in the above screenshot.

3.  Navigate to the Essbase Cloud web interface.
4.  Click on *Utilities*:

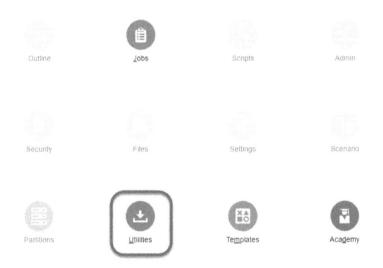

5.  Download the *Command Line Tool:*

ORACLE° Analytics Cloud - Essbase

| Outline | Jobs | Scripts | Admin | Security | Files |

### Utilities

| Name | Provider | Description |
|---|---|---|
| Export Utility | Oracle | Command-line tool for exporting the outline of a cube into a formatted Excel wo |
| Smart View for Essbase | Oracle | Smart View for Essbase |
| Life Cycle Management | Oracle | Backup and restore the Essbase artifacts |
| Command Line Tool | Oracle | Command Line Tool for Essbase platform |

6.  Unzip the file to a location on the computer/server. For example: C:\CLI.

There are several tasks that the CLI can help Administrators accomplish, such as loading data, running calculation scripts, uploading and downloading files from Cloud, and importing and exporting LCM zip files. The CLI gives Administrators a great tool for moving Essbase applications around. This utility also supports a hybrid deployment of on-premises and Essbase Cloud applications.

First, I'll import the on-premises application named Vision that I created earlier to Essbase Cloud.

7.  Open a command window and navigate to the CLI folder:

```
Administrator: Command Prompt

Microsoft Windows [Version 10.0.14393]
(c) 2016 Microsoft Corporation. All rights reserved.

C:\WINDOWS\system32>cd CLI
The system cannot find the path specified.

C:\WINDOWS\system32>cd C:\CLI

C:\cli>
```

8.  Type in the following command, substituting the appropriate credentials and server:

**esscs login –user mark –password WatneyRules2017 – url http://host:port/essbase**

If a secured connection is required, the –url parameter would look something like https://host:securedport. As mentioned before, if the –password parameter is missing, the system will prompt for it.

**Note!**

I must log in to be able to execute commands with CLI, and each command must start with "esscs".

9.  Execute the following command: **esscs LcmImport – zipFileName C:\Vision.zip** (where c:\Vision.zip is the location of your zip file).

```
Administrator: Command Prompt

C:\cli>esscs lcmimport -zipFileName C:\Vision.zip
File "C:\Vision.zip" Uploaded
.........................Status: 200
Details: Completed

C:\cli>
```

The LCM import to the Cloud has been completed:

There are several commands that can be run using the CLI. The list of available commands and syntax includes:

- **Login** - logs into the system:

```
login -user username -password password -url
http://host:port/essbase
```

- **Calc** - executes a calc script:

```
calc -application appname -db cubename -script
scriptfilename
```

- **Dataload** - loads data to a cube:

  ```
  dataload -application appname -db cubename -file
  filename -abortOnError true|false
  ```

- **Dimbuild** - loads a dimension to a cube:

  ```
  dimbuild -application appname -db cubename -rule
  rulesfilename        -file        datafilename        -
  restructureOption optionKeyword
  ```

- **Clear** - clears data and the outline:

  ```
  clear -application appname -db cubename -option
  ALL_DATA
  ```

- **Version** - get the current Essbase version:

  ```
  Version
  ```

- **Listfiles** - lists calculation scripts, text files, rules files, and other artifacts:

  ```
  listfiles -application appname -db cubename -
  type filetype
  ```

- **Download** - downloads artifacts from an Essbase cube:

  ```
  download -application appname -db cubename -file
  filename  -localDirectory  path   -   overwrite
  true|false
  ```

- **Upload** - uploads artifacts to the Cloud:

  ```
  upload -application appname -db cubename -file
  filename
  ```

- **LcmExport** - performs LCM export:

```
lcmExport    -application    appname    -skipdata
true|false        -zipfilename        filename        -
localDirectory path -overwrite true|false
```

- **LcmImport** - performs LCM import:

```
lcmImport    -zipfilename    filename    -overwrite
true|false
```

**Note!** Since OAC is installed on Linux, commands and file names can be case sensitive so beware.

In addition to running EssCLI from a command window, it can be run from a bat file:

```
login -user c          -password         -url http://          :9000/essbase  >output.txt
upload -application Glenn_Test -db Analysis -file C:\clientfiles\DSC\data\Cst_Stat.rul -overwrite tru
upload -application Glenn_Test -db Analysis -file C:\clientfiles\DSC\data\restof2016\extracted\custom
dataload  -application Glenn_Test -db Analysis -rule Cst_Stat.rul -file customer_status_r2106.txt -ab
calc -application Glenn_Test -db Analysis -script Calc_Avg_Subscribers.csc >>output.txt
logout  >>output.txt
```

# DBXTOOL

The DBXTool offers a command line interface to create metadata and data from an Essbase cube regardless if it's on-premises or in Cloud. The DBXTool export creates an Excel Application Workbook with all of the information about the cube, such as application name, database (cube) name, dimensions, hierarchies, and dimension members. Once created, I can use this Application Workbook to create a cube in Essbase Cloud.

**Note!** The LCM Utility and DBXTool support on-premises Essbase 11.1.2.3.500 and higher versions. While it may work on earlier versions, it is not officially supported.

To use the DBXTool,

1. Make sure that you have JRE 1.8 or later installed.

2. Log into the Essbase Cloud web interface and navigate to *Utilities*:

3. Download the *Export Utility*:

**Utilities**

| Name | Provider | Description |
|------|----------|-------------|
| Export Utility | Oracle | Command-line tool for exporting the outline of a cube into a formatted Excel workbook |
| Smart View for Essbase | Oracle | Smart View for Essbase |
| Life Cycle Management | Oracle | Backup and restore the Essbase artifacts |
| Command Line Tool | Oracle | Command Line Tool for Essbase platform |

4.  Extract the downloaded zip file to a local drive. For example, extract to: C:\dbxtool.

5.  Run the export utility (export.bat for Windows or export.sh for Linux) from the dbxtool\bin directory.

**Note!** If you wish to include the DBXTOOL in a batch script use the *CALL* command in Windows or *cams /c* in Linuxin Linux use the *cams /c* option.

The available parameters to include when running the DBXTool utility (export.bat or export.sh) are:

- –server (Cloud instance or on-premises instance)
- –application (app name)
- –cube (cube name)
- –user
- –password (optional – you will be prompted for a password if omitted)
- –path (full path to the folder to which the application workbook file should be exported; if the file already exists, you will be asked if you want to overwrite the existing file or not)
- –build (build method: PARENT-CHILD or GENERATION)
- –data (use only if you want to export input data from the cube to a separate file; data will not be exported if omitted)

6.  At the command prompt, run the following code using the appropriate credentials and server name:

```
C:\dbxtool\bin\export -server myserver:server port -
application Vision -cube Plan1 -user myusername -
password mypassword -path C:\ExportDirectory -build
PARENT-CHILD -data
```

**Note!**

Before importing the application workbook, carefully examine member names for compatibility with Essbase Cloud. For example, if a member name contains the backslash (\) character, the member name would need to be changed (because backslashes are interpreted as escape characters in Cloud and are not allowed).

7. After the export command is executed, a summary will show:

```
Administrator: Command Prompt
INFO: Exporting outline to "C:\Vision_Plan1_1492695734351.xlsx";
Apr 20, 2017 9:42:27 AM oracle.essbase.platform.util.PlatformLogger info
INFO: Outline exported at "C:\Vision_Plan1_1492695734351.xlsx";
Essbase application exported to file : Vision_Plan1.xlsx
Exporting Data...
Essbase Cube Data exported to file : Plan1.zip
Time Taken for execution: 34 secs

C:\dbxtool\bin>
```

Once the Application Workbook is created, it can be edited. Member names can be added, changed, or deleted, and settings like Dense/Sparse can also be modified.

As I learned in the previous missions, the Application Workbook is laid out with worksheets for the cube definition. The information within any worksheet can be edited prior to importing into Essbase Cloud:

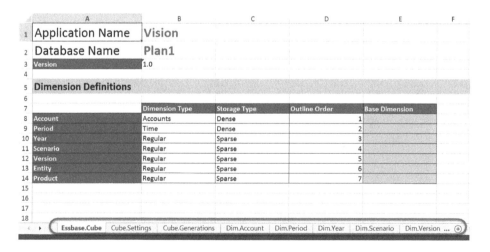

To import the Vision application workbook into the Cloud,

8. Log into Essbase Cloud.

9. In the Applications pane, select *Import*:

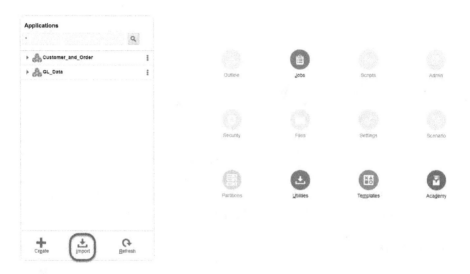

10. Click *Choose File* and Browse to the application workbook file:

11. Click the drop-down next to *Build Option*.

12. From this box choose preferences for how the build should behave. For instance, since there is no cube, select *Create Cube*.

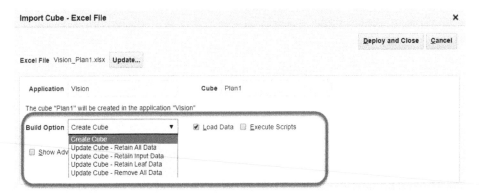

13. Leave the *Load Data* option checked to load exported data.
14. Finally, click *Deploy and Close*:

15. When the build is complete, confirm that the Vision application has been created:

And that concludes the DBXTool topic!

---

**COMMUNICATION: ROSKE TO GIDEON**

[9:05] ROSKE: Gideon, how ya been? Now that I'm in a "dire situation," I don't have to follow social rules anymore. I can be honest with everyone.

You know how I've been playing Werewolf for years? I've started hundreds of others playing this game at conferences like Kscope and i.n.t.e.r.R.e.l. events.

I hate it. It is the most boring game ever. But once I became known as "the Werewolf guy," there was nothing I could do to stop it. If I have to be the moderator one more time… That is the only bonus to being stranded in the Cloud - no one to ask me to play Werewolf.

---

**COMMUNICATION: GIDEON TO ROSKE**

[10:12] GIDEON: Wow, this is like that movie Citizen Kane where you later find out that Rosebud is a sled. Gosh, I sure hope you've already seen Citizen Kane. #SpoilerAlert. You sure fooled me with those

Ultimate Werewolf pajamas and vampire sheet set in
your bunk.
    I'll tell you a good story to cheer you up.
Remember that time when we were playing a video game
at the office? That was fun. If I remember right, you
had to leave suddenly after I started beating you. I
do have to confess though, I actually won an intramural
championship in college playing that game. Feel
better? I sure do. Good times.

# SERVER ACCESS

Even though Oracle is providing all of the servers, I still can
access the "server" in a few different ways. An Administrator can remote
onto the server using a remote desktop protocol like "Putty." Indirect
server access can be handled through SFTP, SSH, and the Essbase Cloud
web interface. Now let's be honest here – this section has the potential to
get really technical. I'll do my best to highlight the important stuff
without getting too much into the weeds and confusing those of you
who are not network security experts.

To start, SFTP and SSH are accessed through My Services.

### Managing SSH Access

From within My Services, an Administrator can view and
manage all SSH keys by navigating to the SSH Access tab. SSH keys are
generated at the time of provisioning and can be used to access the OAC
file system:

What is an SSH key? SSH stands for "secure shell" and is a protocol for accessing a network securely through Public Cloud. SSH authenticates through a private-public key pairing. A public key is placed on any computer needing access to a system, and the public key must match the private host key. Then password authentication is used to finish off the login process.

Keys can be created through My Services, which can then be used to securely log into OAC components directly – in the case of SSH, to access the file system. Both private and public keys can be managed. Access rules can also be designed and applied so that security can be even more restricted.

**Note!**
Important documentation note: "Modifications that you make to the Oracle file system might not be saved after you perform routine lifecycle operations, such as patching, and might even prevent you from performing lifecycle operations."

Administration scripts can also be run via the SSH client software, which is UNIX-based. Only the Oracle Analytics Cloud Administrator can run the SSH client software and administration scripts.

Once the SSH access keys have been created and properly set up, they can be used to access the server. Multiple SSH key pairs can be created. For example, if I need Oracle to look at something on my OAC service instance, I can generate a key pair for them and then revoke it when they are done.

### Managing SFTP Access

For SFTP (Secure File Transfer Protocol), the host & port (URL) and system-generated username are available for both the domain and service. I need to access My Services to gather this information for use.

SFTP allows users to securely transfer (or "FTP") large files directly to the Essbase Cloud instance instead of going direct through the web interface. Notice how I could use FTP as a verb here – it's funny how nouns turn into verbs over time, like "to google." FTP is a network protocol for transferring files and has been around for ages. In more recent years, FTP has been used to transfer files too large to upload through web interfaces.

### Server Access through the Web Interface

The final way that users can access the server is indirectly through the Essbase Cloud web interface. From here, users can manage system files.

**Note!** The only file types that can be uploaded are: .txt, .rul, .msh, and .xml.

To manage files,
1. Log in and navigate to the Essbase Cloud home page.
2. Highlight an Essbase Cloud cube.
3. Click the *Files* icon:

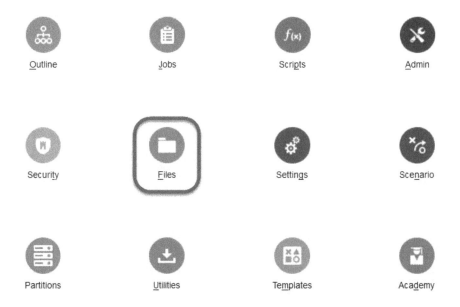

4. A listing of files already uploaded/created on the Essbase Cloud server displays:

5. The files are sorted by file type. Select the down arrow to the right of the *Modified Time* column to download a particular file:

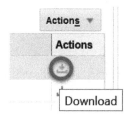

6. Highlight a single file and click the *Actions* button, which shows commands to refresh the file list or delete the highlighted file:

7. Files can be uploaded to the server by using the *Upload Files* pane on the right side of the screen:

8. Click *Browse* to select a local system file:

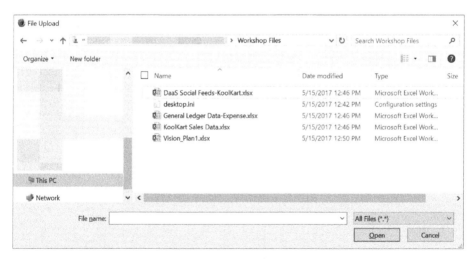

9. Click *Upload* to upload the selected file. A message will appear once the file is successfully uploaded:

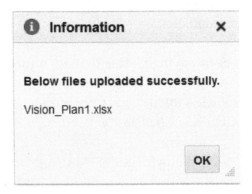

A variety of important files can be found here. System generated files include:

- Essbase outline files
- Dimension rules files
- Data load rules files
- Error files (from dimension and data loads, for example)
- Text files (data files, cube structure files, data structure files, etc.)
- XML files (such as those built from Cube Designer)


# MAXL

Hello, old friend! I didn't think you were going to make it into OAC, and yet here you are. (I am so happy!)

I've learned pretty much all of the tasks involved in building and maintaining Essbase cubes through the many interfaces in Essbase Cloud. However, I certainly don't want to perform all of these tasks manually every day. Essbase Cloud has a scripting alternative to automate almost any task. Our friend, MaxL is the scripting language for both on-premises Essbase and Essbase Cloud, so this should be familiar to anyone who's used MaxL in the on-premises world.

Some of the common actions that MaxL can handle include:

- Loading data to a cube
- Building a dimension
- Running calculation scripts
- Viewing cube statistics

**Note!**
If you've been paying close attention, it might seem like the CLI and MaxL overlap in functionality. That's because they do. Oracle's intention is to eventually replace MaxL with the CLI once it has parity.

Having a good knowledge of MaxL is essential to being administratively efficient with Essbase Cloud. In addition to daily cube updates and administration, developers can also automate repetitive tasks in order to speed up testing cycles, a trick that can save much stress when under tight deadlines.

MaxL is also required in some instances when the Essbase Cloud web interface does not support a feature (yet). Examples include materializing aggregations on ASO cubes, building dimensions from outline files in a single pass, using buffers for ASO loads, and creating replicated partitions.

MaxL is invoked in a very special way in Essbase Cloud: from the CLI via a MaxL file that has been uploaded to the appropriate Essbase Cloud cube under Files.

**Note!**
Only a Service Administrator can invoke and run MaxL commands.

**Note!**
Due to the strict protocols of Public Cloud, only certain file types are allowed to be uploaded and generated in Essbase Cloud. MaxL scripts should use files with extension ".msh".

This invocation method uses the essmsh (*ESS*base *MaxL SH*ell) executable behind the scenes. At that time that this book was authored, there was no visual editor for MaxL available to Essbase Cloud yet.

Important considerations for running MaxL in Essbase Cloud:

1) The Administrator can log into the server and create a shell script to run MaxL and schedule it through a CRON (a time-based Unix scheduler program) job, or run it from EssCLI or from the Job Console.
2) The Administrator can also leverage .msh scripting files that have already been uploaded. The Administrator can use a command window to run MaxL scripted files on-demand.
3) The Service Administrator must know how to properly write MaxL on their own since there is no visual editor. The online documentation is a great starting point!
4) The Service Administrator must have the CLI installed on the computer that they're using to invoke MaxL (refer to the "Command Line Interface" section earlier in this chapter for more on how to get this utility installed). The CLI may be installed to their local laptop/desktop or on a management server.

Let's learn some of the basics of MaxL before I invoke it.

### Basic MaxL Syntax Rules

Essbase Cloud runs on Linux boxes, therefore, case sensitivity and special characters may come into play at times with the CLI and MaxL. In addition, these are two different languages so they have different rules. Some important restrictions:

- Script files can only contain ASCII text
- Every MaxL command must be terminated with a semicolon
- CLI commands do not need a terminating character and should not be terminated with any character
- MaxL and CLI commands are not case sensitive
- All CLI parameters (those preceded with a dash; also, these are different from commands as they are the parameters that are required by commands) must be lowercase
- All passwords are case sensitive

- I do not need to log into MaxL separately – the CLI login passes through
- Artifact names (apps, dbs, calculation scripts, etc.) should match their original case, meaning, how they were initially created. (This is actually not true for MaxL and app/db names only, but let's keep things consistent, yo!)
- Remember, only a Service Administrator can invoke MaxL

Other than that, I can insert tabs, spaces, and new lines as I see fit to make the code easier to read.

**Tip!**

Putting CLI and MaxL commands in all uppercase will make it much easier to identify which words are variables and which are CLI/MaxL commands.

### Output Comments

In order to output text to the "maxl_out" file (this is a log file generated automatically by the system), in MaxL I would use the **ECHO** command. This is similar to the **ECHO** command used in MS-DOS.

There is an important difference between single and double quotes in MaxL, especially when using the **ECHO** command. Single quotes tell the engine to translate the text they enclose literally, while double quotes allow for variable translation. Consider the case where I want to output the system environment variable JAVA_HOME. Here are two different MaxL statements that attempt to do this:

```
ECHO 'JAVA_HOME is $JAVA_HOME';

ECHO "JAVA_HOME is $JAVA_HOME";
```

The first statement with single quotes will output literally **JAVA_HOME is $JAVA_HOME**, while the second will evaluate the variable first and output the desired result of **JAVA_HOME.** Note that the Essbase Cloud server variable value will be read and output, not the one on the local machine since this script is being run on the server via MaxL: `/usr/java/jdk1.8.0_60`.

If I want to output a single quote, I need to enclose the entire statement in double quotes:

```
ECHO "Is Matt Damon's performance in The Martian
Oscar-worthy?";
```

### Log into MaxL

Logging into MaxL is unnecessary in Essbase Cloud. Since MaxL is used with the CLI, logging into the CLI is all that is necessary. The login credentials pass through.

### Redirect Output

Redirecting output is not necessary with Essbase Cloud. With every MaxL script that's run, a corresponding maxl_out.txt file is generated. This file captures the output of what ran in the MaxL script.

### Use Variables with MaxL

There are three types of variables that I can use inside my MaxL scripts:

1) Environment variables from the local operating system. If I want to reference a variable set in the operating system shell, I can reference it directly by name, prefixed with a dollar sign (e.g., $JAVA_HOME)

2) Positional variables passed in on the command line. I can also add parameters that will be translated to variables inside the script. For example, consider the script myscript.mxl that contains these commands (note that $3, $2, and $1 are variables):

```
ECHO "The third variable is $3.";
ECHO "The second variable is $2.";
ECHO "The first variable is $1.";
```

When I execute this script the output will be:

```
The third variable is thirty.
The second variable is twenty.
The first variable is ten.
```

3) Temporary variables that I set inside the MaxL script. I may also want to set variables inside my MaxL scripts. To do this, use the following syntax:

```
SET myvariable = 'ten';
ECHO $myvariable;
```

### MaxL Actions

It can be overwhelming for first-time users to look at the large list of MaxL commands. However, it seems much simpler when I understand that there are only ten core actions.

The following list summarizes what each of these core actions does.

- **Alter** - changes the state of an object
- **Create** - creates a new object
- **Display** - shows information about an object
- **Drop** - deletes a object
- **Execute** - runs a calculation or aggregation process
- **Export** - outputs data or linked reporting objects (LRO's)
- **Grant** - assigns security to users or groups
- **Import** - loads data, dimensions, or LRO's
- **Query** - gets information about an application or cube
- **Refresh** - reloads partitioning information or custom Java function definitions

The following sections illustrate some of the most frequently used MaxL actions and provide commentary on the nuances of the syntax.

**Note!** The maximum size of a MaxL statement is 81,920 characters or bytes. Um, yeah…kudos to anyone who writes a MaxL statement that long.

### Update a Dimension from a Text File

It is possible to update dimensions from text files. The following statement will import dimensions from a text file named Dim_Measures using the rules file named Measures. Both files have already been built in Essbase Cloud. Remember that most dimension files and rules files are system-generated, usually when the Cube Designer or Import process has occurred. Dimension files and rules files can also be migrated from on-premises or other Essbase Cloud cubes. However, if Administrators prefer to update dimensions through the flat file format, this is a good trick to help do that.

```
IMPORT DATABASE KoolKart.Sales DIMENSIONS
 FROM SERVER TEXT DATA_FILE Dim_Measures.txt USING
SERVER RULES_FILE Measures.rul
 ON ERROR WRITE TO
'/esscloud/oracle/12esscs/data/app/KoolKart/Sales/Up
dateDim-Measures_err.txt';
```

Note that the error file is being written to a common Essbase Cloud directory, but the filename contains both the cube name and the dimension being built for easy reference.

**Note!** Due to the strict protocols of Public Cloud, only certain file types are allowed to be uploaded and created in Essbase Cloud. When specifying custom error files, use a file extension of ".txt" or else your file will not be created during processing.

### Run a Calc Script

Of course, MaxL can run a calc script that I've already saved (in this example, the calc script named *Default* is executed).

```
EXECUTE CALCULATION KoolKart.Sales.Default;
```

A nice capability that's often overlooked is the ability to send custom calc commands directly from MaxL, which is incredibly useful when I want to test different settings or commands using variable substitution.

```
EXECUTE CALCULATION
  "SET UPDATECALC OFF;
   CALC ALL;"
ON KoolKart.Sales;
```

### Error Handling

Error handling in MaxL is a two-stage process. The first stage involves redirecting the script after the error occurs so that no more statements are executed. In this example, I am testing for a successful run of a calculation script. If the login fails, I divert the MaxL script immediately to the "calc_error" error handling section.

```
ALTER SYSTEM LOAD APPLICATION KoolKart;
EXECUTE CALCULATION KoolKart.Sales.Default;
IFERROR 'calc_error';
EXIT 0;

DEFINE LABEL 'calc_error;
EXIT 1;
```

The second stage takes place in the operating system command-line environment that runs the .msh script behind the scenes. The script will return a 0 (zero) if everything was successful, but will return a non-zero number if an error was encountered.

### Invoking MaxL

Finally! Now it's time to put this awesome information into action! Let's invoke MaxL.

To log into MaxL through the Essbase Cloud CLI,

1. Open a command window from your local laptop/desktop/management server. Navigate to where the CLI has been installed:

2. Ensure that the JAVA_HOME variable is set based on the installed version of the JDK in the environment (note: set this to the version of JDK installed to your environment – the following displays mine):

The command window is now set up to run a MaxL script. I'll switch back over to that in a second. First, I'm going to pause and create a simple calc script in Scripts. Then I'll create the MaxL script and upload it to Essbase Cloud.

3. Navigate to Essbase Cloud >> *KoolKart* >> *Sales* >> *Scripts* and create a dummy calc script called "CALCALL." Insert only one line into it: **CALC ALL;** and then save and close it.

4.  Use one of the simple MaxL examples mentioned earlier to create the new MaxL script. I'll pick one that can execute the new calc script:

```
1  ALTER SYSTEM LOAD APPLICATION KoolKart;
2  EXECUTE CALCULATION KoolKart.Sales.CALCALL;
3  IFERROR 'calc_error';
4  EXIT 0;
5
6  DEFINE LABEL 'calc_error;
7  EXIT 1;
```

5.  Save the file as "KoolKart_CalcAll.msh".
6.  Navigate to Essbase Cloud >> *KoolKart* >> *Sales* >> *Files*:

7.  Use the right window pane to upload the newly created MaxL script:

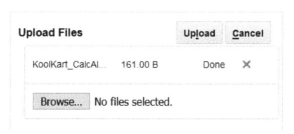

8. Back in the command window, log into the CLI with a Service Administrator ID:

9. The following syntax will execute an already uploaded MaxL script:

```
ESSCS SCRIPT -v -application (AppName) -db (DbName)
-script (ScriptName).msh
```

Remember to use the correct case for the application, cube, and script name. Also, use all lowercase for the parameters:

10. Press *Enter*.

11. Feedback will be sent to the screen, with a success or failure message at the bottom:

```
Command Prompt                                                        —  □  ×
c:\cli2>ESSCS SCRIPT -v -application KoolKart -db Sales -script KoolKart_CalcAll.msh
POST: {"application":"KoolKart","db":"Sales","jobtype":"maxl","parameters":{"script":"KoolKart_CalcAll.msh"}}
RETURN: {
  "job_ID" : 77,
  "appName" : "KoolKart",
  "dbName" : "Sales",
  "jobType" : "MaxL Script",
  "jobfileName" : "KoolKart_CalcAll.msh",
  "userName" : "        ",
  "startTime" : 1495655927000,
  "endTime" : 1495655927000,
  "statusCode" : 100,
  "statusMessage" : "In Progress",
  "jobInputInfo" : {
    "script" : "KoolKart_CalcAll.msh"
  },
  "jobOutputInfo" : {
    "maxLOutputFileName" : "",
    "maxLErrorFileName" : "",
    "errorMessage" : ""
  },
  "links" : [ {
    "rel" : "self",
    "href" : "http://       :9000/essbase/rest/v1/jobs",
    "method" : "POST"
  }, {
    "rel" : "canonical",
    "href" : "http://       :9000/essbase/rest/v1/jobs",
    "method" : "POST"
  }, {
    "rel" : "Job Status",
    "href" : "http://       :9000/essbase/rest/v1/jobs/77",
    "method" : "GET"
  } ]
}
..Status: 200
Details: Completed
```

12. In addition, a "maxl_out.txt" file will appear in the Files library once the script runs:

**Files**

Actions ▾

| Name | Locked | Size | Modified Time | Actions |
|------|--------|------|---------------|---------|
| Sales.rul | | 530.00 bytes | May 22, 2017 5:42:08 PM | ⬇ |
| TimePeriod.rul | | 785.00 bytes | May 22, 2017 5:42:08 PM | ⬇ |
| Measures.rul | | 881.00 bytes | May 22, 2017 5:42:08 PM | ⬇ |
| Sales.xlsx | | 52.49 KB | May 22, 2017 5:42:13 PM | ⬇ |
| KoolKart_Test2.msh | | 84.00 bytes | May 24, 2017 2:58:02 PM | ⬇ |
| KoolKart_CalcAll.msh | | 154.00 bytes | May 24, 2017 2:58:47 PM | ⬇ |
| Dim_Category_Dim.txt | | 784.00 bytes | May 22, 2017 5:42:23 PM | ⬇ |
| Dim_TimePeriod.txt | | 17.87 KB | May 22, 2017 5:42:19 PM | ⬇ |
| Dim_Measures.txt | | 181.00 bytes | May 24, 2017 1:52:06 PM | ⬇ |
| KoolKart_CalcAll_maxl_out.txt | | 906.00 bytes | May 24, 2017 2:58:48 PM | ⬇ |

13. The "maxl_out.txt" file can be downloaded to confirm the details of the script execution. Select the down arrow ⬇ next to this filename on the right hand side of the window:

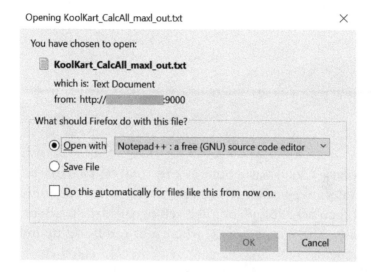

14. This file gives a lot of great information that long-time MaxL users will find familiar:

```
Essbase MaxL Shell 64-bit - Release 12.2.1 (ESB12.2.1.1.105B154)
Copyright (c) 2000, 2017, Oracle and/or its affiliates.
All rights reserved.

MAXL> ALTER SYSTEM LOAD APPLICATION KoolKart;

OK/INFO - 1056090 - System altered.

MAXL> EXECUTE CALCULATION KoolKart.Sales.CALCALL;

OK/INFO - 1012675 - Commit Blocks Interval for the calculation is [0].
OK/INFO - 1012684 - Multiple bitmap mode calculator cache memory usage has a limit of [7142] bitmaps..
OK/INFO - 1012669 - Calculating [ Measures(All members) TimePeriod(All members) Category_Dim(All members)].
OK/INFO - 1012677 - Calculating in serial.
OK/INFO - 1012918 - Essbase is unable to execute the calculation using hybrid mode because the calculation
commands CALC DIM and AGG are not supported in hybrid mode..
OK/INFO - 1012579 - Total calc elapsed time for [CALCALL.csc]: [0.013] seconds.
OK/INFO - 1013274 - Calculation executed.
```

Remember, I can also create a bat file so I can run things over and over again. I must set the java_home command into an EssCS.bat file (right after the Echo command):

```
login -user c... ... -password ... -url http:// ... :9000/essbase  >output.txt
upload -application Glenn_Test -db Analysis -file C:\clientfiles\DSC\data\Cst_Stat.rul -overwrite tru
upload -application Glenn_Test -db Analysis -file C:\clientfiles\DSC\data\restof2016\extracted\custom
dataload  -application Glenn_Test -db Analysis -rule Cst_Stat.rul -file customer_status_r2106.txt -ab
calc -application Glenn_Test -db Analysis -script Calc_Avg_Subscribers.csc >>output.txt
logout  >>output.txt
```

## ESSBASE CLOUD JOBS CONSOLE

Essbase Cloud has a built-in jobs console. This can be useful to Administrators who want to set up jobs for common administration tasks and then schedule them, like setting up data loads to run on a weekly basis. The jobs console is where jobs can be set up initially and run on demand.

From this area, Administrators will be able to:

- Run an existing job on demand
- Deactivate an existing job
- View job status and details for all jobs (other users only see the jobs they ran)

To access the Jobs Console,
1. Log into Essbase Cloud and navigate to the home page.
2. Ensure that the *Sales* cube of the KoolKart application is selected in the home page.

3.  Select the *Jobs* icon:

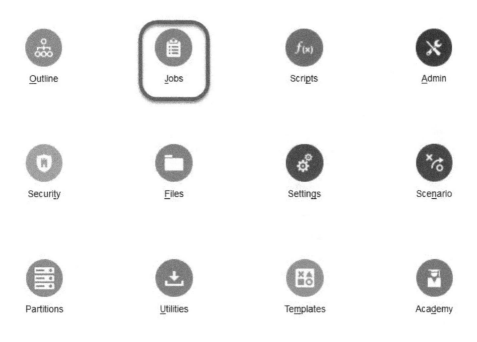

From this main screen, users can view existing jobs, set up new jobs, refresh (on demand or automatically) the jobs list, and set up the maximum number of parallel jobs:

**Note!**

A maximum of 10 jobs can run in parallel by default. The *Settings* area is where the max number can be set. This setting can be changed to a valid number between 1 and 100.

Default information for each job is shown: JobID, affected application and cube, type of job, script name (if applicable), the user running the job, start time, elapsed time, and the status.

The icons next to a job can be used to interact with a job:

The job can be rerun , or the details of the job can be viewed

Job details give information about the job specifics:

**Job Details-Import Excel**

## Input Details

| | |
|---:|:---|
| **Script Name** | KoolKart Sales Data_05112017.xlsx |
| **Load Data** | true |
| **Recreate Application** | false |
| **Create Files** | true |
| **Execute Script** | false |
| **Build Option** | |

## Output Details

| | |
|---:|:---|
| **Result** | Completed |

To set up a new job,

4.  Click the *New Job* button:

There are 0 active jobs. A maximum of 10 Jobs can run in parallel.   Settings   ( New Job )   Auto Refresh   ↻   | Refresh

5.  A series of parameters need to be completed for the job. Different fields will highlight based upon the type of job created. There are multiple job types available – data load, dimension build, calc execution, or clear data:

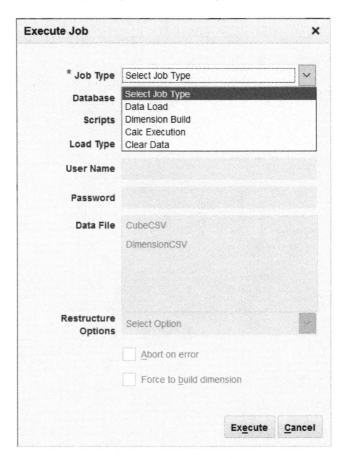

For this example, I'm going to load data. To do this,

6.  Select *Data Load*.

7.  Since the KoolKart.Sales Essbase Cloud cube was already selected before navigating to the jobs console, the Sales has been pre-selected.

8. A script was auto-generated behind the scenes when the KoolKart.Sales cube was created. Select the *Sales* script:

9. Select *File* for *Load Type* field and *CubeCSV* for *Data File*.
10. Since data is being loaded and dimensions are not being built, *Restructure Options* is greyed out.
11. Check the *Abort on error* option.
12. Select *Execute* to kick off the job.

13. A message should appear, indicating that the job is now in progress:

Unless Auto Refresh has been toggled on, the jobs list will need to be refreshed manually. A status icon of $\square$ means that a job is still running. A status icon of ✅ means that a job has completed "successfully" (with no errors). Finally, a status icon of ❌ means that a job has failed, with errors. If applicable, the errors file can be viewed in the Files area.

14. The job completed successfully:

15. Select the *Job Details* icon to the right to see more information about it:

**Job Details-Data Load**

**Input Details**

**Script Name**   Sales

**Data File**   CubeCSV

**Abort on error**   true

**Job Progress**

**Records Processed**   8640

**Records Rejected**   0

**Output Details**

**Result**   Completed

16. Close out of this screen.

## BACKUPS, RESTORES, AND PATCHES

Because OAC belongs to the PaaS (*refresher*: that's "Platform as a Service" for those who can't remember) licensing model, the backup, restore, and patching process is a bit unique and is the responsibility of the customer.

From a general standpoint, Administrators can:

- Start, stop, and restart the OAC Cloud services
- Backup the OAC environments
- Restore the OAC environments from backup
- Patch the OAC environments
- Delete the OAC service
- Scale up or down the OAC service (allocating more or less performance through the shape or OCPU configuration)

All of these activities take place within the OAC Dashboard. Therefore, only an Administrator with the proper authority can make changes and take action to manage their OAC instance.

### Backing up Essbase Cloud

In order to back up the OAC Service, the Administrator needs to log into the OAC Dashboard in My Services.

1. Select the service that needs to be backed up.
2. On the Services tab, select the *Administration* hyperlink.
3. Navigate to the *Backup* tab and click *Configure Backups*:

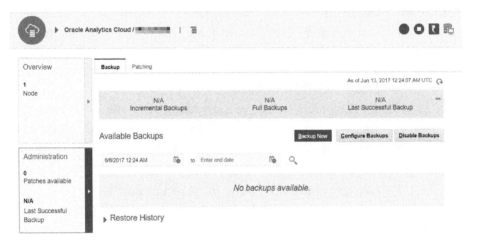

4. Optionally set the amount of time that the backup should be retained.
5. Click *Save*.
6. Click *Backup Now*.
7. A message should appear to indicate success or failure.

The backup can also be scheduled from a shell script and run from a CRON job.

### Restoring Essbase Cloud

In order to restore the OAC Service from a previous backup, the Administrator needs to log into the OAC Dashboard.

1. Select the service that needs to be restored from backup.
2. On the Services tab, select the *Administration* hyperlink.
3. Next to the backup that needs to be used for restore, select the *Manage this service* icon.
4. Click *Restore*.
5. A message should appear to indicate success or failure.

The restore process is an "all or nothing" type of restore. I can't restore specific artifacts using this process. I recommend having an implementation partner like i.n.t.e.r.R.e.l. help you put in specific application backup processes.

### Patching Essbase Cloud

In order to patch the OAC Service, again, the Administrator needs to log into the OAC Dashboard. Administrators have two options here: to patch their service or to rollback an existing path on a service.

**Note!** Patches are cumulative. The most recent patch would contain all of the previous updates within it.

1. Select the service that needs to be patched:
2. On the Services tab, select the *Administration* icon:
3. Next to the patch that needs to be applied, select the *Manage this service* icon.

**Note!** Administrators can also precheck a patch before applying it. To do this, select the *Precheck* option instead in the next step. After the precheck runs, a list of potential conflicts will be shown.

4. Click *Patch*.

5. A message should appear to indicate success or failure.

In the example below, no patches are currently available:

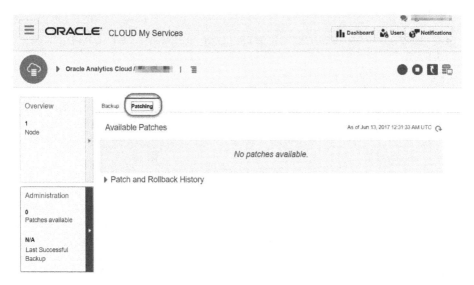

If a patch is applied and causes issues, it can be rolled back.

To rollback a patch,

6. Navigate back to the OAC Dashboard.
7. Select the service that needs to have its patch rolled back.
8. On the Services tab, select the *Administration* icon.
9. Navigate to the *Patches* tab and expand the *Patch and Rollback History* drop-down.
10. Next to the patch that needs to be rolled back, select the *Manage this service* icon.
11. Click *Rollback*.
12. Click *Yes* to confirm that you wish to roll back the patch:
13. A confirmation message should appear once the rollback action completes successfully.

```
LOG ENTRY FOR FLIGHT ENGINEER ROBERT GIDEON
SOL 23, Entry 2

     Mission Administration complete.
```

# CHAPTER 9: ANALYZE DATA IN SMART VIEW

---

LOG ENTRY FOR EDUCATOR MISSION SPECIALIST OPAL
ALAPAT
*SOL 23, Entry 1*

I'm commencing on Mission Smart View. Teaching TBC's analyst how to analyze data using Smart View in Excel? This is going to be a piece of cake. Who doesn't love Excel?

I am happy to announce that Smart View still has all of the functionality in the Cloud as it did on planet Earth…and then some! This means one less worry to keep me up at night. The tool has always been a buffer to those pesky users resistant to change.

(Maybe I should hide this entry in a safe spot so that it not be found by anyone who could possibly think I am referring to them…)

Apparently this Cloud is making me a little hangry. Maybe I should go eat something. Oh great, more Cloud food.

---

## INTRODUCTION TO SMART VIEW

What is Smart View? In case you missed it, Smart View is THE Office add-in for all of the Oracle Business Analytic and Enterprise Performance Management products including Essbase, OBIEE, Planning, Financial Management, Financial Reporting, and now also most Cloud products including Essbase Cloud, PBCS, FCCS, EPRCS, and more. It's Oracle's version of the Swiss Army knife, and that makes me MacGyver.

With Smart View, I can create reports in Word or PowerPoint with live data from Essbase sources. Features like Report Designer, Query Designer, and Cascade (report bursting) give end users powerful reporting capabilities in the tools they know and love: Excel, Word, and PowerPoint (beat that, Excel add-in).

Smart View also brings add-In functionality for all of the Oracle EPM products that need an add-in. I can import Reporting and Analysis documents as images into Microsoft Word or PowerPoint. I can import query-ready or fully formatted grids into Microsoft Excel.

And most recently for OAC, as you know by now if you have been paying attention, cubes can be created and imported from Excel utilizing the Oracle Smart View add-in and a Smart View extension called Cube Designer. I can build cubes from both unstructured spreadsheets or from Cube Designer templates.

## SMART VIEW BASICS

JWE's company The Beverage Company sells beverage products across the United States. JWE wants to find out which products and markets are profitable and which are losing money. To help with their analysis, they want to use Oracle Analytics Cloud with Smart View, which is an end user interface included in the OAC suite.

Did you know Smart View is spelled "Smart View" and not "Smartview?"

**Tip!**

In this mission, I am using Smart View version 11.1.2.5.700. All steps and screenshots will assume this version and could vary depending on the version.

### The Smart View Ribbon

When I launch Microsoft Excel, the Smart View ribbon appears on the menu bar. The Smart View ribbon contains all of the common actions that will be performed across the Oracle products. The Smart View ribbon persists in the menu even when not connected to a source.

Before I connect to Essbase Cloud, though, notice some of the items in the *Smart View* ribbon that will be used later in this book. For instance, one menu option is *Refresh*. Presumably, I'll be using this to refresh data from Essbase.

When I need to send data back into Essbase (for budgeting, say), I'll use the *Submit Data* option:

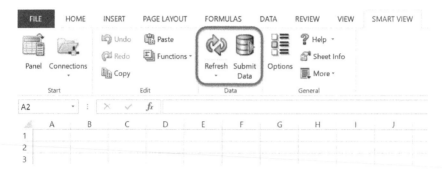

### The Cube Designer Extension

The Cube Designer Smart View extension was released in version 11.1.2.5.620, specifically to assist with creating and updating OAC applications. This extension has been covered in greater detail in other sections of this book:

### Connect to Essbase Cloud with Smart View

To connect to Essbase Cloud via Smart View,

1. Click on the *Panel* button on the Smart View ribbon:

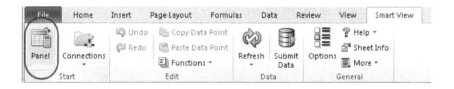

2.  Select *Private Connections*:

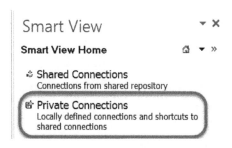

3.  Type in the URL for the Essbase Cloud instance – it will be something like:

    http://workspaceservername:9000/essbase/smartview

    (your Cloud Administrator should be able to provide this):

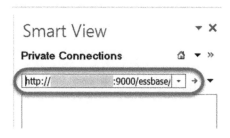

I should be prompted for an ID and password. My login information controls access to various parts of Essbase Cloud. Depending on my security, I might have access to all of Essbase Cloud, access to specific applications and cubes, or no access at all.

**Tip!**

Only get Essbase access to what you need to do your regular job and avoid getting blamed for everything!

4.  Enter your Oracle Analytics ID and password and click *Sign In*:

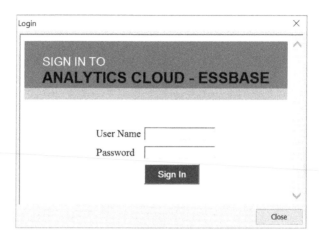

The Essbase cluster that applies to the Essbase Cloud instance will appear:

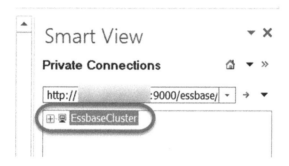

So what exactly is an Essbase cluster? It is basically a really powerful machine that holds the Essbase software and all of the data for the Essbase cubes that have been licensed by the customer. It is maintained by Oracle in the Cloud.

My computer (which in computer terms is called the "client" or "client machine") talks to this server through the Cloud. While all the data is stored on the server, all of the analysis happens on my client. Once I connect to the server, I can pull data back to the client and look at it in Excel. If I change the data, I should send it back to the server so that everyone else in the company can look at the same set of numbers. You've probably heard of the concept a "single version of the truth."

5.  Click the + sign next to *EssbaseCluster*:

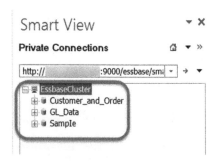

Depending on what's been created, a list of applications will appear. If I click the plus sign next to an application, I will see the cubes (the cube icon denotes Essbase cubes, or cubes).

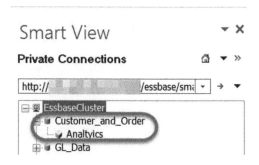

An Essbase application is a collection of one or more Essbase cubes. In the image above, the Customer_and_Order application has one cube, Analytics.

The anticipation is overwhelming – I can't wait to start analyzing data. I'll be using the Basic cube in the Sample application. I'll call it Sample.Basic, for short. First I need to connect the spreadsheet to Sample.Basic.

6.  Expand the *Sample* application.

7.  Right-click on the *Basic* cube and choose *Connect*:

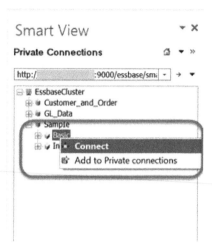

I am now connected to the cube.

8.  Right-click on *Basic* again and there are now a number of options available. Select *Ad hoc analysis*:

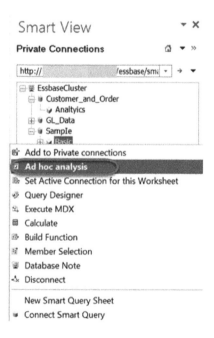

The display in the Smart View spreadsheet will now change to show a high level ad hoc grid:

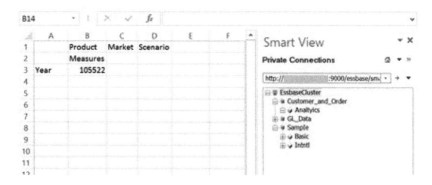

First notice that a new ribbon called "Essbase" now displays in Excel. A number of ribbon actions are available, including Zoom In, Zoom Out, Keep Only, Remove Only, Refresh, and POV:

Also notice that data has been refreshed from the Essbase server and is displayed in the spreadsheet. I see the five dimensions in Sample.Basic along with a single data value.

Before I start zooming and drilling (boy, Essbase sounds really exciting!), let's discuss connection information. The current spreadsheet tab in the Excel workbook is the only one that's connected to Essbase. If I went from Sheet1 to Sheet2, Sheet2 wouldn't be connected. It's possible to click over to Sheet2 and connect it to Essbase, but at the moment it's not.

This does bring up the interesting point that each sheet can be connected to a different Essbase cube or no cube at all. Sheet2 could be connected to Demo.Basic while Sheet1 is connected to Sample.Basic. All this can get a bit confusing. To easily see which data source a worksheet is using, select the Smart View tab and select *Sheet Info*.

All of the important connection information is displayed, including Server, Application, and Database (or Cube):

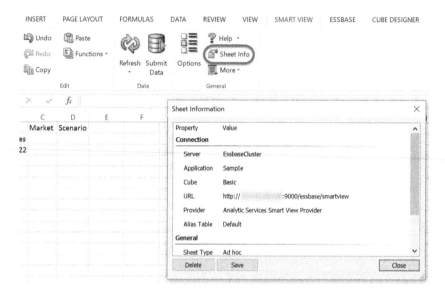

### Ad Hoc Analysis

Now that I understand sheet connections, let's get back to retrieving data and analyzing data.

I am now connected to Essbase via Sample.Basic.

9.  Click on the cell that shows 105,522 and look at the formula bar just above the spreadsheet grid:

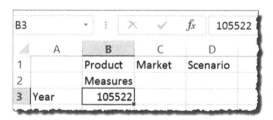

The data point 105,522 represents the total of all the months, products, and markets in my application.

Notice, however, that the content of the cell is not an Excel formula summing up other values. The total is being calculated on the Essbase server and then returned back to me as a plain old number. This is one of the main reasons that Essbase is far faster than, say, a pivot table: all of the detail stays on the Essbase server and only the value I care about is returned to me.

I may also see a floating POV window in my spreadsheet. I'll review this component shortly.

**Tip!**   Since there are no formulas linking this spreadsheet to Essbase (only values), you can send this spreadsheet to people in your company who don't have access to the Essbase server.

10. Select the cell that contains *Measures* (cell B2 if you're following along). Measures tells us nothing, so go ahead and type the word Profit into that cell instead and press *Enter*. The numbers will not change, mainly because you haven't told Essbase to re-refresh the data yet. Choose *Refresh* from the ribbon:

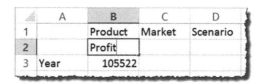

Now I'll turn my attention to the POV ("point of view"). In my current spreadsheet the POV includes the dimensions Product, Market, and Scenario. I am looking at the data value for total products, total markets, and a single scenario (likely Actual, because this is how Essbase Administrators usually design their cubes). I can also toggle these POV dimensions to a floating POV window by clicking the POV icon on the Essbase ribbon:

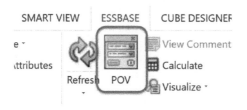

This toggles the POV window on:

This floating window pulls POV dimensions into a floating dialogue (really, the clever developers have just hidden row one). Some users love the floating POV. Others strongly dislike ("hate" is such a harsh word) the floating POV. Simply toggle off the POV using the POV button in the Essbase ribbon (new sheets start with the POV turned off).

11. Practice turning on and off the POV:

Notice the dimensions that were previously in the floating POV – Product, Market and Scenario – are now in the spreadsheet:

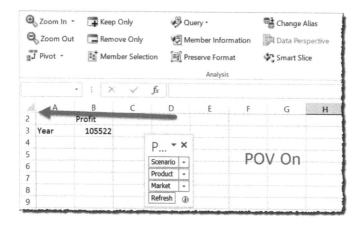

12. To switch back to the floating POV, choose the POV icon again.

Notice that row one is hidden. When the POV window is turned on, the members are actually still there, they're just hidden in the first row of the Excel spreadsheet. This allows me to print the POV on reports or use those hidden rows in formulas to create headings:

I can also easily move these dimensions from the floating POV to the spreadsheet and back again.

13. To move the dimension, grab it by the drop-down arrow. For example, select Scenario and drag it from the POV to the columns section of the spreadsheet, near Profit:

Scenario will be dropped into the grid either above or below profit depending on where the mouse stops:

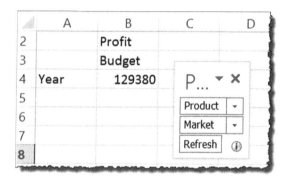

Update the analysis to focus on Budget.

14. Type "Budget" over Scenario and click *Refresh*:

If I spelled Profit or Budget wrong, Essbase will kindly replace the misspelled member name with the dimension name into the POV.

15. Type "Budgets" over Budget in cell B1.

16. Click *Refresh*:

| ▲ | A | B | C | D |
|---|---|---|---|---|
| 2 | | Profit | | |
| 3 | | Budgets | | |
| 4 | Year | 105522 | P... ▾ ✕ | |
| 5 | | | | |
| 6 | | | Scenario ▾ | |
| 7 | | | Product ▾ | |
| 8 | | | Market ▾ | |
| 9 | | | Refresh ⓘ | |

Notice that cell B1 says "Budgets", so when refreshed, Essbase put Scenario in the POV (thinking that a dimension was omitted). Essbase is very particular about spelling. It has no idea that "Budgets" and "Budget" means the same thing, so be careful when typing in the names of members.

**Tip!** While spelling is important, members are not case sensitive. Type in "BuDgEt" and Essbase will refresh the data and replace your funky capitalization with "Budget."

I can also type member names directly in the floating POV.

17. Type "Budget" over scenario in the POV window and click Refresh:

| ▲ | A | B | C | D |
|---|---|---|---|---|
| 2 | | Profit | | |
| 3 | | Budget: | | |
| 4 | Year | 129380 | P... ▾ ✕ | |
| 5 | | | | |
| 6 | | | Budget ▾ | |
| 7 | | | Product ▾ | |
| 8 | | | Market ▾ | |
| 9 | | | Refresh ⓘ | |

I'll go through one more scenario.

18. Open a new spreadsheet and type in the following:

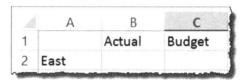

|   | A | B | C |
|---|---|---|---|
| 1 |   | Actual | Budget |
| 2 | East |   |   |

Notice that there isn't a floating POV window and that the spreadsheet is not connected to a cube.

19. Right-click *Sample.Basic* and select *Ad hoc Analysis.*

Voila! The spreadsheet is refreshed based on the member selections for the two dimensions displayed (Market and Scenario). The remaining dimensions are listed in the POV (either in the spreadsheet or floating POV, depending on what you have turned on):

|   | A | B | C | D |
|---|---|---|---|---|
| 1 |   | Year | Measures | Product |
| 2 |   | Actual | Budget |   |
| 3 | East |   | 24161 | 28390 |

If I attempt to type over an existing ad hoc grid that is actively connected to an Essbase cube, I might be prompted with the following message:

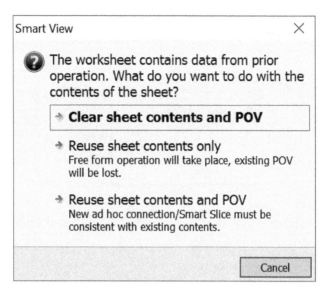

Smart View is asking which of the following options I prefer:

- Remove everything (i.e., start with a blank spreadsheet)
- Keep existing row and column selections, but remove the POV selections
- Keep all existing member selections (i.e., reuse what's there)

If I want to start with a blank spreadsheet with the top level members of each dimension selected, I would choose *Clear sheet contents and POV*. The remaining two options will maintain the spreadsheet as I've defined it and apply the member selections/query to the connected source either with or without the POV.

I do not want to clear the contents of the sheet and I don't have a POV defined so I'll select *Reuse sheet contents only*. Now my spreadsheet is connected to the cube and has refreshed values.

I'll go ahead and close this spreadsheet for now and use the original query going forward. Ready to zoom?

## Zoom In and Out

To utilize the zoom feature,

1. Start with a spreadsheet connected to Sample.Basic that looks like the following:

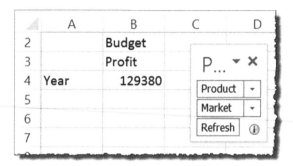

2. Select the cell that says Year (cell A4) and choose Zoom In from the Essbase ribbon:

Though my report might not look exactly like this (depending on my current Essbase Options and Excel formatting), I should see the quarters that make up the total year:

| | A | B | C | D |
|---|---|---|---|---|
| 2 | | Budget | | |
| 3 | | Profit | P... ▾ ✕ | |
| 4 | Qtr1 | 30580 | Product ▾ | |
| 5 | Qtr2 | 32870 | Market ▾ | |
| 6 | Qtr3 | 33980 | Refresh ⓘ | |
| 7 | Qtr4 | 31950 | | |
| 8 | Year | 129380 | | |

3.   Select the Qtr1 cell (cell A4) and again choose Zoom In. This will display the three months that comprise Qtr1.

**Tip!**   There are also mouse shortcuts for zooming in and zooming out. To Zoom In using the mouse, double-click with the *left* mouse button on a member name. To Zoom Out, double-click with the *right* mouse button on a member name.

When I zoom in, I am navigating from the top of a dimension down to the various levels, eventually getting to the bottom of the dimension. Zooming is also known as drilling. In my example, I zoomed (or drilled) from Year to Quarter. If I select Qtr1 and select *Zoom In*, I'll see the three months that make up Qtr1 – Jan, Feb, and Mar. I can zoom on any dimension in Essbase, quickly retrieving the data at various levels across the Essbase cube. For example, I've very quickly refreshed profit data for the three months that make up Qtr1 for all products and markets.

To go back up a dimension from bottom to top, I can *Zoom Out* (or right double-click on a member). I can highlight any of those three months and choose *Zoom Out* from the *Essbase* ribbon. I can select a quarter and choose *Zoom Out* again to get back to where I started.

From the Essbase ribbon, I can choose how I want to zoom. Do I want to zoom to the next level (the default, unless specified differently under the Options) or the bottom level? Be careful with *All Levels* and *Bottom Level*. This could potentially bring back a LOT of members, which will slow performance and create run-away queries on the Essbase server.

4.  Select the drop-down arrow next to Zoom In:

Sometimes I might get a bit overexcited and zoom one too many times (haven't we all been there?). If you ever need to "go back," Smart View provides undo capabilities (that fortunately works excellently for undoing my actions in Smart View but unfortunately doesn't work anywhere else in my life).

To undo my last Essbase action, I won't look under the *Edit* menu in Excel (and I won't click the 🔄 button on the Excel toolbar). I'll simply click the *Undo* button on the *Smart View* ribbon:

Note that there is also a *Redo* button, which can repeat actions I've performed. How many times can I undo or redo? Well, it depends. Select the *Options* button from the Smart View ribbon.

In the Advanced section, I can define the number of actions that Smart View will allow me to undo:

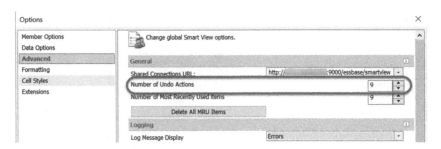

I can type in the number of undo actions I want to allow. Would I ever want to set this setting to 100? No, higher values can impact performance negatively. Keep the *Number of Undo Actions* to a lower number – the default is nine.

### Keep Only/Remove Only

Let's say that I want to remove Year from the report. There are two ways to accomplish this. The first is by using the power of Excel: highlight row eight (or whatever row has Year on it) and choose *Delete* from Excel's *Edit* menu. I can also use the power of Essbase by highlighting the Year cell and choosing *Remove Only* from the *Essbase* ribbon.

5.   *Remove Only* the member *Year*.

Remove Only is the opposite of Keep Only. It will remove the members selected in the spreadsheet. Keep Only is the opposite of Remove Only. Keep Only will keep only the members selected on the spreadsheet. Remove Only and Keep Only both work with multiple cells, as long as the selected cells are all from the same dimension.

6. Keep Only/Remove Only works on multiple cells as well. Select the Qtr1 cell, hold down the control key, and then click the Qtr2 cell. With both cells selected, click *Keep Only*. Cool! Now the spreadsheet includes only Qtr1 and Qtr2:

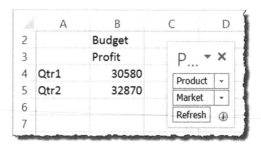

| | A | B | C | D |
|---|---|---|---|---|
| 2 | | Budget | | |
| 3 | | Profit | | |
| 4 | Qtr1 | 30580 | | |
| 5 | Qtr2 | 32870 | | |
| 6 | | | | |
| 7 | | | | |

7. Since this report is fairly useless, click on *Qtr1* and choose *Zoom Out* to return to the previous report.
8. *Zoom In* again to display the quarters above the year.
9. Let's drill down a second dimension. Highlight the *Profit* cell and choose *Zoom In*:

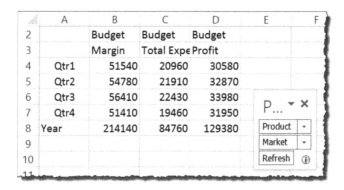

| | A | B | C | D | E | F |
|---|---|---|---|---|---|---|
| 2 | | Budget | Budget | Budget | | |
| 3 | | Margin | Total Expe | Profit | | |
| 4 | Qtr1 | 51540 | 20960 | 30580 | | |
| 5 | Qtr2 | 54780 | 21910 | 32870 | | |
| 6 | Qtr3 | 56410 | 22430 | 33980 | | |
| 7 | Qtr4 | 51410 | 19460 | 31950 | | |
| 8 | Year | 214140 | 84760 | 129380 | | |
| 9 | | | | | | |
| 10 | | | | | | |
| 11 | | | | | | |

## Pivot

To utilize the pivot feature in Smart View,

10. Now select *Margin* and click *Pivot* on the Essbase ribbon. (Notice that you can just *Pivot*, which will pivot the selected dimension within the spreadsheet, or you can *Pivot to POV* which will move the dimension and selected members to the floating POV.) For this example, choose *Pivot >> Pivot*:

The spreadsheet should now look as follows:

| | A | B | C | D | E |
|---|---|---|---|---|---|
| 2 | | | Budget | | |
| 3 | Margin | Qtr1 | 51540 | | |
| 4 | Margin | Qtr2 | 54780 | | |
| 5 | Margin | Qtr3 | 56410 | | |
| 6 | Margin | Qtr4 | 51410 | | |
| 7 | Margin | Year | 214140 | | |
| 8 | Total Expenses | Qtr1 | 20960 | | |
| 9 | Total Expenses | Qtr2 | 21910 | | |
| 10 | Total Expenses | Qtr3 | 22430 | | |
| 11 | Total Expenses | Qtr4 | 19460 | | |
| 12 | Total Expenses | Year | 84760 | | |
| 13 | Profit | Qtr1 | 30580 | | |
| 14 | Profit | Qtr2 | 32870 | | |
| 15 | Profit | Qtr3 | 33980 | | |
| 16 | Profit | Qtr4 | 31950 | | |
| 17 | Profit | Year | 129380 | | |
| 18 | | | | | |

To hide the repeating members for Margin, Total Expenses and Profit for each time period.

11. Select the *Smart View* ribbon and choose *Options*. In the *Data Options* section, check *Repeated Members* under *Suppress Rows:*

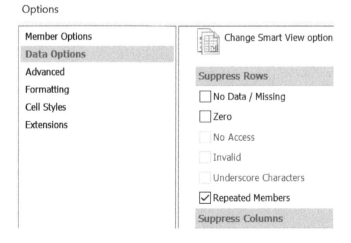

12. Click *Refresh* to update the spreadsheet.

I see how Smart View can show two dimensions on either the row or column axis at the same time. To move the Year dimension up to the columns, I could do that "hiring the temp to rekey" method I mentioned before, or I can do it the Essbase way.

13. Select any of the member names in the Year dimension row, row two (Qtr1, for example), and choose *Pivot*:

| | A | B | C | D | E | F |
|---|---|---|---|---|---|---|
| 2 | | Qtr1 | Qtr2 | Qtr3 | Qtr4 | Year |
| 3 | | Budget | Budget | Budget | Budget | Budget |
| 4 | Margin | 51540 | 54780 | 56410 | 51410 | 214140 |
| 5 | Total Expenses | 20960 | 21910 | 22430 | 19460 | 84760 |
| 6 | Profit | 30580 | 32870 | 33980 | 31950 | 129380 |
| 7 | | | | | | |
| 8 | | | | | P... ▾ ✕ | |
| 9 | | | | | Product ▾ | |
| 10 | | | | | Market ▾ | |
| 11 | | | | | Refresh ⓘ | |
| 12 | | | | | | |

There's also a mouse shortcut for pivoting dimensions: it's called a "right drag-and-drop."

14. Select *Qtr1* using your left mouse button.

15. Now, with the mouse cursor over that cell, hold down the right mouse button. Slightly move the cursor towards column A while holding the right mouse button down. Don't let go of the right mouse button yet:

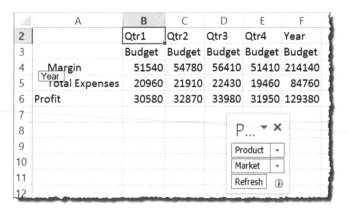

| | A | B | C | D | E | F |
|---|---|---|---|---|---|---|
| 2 | | Qtr1 | Qtr2 | Qtr3 | Qtr4 | Year |
| 3 | | Budget | Budget | Budget | Budget | Budget |
| 4 | Margin | 51540 | 54780 | 56410 | 51410 | 214140 |
| 5 | Year Total Expenses | 20960 | 21910 | 22430 | 19460 | 84760 |
| 6 | Profit | 30580 | 32870 | 33980 | 31950 | 129380 |
| 7 | | | | | | |
| 8 | | | | P... ▾ ✕ | | |
| 9 | | | | Product ▾ | | |
| 10 | | | | Market ▾ | | |
| 11 | | | | Refresh ⓘ | | |
| 12 | | | | | | |

16. Move the white cells over to the cell where you want to pivot the dimension. In our case, drag the members over to cell A3. Okay, now let go of the right mouse button and you should see the dimension pivot to the rows:

| | A | B | C | D | E |
|---|---|---|---|---|---|
| 2 | | | Budget | | |
| 3 | Qtr1 | Margin | 51540 | | |
| 4 | Qtr1 | Total Expenses | 20960 | | |
| 5 | Qtr1 | Profit | 30580 | | |
| 6 | Qtr2 | Margin | 54780 | | |
| 7 | Qtr2 | Total Expenses | 21910 | | |
| 8 | Qtr2 | Profit | 32870 | P... ▾ ✕ | |
| 9 | Qtr3 | Margin | 56410 | Product ▾ | |
| 10 | Qtr3 | Total Expenses | 22430 | Market ▾ | |
| 11 | Qtr3 | Profit | 33980 | Refresh ⓘ | |
| 12 | Qtr4 | Margin | 51410 | | |
| 13 | Qtr4 | Total Expenses | 19460 | | |
| 14 | Qtr4 | Profit | 31950 | | |
| 15 | Year | Margin | 214140 | | |
| 16 | Year | Total Expenses | 84760 | | |
| 17 | Year | Profit | 129380 | | |

While I'm back to having two dimensions on the rows, I've changed the orientation of the two dimensions to show each measure by each time period. If we only want to show Profit for each time period, I could use the *Keep Only* function.

17. Select one of the Profit cells (cell B5, say), and choose *Keep Only*. This will remove all the instances of Margin and Total Expenses (alternatively, I could also have used *Remove Only* on the other two members):

| | A | B | C | D | E | F |
|---|---|---|---|---|---|---|
| 2 | | | Budget | | | |
| 3 | Qtr1 | Profit | 30580 | | | |
| 4 | Qtr2 | Profit | 32870 | | P... ▾ ✕ | |
| 5 | Qtr3 | Profit | 33980 | | | |
| 6 | Qtr4 | Profit | 31950 | | Product ▾ | |
| 7 | Year | Profit | 129380 | | Market ▾ | |
| 8 | | | | | Refresh ⓘ | |

This method is much more efficient than simply adding and deleting rows in Excel.

18. To clean up the report (since it looks a bit silly showing the same member repeatedly in the rows), select one of the instances of *Profit* and choose *Pivot*.

Since there is only one member to be pivoted, Essbase will assume that you want the member to be pivoted up to the page instead of the columns.

19. Move *Profit* back down to the rows.

Remember: "Where is row one in my Excel spreadsheet?" Take a look below:

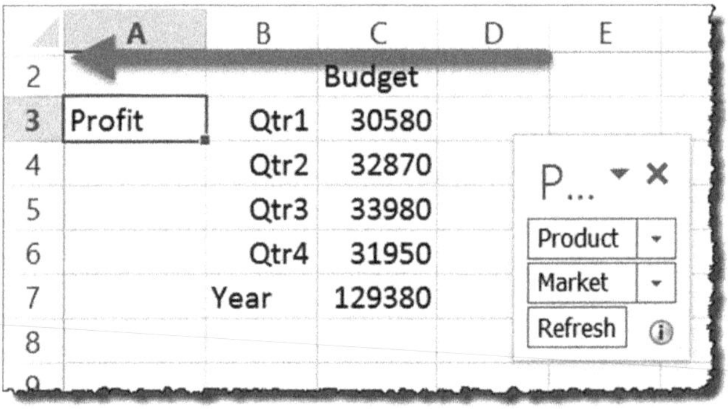

| | A | B | C | D | E |
|---|---|---|---|---|---|
| 2 | | | Budget | | |
| 3 | Profit | Qtr1 | 30580 | | |
| 4 | | Qtr2 | 32870 | | |
| 5 | | Qtr3 | 33980 | | |
| 6 | | Qtr4 | 31950 | | |
| 7 | | Year | 129380 | | |
| 8 | | | | | |

P... ▾ ✕
Product ▾
Market ▾
Refresh ⓘ

This is where Smart View is storing the POV members. Toggle off the floating POV and row one appears like magic!

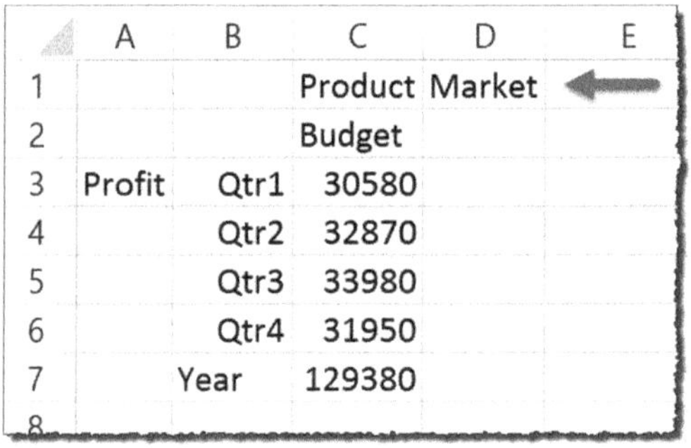

| | A | B | C | D | E |
|---|---|---|---|---|---|
| 1 | | | Product | Market | |
| 2 | | | Budget | | |
| 3 | Profit | Qtr1 | 30580 | | |
| 4 | | Qtr2 | 32870 | | |
| 5 | | Qtr3 | 33980 | | |
| 6 | | Qtr4 | 31950 | | |
| 7 | | Year | 129380 | | |
| 8 | | | | | |

### Multi Member Zoom

I can zoom on more than one member (or more than one dimension) at the same time.

1. Create the following ad hoc query, changing Budget to Actual. Select Qtr1 and Qtr2 so it is highlighted in the spreadsheet:

| | A | B | C | D |
|---|---|---|---|---|
| 1 | | | Product | Market |
| 2 | | | Actual | |
| 3 | Profit | Qtr1 | 30580 | |
| 4 | | Qtr2 | 32870 | |
| 5 | | Qtr3 | 3980 | |
| 6 | | Qtr4 | 31950 | |
| 7 | | Year | 129380 | |

2. Click *Zoom In* from the Essbase ribbon. Notice that Smart View zoomed in on both Qtr1 and Qtr2:

| | A | B | C | D |
|---|---|---|---|---|
| 1 | | | Product | Market |
| 2 | | | Actual | |
| 3 | Profit | Jan | 8024 | |
| 4 | | Feb | 8346 | |
| 5 | | Mar | 8333 | |
| 6 | | Qtr1 | 24703 | |
| 7 | | Apr | 8644 | |
| 8 | | May | 8929 | |
| 9 | | Jun | 9534 | |
| 10 | | Qtr2 | 27107 | |
| 11 | | Qtr3 | 27912 | |
| 12 | | Qtr4 | 25800 | |
| 13 | | Year | 105522 | |

### Refresh the Data

I can refresh the data in a spreadsheet at any time. To refresh the data to the current values in Essbase, select the *Refresh* button:

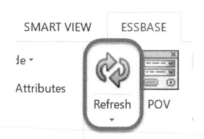

I have multiple options for refreshing data when activating the drop-down arrow. There is an option called *Refresh All Worksheets*. Refresh All Worksheets will refresh all worksheets in a workbook for the cube connection.

This is really helpful in instances when I've created a workbook of reports that I run regularly. For example, I create and update my reporting package each month. With one menu item, I can refresh the data for all reports within my workbook.

### Aliases

Let's take a look at how to best interact with aliases within Smart View.

To view and change alias tables,

1. Using your fancy new Essbase knowledge, create the following query with the floating POV turned off:

|   | A | B | C | D | E | F | G |
|---|---|---|---|---|---|---|---|
| 1 |   |   | Budget | Market |   |   |   |
| 2 |   |   | Qtr1 | Qtr2 | Qtr3 | Qtr4 | Year |
| 3 | Product | Margin | 51540 | 54780 | 56410 | 51410 | 214140 |
| 4 | Product | Total Expenses | 20960 | 21910 | 22430 | 19460 | 84760 |
| 5 | Product | Profit | 30580 | 32870 | 33980 | 31950 | 129380 |

2. *Zoom In* on Product:

|   | A | B | C | D | E | F | G |
|---|---|---|---|---|---|---|---|
| 1 |   |   | Budget | Market |   |   |   |
| 2 |   |   | Qtr1 | Qtr2 | Qtr3 | Qtr4 | Year |
| 3 | 100 | Margin | 15670 | 16890 | 17770 | 15540 | 65870 |
| 4 |   | Total Expenses | 5880 | 6230 | 6330 | 5490 | 23930 |
| 5 |   | Profit | 9790 | 10660 | 11440 | 10050 | 41940 |
| 6 | 200 | Margin | 14920 | 15390 | 15580 | 15450 | 61340 |
| 7 |   | Total Expenses | 6440 | 6550 | 6750 | 5650 | 25390 |
| 8 |   | Profit | 8480 | 8840 | 8830 | 9800 | 35950 |
| 9 | 300 | Margin | 11580 | 12620 | 12850 | 11650 | 48700 |
| 10 |   | Total Expenses | 4610 | 4940 | 5140 | 4650 | 19340 |
| 11 |   | Profit | 6970 | 7680 | 7710 | 7000 | 29360 |
| 12 | 400 | Margin | 9370 | 9880 | 10210 | 8770 | 38230 |
| 13 |   | Total Expenses | 4030 | 4190 | 4210 | 3670 | 16100 |
| 14 |   | Profit | 5340 | 5690 | 6000 | 5100 | 22130 |
| 15 | Diet | Margin | 14340 | 14910 | 15180 | 14250 | 58680 |
| 16 |   | Total Expenses | 5430 | 5690 | 5800 | 5040 | 21960 |
| 17 |   | Profit | 8910 | 9220 | 9380 | 9210 | 36720 |
| 18 | Product | Margin | 51540 | 54780 | 56410 | 51410 | 214140 |
| 19 |   | Total Expenses | 20960 | 21910 | 22430 | 19460 | 84760 |
| 20 |   | Profit | 30580 | 32870 | 33980 | 31950 | 129380 |

**Note!**

Product does not equal the total sum of the products listed underneath it, but it does equal the sum of products 100, 200, 300, and 400. Diet is a custom total that includes select products from the other product groupings. Diet is called an alternate hierarchy.

Product 100 is doing very well this year, especially compared to product 400. "100" is the member name of a specific Product member. Member names are the short, "computer-like" ways of referencing things and are completely unintuitive to the average user. Essbase allows member names to have longer, more user-friendly descriptions for members called "aliases." For instance, the alias for 100 is Cola. So how do I change the display from member names to aliases?

3.   On the Essbase ribbon, choose Change Alias.

A list of available Alias tables for the connected Essbase cube will display.

4.   Select the *Default* alias table:

The spreadsheet will refresh with the aliases:

| | A | B | C | D | E | F | G |
|---|---|---|---|---|---|---|---|
| 1 | | | Budget | Market | | | |
| 2 | | | Qtr1 | Qtr2 | Qtr3 | Qtr4 | Year |
| 3 | Colas | Margin | 15670 | 16890 | 17770 | 15540 | 65870 |
| 4 | | Total Expenses | 5880 | 6230 | 6330 | 5490 | 23930 |
| 5 | | Profit | 9790 | 10660 | 11440 | 10050 | 41940 |
| 6 | Root Beer | Margin | 14920 | 15390 | 15580 | 15450 | 61340 |
| 7 | | Total Expenses | 6440 | 6550 | 6750 | 5650 | 25390 |
| 8 | | Profit | 8480 | 8840 | 8830 | 9800 | 35950 |
| 9 | Cream Soda | Margin | 11580 | 12620 | 12850 | 11650 | 48700 |
| 10 | | Total Expenses | 4610 | 4940 | 5140 | 4650 | 19340 |
| 11 | | Profit | 6970 | 7680 | 7710 | 7000 | 29360 |
| 12 | Fruit Soda | Margin | 9370 | 9880 | 10210 | 8770 | 38230 |
| 13 | | Total Expenses | 4030 | 4190 | 4210 | 3670 | 16100 |
| 14 | | Profit | 5340 | 5690 | 6000 | 5100 | 22130 |
| 15 | Diet Drinks | Margin | 14340 | 14910 | 15180 | 14250 | 58680 |
| 16 | | Total Expenses | 5430 | 5690 | 5800 | 5040 | 21960 |
| 17 | | Profit | 8910 | 9220 | 9380 | 9210 | 36720 |
| 18 | Product | Margin | 51540 | 54780 | 56410 | 51410 | 214140 |
| 19 | | Total Expenses | 20960 | 21910 | 22430 | 19460 | 84760 |
| 20 | | Profit | 30580 | 32870 | 33980 | 31950 | 129380 |

I can type in either the member name or the alias and Essbase will be able to find it. For instance, below Product, type in the word "100-20" (without the quotes). "100-20" is the actual product member name. Refresh the data and see that Essbase replaced 100-20 with Diet Cola. Diet Cola is the alias.

**Tip!** Some member names are numbers. To type in a member name that Essbase could confuse with a number (like "100"), type in a single apostrophe before the member name. For "100", you would type in: '100. This tells Excel (and Essbase) that this is text and not a number.

Since some companies have multiple ways of referring to the same items (for instance, product 100 might be called "Cola" in the Northeast and "pop" in the Northwest), Essbase allows up to 32 different aliases for each member. Right now I'm using the Default alias (which belongs to an alias table called "Default"), but if my application has other descriptions for members beyond the defaults (called "alternate alias tables"), I can choose a different alias table in the *Change Alias* option on the Essbase ribbon.

**Note!**   Sample.Basic comes with another alias table called Long Names, in addition to Default.

### Member and Data Options

As mentioned before, the report I'm making might not look identical to the screenshots in this book. This could be due to changes in the dimension members or different zoom options. However, the most common reason for this is that my Options have been changed. Most options are worksheet-specific settings that control how Smart View operates. All of these settings are found by selecting the *Options* icon on the *Smart View* ribbon.

Some of the options are Global, which means they apply to all workbooks and any future workbooks and worksheets. The Global options are those under the Advanced, Extensions, and Cell Styles sections.

Sheet level options are those that are specific to each worksheet. New worksheets will use the default options until a change is made. Changes in options for one worksheet will not impact other worksheets and workbooks. Once the sheet level settings are changed for a worksheet, those settings will be remembered for that worksheet. Sheet level options are those under the Member Options, Data Options, and Formatting sections.

If I don't like the default options, I can change them! I'll update the settings under the Member Options, Data Options, and Formatting sections to my preference, then simply select the drop-down on the *OK* button and choose *Save As Default Options*:

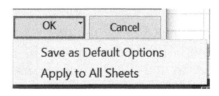

To reset the default options to those that are set during the installation and configuration, click *Reset* on the Options window:

Follow along to see how this works.

5.  On the Smart View ribbon, select *Options*. Under the Data Options section, make sure *Repeated Members* is checked:

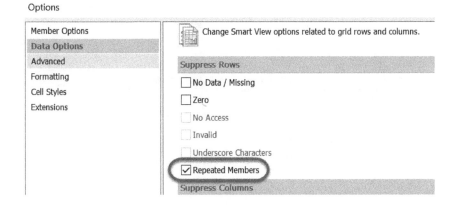

6. Select the drop-down arrow next to OK. Choose *Save as Default Options*:

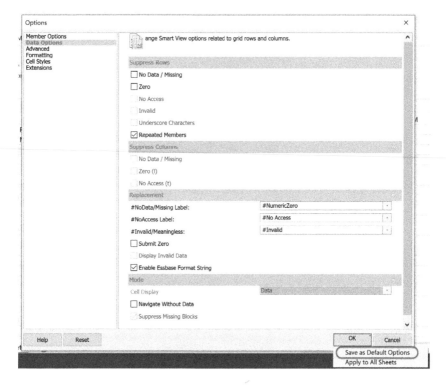

7. Open a new worksheet. Right-click on Sample.Basic and select *Ad hoc analysis.*

8. Double-click on *Year* to zoom into it.

9. Double-click on *Product* to zoom in on that. Notice that the product members are not repeated for each quarter:

| | A | B | C | D |
|---|---|---|---|---|
| 1 | | | Market | Scenario |
| 2 | | | Measures | |
| 3 | Colas | Qtr1 | 7048 | |
| 4 | | Qtr2 | 7872 | |
| 5 | | Qtr3 | 8511 | |
| 6 | | Qtr4 | 7037 | |
| 7 | | Year | 30468 | |
| 8 | Root Beer | Qtr1 | 6721 | |
| 9 | | Qtr2 | 7030 | |
| 10 | | Qtr3 | 7005 | |
| 11 | | Qtr4 | 7198 | |
| 12 | | Year | 27954 | |
| 13 | Cream Soda | Qtr1 | 5929 | |
| 14 | | Qtr2 | 6769 | |
| 15 | | Qtr3 | 6698 | |
| 16 | | Qtr4 | 6403 | |
| 17 | | Year | 25799 | |

10. For this worksheet, go back to *Options* on the Smart View ribbon. Under the *Data Options* section, uncheck *Repeated Members* under *Suppress Rows*.

11. Click *OK* (not the Save as Default Options option; just OK).

12. Then click *Refresh*. The spreadsheet should now have repeated product members for each quarter:

|    | A | B | C | D |
|----|---|---|---|---|
| 1 |  |  | Market | Scenario |
| 2 |  |  | Measures |  |
| 3 | Colas | Qtr1 | 7048 |  |
| 4 | Colas | Qtr2 | 7872 |  |
| 5 | Colas | Qtr3 | 8511 |  |
| 6 | Colas | Qtr4 | 7037 |  |
| 7 | Colas | Year | 30468 |  |
| 8 | Root Beer | Qtr1 | 6721 |  |
| 9 | Root Beer | Qtr2 | 7030 |  |
| 10 | Root Beer | Qtr3 | 7005 |  |
| 11 | Root Beer | Qtr4 | 7198 |  |
| 12 | Root Beer | Year | 27954 |  |
| 13 | Cream Soda | Qtr1 | 5929 |  |
| 14 | Cream Soda | Qtr2 | 6769 |  |

13. Finally, open a new worksheet.
14. Right-click on Sample.Basic and select *Ad hoc analysis.*
15. Double-click on Year to zoom into it.
16. Double-click on Product to zoom in on that.

Notice that the product members are not repeated for each quarter, using the original default settings defined. I can even close and open the workbook. The worksheet-specific settings will remain.

Now that I have a good understanding of how options are applied to worksheets, I'll review the different option settings. The options are categorized into six groups: Member Options, Data Options, Advanced, Formatting, Cell Styles, and Extensions:

Options

| Member Options |
| Data Options |
| Advanced |
| Formatting |
| Cell Styles |
| Extensions |

When I zoom in, I tend to want to see the members that comprise the current member. When I zoom in on Year, I most likely want to see the quarters. Likewise, a zoom in on Qtr1 should show the first three months of the year. Some impatient people don't like passing through the levels in the middle on the way to the bottom level of a dimension. To control how far Essbase drills with each zoom, go to the Member Options section. Under General, I can choose the Zoom In Level:

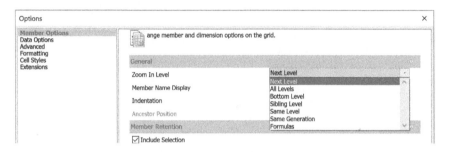

Right now, Zoom In is set to *Next Level* (the default for the sheet). This means that when I drill into Year, I see the quarters. I can override this default by changing the Zoom In Level selection. If, when I drill into Year, I want to see every single member in the Year dimension, I'll set my Zoom In to *All Levels*. If I then drilled on Year, I'd see every month and every quarter. If I want to jump from the Year down to all the months without showing any of the quarters, I'll select *Bottom Level*.

**Tip!**     Before drilling into a dimension that has thousands of members, make sure that the Zoom level is not set to *All Levels* or *Bottom Level*. Sample.Basic has no dimension with more than 25 members, so I'm safe for the moment.

The Member Retention options are related to the Zoom In setting:

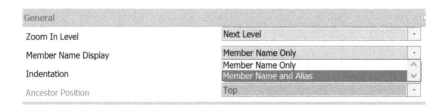

This option allows me to define what happens to the member that I drill on – do I want to keep it as part of the grid or remove it? If *Include Selection* is checked and I zoom in on Year, Year will still remain. If I uncheck this option, when I zoom in on Year I will only see the children of Year. The *Within Selected Group* option will perform ad hoc operations like Zoom In/Out and Keep/Remove Only on a selected range of cells, excluding any unselected cells. *Remove Unselected Groups* will remove all members except for the selected member and refresh members when zooming.

The default option for Member Name Display is *Member Name Only* (which is a little confusing because you can toggle between member name and alias). Basically this option allows you to either view the member name or the alias but not both at the same time.

The *Member Name and Alias* option allows you to view both at the same time when the dimension is in the rows:

| General | | |
|---|---|---|
| Zoom In Level | Next Level | |
| Member Name Display | Member Name Only | |
| Indentation | Member Name Only<br>Member Name and Alias | |
| Ancestor Position | Top | |

By choosing *Member Name and Alias,* an additional column is added to the spreadsheet:

| | A | B | C | D | E | F |
|---|---|---|---|---|---|---|
| 1 | | | | | Market | Scenario |
| 2 | | | | | Measures | |
| 3 | 100 | Colas | Qtr1 | Qtr1 | 7048 | |
| 4 | | | Qtr2 | Qtr2 | 7872 | |
| 5 | | | Qtr3 | Qtr3 | 8511 | |
| 6 | | | Qtr4 | Qtr4 | 7037 | |
| 7 | | | Year | Year | 30468 | |
| 8 | 200 | Root Beer | Qtr1 | Qtr1 | 6721 | |
| 9 | | | Qtr2 | Qtr2 | 7030 | |
| 10 | | | Qtr3 | Qtr3 | 7005 | |
| 11 | | | Qtr4 | Qtr4 | 7198 | |
| 12 | | | Year | Year | 27954 | |
| 13 | 300 | Cream Soda | Qtr1 | Qtr1 | 5929 | |
| 14 | | | Qtr2 | Qtr2 | 6769 | |
| 15 | | | Qtr3 | Qtr3 | 6698 | |
| 16 | | | Qtr4 | Qtr4 | 6403 | |
| 17 | | | Year | Year | 25799 | |

Notice in the grid below that the detail beneath each member is indented (for example, the quarters underneath the Year member).

| | A | B | C | D |
|---|---|---|---|---|
| 1 | | | Market | Scenario |
| 2 | | | Measures | |
| 3 | Colas | Qtr1 | 7048 | |
| 4 | Colas | Qtr2 | 7872 | |
| 5 | Colas | Qtr3 | 8511 | |
| 6 | Colas | Qtr4 | 7037 | |
| 7 | Colas | Year | 30468 | |
| 8 | Root Beer | Qtr1 | 6721 | |
| 9 | Root Beer | Qtr2 | 7030 | |
| 10 | Root Beer | Qtr3 | 7005 | |
| 11 | Root Beer | Qtr4 | 7198 | |
| 12 | Root Beer | Year | 27954 | |
| 13 | Cream Soda | Qtr1 | 5929 | |
| 14 | Cream Soda | Qtr2 | 6769 | |

For those who went to accounting school prior to 1990, it might seem better to indent the totals.

On the *Indentation* section under Member Options, you can switch the indentation from *Subitems* to *Totals* (or select *None* for no indentation):

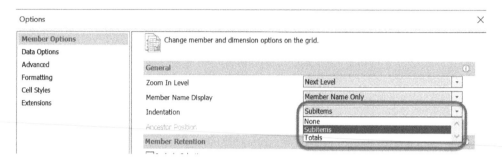

The next time I refresh my data, each summary total will be further indented. See the example below where Year is further indented from the quarters:

|  | A | B | C | D | E |
|---|---|---|---|---|---|
| 1 |  |  | Market | Scenario |  |
| 2 |  |  | Profit | Inventory | Ratios |
| 3 | Colas | Qtr1 | 7048 | 29448 | 57.40178857 |
| 4 |  | Qtr2 | 7872 | 29860 | 57.28473167 |
| 5 |  | Qtr3 | 8511 | 3646 | 57.39 9978 |
| 6 |  | Qtr4 | 7037 | 35811 | 56 99467561 |
| 7 |  | Year | 30468 | 2944 | 57.27288145 |
| 8 | Root Beer | Qtr1 | 6721 | 33 00 | 55.38738874 |
| 9 |  | Qtr2 | 7030 | 31361 | 55.49797453 |
| 10 |  | Qtr3 | 700 | 35253 | 55.06764011 |
| 11 |  | Qtr4 | 198 | 32760 | 56.21773123 |
| 12 |  | Year | 27954 | 33000 | 55.53966595 |
| 13 | Cream Soda | Qtr1 | 5929 | 28865 | 54.11926491 |

To turn off indentation entirely, choose *None* under Indentation.

In the Data Options section, review the available suppression alternatives for Suppress Rows: No Data/Missing, Zero, and Repeated Members.

17. Uncheck the box for *No Data / Missing:*

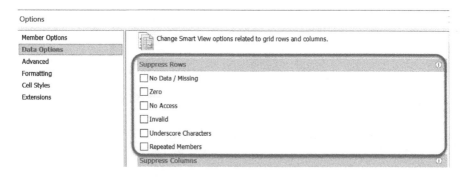

**Note!** The Suppress Rows options *Invalid* and *Underscore Characters* are supported for Hyperion Financial Management only.

Under the Replacement section, notice the #NoData/Missing Label:

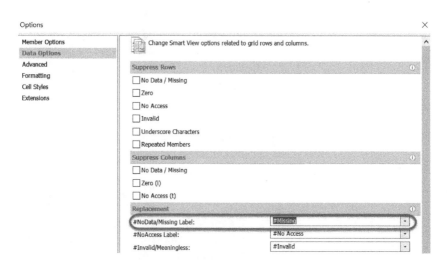

18. Make sure #NoData/Missing label is set and click *OK*.

19. Create the following spreadsheet:

| | A | B | C | D |
|---|---|---|---|---|
| 1 | | Year | Market | Scenario |
| 2 | | Profit | | |
| 3 | Product | 105522 | | |

20. Zoom into the next level for Product.
21. Zoom into the next level for Market.

Notice that Fruit Sodas for the South Region does not have any data and is showing a '#Missing':

| | A | B | C | D |
|---|---|---|---|---|
| 1 | | | Year | Scenario |
| 2 | | | Profit | |
| 3 | East | Colas | 12656 | |
| 4 | | Root Beer | 2534 | |
| 5 | | Cream Soda | 2627 | |
| 6 | | Fruit Soda | 6344 | |
| 7 | | Diet Drinks | 2408 | |
| 8 | | Product | 24161 | |
| 9 | West | Colas | 3549 | |
| 10 | | Root Beer | 9727 | |
| 11 | | Cream Soda | 10731 | |
| 12 | | Fruit Soda | 5854 | |
| 13 | | Diet Drinks | 8087 | |
| 14 | | Product | 29861 | |
| 15 | South | Colas | 4773 | |
| 16 | | Root Beer | 6115 | |
| 17 | | Cream Soda | 2350 | |
| 18 | | Fruit Soda | #Missing | |
| 19 | | Diet Drinks | 4912 | |

The South is not a big fan of Fruit Soda. Data is missing (denoted by Essbase with the term "#Missing"). A missing value in Essbase is very different from a value of zero. A profit of zero means that my sales were cancelled out exactly by my expenses. A profit of #Missing means that I have neither sales nor expenses at this particular combination. Data for South, Fruit Soda, Profit for the year simply does not exist.

If I don't want to see #Missing on my reports, I can replace it with something else. I'll go to my Display options and change the #NoData/Missing label to something that will look better in my report:

22. Under *Options >> Data Options >> Replacement*, change the #NoData/Missing label to #NumericZero:

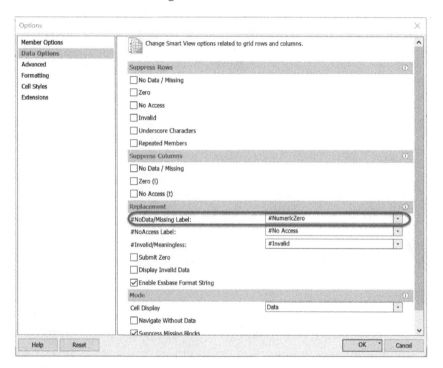

23. Click *OK* and *Refresh* and the ad hoc report should look like this:

|    | A     | B          | C      | D        |
|----|-------|------------|--------|----------|
| 1  |       |            | Year   | Scenario |
| 2  |       |            | Profit |          |
| 3  | East  | Colas      | 12656  |          |
| 4  |       | Root Beer  | 2534   |          |
| 5  |       | Cream Soda | 2627   |          |
| 6  |       | Fruit Soda | 6344   |          |
| 7  |       | Diet Drinks| 2408   |          |
| 8  |       | Product    | 24161  |          |
| 9  | West  | Colas      | 3549   |          |
| 10 |       | Root Beer  | 9727   |          |
| 11 |       | Cream Soda | 10731  |          |
| 12 |       | Fruit Soda | 5854   |          |
| 13 |       | Diet Drinks| 8087   |          |
| 14 |       | Product    | 29861  |          |
| 15 | South | Colas      | 4773   |          |
| 16 |       | Root Beer  | 6115   |          |
| 17 |       | Cream Soda | 2350   |          |
| 18 |       | Fruit Soda | 0      |          |

**Tip!**

The most common #Missing labels are: N/A, #numericzero (0), -, and blank.

In general, there will be lots of intersections in my applications that contain no data value, and retrieving them into a report takes unnecessary time and space. If I have 100,000 products and 5,000 stores, but only 2,000 products might be sold each day at each store, do I really want to see a report that's 98% empty? If not, I can check the box for the *No Data / Missing* option under *Suppress Rows*:

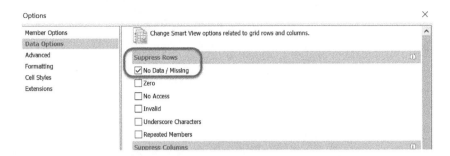

This will suppress any rows where the data for the row is missing. If a single column has a value, even a zero, the row will not be suppressed.

If I also don't want to see intersections where all the values in the row are zero, I'll check the box to suppress Zero as well. I can also suppress rows for which I have no access (No Access check box) or rows that are invalid.

*Navigate Without Data* under the Mode section allows me to set up my spreadsheet, defining the layout without the added time of retrieving data. This can shorten report creation time as I don't have to wait for Essbase to send the data:

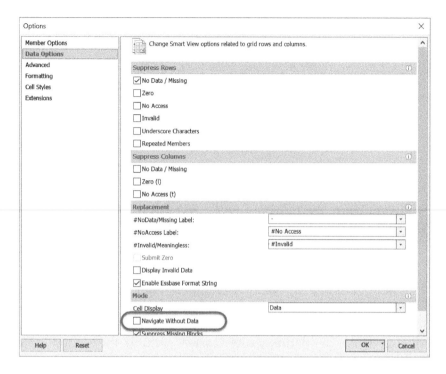

## Change Data

So far, all of my work with the add-in has been for reporting and analysis.

To change data,

1. Using the techniques you've learned to this point, create a new report that looks like the following:

| | A | B | C |
|---|---|---|---|
| 1 | | Cola | Jan |
| 2 | | Actual | Budget |
| 3 | | Sales | Sales |
| 4 | New York | 678 | 640 |
| 5 | Massachusetts | 494 | 460 |
| 6 | Florida | 210 | 190 |
| 7 | Connecticut | 310 | 290 |
| 8 | New Hampshire | 120 | 110 |
| 9 | East | 1812 | 1690 |

**Tip!** To make a quick report, you can always type the member names into a blank spreadsheet. Click *Refresh*. Make sure that each intersection is represented by all dimensions.

The budget for Cola sales in New York is looking a little light, so I'll raise it to 700.

2. Type 700 into cell C4 (or wherever the report has the intersection of New York and Budget). Note the cell color changes to a pale yellow, indicating an adjusted number (though you must be using Cell Styles, discussed later in this chapter):

| | A | B | C | D |
|---|---|---|---|---|
| 1 | | Cola | Jan | |
| 2 | | Actual | Budget | Variance |
| 3 | | Sales | Sales | Sales |
| 4 | New York | 678 | 700 | 38 |
| 5 | Massachusetts | 494 | 460 | 34 |
| 6 | Florida | 210 | 190 | 20 |
| 7 | Connecticut | 310 | 290 | 20 |
| 8 | New Hampshire | 120 | 110 | 10 |
| 9 | East | 1812 | 1690 | 122 |

As of Smart View version 11.1.2.5, I have three options for submitting data (granted that I am on the Essbase ribbon):

- **Submit Data** - submit data to the cube
- **Submit Data Without Refresh** - submit data to the cube without first refreshing the data
- **Submit Data Range** - submit a defined set of cells or cell range(s) to the cube

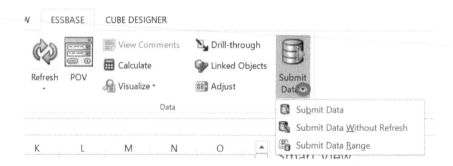

For this exercise, I will use the generic *Submit Data* option.

3. Choose *Submit Data* on the Smart View ribbon:

Or the Essbase ribbon:

The data will automatically refresh, showing I saved the 700 data value.

4. Now type "Variance" next to *Budget* in cell D2 and click *Refresh*:

| | A | B | C | D |
|---|---|---|---|---|
| 1 | | Cola | Jan | |
| 2 | | Actual | Budget | Variance |
| 3 | | Sales | Sales | Sales |
| 4 | New York | 678 | 700 | -22 |
| 5 | Massachusetts | 494 | 460 | 34 |
| 6 | Florida | 210 | 190 | 20 |
| 7 | Connecticut | 310 | 290 | 20 |
| 8 | New Hampshire | 120 | 110 | 10 |
| 9 | East | 1812 | 1690 | 122 |

This isn't going to make any sense, but I want to show a possible scenario that I could run into in my application.

5. Type 50 in cell D4 (you're saying "what in the ..." but trust me). The cell shading will change to yellow:

| | A | B | C | D |
|---|---|---|---|---|
| 1 | | Cola | Jan | |
| 2 | | Actual | Budget | Variance |
| 3 | | Sales | Sales | Sales |
| 4 | New York | 678 | 700 | 50 |
| 5 | Massachusetts | 494 | 460 | 34 |
| 6 | Florida | 210 | 190 | 20 |
| 7 | Connecticut | 310 | 290 | 20 |
| 8 | New Hampshire | 120 | 110 | 10 |
| 9 | East | 1812 | 1690 | 122 |

6. Now select *Submit Data* on the Smart View or Essbase ribbon.

Was the data saved to Essbase? Nope. Depending on the Essbase cube and security, there will be some data points where I can't save data. In the case of Variance, this member is dynamically calculated and never stores any data. The other common causes are insufficient rights and sending numbers into summary members (also called upper-level members).

One cool feature I want to illustrate along with Submit Data is the Adjust feature. In Smart View, I can select a single cell or multiple cells and click the *Adjust* button.

A window will display with some built in financial calculations to adjust the data set you've selected.

The options are:

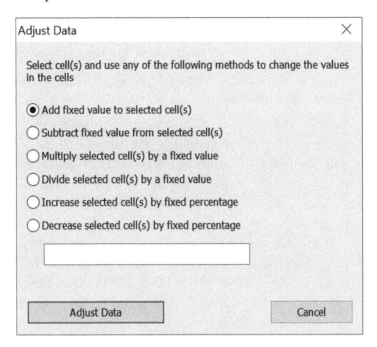

- **Add fixed value to selected cell(s)** - Adds the entered value to the original value(s) in the selected cell(s)
- **Subtract fixed value from selected cell(s)** - Subtracts the entered value from the original value(s) in the selected cell(s)
- **Multiply selected cell(s) by a fixed value** - Multiplies the original value(s) in the selected cell(s) by the entered value
- **Divide selected cell(s) by a fixed value** - Divides the original value(s) in the selected cell(s) by the entered value
- **Increase selected cell(s) by a fixed percentage** - Increases the original value(s) in the selected cell(s) by the percentage entered. For example, to increase the original value(s) by 5%, enter "5".
- **Decrease selected cell(s) by a fixed percentage** - Decreases the original value(s) in the selected cell(s) by the percentage entered. For example, to decrease the original value(s) by 5%, enter a value of "5".

When data is adjusted, it has not been submitted to the server. I have to click Submit Data to commit the changes back to the Essbase cube.

**Note!**   When using Adjust, I must have write security for the intersections of data.

If I submit 735 over the budgeted 700 value, math wizards in the audience will immediately note that 735+460+190+290+110 does not equal 1,690. It's actually 95 short because I haven't told the Essbase server to recalculate the totals. Depending on the type of Essbase cube, I may need to run an additional calculation to aggregate data to all levels of the cube. If my cube is a block storage cube, many of the summary members may be "stored," meaning that Essbase stores the pre-calculated totals to speed retrieval. This aligns with the common Essbase belief that analysis tends to start at the top of the hierarchy and then drill down.

**Note!**   One of the major differences between Essbase and a relational database is that relational databases assume that you want to look at detail (so displaying totals is much slower) and Essbase assumes that you want to look at summaries (though detailed data is not any slower).

Other members may be "dynamically calculated" (though the cool kids say "dynamic calc"), meaning that Essbase calculates those members at the time the user requests them. While some members in Sample.Basic are dynamically calculated (the upper level Measures, for instance), it's usually best to assume that I should recalculate after submitting data to a block storage cube.

7.  Assuming you have access to recalculate the cube, choose *Calculate* from the Essbase ribbon:

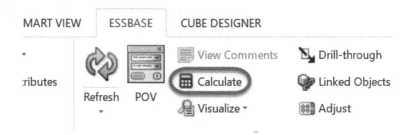

This will pull up a list of calculation scripts for which I have access. I can filter this list by cube.

8. Select the calc script you wish to run and click *Launch*. In this example, choose the Default calculation script (which basically calculates everything in the cube) for the Sample.Basic cube:

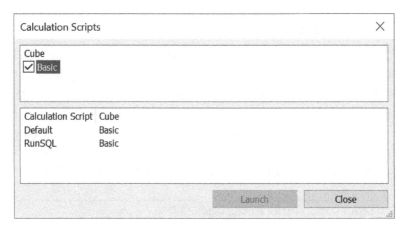

Smart View will check with the Essbase server every few seconds to see if the calculation has completed yet. I can always continue to work in Excel in the meantime, I just won't work with this Essbase cube unless I'm OK with potentially erroneous results.

While the Default calculation for Sample.Basic will always take just a few seconds, complex calculations against large cubes can take several minutes or even hours. I'll be patient and Smart View will let me know when the calculation is finished.

9.  Once the calculation message appears, click *Refresh* to refresh the calculated data and you should see the correct value for East with the additional 95 in it:

|   | A | B | C | D |
|---|---|---|---|---|
| 1 |  | Cola | Jan |  |
| 2 |  | Actual | Budget | Variance |
| 3 |  | Sales | Sales | Sales |
| 4 | New York | 678 | 700 | 50 |
| 5 | Massachusetts | 494 | 460 | 34 |
| 6 | Florida | 210 | 190 | 20 |
| 7 | Connecticut | 310 | 290 | 20 |
| 8 | New Hampshire | 120 | 110 | 10 |
| 9 | East | 1812 | 1750 | 122 |

## Logging Off

I can disconnect from a spreadsheet if I choose. Simply right-click on the Essbase cube and select *Disconnect*. I can also just close the spreadsheet and this will end my connection to the active Essbase cube for the spreadsheet.

Can you believe it? I've already refreshed and analyzed data in Essbase. I've successfully connected to an Essbase data source, zoomed and pivoted, and set a number of options for analysis. Wahoo!

---

**COMMUNICATION: ROSKE TO ALAPAT**

[11:32] ROSKE: Opal, now that I have implemented PBCS in the Cloud, I can appreciate how much we are both "true nerds." We eat, sleep, and breathe Oracle and EPM. We know the language, "Hyperion," backwards and forwards. Backwards, it's "Noirepyh," but I don't need to tell you that. For goodness sake, we both scored 96% on the "What Percent Geek Are You" test,

my kindred soul. Others only aspire to our level of
coolness, known only as "Essbase Cool."

## BECOME A POWER USER

Up until this point, I've primarily been navigating my way to
data by zooming in or out, using keep/remove only, or just typing
members into my spreadsheet. In this section, I'll introduce you to
member selection capabilities, the Smart View Query Designer, the POV
Manager, and more; all tools that will help me get the information I need
faster and easier.

The TBC division of JWE has just requested a detailed market
report analyzing financials by state…just as I was about to duck out for
the weekend. Despite my attempts to avoid their Finance person at the
end of the day on Friday (one can only hide in the copy room for so long),
he catches me with a demand to work the weekend to get the state
analysis done. "Opal, pull out all stops to get this done." Argh. However,
I *am* trying to save Edward.

I'm a problem solver so I create this sheet by opening up a blank
spreadsheet, typing Measures into cell B1, Product into C1, Scenario into
D1, all the months into B2:B13, and all the states into the cells starting at
A3:

| | A | B | C | D | E | F | G | H | I | J | K | L | M |
|---|---|---|---|---|---|---|---|---|---|---|---|---|---|
| 1 | | Product | Profit | Scenario | | | | | | | | | |
| 2 | | Jan | Feb | Mar | Apr | May | Jun | Jul | Aug | Sep | Oct | Nov | Dec |
| 3 | New York | 512 | 601 | 543 | 731 | 720 | 912 | 857 | 570 | 516 | 766 | 721 | 753 |
| 4 | Massachusetts | 519 | 498 | 515 | 534 | 548 | 668 | 688 | 685 | 563 | 477 | 499 | 518 |
| 5 | Florida | 336 | 361 | 373 | 408 | 440 | 491 | 545 | 529 | 421 | 373 | 337 | 415 |
| 6 | Connecticut | 321 | 309 | 290 | 272 | 253 | 212 | 198 | 175 | 231 | 260 | 310 | 262 |
| 7 | New Hampshire | 44 | 74 | 84 | 86 | 99 | 125 | 139 | 136 | 93 | 81 | 75 | 89 |
| 8 | California | 1034 | 1047 | 1048 | 1010 | 1093 | 1185 | 1202 | 1269 | 1122 | 1053 | 923 | 978 |
| 9 | Oregon | 444 | 417 | 416 | 416 | 400 | 402 | 414 | 412 | 409 | 421 | 467 | 444 |
| 10 | Washington | 405 | 412 | 395 | 368 | 378 | 372 | 372 | 392 | 394 | 397 | 385 | 371 |
| 11 | Utah | 237 | 251 | 256 | 277 | 262 | 246 | 276 | 248 | 217 | 269 | 309 | 307 |
| 12 | Nevada | 219 | 267 | 289 | 330 | 365 | 411 | 493 | 451 | 268 | 317 | 281 | 348 |
| 13 | Texas | 504 | 547 | 531 | 507 | 547 | 556 | 556 | 595 | 552 | 531 | 497 | 502 |

This, however, would mean coming in on Saturday. Is there
another way to get this done and save my plans for organizing the sock

drawer? Yes! I can use a previously ignored menu item called *Member Selection*.

### Member Selection

Member Selection is like my own personalized temp typist. Now I'll see how handy it can be at generating spreadsheets like the one above. First, I'll make Member Selection (often shortened to Member Select) type in my states for me.

1.  In a blank worksheet, right-click on *Sample.Basic* and select *Ad hoc analysis*. Drag the *Market* dimension to rows and the *Year* dimension to the column. Move *Measures* back to the POV. The spreadsheet should look something like this:

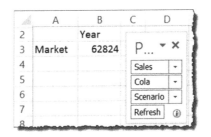

2.  Select cell A3 and then choose the *Member Selection* button:

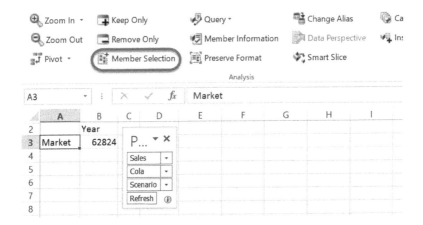

The Member Selection window will display:

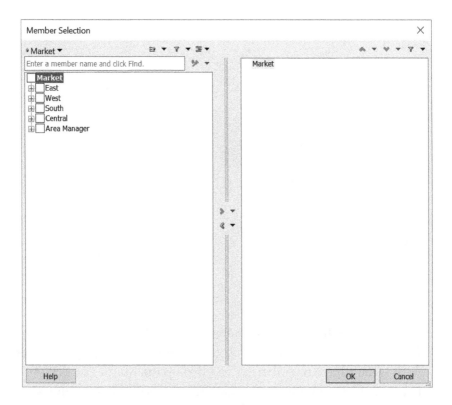

Notice that the dimension that comes up is Market. Smart View will refresh the dimension based on what's in the cell that I selected.

I could also see a Dimension Name Resolution screen which allows me to pick the desired dimension and the desired orientation for the spreadsheet (e.g., vertical position to list members down the page). Layout is very important when defining queries and using member selection.

Back to the task at hand. Let me take a closer look at the Member Selection window.

The upper left hand corner shows the current dimension selected:

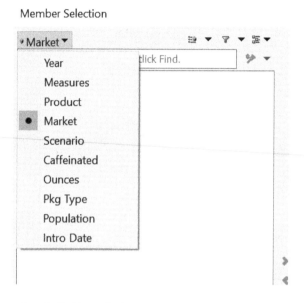

Notice the full list of dimensions is listed. I could, if I had a hankering to, change the dimension for the selected cell (e.g., Market to Product). I don't have a hankering so I'll keep the Market dimension for the current cell. The members in the left box should list for the Market dimension.

3.  Click the plus sign next to *East* and it will expand to show the states in the East.

Notice that I am viewing this dimension by "Hierarchy":

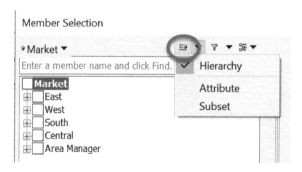

I could also choose to view the members of the Market dimension by Attribute or Subset. For now I'll leave the selection as Hierarchy.

4.  Click the check box next to all of the East states:

5.  Click the arrow  ⟩  button.

I should now see five of the fifty most important states in the USA appear in the box to the right under Selection.

6.  Use this same method to add the states under West, South, and Central to the list on the right.

I should now be looking at the following:

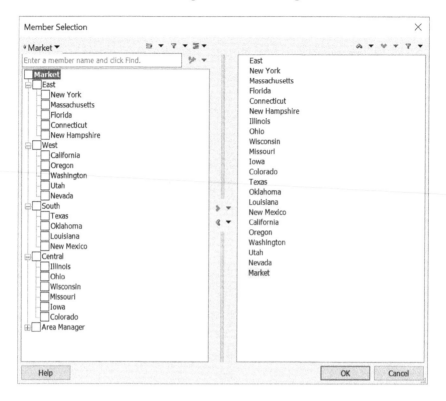

If I was an obsessive-compulsive type and wanted to manually alphabetize my state names before entering them into the sheet, I would highlight the state I want to rearrange in the list and then click either the *Move Item Up* or *Move Item Down* button.

If I want to jump a member all the way to the top, I'd select the drop-down arrow and choose *Move to Top*:

If I accidentally add any member more than once, I'd highlight the member to remove and choose the < icon.

To clear the whole list, I'd select the drop-down arrow and choose *Remove All*:

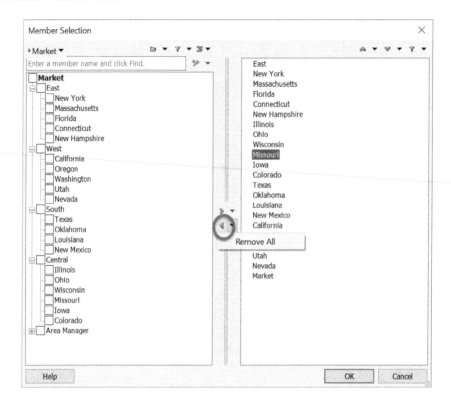

7. Assuming your list is complete (and alphabetized if that's how you roll), click *OK* and you'll be able to watch while Essbase enters the states down the left side of the spreadsheet:

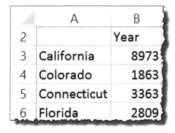

**Note!** After you use Member Selection to type in your members, you will need to click Refresh. Member Selection does not do a refresh on its own.

Now I'll use a slightly different method to type in the months.

8.  Select cell *B2* and choose *Member Selection*. The Year dimension should appear.

Be default, I am viewing the Year hierarchy in the member selection window by Hierarchy:

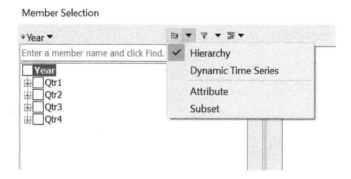

9.  Click the filter icon and choose *Level* (notice the default is set to *None*):

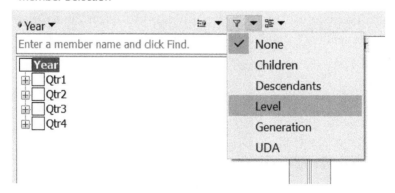

The filter icon allows me to search for a specific set of members in a hierarchy. For any member in the selected dimension, I could easily select the member itself (*None*), its children, its descendants, members at the same level or generation of the selected member, or members for specific user defined attribute (UDA).

Remember for my example that the months are level-0 since they don't have any children (through no lack of trying, mind you).

10. Enter the level number. In this case, 0:

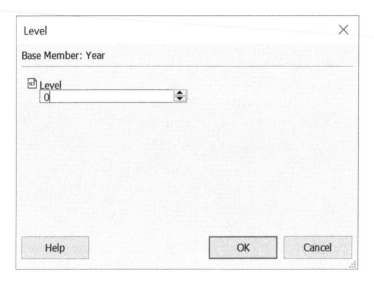

**Tip!**
You could also use the arrow keys to select the available levels for the selected dimension.

11. Click *OK* and you will see that the level-0 months are available in the members section. Note they haven't been selected yet. I've only filtered them in the members section:

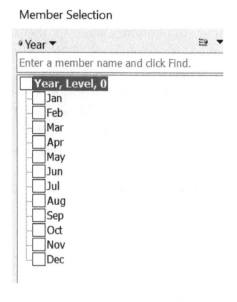

12. Click the drop-down box just to the right of the filter icon to select *Check Base Members* (much easier than having to manually check month by month):

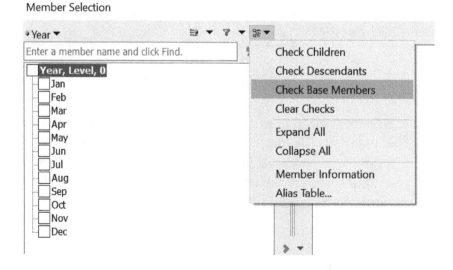

I can also choose to *Check Children* or *Check Descendants* of filtered members, depending on what I'm attempting to select. If I want to clear all check marks, I'd select *Clear Checks*.

13. Now move the months over to the selection section by clicking the right arrow icon.

Notice the two small icons at the bottom of the Member Selection window: Show Formatting Bar and Fill Horizontally. These are toggle options that should be selected or deselected. Because the Year dimension is in the columns, the selected members will be inserted horizontally by default. I could change this to list down the rows by unselecting the Fill Horizontally icon:

14. Leave the default for horizontal placement of members. Click *OK* and the months are placed across the columns in the spreadsheet:

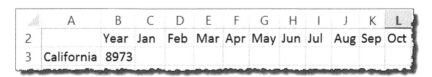

15. Remember to click *Refresh* to see the data.

**Tip!**

Member selection just selects members from the source dimensions. It may not create a usable report. For example, if you selected Fill Vertical for the months in the example above, Smart View would add the members vertically in column B, creating a problematic resulting format.

What about changing the members that are displayed in my floating POV? Remember earlier in the book that I could change the selected member by just typing a member name over the current name in the floating POV window. I can also use Member Selection, following a similar process.

16. Before I get there, let's do one thing. If necessary, select *Change Alias* from the Essbase ribbon and select Default. Remember, this is the way you toggle back and forth between member names and aliases in Smart View.

**Tip!** While you can select multiple members in the floating POV, Smart View will only display data for a single member from each POV dimension.

17. Select the drop-down arrow next to Product and choose the ellipses (…).

The Member Selection window is launched:

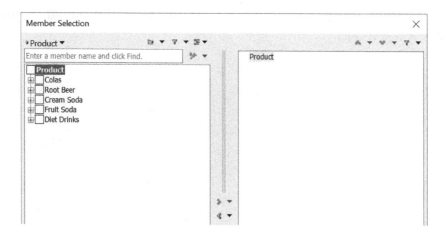

Let's say I want to perform analysis on the Diet Drinks.

18. Remove any other selections that currently exist. Check the *Diet Drinks* check box and then select children under the right arrow icon:

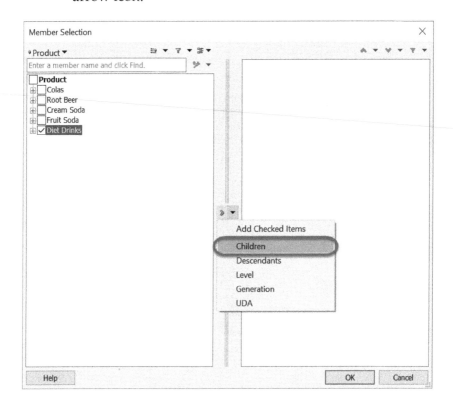

The children of Diet Drinks are automatically added to the Selection section:

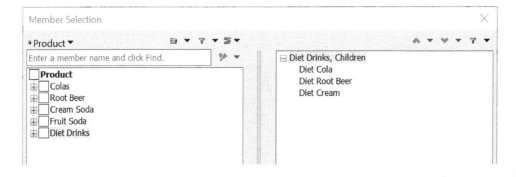

19. Click *OK*.

Now in the Product drop-down, all selected members are available:

20. Change the selection from Product to Diet Drinks and click *Refresh* to see the new data.
21. Go back to the Member Selection for Product.
22. Choose the drop-down option for Dimension and note that you can select the members for all of the dimensions in the POV.
23. Go ahead and select the Scenario dimension:

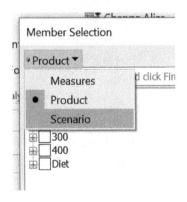

24. Select the *Check Base Members* of Scenario and move them into the selection section:

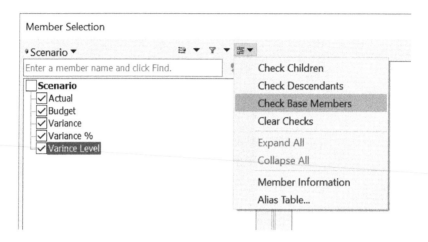

25. Now choose the Measures dimension:

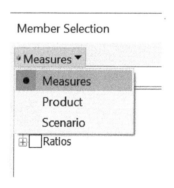

26. Type in sal* in the text box next to the flashlight icon to search for the member beginning with the letters "sal*":

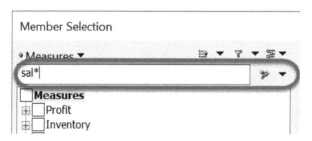

27. In the drop-down next to the flashlight, choose *Check All Found*. This option will find all matches to the search criteria and check them (so they are easily moved to the selection panel of the Member Selection window):

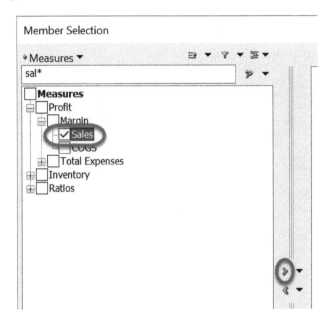

Note that I can also find the next or previous member in the hierarchy from the selected member that matches the search criteria.

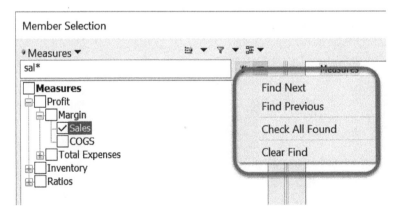

**Tip!**

Use the * as a wildcard when searching in Member Selection. Wildcards only work as trailing wildcards.

28. Move the *Sales* member over to the Selection section.

29. Lastly, let's go back to the Product dimension. In the filter drop-down, select *Generation*:

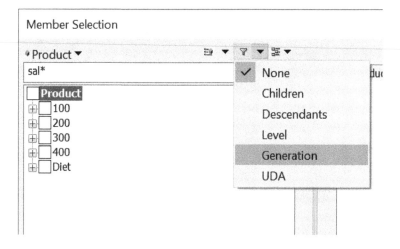

30. Type in or select 2 as the Generation and click *OK*.

31. Move the Gen2 products into the selection section. Click *OK* to finally close the Member Selection window:

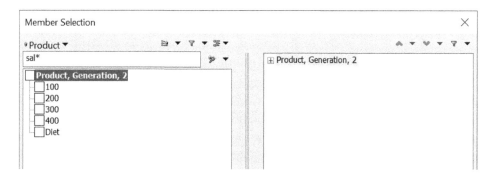

32. Check out the new member selections in the floating POV:

I'll walk through one more use case for member selection. I want to create a report that just pulls in the level-0 members under the East region. Follow along to learn the easiest way to build this query.

1. Create the following starting point query using your growing Smart View skills:

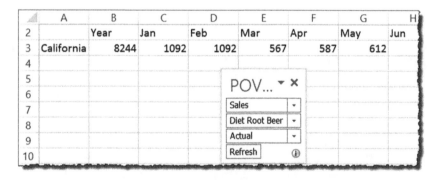

2. Select cell A3 and choose *Member Selection* from the Essbase ribbon.

3. In the Member Selection window, remove the selection for *California*. Check the box next to *East*.

4.  In the drop-down arrow key to move over the selected member, choose *Level*:

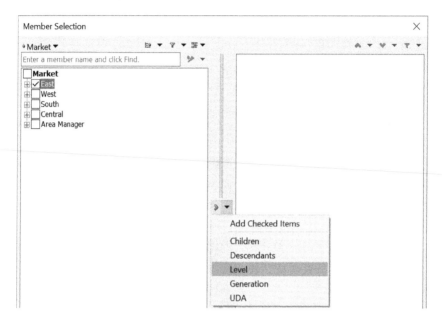

5.  Enter a zero:

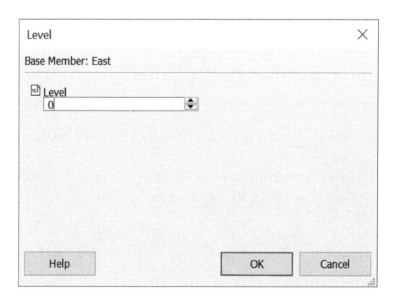

6.  Click *OK*. The level-0 members under East are added to the selection panel:

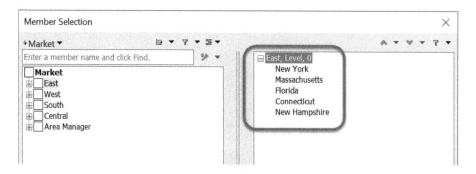

7.  Click *OK* and you are off and running.

In summary, there are many ways to filter members in my dimensions for reporting and analysis. Remembering the Essbase terminology and knowing the hierarchies will be important in effectively using Member Selection. When searching for members to add to analysis, dimensions can be filtered by:

- Children
- Descendants
- Level
- Generation
- Attribute
- UDA
- Subset (which is really just another way to filter by attribute)
- Search using wildcards

I can then check all of the desired members in a single swoop for my analysis by using the options Check Children, Check Descendants, or Check Base Members.

### Dynamic Time Series

My boss has a new request: while I have data for the entire year, he wants a report with sales through May along with a year to date total at the end.

1.  Create the following starting point query:

| | A | B | C | D |
|---|---|---|---|---|
| 1 | | Sales | Diet Root Beer | Actual |
| 2 | | Year | | |
| 3 | East | 3777 | | |

2.  Use Member Selection to select the months Jan to May.

Next I want to add a year to date column. How could I accomplish that? I could add an Excel total column to the right of column F to sum the values in January through May, but if Dynamic Time Series has been turned on, all I have to do is refresh this information. (Oh right, time can now be spent actually analyzing the data versus getting and calculating the data.) Dynamic Time Series will be based on my Periods or Year dimension and is not applicable to other dimensions.

Dynamic Time Series means that Essbase will take and dynamically add up time periods up to whatever period I specify just as if that member was stored in the outline. For instance, if I ask for Q-T-D (Q-T-D is short for Quarter-To-Date) through May, Essbase will total the data for April and May (since those are the months in the quarter containing May) and put them into a Q-T-D member. This member can then be pivoted and for the most part treated just like a stored member.

Sample.Basic has two Dynamic Time Series members (often abbreviated as "DTS members"): Q-T-D and H-T-D. H-T-D stands for History-To-Date. Other common DTS members include Y-T-D (Year-To-Date), M-T-D (Month-To-Date), W-T-D (Week-To-Date), S-T-D (No, not a disease but Season-To-Date), P-T-D (Period-To-Date), and D-T-D (Day-To-Date).

3. Since you want January through May to be totaled, select *H-T-D* and add it to the right side of our starting point query. Select cell G2 in your spreadsheet (to the right of May). Type in "H-T-D(May)" and click *Refresh*:

|  | A | B | C | D | E | F | G |
|---|---|---|---|---|---|---|---|
| 1 |  | Sales | Diet Root Beer | Actual |  |  |  |
| 2 |  | Jan | Feb | Mar | Apr | May | H-T-D(May) |
| 3 | East | 310 | 310 | 312 | 314 | 317 | 1563 |

The year to date value (named H-T-D or History-To-Date in Sample.Basic's example) is returned with no further calculation.

I can also select dynamic time series members via Member Selection.

4. Select cell G2 and click *Member Selection*. Change the member view selection 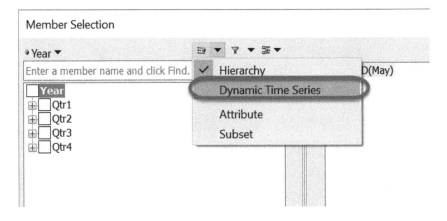 from Hierarchy to *Dynamic Time Series*:

5.  Check the *Q-T-D* option and click the > arrow to move it to the right panel:

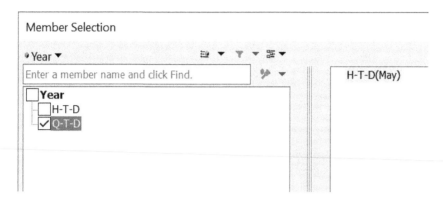

6.  When prompted, select the Month that should be used as the basis for the quarter to date calculation. In our example, choose *May*:

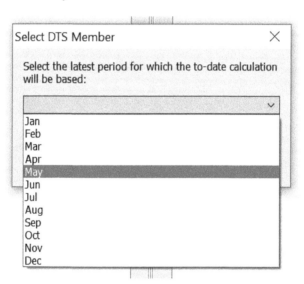

7.  Click *OK* twice to complete the member selection steps which should now have both H-T-D and Q-T-D. Once you are back in the spreadsheet, click *Refresh* and the values are refreshed:

|  | A | B | C | D | E | F | G | H |
|---|---|---|---|---|---|---|---|---|
| 1 |  | Sales | Diet Root Beer | Actual |  |  |  |  |
| 2 |  | Jan | Feb |  | Mar | Apr | May | H-T-D(May) | Q-T-D(May) |
| 3 | East | 310 |  | 310 | 312 | 314 | 317 | 1563 | 631 |

**Note!**

You can also type in DTS members directly. To specify a specific month, put it in parentheses after the member. For instance to get Q-T-D through March, type in "Q-T-D(Mar)". There is no space between the member and the parenthesis. The member entered must always be the level-0 members of the time dimension.

## Substitution Variables

Another retrieval alternative available to me is substitution variables. These objects are created to help in Essbase maintenance as well as reporting (that's the part I care about). A substitution variable is a holding place for information that changes on a periodic basis and is used in a number of places. Current month, current year, and prior year are all examples of common substitution variables. Smart View supports them, too. To use a substitution variable in Smart View, simply type an ampersand ("&") in front of the variable name in the spreadsheet where you'd like to display the member:

|  | A | B |
|---|---|---|
| 1 |  | Measures |
| 2 | &curmo | 8333 |

Click *Refresh* and the member assigned to the variable will display. So now when my boss requests that last-minute report, I can type in the substitution variable and immediately refresh the report. Awesome!

### Attribute Dimensions

All the analysis of Sample.Basic up to this point has been done using five dimensions. There are five other dimensions in Sample.Basic that I could be using but I've been ignoring them. These dimensions are known as "Attribute dimensions," and they are alternate ways of summarizing my base (sometimes called "standard" or "stored") dimensions. I won't see Attribute dimensions unless I specifically reference them in an analysis.

I can click *Insert Attributes* from the Essbase ribbon and select the desired attribute to add to my spreadsheet:

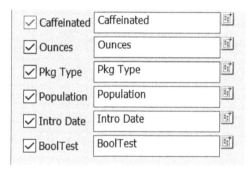

Thankfully, I am covering these dimensions now since JWE has been wowed with the detailed state analysis and an additional analysis by caffeinated products.

**Note!**
Unlike base dimensions, the totals for attribute dimensions are not pre-calculated in Essbase. As such, retrieval of attribute dimensions will often be slower as Essbase dynamically calculates the results. Also watch out for instances where dynamically calculated member values are off due to the use of Attribute dimensions. Hopefully, these have been caught but adjustments might have to be made if there are any calculation issues with Attributes.

Sample.Basic has five attribute dimensions: Caffeinated, Ounces, Pkg Type, Intro Date, and Population. The first four of these are alternate ways of rolling up the Product dimension. Population is an alternate way of rolling up the Market dimension. As an example, I'll limit the report I just made to only caffeinated drinks for all products.

8. First type "Products" into C1, replacing the member reference for *Diet Root Beer*. Click *Refresh.*
9. Type "Caffeinated" into cell E1. Click *Refresh* and the Caffeinated attribute dimension is now referenced in the query:

| | A | B | C | D | E | F | G | H |
|---|---|---|---|---|---|---|---|---|
| 1 | | Sales | Products | Actual | Caffeinated | | | |
| 2 | | Jan | Feb | Mar | Apr | May | H-T-D(May) | Q-T-D(May) |
| 3 | East | 6780 | 6920 | 6921 | 7213 | 7341 | 35175 | 14554 |

Since I haven't been getting much sleep lately, I'll focus just on Caffeinated products.

10. Zoom in on *Caffeinated* to see the data broken up by Caffeinated_True and Caffeinated_False:

| | A | B | C | D | E | F | G | H | I |
|---|---|---|---|---|---|---|---|---|---|
| 1 | | | Sales | | Product | Actual | | | |
| 2 | | | Jan | Feb | Mar | Apr | May | H-T-D(May) | Q-T-D(May) |
| 3 | Caffeinated_True | East | 4578 | 4559 | 4641 | 4871 | 4980 | 23629 | 9851 |
| 4 | Caffeinated_False | East | 2202 | 2361 | 2280 | 2342 | 2361 | 11546 | 4703 |
| 5 | Caffeinated | East | 6780 | 6920 | 6921 | 7213 | 7341 | 35175 | 14554 |

**Tip!**

What do you think is the fastest way to find which products are Caffeinated? You might think zooming in on Product, which will certainly work, but depending on how you zoom you may have to step through two or more levels. The super-fast method to pull up this list is to zoom in on Caffeinated_True.

11. Zoom in on *Caffeinated_True* and the query displays the list with a single double-click:

| | A | B | C | D | E |
|---|---|---|---|---|---|
| 1 | | | | Sales | Produc |
| 2 | | | | Jan | Feb |
| 3 | Caffeinated_True | Cola | East | 1812 | |
| 4 | Caffeinated_True | Diet Cola | East | 200 | |
| 5 | Caffeinated_True | Old Fashioned | East | 647 | |
| 6 | Caffeinated_True | Diet Root Beer | East | 310 | |
| 7 | Caffeinated_True | Dark Cream | East | 999 | |
| 8 | Caffeinated_True | Vanilla Cream | East | 500 | |
| 9 | Caffeinated_True | Diet Cream | East | 110 | |
| 10 | Caffeinated_False | Product | East | 2202 | |
| 11 | Caffeinated | Product | East | 6780 | |

Can I use Member Selection with Attribute dimensions? Absolutely, but I need to first add the attribute to the spreadsheet (just as I did with the Caffeinated attribute dimension). I'll go ahead and create another analysis, this time with the Population attribute dimension. JWE is going to want to see sales broken down by Population.

1. Create the following starting point query:

| | A | B | C | D | E |
|---|---|---|---|---|---|
| 1 | | Year | Market | Product | Scenario |
| 2 | | Sales | | | |
| 3 | Population | 400855 | | | |

By typing "Population" into cell A3, I can now use Member Selection to pick and choose my desired members. (I could also Zoom In and Keep Only too, but I'd like to show you the interface for selecting attribute members).

2. Select cell A3 and choose *Member Selection*.

All of the same member selection options are available for Attribute dimensions (that are applicable; e.g., UDAs and Attributes are not available for attribute dimensions).

3.  Select the filter icon and filter the Population hierarchy for level-1 members:

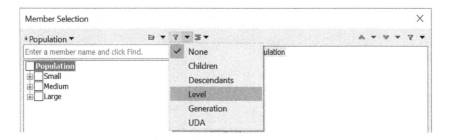

4.  Select the *Check Base Members* option to select all of the level-1 members. Use the > key to select the members and click *OK*. Click *Refresh*.

|   | A | B | C | D | E |
|---|---|---|---|---|---|
| 1 |  | Year | Market | Product | Scenario |
| 2 |  | Sales |  |  |  |
| 3 | Population | 400855 |  |  |  |
| 4 | Small | 216321 |  |  |  |
| 5 | Medium | 84091 |  |  |  |
| 6 | Large | 100443 |  |  |  |

I'll walk through one more analysis example using attributes. This time I am going to filter members in the Product dimension using attribute dimensions (this is really just another way to get to the same answer, but in some cases this member selection method can be more efficient).

5. Create the following starting point query:

| | A | B | C | D |
|---|---|---|---|---|
| 1 | | Year | Market | Actual |
| 2 | | Sales | | |
| 3 | Product | 400855 | | |

6. Select cell A3 (*Product*) and choose *Member Selection*. From the
   ⊟ ▾  icon, select *Attribute*:

7. A new window will display. Click the magnifying glass icon;
   this will launch another window.

8.  Choose the *Intro Date* attribute dimension:

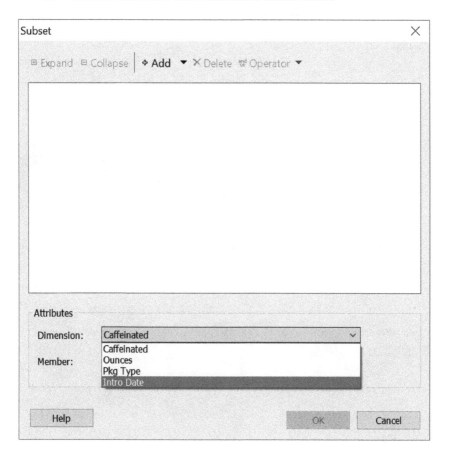

9. Select the member *Intro Date 3-25-1996* and click *Add.* The member is added to the subset:

10. If the wrong date is mistakenly selected, choose the correct date and select *Set* to confirm it.
11. Click *OK* twice.

12. The members listed in member selection are those that have an introduction date of 3-25-1995. You can then use the Check options to select the members:

Member Selection

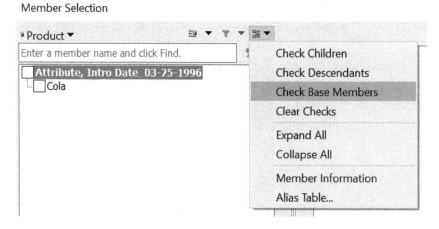

The resulting spreadsheet displays the filtered Product members. Note that the attribute member itself does not display; I simply used this method to quickly filter the product members:

|   | A | B | C | D |
|---|---|---|---|---|
| 1 |  | Year | Market | Actual |
| 2 |  | Sales |  |  |
| 3 | Product | 400855 |  |  |
| 4 | Cola | 62824 |  |  |

**Tip!**

Another way to perform analysis on attribute dimensions: insert a column before column A and either type the Attribute dimension name (e.g., Ounces) into A3 or use member selection, select the attribute dimension members. Click *Refresh*:

|  | A | B | C | D | E |
|---|---|---|---|---|---|
| 1 |  |  | Year | Market | Actual |
| 2 |  |  | Sales |  |  |
| 3 | Ounces | Product | 400855 |  |  |

I can also use the Insert Attributes option to insert selected attribute dimensions on the worksheet:

1. Create the following starting point query:

|  | A | B | C | D |
|---|---|---|---|---|
| 1 |  | Year | Market | Actual |
| 2 |  | Sales |  |  |
| 3 | Product | 400855 |  |  |
| 4 | Colas | 106134 |  |  |
| 5 | Cola | 62824 |  |  |
| 6 | Diet Cola | 30469 |  |  |
| 7 | Caffeine Free Cola | 12841 |  |  |
| 8 | Root Beer | 109086 |  |  |
| 9 | Fruit Soda | 84230 |  |  |
| 10 | Cream Soda | 101405 |  |  |
| 11 | Diet Drinks | 105678 |  |  |

2. Select *Insert Attributes* on the Essbase ribbon:

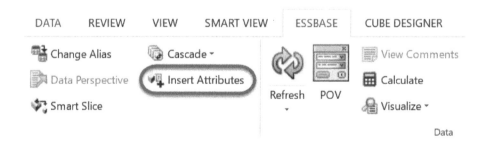

| DATA | REVIEW | VIEW | SMART VIEW | ESSBASE | CUBE DESIGNER |

Change Alias     Cascade ▾                View Comments

Data Perspective     Insert Attributes             Calculate

Smart Slice                 Refresh   POV      Visualize ▾

                                                         Data

3. Uncheck all attribute dimensions but *Intro Date.* Select the Member Selector 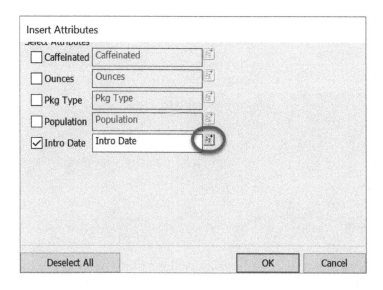 icon next to Intro Date:

Insert Attributes

Select Attributes

| ☐ Caffeinated | Caffeinated | |
| ☐ Ounces | Ounces | |
| ☐ Pkg Type | Pkg Type | |
| ☐ Population | Population | |
| ☑ Intro Date | Intro Date | |

Deselect All                    OK          Cancel

4. Select *Intro Date_03-25-1996*:

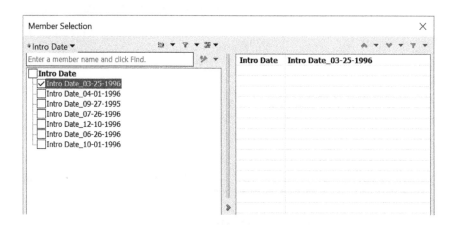

Member Selection                                                              ✕

● Intro Date ▼                    ☰ ▼  ⏷ ▼ ☰ ▼                          ⏶ ▼  ⏷ ▼ ⏷ ▼

Enter a member name and click Find.    ⚡ ▼    **Intro Date    Intro Date_03-25-1996**

☐ **Intro Date**
  ☑ Intro Date_03-25-1996
  ☐ Intro Date_04-01-1996
  ☐ Intro Date_09-27-1995
  ☐ Intro Date_07-26-1996
  ☐ Intro Date_12-10-1996
  ☐ Intro Date_06-26-1996
  ☐ Intro Date_10-01-1996

5.   Click *OK* >> *OK*:

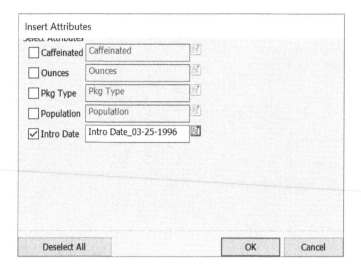

Now the only members and values that are valid are those with an intro date of 03-25-1996:

|  | A | B | C | D | E |
|---|---|---|---|---|---|
| 1 |  | Year | Market | Actual | Intro Date_03-25-1996 |
| 2 |  | Sales |  |  |  |
| 3 | Product | 62824 |  |  |  |
| 4 |   Colas | 62824 |  |  |  |
| 5 |     Cola | 62824 |  |  |  |
| 6 |     Diet Cola | #Invalid |  |  |  |
| 7 |     Caffeine Free Cola | #Invalid |  |  |  |
| 8 |   Root Beer | #Invalid |  |  |  |
| 9 |   Fruit Soda | #Invalid |  |  |  |
| 10 |   Cream Soda | #Invalid |  |  |  |
| 11 |   Diet Drinks | #Invalid |  |  |  |

## Analysis, Analysis, Analysis

JWE has just made a new list of information requests. Answer the questions below and see if you think I will be working for sols and sols:

- How many different caffeinated products are sold in Massachusetts for the year?

- What were the sales for Actual Cola for the East Region for Jan, Feb, Mar?
- What were Actual, Budget and Variance for the Margin on the Cola products for Q1 for the West region?
- What were the top selling products for the year for all markets?
- What were the product codes for the top selling products for the year for all markets?
- Which product had the highest negative Actual to Budget variance for Sales for all regions?
- For that product, what two regions had the most impact on the negative variance?
- Which region had the highest total expenses as a percent to total sales?
- What were the bottom three performing states for Profit, total Products, for the year?
- What size population (small, medium, large) are those three states?
- Which packaging type sold more in Small Populations?
- What were the two top selling months for diet products for all regions for the year?
- What two states purchased the most diet products for the Q2?
- What state beginning with the letter C had the top sales for the year for all products?

And here are the answers!

- How many different caffeinated products are sold in Massachusetts for the year?
  - Four different caffeinated products are sold in MA
- What were the sales for Actual Cola for the East Region for Jan, Feb, Mar?
  - $1,812 $1,754 $1,805
- What were Actual, Budget and Variance for the Margin on the Cola products for Q1 for the West region?
  - $2,065 $2,570 ($505)
- What were the top selling products for the year for all markets?

- o   Cola, Dark Cream, Old Fashioned
- What were the product codes for the top selling products for the year for all markets?
  - o   100-10, 300-10, 200-10
- Which product had the highest negative Actual to Budget variance for Sales for all product?
  - o   100-10
- What regions had the most impact on the negative variance?
  - o   West, South
- Which region had the highest total expenses as a percent to total sales?
  - o   South
- What were the bottom three performing states for Profit, total Products, for the year?
  - o   New Mexico, New Hampshire, Missouri
- What size population are those three states?
  - o   Small, small, small
- Which packaging type sold more in Small Populations?
  - o   Bottle
- What were the two top selling months for diet products for all regions for the year?
  - o   July and August
- What two states purchased the most diet products for the Q2?
  - o   California and Illinois
- What state beginning with the letter C had the top sales for the year for all products?
  - o   California

If I've been doing my job in this chapter, you should NOT have to work the weekend. At this point you might think you're done, but I still have a ways to go. Hold tight; it will be worth it. Next I will review smart queries.

### Smart Query

Smart Query is a tool that can create a complex query using multiple sets, filters, unions and joins for Essbase data sources. Once a

Smart Query is created, it can be saved, reused and shared for ad hoc analysis. It can also be used in other Smart Queries.

The process to define a Smart Query is:

1) Define the Set(s)
2) Define the Set Filter(s)
3) Build the Smart Query
4) Set Options and Save the Query

I'll now knock out the new report request.

1. Within Smart View and Excel, navigate to the Smart View panel by selecting the *Panel* icon.
2. Under the Shared Connections for Essbase, expand the tree to find Sample.Basic. Right-click on *Sample.Basic* and select *New Smart Query Sheet* (or click *New Smart Query Sheet* at the bottom of the Smart View panel):

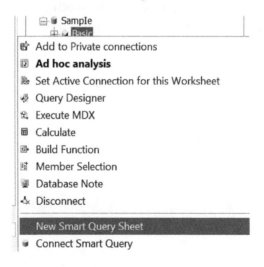

The Smart Query panel will display with the default dimensions for the Essbase source:

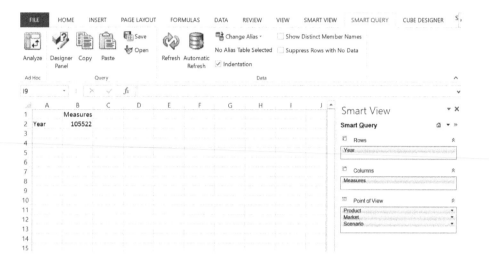

Like in Query Designer, I can drag dimensions to rows, columns, and the point of view. I can then further select members for the set. In addition to normal member selection methods, I can use MDX expressions to choose members from a dimension.

3.  Drag *Product* to the rows:

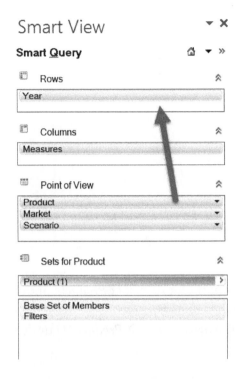

Within the point of view use the arrow keys to navigate to difererent dimensions in the rows, columns, or point of view (or select the ⌃ icon to display all point of view dimensions):

4.  Drag *Markets* to the columns. Drag *Measures* and *Years* to the point of view. The resulting Smart Query should look as follows:

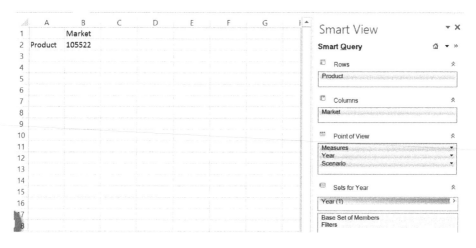

5.  In the Smart Query, select *Products* under Rows. The Sets for Products becomes active.

6.  Select the arrow next to *Product (1)* under *Sets for Products*:

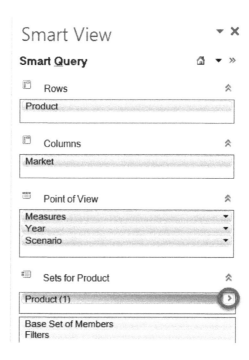

The following menu will display, providing different alternatives for further defining the member selection for the Product dimension:

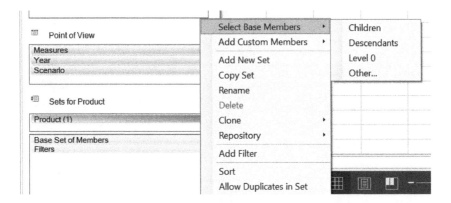

7.  Choose *Select Base Members >> Other*. When the Member Selection dialogue displays, choose products *100-10* and *100-20*:

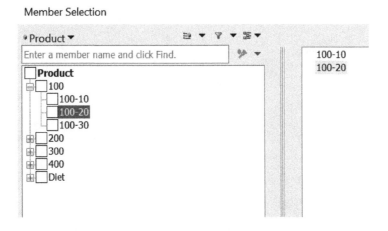

8.  Click *OK*.
9.  Repeat the steps to select *Actual* for Scenario and *Sales* for Measures. *Year* is already defined for the Year dimension so no change is required.

10. Select *Market* under columns. Choose *Select Base Members >> Level 0*:

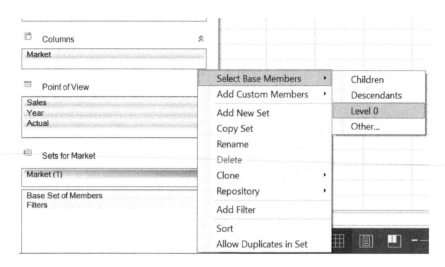

Notice that the Smart Query worksheet is updated for the member selections:

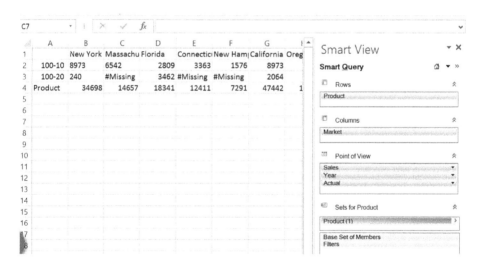

11. Click *Save* from the Smart Query ribbon:

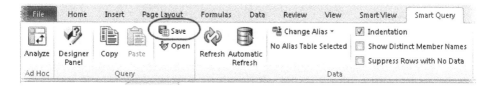

12. Name the set "Request 1" and optionally add a description:

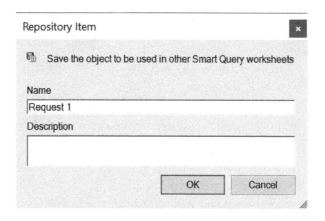

I've just defined my first set!

...But I'm not finished. I have a listing of all of the markets for Cola and Diet Cola. But which markets have the worst sales for product 100-10? I'll add a Smart Query Filter to apply to the set.

13. Select the *Market* dimension. Under the Sets for Market, click the arrow key. Choose *Add Filter:*

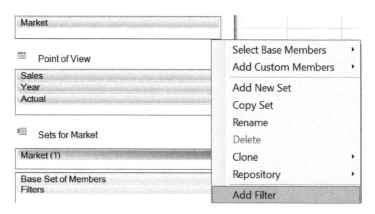

14. Choose *Select Top/Bottom*:

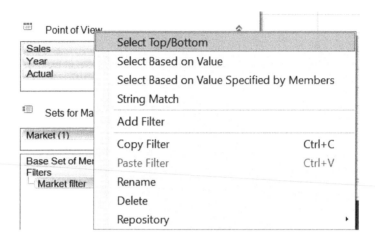

From this dialogue window, I can choose between the *Top* and *Bottom*. I can apply this based on *Count, Percent,* or *Sum*.

15. For the report request select *Bottom*.
16. Change the setting to *Count* with the number set to *5*:

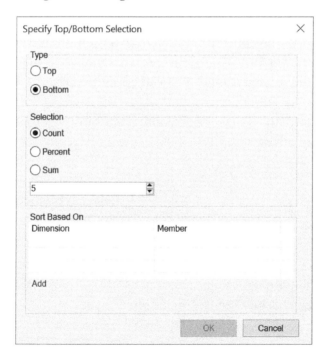

17. Click *Add*.

18. Select *Measures* from the dimension drop-down in the upper left hand corner. Select *Sales* and move it over to the right panel:

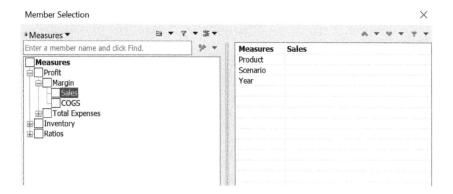

19. Click *OK* and the resulting filter definition should display:

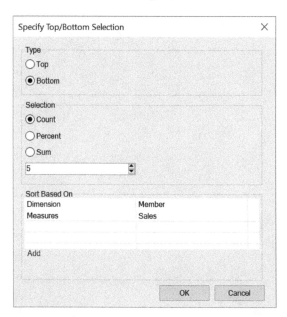

20. Click *Add*.

21. Select *Product* from the dimension drop-down in the upper left hand corner. Select *100-10* and move it over to the right panel.

22. Click *OK*:

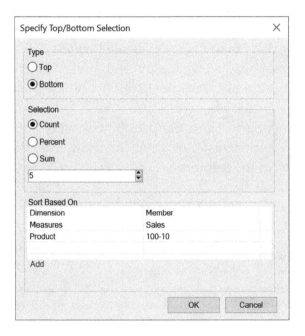

23. Click *OK*.

The filter is applied to the Smart Query:

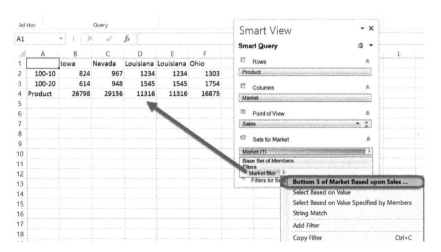

24. Click *Save* from the Smart Query window to save Request 1 with the updated filter.

Request 1 is complete. Now I need to create a Smart Query for Request 2. I could start from scratch but Request 2 is similar to Request 1 so I'll modify that Smart Query to create Request 2. I can accomplish this two different ways: I can copy and paste Smart Query across spreadsheets. I could also save the Request 1 Smart Query with a new name. The Save feature also works like a "Save As."

Follow along to learn the possibilities with Copy & Reuse of Smart Query components; I'm going to show you the roundabout method to hit all of the features.

25. Select *Copy* from the Smart Query ribbon:

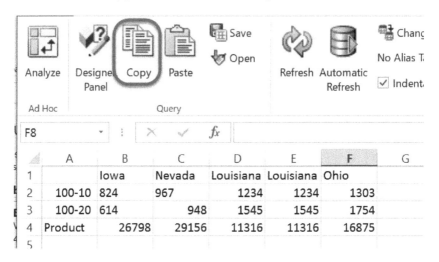

26. Select a new spreadsheet. Click *Paste* from the Smart View panel, pasting the Smart Query definition into the active sheet:

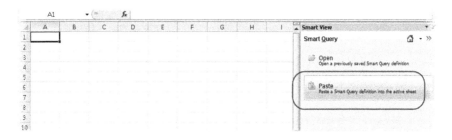

27. Select *Product*. Under *Sets for Product* choose *Select Base Members >> Other*:

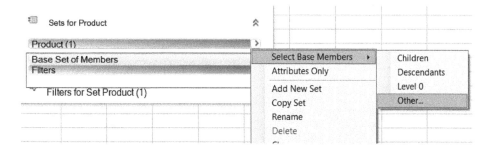

28. Change the member selection to *200-10* and *200-20*:

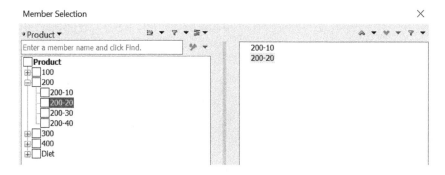

29. Click *OK*.

30. Select *Market*. Under *Sets for Market,* click the arrow next to *Market* filter. Select *Bottom 5 of Market Based upon Sales…*:

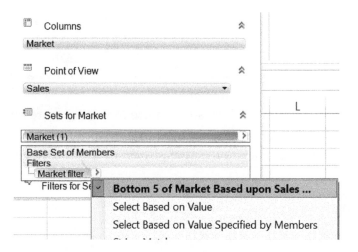

31. Update the filter to select the top five markets based on sales for 200-10:

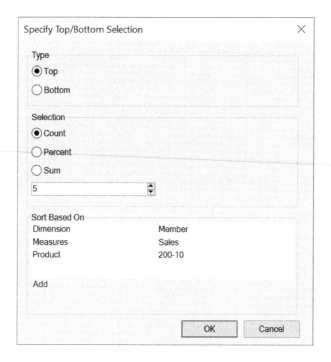

32. Click *OK* twice.

The Smart Query results are updated:

|   | A | B | C | D | E | F |
|---|---|---|---|---|---|---|
| 1 |   | Central | West | Illinois | Ohio | California |
| 2 | 200-10 | 17233 | 9235 | 7152 | 3811 | 3728 |
| 3 | 200-20 | 11973 | 14957 | 6786 | 1676 | 8244 |

Now I'll save the filters so I can use them for future queries.

33. Navigate back to the spreadsheet containing Request 1.

34. Right-click on the *Bottom 5 Market based upon 100-10...* and
    select *Repository >> Save Filter:*

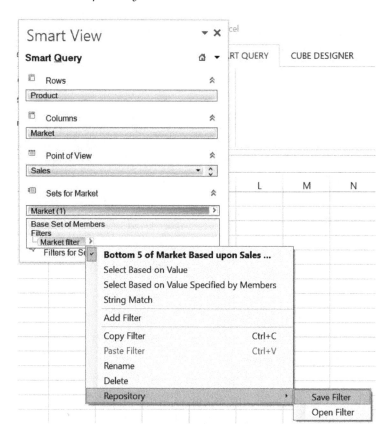

35. Enter a name and description for the filter:

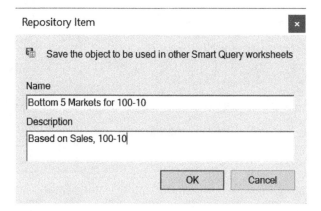

36. Click *OK*.
37. Navigate to the spreadsheet containing Request 2.
38. Right-click on the *Top 5 Markets Based upon 200-10...* and select *Repository >> Save Filter*. Enter a name and description for the filter:

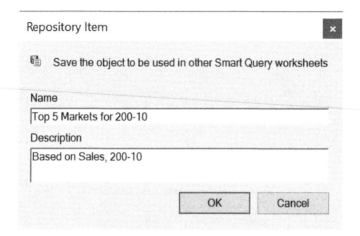

39. Click *OK*.

Two requests complete!

40. Navigate to the spreadsheet with Request 1.
41. Select *Copy* from the Smart Query ribbon:

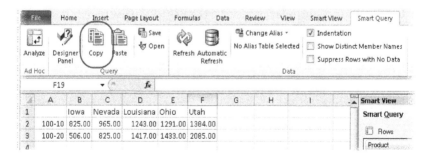

42. In a blank worksheet, click *Paste* from the Smart Query panel:

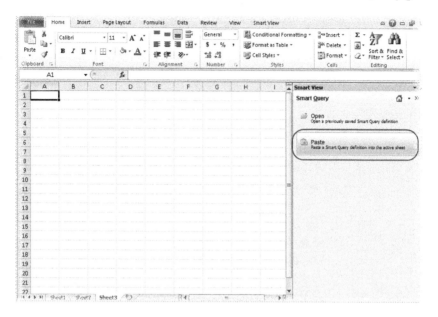

43. Under Sets for Market, select the > arrow and choose *Add Filter:*

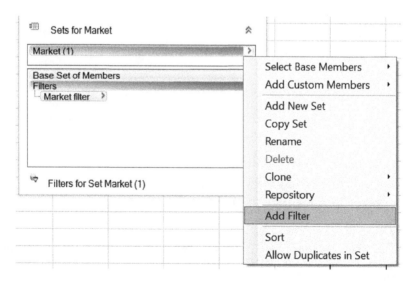

A new filter is added to the Smart Query definition for Markets.

44. Select the > arrow next to *Market filter (2)* and choose *Repository >> Open Filter:*

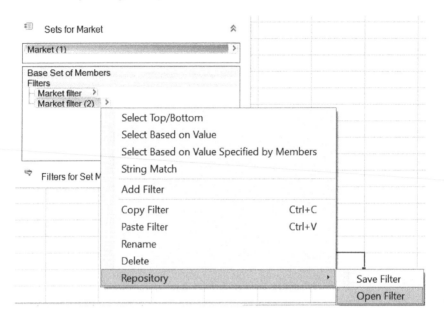

45. Select the *Top 5 Markets for 200-10* filter:

| Repository | | | | | × |
|---|---|---|---|---|---|
| Name | | Description | Cube | Applica... | Server |
| Top 5 Markets for 200-10 | | | Basic | Sample | Essba: |

46. Click *OK.*

The Smart Query definitions and results are updated, showing the five markets from each filter (note that there are nine because Ohio exists in both filter results):

| | A | B | C | D | E | F | G | H | I | J |
|---|---|---|---|---|---|---|---|---|---|---|
| 1 | | Iowa | Nevada | Louisiana | Louisiana | Ohio | Central | West | Illinois | California |
| 2 | 100-10 | 824 | 967 | 1234 | 1234 | 1303 | 14153 | 14862 | 5190 | 8973 |
| 3 | 100-20 | 614 | 948 | 1545 | 1545 | 1754 | 12802 | 8923 | 4099 | 2064 |
| 4 | Product | 26798 | 29156 | 11316 | 11316 | 16875 | 129680 | 132931 | 34218 | 47442 |

This is called a "union" of a filter set. JWE requested to see Profit for all products so I need to modify the member selections for Products and Measures.

47. Select *Product* under Rows. Under *Sets for Product*, select *Select Base Members >> Level 0*:

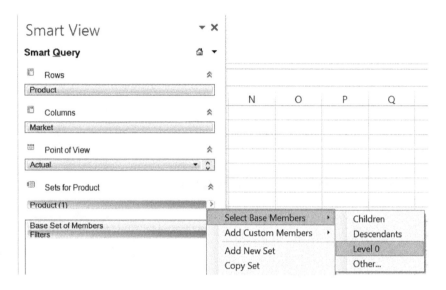

48. Select Measure (Sales) under Point of View. Under Sets for Measures, select *Select Base Members >> Other*:

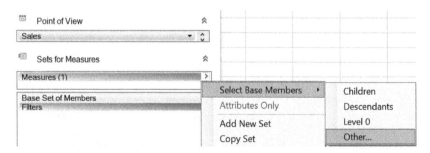

49. In the Member Selection window, remove *Sales* and select *Profit*:

50. Click *OK*.

The final report request is complete:

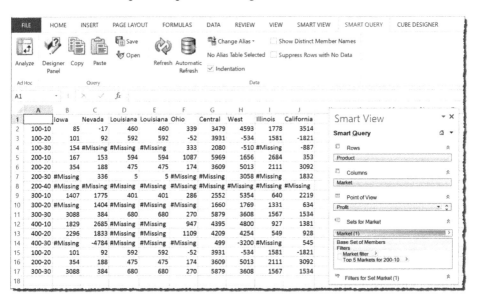

51. Click *Save* from the Smart Query ribbon. Enter a name and description for Request 3:

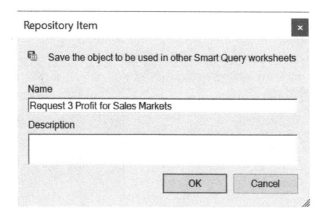

52. Click *OK*.

I've just skimmed the surface of how Smart Query sets can be defined. Within a set definition, I can choose members based on functions like Children, Descendants, or Level 0.

I can choose *Other* to launch the Member Selection window:

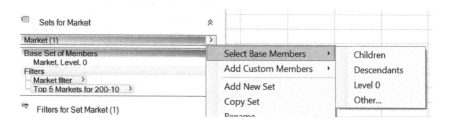

I can also add Custom Members like Totals or Counts:

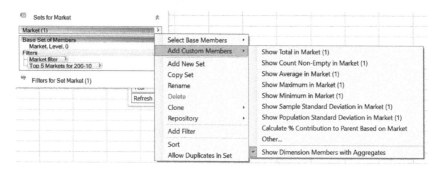

In my example, my Smart Queries just contained one set but I can select many sets in a single Smart Query definition. To add a new set, choose *Add New Set* from the menu:

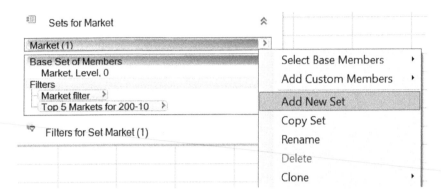

I can save a set definition for use in future Smart Query definitions or I can open a saved set by selecting *Repository >> Save Set* or *Open Set*:

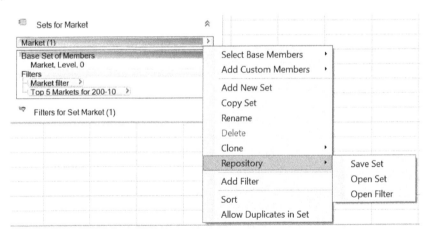

I can define custom filters or used a filter wizard to filter data based on a value or based on a value for specific members:

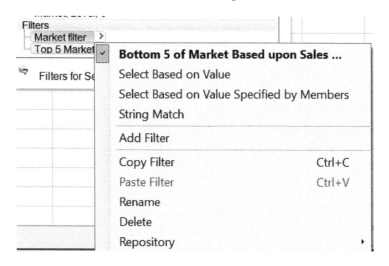

The *Select Based on Value* menu option launches the following dialogue window:

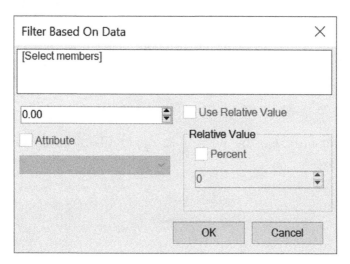

The Member Selection window is displayed when I click on *[Select members]*:

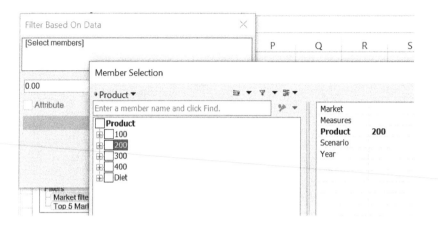

I can then set the comparison criteria and the amount to be applied in the filter:

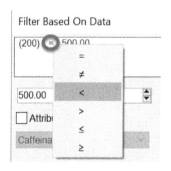

I can also use the wizard to apply filters based on attribute dimensions:

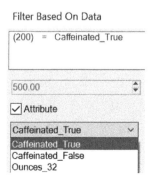

Multiple filters can be added to a Smart Query definition. The prior example showed us a union of two filters.

I can also create an "intersection" of filters. Intersections will combine only members that belong to all member sets. For example, JWE wants to only see the markets that contain "io" in its name from Request 1 – bottom five markets based on Sales for product 100-10.

53. From the first Market filter >, choose *Add Filter:*

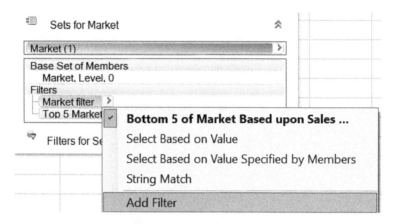

54. Select *String Match*:

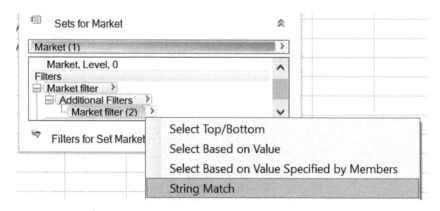

55. Enter "io." Choose *Contains* and check *Ignore Case*:

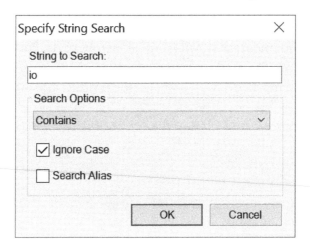

56. Click *OK* and the intersection is created:

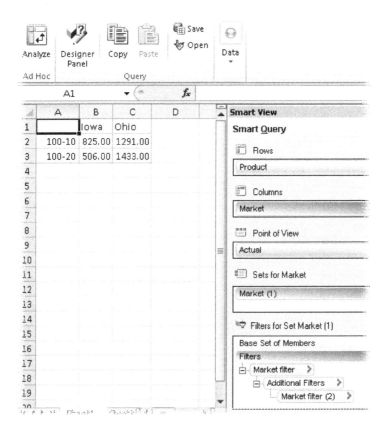

Members from one set that are not members of the other specified set are selected. Simply choose the *Exclude* option when adding the additional features:

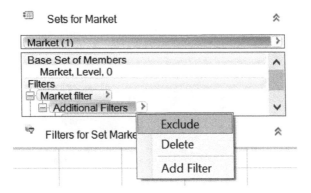

And then, of course, I can save and reuse these filter definitions.

In the Smart Query ribbon, I can choose options to format and show and suppress specific members/rows:

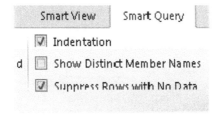

I can also change the alias table used in the result set:

At any point within a Smart Query, I can jump into ad hoc mode by clicking *Analyze* from the Smart Query ribbon:

| | Iowa | Nevada | Louisiana | Louisiana | Ohio | Central | West | Illinois | California |
|---|---|---|---|---|---|---|---|---|---|
| 100-10 | 85 | -17 | 460 | 460 | 339 | 3479 | 4593 | 1778 | 3514 |
| 100-20 | 101 | 92 | 592 | 592 | -52 | 3931 | -534 | 1581 | -1821 |
| 100-30 | 154 | #Missing | #Missing | #Missing | 333 | 2080 | -510 | #Missing | -887 |
| 200-10 | 167 | 153 | 594 | 594 | 1087 | 5969 | 1656 | 2684 | 353 |
| 200-20 | 354 | 188 | 475 | 475 | 174 | 3609 | 5013 | 2111 | 3092 |
| 200-30 | #Missing | 336 | 5 | 5 | #Missing | #Missing | 3058 | #Missing | 1832 |
| 200-40 | #Missing | #Missing | #Missing | #Missing | #Missing | #Missing | #Missing | #Missing | #Missing |
| 300-10 | 1407 | 1775 | 401 | 401 | 286 | 2552 | 5354 | 640 | 2219 |
| 300-20 | #Missing | 1404 | #Missing | #Missing | #Missing | 1660 | 1769 | 1331 | 634 |
| 300-30 | 3088 | 384 | 680 | 680 | 270 | 5879 | 3608 | 1567 | 1534 |
| 400-10 | 1829 | 2685 | #Missing | #Missing | 947 | 4395 | 4800 | 927 | 1381 |
| 400-20 | 2296 | 1833 | #Missing | #Missing | 1109 | 4209 | 4254 | 549 | 928 |
| 400-30 | #Missing | -4784 | #Missing | #Missing | #Missing | 499 | -3200 | #Missing | 545 |
| 100-20 | 101 | 92 | 592 | 592 | -52 | 3931 | -534 | 1581 | -1821 |
| 200-20 | 354 | 188 | 475 | 475 | 174 | 3609 | 5013 | 2111 | 3092 |
| 300-30 | 3088 | 384 | 680 | 680 | 270 | 5879 | 3608 | 1567 | 1534 |

Try that now!

| | Profit | Actual | Year | | | | | | |
|---|---|---|---|---|---|---|---|---|---|
| | Iowa | Nevada | Louisiana | Louisiana | Ohio | Central | West | Illinois | California |
| 100-10 | 85 | -17 | 460 | 460 | 339 | 3479 | 4593 | 1778 | 3514 |
| 100-20 | 101 | 92 | 592 | 592 | -52 | 3931 | -534 | 1581 | -1821 |
| 100-30 | 154 | #Missing | #Missing | #Missing | 333 | 2080 | -510 | #Missing | -887 |
| 200-10 | 167 | 153 | 594 | 594 | 1087 | 5969 | 1656 | 2684 | 353 |
| 200-20 | 354 | 188 | 475 | 475 | 174 | 3609 | 5013 | 2111 | 3092 |
| 200-30 | #Missing | 336 | 5 | 5 | #Missing | #Missing | 3058 | #Missing | 1832 |
| 200-40 | #Missing | #Missing | #Missing | #Missing | #Missing | #Missing | #Missing | #Missing | #Missing |
| 300-10 | 1407 | 1775 | 401 | 401 | 286 | 2552 | 5354 | 640 | 2219 |
| 300-20 | #Missing | 1404 | #Missing | #Missing | #Missing | 1660 | 1769 | 1331 | 634 |
| 300-30 | 3088 | 384 | 680 | 680 | 270 | 5879 | 3608 | 1567 | 1534 |
| 400-10 | 1829 | 2685 | #Missing | #Missing | 947 | 4395 | 4800 | 927 | 1381 |
| 400-20 | 2296 | 1833 | #Missing | #Missing | 1109 | 4209 | 4254 | 549 | 928 |
| 400-30 | #Missing | -4784 | #Missing | #Missing | #Missing | 499 | -3200 | #Missing | 545 |
| 100-20 | 101 | 92 | 592 | 592 | -52 | 3931 | -534 | 1581 | -1821 |
| 200-20 | 354 | 188 | 475 | 475 | 174 | 3609 | 5013 | 2111 | 3092 |
| 300-30 | 3088 | 384 | 680 | 680 | 270 | 5879 | 3608 | 1567 | 1534 |

JWE has entered a few last transactions that could impact the data and they want you to rerun the data. On a day before Smart Query, this would have likely caused me several broken pencils and a bit tongue. But I have Smart Query and this will literally take me a few seconds (booting up the computer will take longer).

1.  Once the computer is booted up, open Excel.
2.  Select the Smart View ribbon and choose *Panel*.
3.  From the *Home* drop-down, select *Smart Query*:

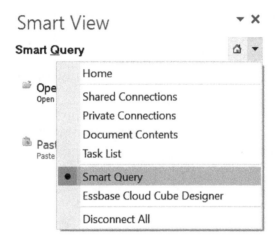

4.  Click *Open* and the local repository of saved Smart Queries displays:

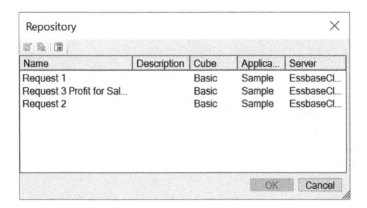

From this window, I can rename and delete Smart Queries.

The Smart Queries are stored locally under your Windows ID. The Smart Queries are not stored on Essbase Cloud and cannot be opened by other users by using the *Open* feature. I can, however, share Smart Queries with other users by simply sending them the spreadsheet.

5. Select Request 1. Enter the login ID and password, if prompted, and the Smart Query will rerun with the new transactions considered.
6. Repeat steps 3-5 for Requests 2 and 3.

This time I'll just email the spreadsheet containing the three Smart Queries with instructions on how to run the queries (just in case there are any last minute transactions).

What are the ad hoc and query options of Smart View?

|  | Regular Ad Hoc Query | Query Designer | Smart Query |
|---|---|---|---|
| You know the query layout at the beginning | Good | Best | Best |
| Apply Data filters | N | Y | Y |
| Your list of members changes often and you need to include new members automatically | N | Y | Y |
| You've drilled into a query and want to get back to the original starting point | Good | Better | Best |
| Reusable Query | Good | Better | Best |
| Complex, reusable member sets and filters using unions, complements, and intersections | N | N | Y |
| Allows free form MDX | N | Y | Y |

### Copy Data Points

One of the coolest features in Smart View is the copy and paste data points feature. This feature allows you to copy data points from spreadsheet to spreadsheet, spreadsheet to Word document, PowerPoint to spreadsheet, and more. What's the coolest is that the data points remained linked to the cube (yes, I am still a geek!), so if the underlying data changes, I can just refresh the copied data points.

**Note!**
You may want to toggle off the floating POV so that the point of view members will be pasted into the target (for reference). It is not required but will help you remember the data intersections displayed.

1.  Create the following spreadsheet. To copy and paste data points, select the grid to copy in Excel:

|   | A | B | C | D | E |
|---|---|---|---|---|---|
| 1 |   | Market | Sales | Actual |   |
| 2 |   | Qtr1 | Qtr2 | Qtr3 | Qtr4 |
| 3 | Colas | 25048 | 27187 | 28544 | 25355 |
| 4 | Root Beer | 26627 | 27401 | 27942 | 27116 |
| 5 | Cream Soda | 23997 | 25736 | 26650 | 25022 |
| 6 | Fruit Soda | 20148 | 21355 | 22079 | 20648 |
| 7 | Product | 95820 | 101679 | 105215 | 98141 |
| 8 |   |   |   |   |   |

2.  Select *Copy* from the Smart View ribbon:

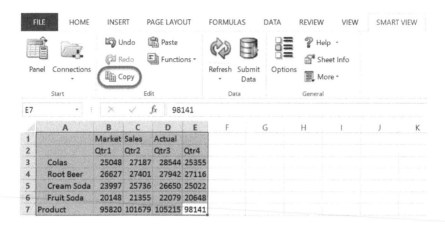

3.  Select a new spreadsheet and select *Paste:*

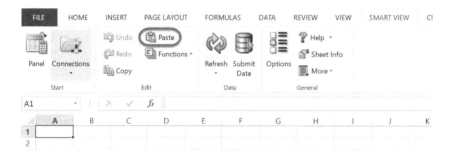

The copied grid will be pasted into the spreadsheet:

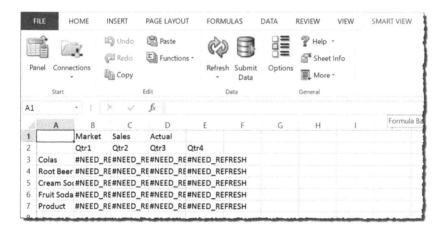

4.   Click *Refresh* to refresh the data points.

| | A | B | C | D | E |
|---|---|---|---|---|---|
| 1 | | Market | Sales | Actual | |
| 2 | | Qtr1 | Qtr2 | Qtr3 | Qtr4 |
| 3 | Colas | 25048 | 27187 | 28544 | 25355 |
| 4 | Root Beer | 26627 | 27401 | 27942 | 27116 |
| 5 | Cream Soda | 23997 | 25736 | 26650 | 25022 |
| 6 | Fruit Soda | 20148 | 21355 | 22079 | 20648 |
| 7 | Product | 95820 | 101679 | 105215 | 98141 |

Each cell that contains a number is a single data point. When I use the Copy/Paste data feature, I am no longer operating with an ad hoc grid (I cannot zoom or pivot data points). Each data point is a self-contained component. Each individual cell (or data point) has linked information about the data point (server, application, cube/database, member intersection for all dimensions and alias table):

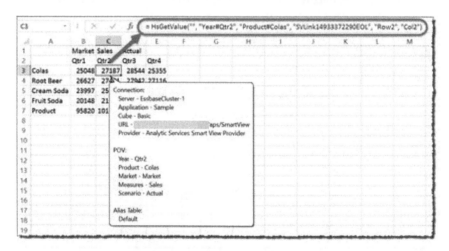

Because the data point stores this information, it is fully refreshable. As the underlying data changes, I'll simply click *Refresh* to see the up to date information.

The header information like Colas and Qtr1 is just text. This means I could change this information, but it will not change the data point and what is refreshed.

**Note!**   Mouse over a data point to see the connection information.

That's good and all but what about Word or PowerPoint? I have new report requests to fill. The real benefit of copying data points is using this feature with Word and PowerPoint.

5. Simply open a Word or PowerPoint document and choose *Paste* from the Smart View ribbon:

6. After pasting the data points into Word (or PowerPoint), hit *Refresh* to pull in the current data values.

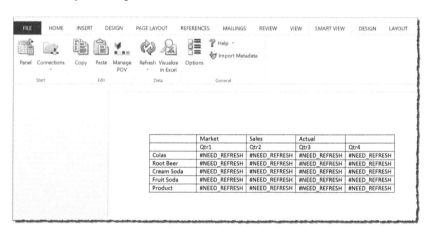

Voila! Essbase numbers in a Word document (can't nobody hold you down!).

|  | Market | Sales | Actual |  |
|---|---|---|---|---|
|  | Qtr1 | Qtr2 | Qtr3 | Qtr4 |
| Colas | 25048 | 27187 | 28544 | 25355 |
| Root Beer | 26627 | 27401 | 27942 | 27116 |
| Cream Soda | 23997 | 25736 | 26650 | 25022 |
| Fruit Soda | 20148 | 21355 | 22079 | 20648 |
| Product | 95820 | 101679 | 105215 | 98141 |

Just like Excel, each one of the numbers is a single self-contained data point. Colas and Qtr1 headers are plain ol' text and not tied to Essbase.

For example, in the Word document, I'll change the headers to "Quarter One," "Quarter Two," "Quarter Three," and "Quarter Four" (these are not valid member names or aliases). What do you think will happen when I click Refresh?

A successful refresh happens. These "headers" are not tied to the data points. I didn't change information related to the data point so it refreshes as normal:

|  | Market | Sales | Actual |  |
|---|---|---|---|---|
|  | Quarter One | Quarter Two | Quarter Three | Quarter Four |
| Colas | 25048 | 27187 | 28544 | 25355 |
| Root Beer | 26627 | 27401 | 27942 | 27116 |
| Cream Soda | 23997 | 25736 | 26650 | 25022 |
| Fruit Soda | 20148 | 21355 | 22079 | 20648 |
| Product | 25731 | 26787 | 27495 | 25665 |

So what if I am looking at Essbase data in Word or PowerPoint and I want to further analyze that data set? Simple.

7.  Select the desired data point and click the *Visualize in Excel* button on the Smart View ribbon to pull the grid back into Excel where you can perform further analytics:

This step brings me to a linked query in Excel:

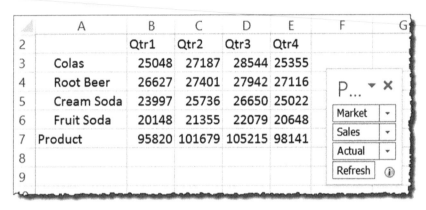

|          | Qtr1  | Qtr2   | Qtr3   | Qtr4  |
|----------|-------|--------|--------|-------|
| Colas    | 25048 | 27187  | 28544  | 25355 |
| Root Beer | 26627 | 27401 | 27942  | 27116 |
| Cream Soda | 23997 | 25736 | 26650 | 25022 |
| Fruit Soda | 20148 | 21355 | 22079 | 20648 |
| Product  | 95820 | 101679 | 105215 | 98141 |

8.  Do you have to copy the full grid? Nope, you can just copy a single data point (the data):

|           | Market | Sales  | Actual |       |
|-----------|--------|--------|--------|-------|
|           | Qtr1   | Qtr2   | Qtr3   | Qtr4  |
| Colas     | 25048  | 27187  | 28544  | 25355 |
| Root Beer | 26627  | 27401  | 27942  | 27116 |
| Cream Soda | 23997 | 25736  | 26650  | 25022 |
| Fruit Soda | 20148 | 21355  | 22079  | 20648 |
| Product   | 95820  | 101679 | 105215 | 98141 |

I want to highlight Q3 sales of Colas #NEED_REFRESH

9.  Click *Refresh* and you have dynamic content in Word (or PowerPoint).

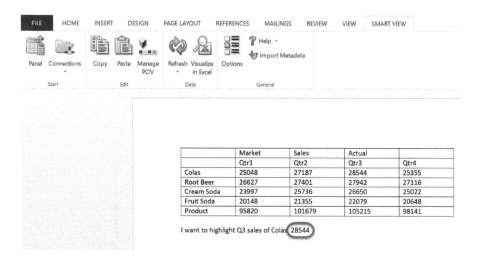

| | Market | Sales | Actual | |
|---|---|---|---|---|
| | Qtr1 | Qtr2 | Qtr3 | Qtr4 |
| Colas | 25048 | 27187 | 28544 | 25355 |
| Root Beer | 26627 | 27401 | 27942 | 27116 |
| Cream Soda | 23997 | 25736 | 26650 | 25022 |
| Fruit Soda | 20148 | 21355 | 22079 | 20648 |
| Product | 95820 | 101679 | 105215 | 98141 |

I want to highlight Q3 sales of Colas 28544

I can also copy and paste data points from Smart Queries.

I've now been through the advanced analytics portion of the chapter, analyzing data at the speed of light (well, almost the speed of light, for relativistic reasons). I am finally to be free for the weekend. I'll next turn my attention to dynamic formatted reporting with Smart View and Essbase.

## CREATE FORMATTED REPORTS

The weekend has been wonderfully relaxing. Bright and early Monday morning, however, a request comes in to create formatted reports. I'll now go through ins and outs of formatting with Smart View.

Smart View provides two ways to format: Excel formatting and Smart View formatting. In this section, I'll show you more reporting capabilities with Smart Slices and Report Designer.

### Use Excel Formatting

Everything I've done up to this point has been fairly ad hoc and formatting has been kept to a minimum. One of the reasons I am using Excel to display my data is that it's a great place to pretty up boring numbers (or as I used to say back on the farm: "making 'em look fancy"). Essbase will still be used as the source of the data, but Excel will provide all of my formatting.

1.  Using what you've learned so far, create the following P&L statement using Sample.Basic:

| | A | B | C | D |
|---|---|---|---|---|
| 1 | | Product | Market | Year |
| 2 | | Actual | Budget | |
| 3 | Sales | 400855 | 373080 | |
| 4 | COGS | 179336 | 158940 | |
| 5 | Margin | 221519 | 214140 | |
| 6 | Marketing | 66237 | 49520 | |
| 7 | Payroll | 48747 | 35240 | |
| 8 | Misc | 1013 | - | |
| 9 | Total Expenses | 115997 | 84760 | |
| 10 | Profit | 105522 | 129380 | |

I now have a P&L statement but it doesn't look that great. What I really need to do is apply some formatting to this spreadsheet. I am in Excel so I can use all the power that is Microsoft for formatting my spreadsheets.

2.  Before you start formatting with Excel, select *Options* from the Smart View ribbon. Look at the *Formatting* section:

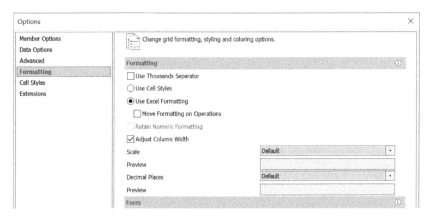

Use Excel Formatting is the key setting to tell Essbase that I want to leverage Excel formatting in my ad hoc grids. Excel formatting will be retained on most operations. However, when I pivot, I may not get what I had planned. The cell itself will maintain the formatting (e.g., in cell C4 I've formatted the data value to be bold with commas but after pivoting C4 holds the member Jan which is bold with commas). However, I have an option available *Move Formatting on Operations*:

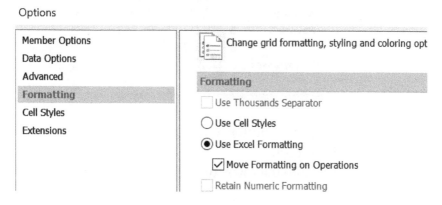

Move Formatting on Operations applies my Excel formatting selections to expanded cells when I zoom in. This formatting also moves with the data when I pivot members.

I can set data scaling if I need to scale Essbase numbers for my report. If I want the column to automatically adjust based on the member length, I'll check Adjust Column Width.

Retain Numeric Formatting will maintain the Scale and Decimal settings during drilling actions. I can also set the Use Thousands separator.

3. Check the box to *Use Excel Formatting*. Click *OK* and you're ready.

4. So what are you waiting for? Format your sheet to look like the following using normal Excel formatting options:

|  | A | B | C | D |
|---|---|---|---|---|
| 1 |  | Product | Market | Year |
| 2 |  | Actual | Budget |  |
| 3 | Sales | $ 400,855 | $ 373,080 |  |
| 4 | COGS | $ 179,336 | $ 158,940 |  |
| 5 | *Margin* | *$ 221,519* | *$ 214,140* |  |
| 6 | Marketing | $ 66,237 | $ 49,520 |  |
| 7 | Payroll | $ 48,747 | $ 35,240 |  |
| 8 | Misc | $ 1,013 | - |  |
| 9 | *Total Expenses* | *$ 115,997* | *$ 84,760* |  |
| 10 | Profit | $ 105,522 | $ 129,380 |  |

5. Click the *Refresh* button and notice the formatting remains.
6. Save this report.
7. Drag *Year* into the rows (or select cell D1 and click *Pivot*).

Oh no! What happened to my formatting?

|  | A | B | C | D |
|---|---|---|---|---|
| 1 |  |  | Product | Market |
| 2 |  |  | Actual | Budget |
| 3 | Year | Sales | $ 400,855 | 373080 |
| 4 |  | COGS | $ 179,336 | 158940 |
| 5 |  | *Margin* | *$ 221,519* | *214140* |
| 6 |  | Marketing | $ 66,237 | 49520 |
| 7 |  | Payroll | $ 48,747 | 35240 |
| 8 |  | Misc | $ 1,013 | - |
| 9 |  | *Total Expenses* | *$ 115,997* | *84760* |
| 10 |  | Profit | $ 105,522 | 129380 |

If I change the grid layout by adding, removing, or moving dimensions, or if I drill into a report, I can probably count on some formatting issues. So the biggest lesson learned from this chapter: **Always format last!**

8. Click *Undo* (remember this is on the Smart View tab) to get back to our pretty report. Let's continue with other formatting capabilities.

At this point, I want to finalize the layout. Once I add formulas and formatting, I need to be wary of changes to the layout. While I have improved support for formatting on drills and pivots, there is still the possibility of rework or updates to the formulas and/or formatting. So I'll ask myself: am I sure this is the final layout? Really sure? If so, then I am ready to move on to the next step.

Since this is the data layout I want to see on my final report, I'll add some spacing to the report by moving my row, column, and page members around. My data is a bit cramped at the moment, so I'll space it out by inserting some blank rows.

9. Highlight the rows (by clicking the row number) and select *Insert >> Rows* from the Excel menu. Make your spreadsheet look like the following:

| | A | B | C | D |
|---|---|---|---|---|
| 1 | | Product | Market | Year |
| 2 | | | | |
| 3 | | | | |
| 4 | | | | |
| 5 | | Actual | Budget | |
| 6 | Sales | $ 400,855 | $ 373,080 | |
| 7 | COGS | $ 179,336 | $ 158,940 | |
| 8 | *Margin* | *$ 221,519* | *$ 214,140* | |
| 9 | Marketing | $ 66,237 | $ 49,520 | |
| 10 | Payroll | $ 48,747 | $ 35,240 | |
| 11 | Misc | $ 1,013 | - | |
| 12 | *Total Expenses* | *$ 115,997* | *$ 84,760* | |
| 13 | **Profit** | $ 105,522 | $ 129,380 | |

Even though I've inserted a bunch of extra lines, this is still a valid Essbase retrieval.

10. Click *Refresh* to just prove it.

As Smart View is scanning the sheet, it will often run into names it doesn't recognize. The refresh will still function even though unknown names are present.

I can use this to my advantage by adding extraneous text to my refresh knowing that the refresh will continue to work just fine. Extra text can include header information, such as the company or the name of the report.

11. In this case, add a title and headers for the POV:
   a.  In cell A2, "Profit and Loss Statement:"
   b.  In cell A3, "for"
   c.  In cell A4, "Product:"
   d.  In cell A5, "Market:"
   e.  In cell A6, "Period":

The top of the refresh should now look like this:

| | A | B | C | D |
|---|---|---|---|---|
| 1 | | | | |
| 2 | | **Profit and Loss Statement** | | |
| 3 | | for | | |
| 4 | Product: | Product | | |
| 5 | Market: | Market | | |
| 6 | Period: | Year | | |
| 7 | | | | |
| 8 | | **Actual** | **Budget** | |
| 9 | **Sales** | $ 400,855 | $ 373,080 | |
| 10 | **COGS** | $ 179,336 | $ 158,940 | |
| 11 | *Margin* | *$ 221,519* | *$ 214,140* | |
| 12 | **Marketing** | $  66,237 | $  49,520 | |
| 13 | **Payroll** | $  48,747 | $  35,240 | |
| 14 | **Misc** | $   1,013 | - | |
| 15 | *Total Expenses* | *$ 115,997* | *$  84,760* | |
| 16 | **Profit** | $ 105,522 | $ 129,380 | |
| 17 | | | | |

12. Click *Refresh* and note that the text was saved.

**Tip!**

Smart View will support merged cells. In the example above, I could have each merged and centered the B-D4 Markets, B-D5 Products, and B-D6 Year cells.

**Tip!**

Be careful not to add text that matches a member name or Essbase will try to refresh it and may give you weird error messages. In the example above, I added a ":" to make the text different from the dimension or member names Product, Market and Year.

At times, I may want to add formulas to my report to calculate things that aren't in Essbase. I am of the belief that, whenever possible, I should try to add these types of calculations to the Essbase cube itself. The main reason is that if I add the calculation to Essbase anyone else will be guaranteed to calculate that value the exact same way I do. This prevents the embarrassing situation of two people walking into a meeting with different ideas of what Profit as a percent of Sales was last month. This is likely to get one or both people fired (usually, they'll fire the one who has the lower Profit number). If both people were getting their Profit % from Essbase, then they'd at least have the same number.

The other benefit of performing the calculation in Essbase is that the next time I need the calculation, I don't have to remember how I calculated it last time. There's a member waiting for me to use with the calculation already defined. Sample.Basic, for instance, has members called Profit % and Margin % in the Measures dimension.

13. Type Profit % into cell A18 and click *Refresh*. Profit as a percent of Sales is about 26% for the year:

| | A | B | C | |
|---|---|---|---|---|
| 1 | | | | |
| 2 | | Profit and Loss Statement | | |
| 3 | | for | | |
| 4 | Product: | Product | | |
| 5 | Market: | Market | | |
| 6 | Period: | Year | | |
| 7 | | | | |
| 8 | | Actual | Budget | |
| 9 | Sales | $ 400,855 | $ 373,080 | |
| 10 | COGS | $ 179,336 | $ 158,940 | |
| 11 | *Margin* | $ 221,519 | $ 214,140 | |
| 12 | Marketing | $ 66,237 | $ 49,520 | |
| 13 | Payroll | $ 48,747 | $ 35,240 | |
| 14 | Misc | $ 1,013 | - | |
| 15 | *Total Expenses* | $ 115,997 | $ 84,760 | |
| 16 | Profit | $ 105,522 | $ 129,380 | |
| 17 | | | | |
| 18 | Profit % | 26.3 | 34.7 | |

While adding all of my calculations to Essbase may be great in theory, there are plenty of times when a calculation will occur to me on the spot and I don't want to bother my Essbase Administrator by asking her to add the calculation to the cube. For instance, say I want to add a line to my report that calculates Total Expenses as a percent of Sales. Expense % is not a member in the cube.

14. Type in the following:
   a. In cell A19, "Expense %"
   b. In cell B19, "=B15/B9*100"
15. Right-click column C and insert a column. Resize to be smaller than the other columns.
16. Copy the formula in cell B19 to cell D19.

The report should now look like this:

| B19 | ▾ | ⋮ | ✕ | ✓ | fx | =B15/B9*100 |

| | A | B | C | D | E |
|---|---|---|---|---|---|
| 1 | | | | | |
| 2 | | **Profit and Loss Statement** | | | |
| 3 | | for | | | |
| 4 | Product: | Product | | | |
| 5 | Market: | Market | | | |
| 6 | Period: | Year | | | |
| 7 | | | | | |
| 8 | | **Actual** | | **Budget** | |
| 9 | Sales | $ 400,855 | | $ 373,080 | |
| 10 | COGS | $ 179,336 | | $ 158,940 | |
| 11 | *Margin* | *$ 221,519* | | *$ 214,140* | |
| 12 | Marketing | $ 66,237 | | $ 49,520 | |
| 13 | Payroll | $ 48,747 | | $ 35,240 | |
| 14 | Misc | $ 1,013 | | $ - | |
| 15 | *Total Expenses* | *$ 115,997* | | *$ 84,760* | |
| 16 | Profit | $ 105,522 | | $ 129,380 | |
| 17 | | | | | |
| 18 | Profit % | 26.3 | | 34.7 | |
| 19 | Expense % | 28.9 | | 22.7 | |

Formulas can be in the rows or the columns just like a normal Excel spreadsheet.

17. Refresh the data and something really cool will happen: the Expense % formulas remain.

**Note!** By default, Smart View will retain formulas (the *Preserve Formulas and Comments in ad hoc operations* option is checked).

Your report template is now complete.

18. In cell B5, type in *East*. Click *Refresh* and the report refreshes for the East region:

| | A | B | C | D |
|---|---|---|---|---|
| 1 | | | | |
| 2 | | Profit and Loss Statement | | |
| 3 | | for | | |
| 4 | Product: | Product | | |
| 5 | Market: | East | | |
| 6 | Period: | Year | | |
| 7 | | | | |
| 8 | | Actual | Budget | |
| 9 | Sales | $ 87,398 | $ 78,950 | |
| 10 | COGS | $ 37,927 | $ 32,250 | |
| 11 | *Margin* | *$ 49,471* | *$ 46,700* | |
| 12 | Marketing | $ 14,721 | $ 11,210 | |
| 13 | Payroll | $ 10,389 | $ 7,100 | |
| 14 | Misc | $ 200 | $ - | |
| 15 | *Total Expenses* | *$ 25,310* | *$ 18,310* | |
| 16 | Profit | $ 24,161 | $ 28,390 | |
| 17 | | | | |
| 18 | Profit % | 27.6 | 36.0 | |
| 19 | Expense % | 29.0 | 23.2 | |

19. Type *Jan* in cell B6. Click *Refresh:*

| | A | B | C | D |
|---|---|---|---|---|
| 1 | | | | |
| 2 | | Profit and Loss Statement | | |
| 3 | | for | | |
| 4 | Product: | Product | | |
| 5 | Market: | East | | |
| 6 | Period: | Jan | | |
| 7 | | | | |
| 8 | | Actual | Budget | |
| 9 | Sales | $ 6,780 | $ 6,180 | |
| 10 | COGS | $ 3,007 | $ 2,590 | |
| 11 | *Margin* | *$ 3,773* | *$ 3,590* | |
| 12 | Marketing | $ 1,161 | $ 890 | |
| 13 | Payroll | $ 865 | $ 620 | |
| 14 | Misc | $ 15 | $ - | |
| 15 | *Total Expenses* | *$ 2,041* | *$ 1,510* | |
| 16 | Profit | $ 1,732 | $ 2,080 | |
| 17 | | | | |
| 18 | Profit % | 25.5 | 33.7 | |
| 19 | Expense % | 30.1 | 24.4 | |

One of my favorite Excel features is the built-in conditional formatting. I can create a dashboard-like report with traffic lighting indicators to understand how I am performing in relation to other data sets or specific criteria that I determine. This is an Excel feature but let's see how I can apply it to data from Essbase.

20. Select the data cells that correspond to *Profit %*:

| | A | B | C | D |
|---|---|---|---|---|
| 1 | | | | |
| 2 | | **Profit and Loss Statement** | | |
| 3 | | for | | |
| 4 | Product: | Product | | |
| 5 | Market: | Market | | |
| 6 | Period: | Year | | |
| 7 | | | | |
| 8 | | **Actual** | | **Budget** |
| 9 | **Sales** | **$ 400,855** | | **$ 373,080** |
| 10 | **COGS** | **$ 179,336** | | **$ 158,940** |
| 11 | *Margin* | *$ 221,519* | | *$ 214,140* |
| 12 | **Marketing** | **$ 66,237** | | **$ 49,520** |
| 13 | **Payroll** | **$ 48,747** | | **$ 35,240** |
| 14 | **Misc** | **$ 1,013** | | - |
| 15 | *Total Expenses* | *$ 115,997* | | *$ 84,760* |
| 16 | Profit | $ 105,522 | | $ 129,380 |
| 17 | | | | |
| 18 | **Profit %** | 26.3 | | 34.7 |
| 19 | **Espense %** | 30.1 | | 24.4 |

21. Select *Conditional Formatting* on the Excel Home ribbon. Choose the *Color Scales >> Green/Yellow* option:

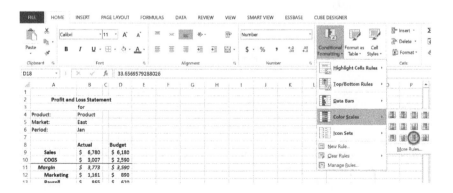

The final report should look as follows:

| | A | B | C | D |
|---|---|---|---|---|
| 1 | | | | |
| 2 | | **Profit and Loss Statement** | | |
| 3 | | for | | |
| 4 | Product: | Product | | |
| 5 | Market: | East | | |
| 6 | Period: | Jan | | |
| 7 | | | | |
| 8 | | **Actual** | | **Budget** |
| 9 | **Sales** | $ 6,780 | | $ 6,180 |
| 10 | COGS | $ 3,007 | | $ 2,590 |
| 11 | *Margin* | *$ 3,773* | | *$ 3,590* |
| 12 | Marketing | $ 1,161 | | $ 890 |
| 13 | Payroll | $ 865 | | $ 620 |
| 14 | Misc | $ 15 | | $ - |
| 15 | *Total Expenses* | *$ 2,041* | | *$ 1,510* |
| 16 | **Profit** | $ 1,732 | | $ 2,080 |
| 17 | | | | |
| 18 | **Profit %** | 25.5 | | 33.7 |
| 19 | **Expense %** | 30.1 | | 24.4 |

I can apply color scales, data bars, icons, and more in Excel conditional formatting.

Before I save the workbook, I'll blank out all of my numbers (I'll keep my formulas, though). This makes the file size that much smaller, thereby making the file that much faster to open next time.

The next time I want to use this report, I'll open it up, connect to the cube, use Member Select to select my Market, Product, and Scenario members (or just type them in), and finally choose *Refresh*. Isn't this a cool Product Analysis report for The Beverage Company?

| | A | B | C | D | E | F | G | H |
|---|---|---|---|---|---|---|---|---|
| 2 | | | | | | | | |
| 3 | | | Product Analysis Report | | | | | |
| 4 | | | | | | | P... ▾ × | |
| 5 | | Qtr1 | Qtr2 | Qtr3 | Qtr4 | Year | Sales ▾ | |
| 6 | Colas | ⬆ $25,048.00 | ⬆ $27,187.00 | ⬆ $28,544.00 | ↗ $25,355.00 | $106,134.00 | Market ▾ | |
| 7 | Root Beer | ⬆ $26,627.00 | ⬆ $27,401.00 | ⬆ $27,942.00 | ⬆ $27,116.00 | $109,086.00 | Actual ▾ | |
| 8 | Cream Soda | ↗ $23,997.00 | ↗ $25,736.00 | ↗ $26,650.00 | ↗ $25,022.00 | $101,405.00 | Refresh ⓘ | |
| 9 | Fruit Soda | ⬇ $20,148.00 | ⬇ $21,355.00 | ⬇ $22,079.00 | ⬇ $20,648.00 | $ 84,230.00 | | |
| 10 | Diet Drinks | ⬆ $25,731.00 | ⬆ $26,787.00 | ⬆ $27,495.00 | ⬆ $25,665.00 | $105,678.00 | | |
| 11 | Product | $ 95,820.00 | $ 101,679.00 | $ 105,215.00 | $ 98,141.00 | $400,855.00 | | |

**Note!** In the example above, zooming in on Colas should also expand the formatting (if you have *Use Excel Formatting* on).

### Print POV in Headers and Footers

Because POV members are hidden in row one, I can include them in standard headers and footers for the report.

Another way to print the POV in Excel headers and footers is to use the POV{} function.

22. In Excel, navigate to the Insert tab >> Text >> Header & Footer. Type in the statement POV:{} in the header or footer to pull in the current POV selections:

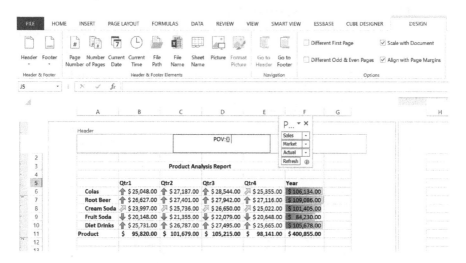

23. The POV should display in the header or footer when you print the spreadsheet:

POV:{Measures-Sales, Market-Market, Scenario-Actual}

**Product Analysis Report**

|  | Qtr1 | Qtr2 | Qtr3 | Qtr4 | Year |
|---|---|---|---|---|---|
| Colas | ⬆ $25,048.00 | ⬆ $27,187.00 | ⬆ $28,544.00 | ⬇ $25,355.00 | $106,134.00 |
| Root Beer | ⬆ $26,627.00 | ⬆ $27,401.00 | ⬆ $27,942.00 | ⬆ $27,116.00 | $109,086.00 |
| Cream Soda | ⬇ $23,997.00 | ⬇ $25,736.00 | ⬇ $26,650.00 | ⬇ $25,022.00 | $101,405.00 |
| Fruit Soda | ⬇ $20,148.00 | ⬇ $21,355.00 | ⬇ $22,079.00 | ⬇ $20,648.00 | $ 84,230.00 |
| Diet Drinks | ⬆ $25,731.00 | ⬆ $26,787.00 | ⬆ $27,495.00 | ⬆ $25,665.00 | $105,678.00 |
| Product | $ 95,820.00 | $ 101,679.00 | $ 105,215.00 | $ 98,141.00 | $400,855.00 |

## Multi-Grid/Multi-Source Reports

There are certain times when I'll want to have two sets of Essbase data on a single Excel sheet. Say I wanted to create a report that had Actual on the top half of the page and Budget on the bottom half:

| | B | C | D | E | F | G |
|---|---|---|---|---|---|---|
| 2 | | | Market | Product | Actual | |
| 3 | | Qtr1 | Qtr2 | Qtr3 | Qtr4 | Year |
| 4 | Sales | 95,820 | 101,679 | 105,215 | 98,141 | 400,855 |
| 5 | COGS | 42,877 | 45,362 | 47,343 | 43,754 | 179,336 |
| 6 | **Margin** | 52,943 | 56,317 | 57,872 | 54,387 | 221,519 |
| 7 | | | | | | |
| 8 | Marketing | 15,839 | 16,716 | 17,522 | 16,160 | 66,237 |
| 9 | Payroll | 12,168 | 12,243 | 12,168 | 12,168 | 48,747 |
| 10 | Misc | 233 | 251 | 270 | 259 | 1,013 |
| 11 | **Total Expenses** | 28,240 | 29,210 | 29,960 | 28,587 | 115,997 |
| 12 | | | | | | |
| 13 | **Profit** | 24,703 | 27,107 | 27,912 | 25,800 | 105,522 |
| 14 | | | | | | |
| 15 | | | Market | Product | Budget | |
| 16 | | Qtr1 | Qtr2 | Qtr3 | Qtr4 | Year |
| 17 | Sales | 89,680 | 95,240 | 98,690 | 89,470 | 373,080 |
| 18 | COGS | 38,140 | 40,460 | 42,280 | 38,060 | 158,940 |
| 19 | **Margin** | 51,540 | 54,780 | 56,410 | 51,410 | 214,140 |
| 20 | | | | | | |
| 21 | Marketing | 11,900 | 12,700 | 13,370 | 11,550 | 49,520 |
| 22 | Payroll | 9,060 | 9,210 | 9,060 | 7,910 | 35,240 |
| 23 | Misc | - | - | - | - | - |
| 24 | **Total Expenses** | 20,960 | 21,910 | 22,430 | 19,460 | 84,760 |
| 25 | | | | | | |
| 26 | **Profit** | 30,580 | 32,870 | 33,980 | 31,950 | 129,380 |

So is it possible in Smart View? Yes, it is! The grids may be connected to the same or different Essbase data sources.

1.  Open a blank worksheet.
2.  Open the Smart View panel and connect to Essbase Cloud and *Sample.Basic.*
3.  Select a range of cells (it must be a range of cells and not a single cell). Right-click on *Basic* and select *Ad hoc analysis:*

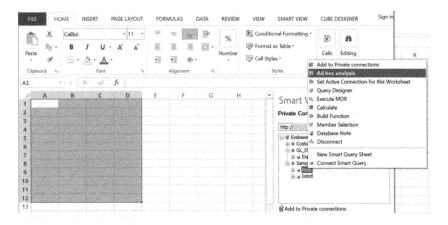

**Tip!** Be careful with how many cells you select in the starting range. Any empty rows are still considered part of the grid and might give you unwanted whitespace.

4.  When prompted, click *Yes* to change the sheet to support multiple grids:

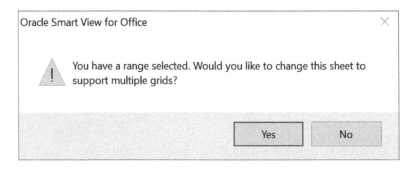

5. In the spreadsheet, use member selection and/or zooming to create the following grid:

|   | A | B | C | D |
|---|---|---|---|---|
| 1 |  | Jan | Market |  |
| 2 |  | Actual | Budget | Variance |
| 3 |  | Sales | Sales | Sales |
| 4 | Colas | 8314 | 8980 | -666 |
| 5 | Root Beer | 8716 | 8500 | 216 |
| 6 | Cream Soda | 7874 | 6650 | 1224 |
| 7 | Fruit Soda | 6634 | 5350 | 1284 |
| 8 | Diet Drinks | 8454 | 8260 | 194 |
| 9 | Product | 31538 | 29480 | 2058 |

6. Select a range of cells below the first ad hoc grid. Right-click on *Basic* and select *Ad hoc analysis:*

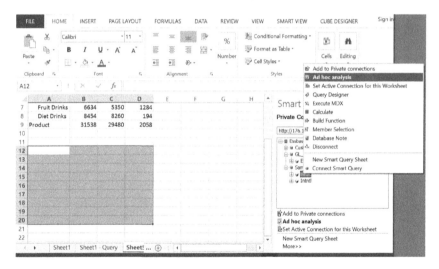

7. Use member selection and/or zooming to create the second grid. Update both grids to use the *Sales* member in the Measures dimension:

| | A | B | C | D |
|---|---|---|---|---|
| 1 | | Jan | Market | |
| 2 | | Actual | Budget | Variance |
| 3 | | Sales | Sales | Sales |
| 4 | Colas | 8314 | 8980 | -666 |
| 5 | Root Beer | 8716 | 8500 | 216 |
| 6 | Cream Soda | 7874 | 6650 | 1224 |
| 7 | Fruit Soda | 6634 | 5350 | 1284 |
| 8 | Diet Drinks | 8454 | 8260 | 194 |
| 9 | Product | 31538 | 29480 | 2058 |
| 10 | | | | |
| 11 | | | | |
| 12 | | Feb | Market | |
| 13 | | Actual | Budget | Variance |
| 14 | | Sales | Sales | Sales |
| 15 | Colas | 8327 | 9040 | -713 |
| 16 | Root Beer | 8960 | 8730 | 230 |
| 17 | Cream Soda | 8046 | 6800 | 1246 |
| 18 | Fruit Soda | 6736 | 5430 | 1306 |
| 19 | Diet Drinks | 8610 | 8410 | 200 |
| 20 | Product | 32069 | 30000 | 2069 |

8. Once you've finalized the layout you can apply formatting, just as learned earlier in this chapter.

**Tip!**

**Excel Formatting Hints for Multiple Grids:**
- Make sure Use Excel Formatting is turned on for the worksheet
- Apply no borders to the cells
- Change background to white
- Change text to white to hide headers and rows (do not delete grid headers or POV members because that could impact your ability to refresh)
- Apply lines, bolding, etc.
- Adjust row size to help with white space

### Butterfly Report

Using the multi-grid features of Smart View, I can create a "butterfly" report, a report that has data points before member names. Follow along.

1. In a new spreadsheet, right-click on *Sample.Basic* and select *Ad hoc analysis.*
2. Using zooming, member selection, or direct typing, create the following grid:

|   | A | B | C |
|---|---|---|---|
| 1 |  | Year | Market |
| 2 |  | Actual | Budget |
| 3 |  | Sales | Sales |
| 4 | Colas | 106134 | 114310 |
| 5 | Root Beer | 109086 | 106740 |
| 6 | Cream Soda | 101405 | 85230 |
| 7 | Fruit Soda | 84230 | 66800 |
| 8 | Diet Drinks | 105678 | 103300 |
| 9 | Product | 400855 | 373080 |

3. At this point you have a standard grid. Insert a column between Actual and Budget. Using Excel functionality, copy and paste the product names from column A to the new blank column, column C.
4. Click *Refresh* and you have a butterfly report!
5. Apply some Excel formatting.
6. Save the report:

|   | A | B | C | D | E |
|---|---|---|---|---|---|
| 1 |  | Sales |  | Year | Market |
| 2 |  | **Actual** |  | **Budget** |  |
| 3 |  | $ 106,134.00 | Colas | $ 114,310.00 |  |
| 4 |  | $ 109,086.00 | Root Beer | $ 106,740.00 |  |
| 5 |  | $ 101,405.00 | Cream Soda | $ 85,230.00 |  |
| 6 |  | $ 84,230.00 | Fruit Soda | $ 66,800.00 |  |
| 7 |  | $ 105,678.00 | Diet Drinks | $ 103,300.00 |  |
| 8 |  | **$400,855.00** | **Product** | **$373,080.00** |  |

## Multi-Source Report with Data Points

I can also create a multi-source report using data points. While multi-grid spreadsheets are the recommended method, I'll review this alternative so I'll have covered the full bag of Smart View tricks.

1. Create the following grid in a separate worksheet, sourced from Sample.Basic:

| | A | B | C | D | E | F |
|---|---|---|---|---|---|---|
| 1 | | Actual | Product | | | |
| 2 | | Qtr1 | Qtr2 | Qtr3 | Qtr4 | Year |
| 3 | | Sales | Sales | Sales | Sales | Sales |
| 4 | East | 20621 | 22449 | 22976 | 21352 | 87398 |
| 5 | West | 31674 | 33572 | 35130 | 32555 | 132931 |
| 6 | South | 12113 | 12602 | 13355 | 12776 | 50846 |
| 7 | Central | 31412 | 33056 | 33754 | 31458 | 129680 |
| 8 | Market | 95820 | 101679 | 105215 | 98141 | 400855 |

2. Create the following grid in a separate worksheet, sourced from Sample.Interntl:

| | A | B | C | D | E | F |
|---|---|---|---|---|---|---|
| 1 | | Product | Actual | | | |
| 2 | | Qtr1 | Qtr2 | Qtr3 | Qtr4 | Year |
| 3 | | Sales | Sales | Sales | Sales | Sales |
| 4 | US | 95820 | 101679 | 105215 | 98141 | 400855 |
| 5 | Canada | 16461.27 | 16505.64 | 16781.04 | 16351.11 | 66099.06 |
| 6 | Europe | 21335.923 | 26254.93 | 28680.47 | 24925.64 | 101196.963 |
| 7 | Market | 133617.193 | 144439.57 | 150676.51 | 139417.75 | 568151.023 |

3.  Select the first grid from the worksheet and select *Copy* from the Smart View ribbon:

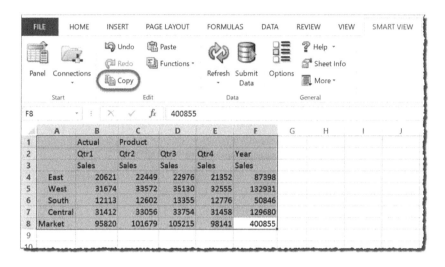

4.  Select a blank worksheet and select *Paste,* pasting the data points into a blank worksheet:

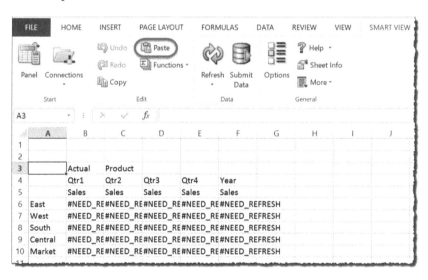

Behind the scenes, the Paste Data Points feature is creating a report with each cell using the HSGetValue function.

5. Repeat the same steps for the second grid, copying and pasting the data points below the first grid.

Notice each data cell is an individual data point that is tied to a specific intersection of dimension members, cube, and server:

| | A | B | C | D | E | F | G |
|---|---|---|---|---|---|---|---|
| 1 | | | | | | | |
| 2 | | | | | | | |
| 3 | | Actual | Product | | | | |
| 4 | | Qtr1 | Qtr2 | Qtr3 | Qtr4 | Year | |
| 5 | | Sales | Sales | Sales | Sales | Sales | |
| 6 | East | #NEED_RE | #NEED_RE | #NEED_RE | #NEED_RE | #NEED_REFRESH | |
| 7 | West | #NEED_RE | #NEED_RE | #NEED_RE | #NEED_RE | #NEED_REFRESH | |
| 8 | South | #NEED_RE | #NEED_RE | #NEED_RE | #NEED_RE | #NEED_REFRESH | |
| 9 | Central | #NEED_RE | #NEED_RE | #NEED_RE | #NEED_RE | #NEED_REFRESH | |
| 10 | Market | #NEED_RE | #NEED_RE | #NEED_RE | #NEED_RE | #NEED_REFRESH | |
| 11 | | | | | | | |
| 12 | | Product | Actual | | | | |
| 13 | | Qtr1 | Qtr2 | Qtr3 | Qtr4 | Year | |
| 14 | | Sales | Sales | Sales | Sales | Sales | |
| 15 | US | #NEED_RE | #NEED_RE | #NEED_RE | #NEED_RE | #NEED_REFRESH | |
| 16 | Canada | #NEED_RE | #NEED_RE | #NEED_RE | #NEED_RE | #NEED_REFRESH | |
| 17 | Europe | #NEED_RE | #NEED_RE | #NEED_RE | #NEED_RE | #NEED_REFRESH | |
| 18 | Market | #NEED_RE | #NEED_RE | #NEED_RE | #NEED_RE | #NEED_REFRESH | |

6. Click *Refresh* to refresh the data for each data point. From this point you can follow the same formatting steps for the spreadsheet.

**Tip!**

**Excel Formatting Hints for Reports using Data Points**:
- Apply no borders to the cells
- Change background to white
- Change text to white to hide headers and rows (do *not* delete grid headers or POV members because that could impact your ability to refresh)
- Apply lines, bolding, etc.
- Adjust row size to help with white space

I can then refresh the report daily, monthly, or as necessary and the current data stored in Essbase will display.

Notice that if I select the data point a tool tip will display, showing me the attributes about the data point. Notice also that all of the data points reference Product. What if I wanted to run this report for product category for Colas? How do I change each cell and, more importantly, is there a way to change it once for all data points?

I'll show you how you can do this once for each data source.

7. Select a data point in our multi-source report and choose *Functions >> Manage POV* on the Smart View ribbon:

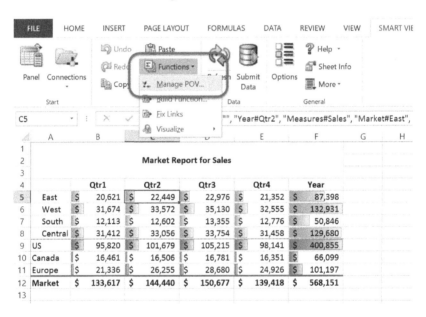

The POV Manager will display showing the two Smart View queries used for the data points (two in this case because I have one for Sample.Basic and one for Sample.Interntl):

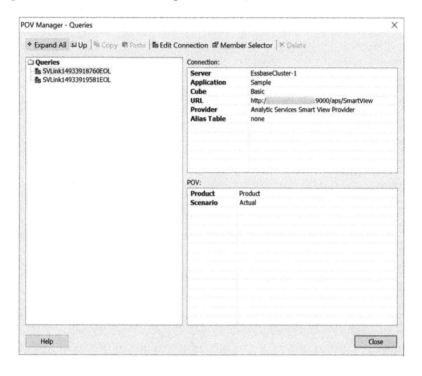

8. For each SVLinkxxx (one for Sample.Basic and one for Sample.Interntl), change the Product dimension selection from Product to *Colas* by highlighting Product in the POV section and using the Member Selection window:

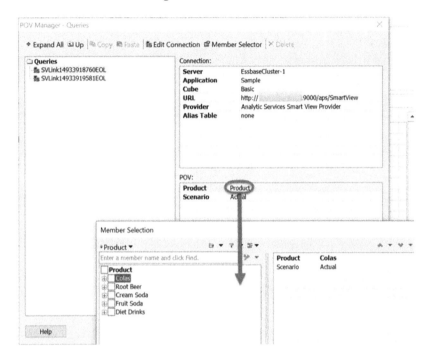

9. Repeat the member selection steps so that both SVLinks are updated to point to *Colas*:

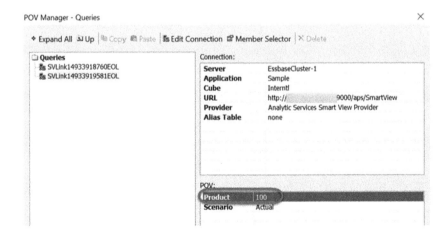

10. Click *Close*. Choose *Refresh* and note all of the data points are updated for the product category *Colas*:

| | A | B | C | D | E |
|---|---|---|---|---|---|
| 1 | | | | | |
| 2 | | | Market Report for Sales | | |
| 3 | | | | | |
| 4 | | Qtr1 | Qtr2 | Qtr3 | Qtr4 |
| 5 | East | $ 6,292 | $ 7,230 | $ 7,770 | $ 6,448 |
| 6 | West | $ 6,950 | $ 7,178 | $ 7,423 | $ 6,755 |
| 7 | South | $ 3,732 | $ 4,078 | $ 4,457 | $ 4,013 |
| 8 | Central | $ 8,074 | $ 8,701 | $ 8,894 | $ 8,139 |
| 9 | US | $ 25,048 | $ 27,187 | $ 28,544 | $ 25,355 |

As I copy and paste new data points into a target, more queries are added. It will become difficult to tell which SVLinkxxx belongs to which data points, so keep this in mind while using data points and the POV Manager.

Another alternative is to use HsGetValue formulas and have the formulas reference a cell with the desired data/point of view.

### Create a Report in Word or PowerPoint

As I mentioned earlier, Smart View works with Excel as well as Word and PowerPoint. Integration with all of the Office products is bread and butter for Smart View. The easiest way to get data into Word or PowerPoint is to copy and paste data points just as I did in the Power User section. I can copy and paste data points from:

- Excel to Word and PowerPoint
- Word to Word and PowerPoint
- PowerPoint to Word and PowerPoint

These live data points are tied to a specific server, cube and dimension member intersection (just like the data points in Excel). This means I can refresh them at any time and get the most current data.

When creating reports in Word or PowerPoint, make sure to apply Excel formatting first, before copying and pasting data points to

Word and PowerPoint. The numeric formatting is preserved as I copy and paste the data points. Member formatting, however, is not saved. I'll need to apply the desired formatting in Word or PowerPoint.

I'll now create a report in Word.

1. Pull up the saved butterfly report. Select the grid and choose *Copy* from the Smart View ribbon:

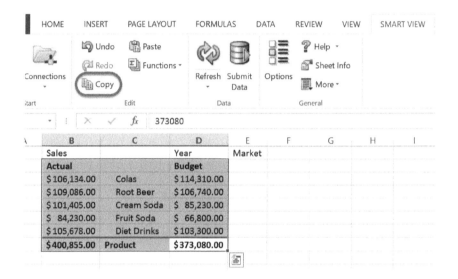

2. Open a blank Word document. Add a title and text to the word document (just to give you a feel for what is possible).

3. Find the desired location for the copied grid and choose *Paste* from the Smart View ribbon:

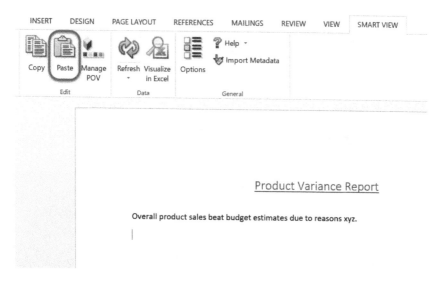

4. Click *Refresh* and the result should look similar to as follows:

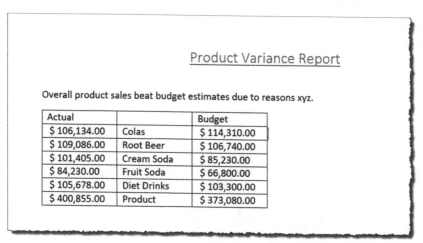

As the underlying data changes, I can simply click *Refresh* to pull in the current data set. In this basic example, I've shown how to pull in data from a single source but I can also create multi-source reports in Word and PowerPoint.

I can change the POV for the data points just as I did in Excel.

5.  Choose a data point and select *Manage POV* from the Smart View ribbon. Change the Market member selection to *West*:

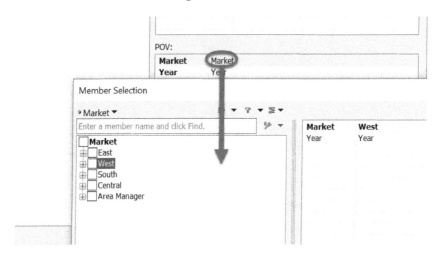

6.  Click *Close* to close the POV Manager and click *Refresh*.

The data points in the report should be updated to reflect the new member selections. I'll make sure to add West to the title of the report (so consumers will understand the data set they are viewing):

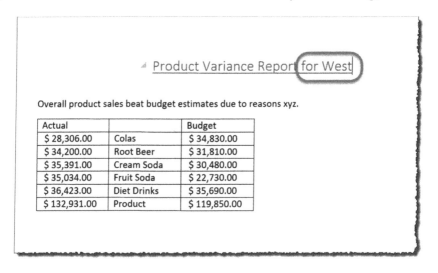

7.  Follow these same steps to create a presentation in PowerPoint.

When data points are inserted into PowerPoint, they appear as floating text boxes:

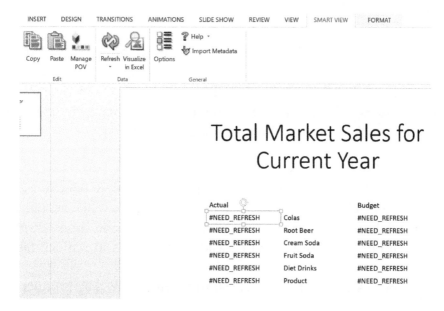

8. You can move each text box to its desired placement. Click *Refresh* to pull in the data. Add formatting to the text boxes as necessary to create a nicely formatted presentation:

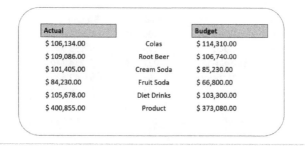

Don't forget the ability to *Visualize in Excel* (amaze your boss with immediate answers during presentation reviews).

**Tip!**

To Visualize in Excel, you must select a specific data point (not the table).

Now that JWE is happy with my nicely formatted reports in Excel, Word, and PowerPoint, they've asked me to create the same version of the P&L report for each different product (and I have over 1,000 products). This is a good time to introduce the magician known as Cascade (I click a button and reports magically appear).

### Cascade

Now I'd like to run the same report for multiple selections. On the report I just built, I want to run it for every region. While I could use Member Select to pick each region (East, Central…) and choose *Refresh* after each one, a feature called Cascade will do this in a much faster manner.

For this example, I've been asked to create a P&L by product.

1. Open the saved P&L report and connect to Sample.Basic:

|    | A | B | C | D | E |
|----|---|---|---|---|---|
| 1  | | | | | |
| 2  | | **Profit and Loss Statement** | | | |
| 3  | | for | | | |
| 4  | Product: | Product | | | |
| 5  | Market: | Market | | | |
| 6  | Period: | Year | | | |
| 7  | | | | | |
| 8  | | **Actual** | | **Budget** | |
| 9  | **Sales** | $ 400,855 | | $ 373,080 | |
| 10 | COGS | $ 179,336 | | $ 158,940 | |
| 11 | *Margin* | $ 221,519 | | $ 214,140 | |
| 12 | Marketing | $  66,237 | | $  49,520 | |
| 13 | Payroll | $  48,747 | | $  35,240 | |
| 14 | Misc | $   1,013 | | - | |
| 15 | *Total Expenses* | $ 115,997 | | $  84,760 | |
| 16 | Profit | $ 105,522 | | $ 129,380 | |
| 17 | | | | | |
| 18 | Profit % | 26.3 | | 34.7 | |

I can choose whether I want to cascade the results to a new workbook or the same workbook. I can also cascade the results with each member to its own workbook.

2.  Click the *Cascade >> New Workbook* option on the Essbase ribbon:

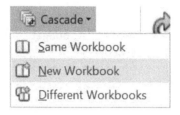

Using my example, you receive the following error message:

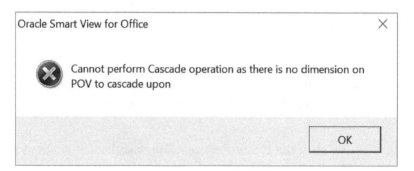

The dimension for which I am cascading (or bursting) must be in the POV. So I need to move Product into the POV. There is little chance that I can do this without impacting the formatting. Valid ways to get Product into the POV are:

- Delete Product from the cell and click Refresh
- Delete the row containing Product and click Refresh
- Select Product and choose *Pivot >> Pivot to POV*
- Just start over

3. Go ahead and pick one of the options above or another that you choose. Correct any formatting so that the result is as follows, with Product in the floating POV:

|  | A | B | C | D | E |
|---|---|---|---|---|---|
| 2 |  |  |  |  |  |
| 3 |  | Profit and Loss Report |  |  |  |
| 4 |  |  |  | P... ▾ ✕ |  |
| 5 |  | **Actual** | **Budget** | Product ▾ |  |
| 6 | *Sales* | *$ 400,855* | *$ 373,080* | Market ▾ |  |
| 7 | COGS | $ 179,336 | $ 158,940 | Year ▾ |  |
| 8 | Margin | $ 221,519 | $ 214,140 | Refresh ⓘ |  |
| 9 | Marketing | $ 66,237 | $ 49,520 |  |  |
| 10 | *Payroll* | *$ 48,747* | *$ 35,240* |  |  |
| 11 | Misc | $ 1,013 | $  -  |  |  |
| 12 | Total Expenses | 115997 | 84760 |  |  |
| 13 | Profit | 105522 | 129380 |  |  |

I now am starting to really appreciate the importance of finalizing the layout before applying formatting.

4. Now click the *Cascade >> New Workbook* button on the Essbase ribbon.
5. Using the Member Selection, filter the Product for *Children* (a.k.a. Product Category):

Member Selection

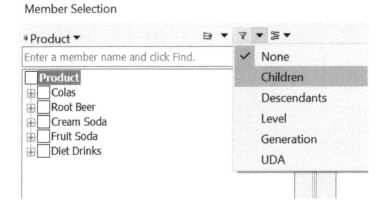

6. Click the option to *Check Base Members* and move them into the selection panel:

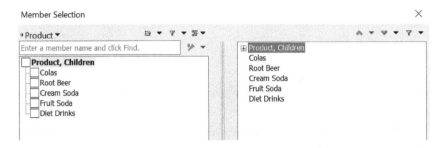

7. Click *OK* and a new workbook will be created with a worksheet for each product category:

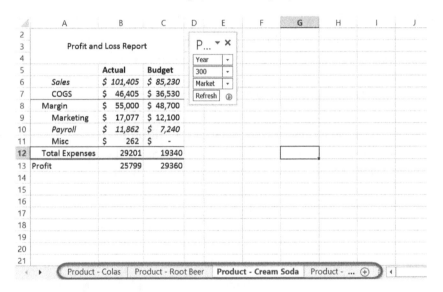

Even if directed back to the original spreadsheet, don't fear, the new workbook is there. Was it really that easy to generate reports for all of my product categories? Yes, it was: imagine the possibilities. I now have a number of reports created in a just a few seconds. Imagine running this for hundreds of stores. Go have a venti latte with the time I've just saved you.

**Note!** The tabs in the cascaded workbook are renamed to either the member name or alias depending on what you have selected for the current connection.

### Smart View Formatting

Now that I've covered Excel formatting options along with some other import report creation "how to's," I'll turn my attention to Smart View formatting options.

I can use either Excel formatting or Smart View formatting but not both. I've already reviewed the most common and, in my opinion, best formatting option for formatting reports, which is Excel. I still must, however, cover two other options available. Smart View formatting can be helpful when operating in ad hoc analysis mode (though with the *Move Formatting on Operations* feature, the use case for Smart View formatting is reduced). Let's look at basic Smart View formatting features.

First I'll have to turn off Excel formatting.

8. Go to *Options* on the Smart View ribbon.
9. Under the Formatting section, change the option from Use Excel Formatting to *Use Cell Styles* and click *OK*:

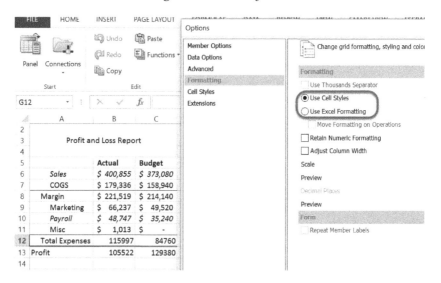

10. Click *Refresh* and the Excel formatting disappears:

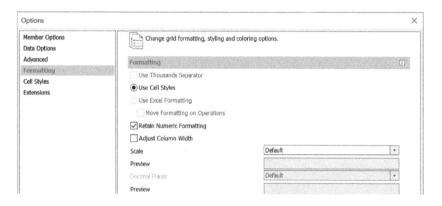

| | A | B | C | D | E |
|---|---|---|---|---|---|
| 2 | Profit and Loss Report | | | | |
| 3 | | | | | |
| 4 | | | | | |
| 5 | | Actual | Budget | | |
| 6 | Sales | 400855 | 373080 | | |
| 7 | COGS | 179336 | 158940 | | |
| 8 | Margin | 221519 | 214140 | | |
| 9 | Marketing | 66237 | 49520 | | |
| 10 | Payroll | 48747 | 35240 | | |
| 11 | Misc | 1013 | 0 | | |
| 12 | Total Expenses | 115997 | 84760 | | |
| 13 | Profit | 105522 | 129380 | | |

11. Go back to the options tab and check the *Retain Numeric Formatting:*

12. Apply numeric formatting to the grid:

| | A | B | C |
|---|---|---|---|
| 2 | Profit and Loss Report | | |
| 3 | | | |
| 4 | | | |
| 5 | | Actual | Budget |
| 6 | Sales | $ 400,855 | $ 373,080 |
| 7 | COGS | $ 179,336 | $ 158,940 |
| 8 | Margin | $ 221,519 | $ 214,140 |
| 9 | Marketing | $ 66,237 | $ 49,520 |
| 10 | Payroll | $ 48,747 | $ 35,240 |
| 11 | Misc | $ 1,013 | $ - |
| 12 | Total Expenses | $ 115,997 | $ 84,760 |
| 13 | Profit | $ 105,522 | $ 129,380 |

13. Click *Refresh*.

The numeric formatting is retained! However, my excitement will be short lived.

14. Zoom out on *Market* (double right-click or select *Zoom Out* from the Essbase ribbon).
15. Zoom in on *Market*.
16. Continue to zoom in and out and pivot on the dimensions.

The numeric formatting might be retained for a few zooms, but I will end up with an unformatted grid eventually. Numeric formatting when applying a scale, however, will be retained.

17. Under *Options >> Formatting*, change the Scale to 1 (to scale to the thousands):

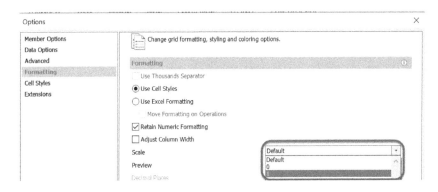

18. Click *Refresh*.

19. Zoom in and out and notice that the scaling remains:

|   | A | B | C | D |
|---|---|---|---|---|
| 1 |   |   | Product | Year |
| 2 | Profit and Loss Report |   |   |   |
| 3 |   |   |   |   |
| 4 |   |   |   |   |
| 5 |   |   | Actual | Budget |
| 6 | Market | Margin | 22151.9 | 21414 |
| 7 | Market | Marketir | 6623.7 | 4952 |
| 8 | Market | Payroll | 4874.7 | 3524 |
| 9 | Market | Misc | 101.3 | 0 |
| 10 | Market | Marketir | 6623.7 | 4952 |
| 11 | Market | Payroll | 4874.7 | 3524 |
| 12 | Market | Misc | 101.3 | 0 |
| 13 | Market | Total Exper | 11599.7 | 8476 |
| 14 | Market | Profit | 10552.2 | 12938 |

**Note!** Scale is supported in both Excel formatting and Smart View formatting.

### Preserve Formatting

Another formatting feature available in Smart View, Preserve Formatting, is the ability to save the formatting selected for data cells. Any Excel formatting will be saved for the highlighted cells. The formatting remains for those cells through zooming operations but it will not apply to new data cells that are returned to the spreadsheet. This feature is more helpful while performing ad hoc analysis, as opposed to creating formatted reports.

1. Open a blank worksheet and refresh data for *Sample.Basic* (see our query below to follow along).
2. Zoom in on *Measures*.

3. Set the formatting for the data cells to $. Make sure *Use Excel Formatting* under *Options >> Formatting* is not selected and *Use Cell Styles* is selected.

4. Select the data cells with the formatting defined (just the data cells). Select *Preserve Format* from the Essbase ribbon:

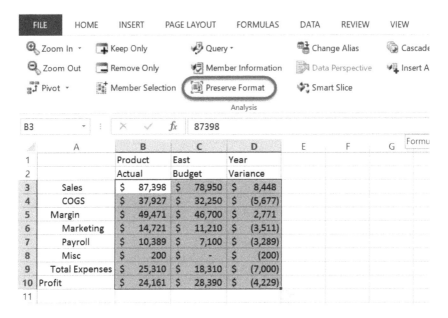

Now when I perform a refresh or basic drilling, the cell formatting will remain for the selected cells.

5. Zoom out on *Sales*.

6. Zoom out on *Profit*.

7. Zoom back down the *Measures* dimension.

The formatting is retained.

8.  Zoom into *Year* and you should see the formatting retained as quarters are displayed across the columns:

| | A | B | C | D | E | F | G | H | I | J |
|---|---|---|---|---|---|---|---|---|---|---|
| 1 | | | | | | | | | | |
| 2 | | | East | Product | | | | | | |
| 3 | | | Qtr1 | | | Qtr2 | | | Qtr3 | |
| 4 | | | | | | | | | | |
| 5 | | Actual | Budget | Variance | Actual | Budget | Variance | Actual | Budget | Variance |
| 6 | Sales | $ 2,062 | $ 1,895 | $ 167 | $ 2,245 | $ 2,059 | $ 186 | $ 2,298 | $ 2,110 | $ 188 |
| 7 | COGS | $ 908 | $ 784 | $ (124) | $ 959 | $ 826 | $ (133) | $ 1,006 | $ 864 | $ (142 |
| 8 | Margin | $ 1,154 | $ 1,111 | $ 43 | $ 1,286 | $ 1,233 | $ 53 | $ 1,291 | $ 1,246 | $ 45 |
| 9 | Marketing | $ 352 | $ 269 | $ (83) | $ 371 | $ 289 | $ (82) | $ 392 | $ 305 | $ (87 |
| 10 | Payroll | $ 260 | $ 186 | $ (74) | $ 260 | $ 189 | $ (71) | $ 260 | $ 186 | $ (74 |
| 11 | Misc | $ 5 | - | $ | $ (5) | $ 5 | - | $ (5) | $ 5 | - | $ (5 |
| 12 | Total Expenses | $ 616 | $ 455 | $ (161) | $ 637 | $ 478 | $ (159) | $ 657 | $ 491 | $ (166 |
| 13 | Profit | $ 538 | $ 656 | $ (118) | $ 650 | $ 755 | $ (105) | $ 635 | $ 755 | $ (120 |

The formatting is retained. However, if I zoomed in on a dimension that was listed down the row, the formatting would only remain on the data cells that were originally highlighted.

9.  Keep only on *Qtr1* and *Sales*.
10. Zoom in on *Product*:

| | A | B | C | D | E |
|---|---|---|---|---|---|
| 1 | | | | | |
| 2 | | | Qtr1 | East | |
| 3 | | | | | |
| 4 | | | Actual | Budget | Variance |
| 5 | Colas | Sales | 629.2 | 593 | 36.2 |
| 6 | Root Beer | Sales | 572.6 | 546 | 26.6 |
| 7 | Cream Soda | Sales | 486.8 | 368 | 118.8 |
| 8 | Fruit Soda | Sales | 373.5 | 388 | -14.5 |
| 9 | Diet Drinks | Sales | 188.4 | 170 | 18.4 |
| 10 | Product | Sales | $ 2,062 | $ 1,895 | $ 167 |

The preserved format is only preserved for the original data cells.

**Note!** Preserve formatting is tied to specific member combinations. If you drill down, next levels will not have the applied formatting.

The following chart provides a quick comparison of the formatting features:

| | Preserve Formatting | Use Excel Formatting |
|---|---|---|
| Use When | Ad hoc Analysis | Report Templates |
| Applies to Data Cells | Y | Y |
| Applies to Members | N | Y |
| Retains formatting on drill | Y (for selected cells) | N |
| Retains formatting on POV change | Y | Y |
| Retains formatting on pivot | Y (for selected cells) | N |
| Provides the fastest retrievals | N | Y |

### Cell Style Options

Cell Styles will apply specific formatting (fonts, borders, and backgrounds) to member and data cells. Formatting can be assigned by different characteristics of members and data cells. I may also want to highlight a specific member or data points for a particular reason. For example, I recommend using cell styles for members or data points that may have drill through reports associated with them. If I am inputting data, I may want to apply a special format to highlight intersections with write access.

JWE now wants a budget input template for quarter one sales.

1. Create the following query to follow along as you learn how to use Styles:

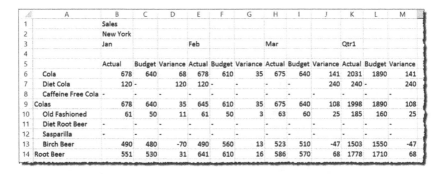

| | A | B | C | D | E | F | G | H | I | J | K | L | M |
|---|---|---|---|---|---|---|---|---|---|---|---|---|---|
| 1 | | Sales | | | | | | | | | | | |
| 2 | | New York | | | | | | | | | | | |
| 3 | | Jan | | | Feb | | | Mar | | | Qtr1 | | |
| 4 | | | | | | | | | | | | | |
| 5 | | Actual | Budget | Variance | Actual | Budget | Variance | Actual | Budget | Variance | Actual | Budget | Variance |
| 6 | Cola | 678 | 640 | 68 | 678 | 610 | 35 | 675 | 640 | 141 | 2031 | 1890 | 141 |
| 7 | Diet Cola | 120 | - | | 120 | 120 | - | - | - | 240 | 240 | - | 240 |
| 8 | Caffeine Free Cola | - | - | - | - | - | - | - | - | - | - | - | - |
| 9 | Colas | 678 | 640 | 35 | 645 | 610 | 35 | 675 | 640 | 108 | 1998 | 1890 | 108 |
| 10 | Old Fashioned | 61 | 50 | 11 | 61 | 50 | 3 | 63 | 60 | 25 | 185 | 160 | 25 |
| 11 | Diet Root Beer | - | - | - | - | - | - | - | - | - | - | - | - |
| 12 | Sasparilla | - | - | - | - | - | - | - | - | - | - | - | - |
| 13 | Birch Beer | 490 | 480 | -70 | 490 | 560 | 13 | 523 | 510 | -47 | 1503 | 1550 | -47 |
| 14 | Root Beer | 551 | 530 | 31 | 641 | 610 | 16 | 586 | 570 | 68 | 1778 | 1710 | 68 |

2. Select the *Options* button from the Smart View ribbon.
3. First check that *Use Excel Formatting* is unselected and *Use Cell Styles* is selected on the Formatting section. (Also, make sure scaling is set to zero or you'll go crazy wondering why your numbers are off.)
4. To use Cell Styles, choose the Cell Styles section:

5. Expand the *Analytic Services* option. Expand *Member cells* to
   set member properties or expand *Data cells* to set data cell
   properties:

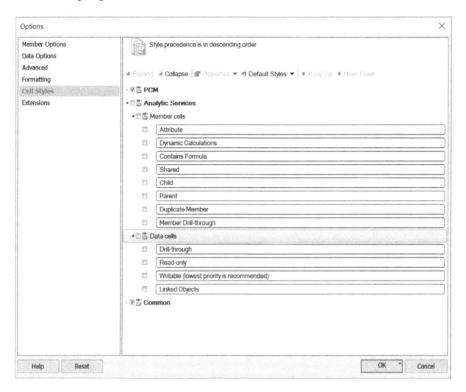

**Note!**

What's Analytic Services? Back in the old days just as
System 9 was introduced and when Hyperion still owned
Hyperion, Essbase was renamed to Analytic Services.
Thank goodness for Oracle as they have now brought
home our beloved Essbase name back to us. Still, you may
see references to "Analytic Services" throughout the
Oracle EPM products. Just think "Essbase" when you see
this.

Now I'm going to change the cell style for parents.

6.  Check the box next to *Parent* to enable a properties box:

@ Expand  @ Collapse | 🖅 Properties ▼  ⤺ Default Styles ▼ | ⬆ Move Up  ⬇ Move Down

▷ ☑ 🗟 **PCM**

◢ ☑ 🗟 **Analytic Services**

   ◢ ☑ 🗟 Member cells

      ☐   Attribute

      ☐   Dynamic Calculations

      ☐   Contains Formula

      ☐   Shared

      ☐   Child

      ☑☐   Parent

      ☐   Duplicate Member

      ☐   Member Drill-through

   ◢ ☐ 🗟 Data cells

      ☐   Drill-through

      ☐   Read-only

      ☐   Writable (lowest priority is recommended)

      ☐   Linked Objects

▷ ☑ 🗟 **Common**

I can set the properties for Font, Background, and Border.

7.  From the Properties drop-down, choose *Font*:

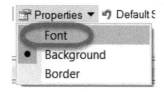

8. Change the font to bold, font size 11, and a nice tone (navy is the new black):

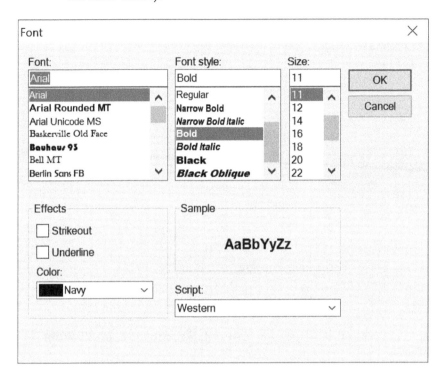

9. Click *OK* and then click *OK* again to save the settings and close the Options window.

10. *Refresh* data.

Here is the result:

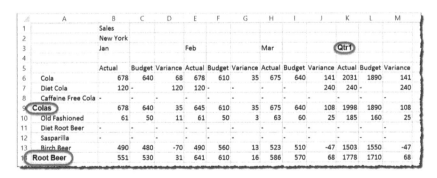

Notice for any member that is a parent that the font is now bold and a nice, earthy navy tone. Any member that is a child only (level-0) is set to the default formatting.

11. If you wanted all members to have the same formatting, go back to the *Options >> Cell Styles* tab and set the same font properties for the Child section. In our example, let's change the font color to *Navy* but leave the font *Regular*:

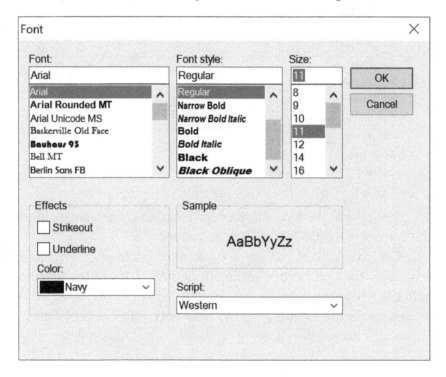

A member can meet more than one criterion. Qtr1 is both a parent and a child.

Use the Move Up or Move Down buttons to define the order of precedence for how cell styles should be applied (I want Parent to have the first priority):

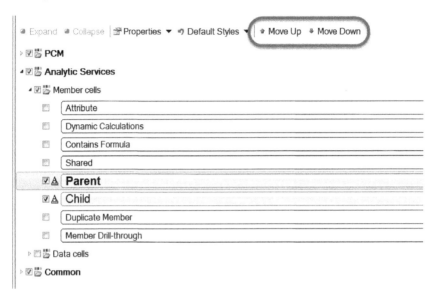

The cells at the top of the list have higher precedence while cells at the bottom of the list have lower precedence.

On Data cells, I can set a background color for writable cells (along with font or border settings). Setting a background color is beneficial when developing budgeting input sheets for end user submissions. In the example below, read-only cells are set to gray and writable cells are set to yellow:

Here is an example of a budget entry spreadsheet with Cell Styles applied for a user who has been assigned write access to the budget scenario for level-0 products:

| | A | B | C | D | E | F | G | H | I | J | K | L | M |
|---|---|---|---|---|---|---|---|---|---|---|---|---|---|
| 1 | | Sales | | | | | | | | | | | |
| 2 | | New York | | | | | | | | | | | |
| 3 | | Jan | | | Feb | | | Mar | | | Qtr1 | | |
| 4 | | | | | | | | | | | | | |
| 5 | | Actual | Budget | Variance | Actual | Budget | Variance | Actual | Budget | Variance | Actual | Budget | Variance |
| 6 | Cola | 678 | 640 | 68 | 678 | 610 | 35 | 675 | 640 | 141 | 2031 | 1890 | 141 |
| 7 | Diet Cola | 120 | - | | 120 | 120 | - | | - | | 240 | 240 | - | | 240 |
| 8 | Caffeine Free Cola | - | | | | | | | | | | | |
| 9 | Colas | 678 | 640 | 35 | 645 | 610 | 35 | 675 | 640 | 108 | 1998 | 1890 | 108 |
| 10 | Old Fashioned | 61 | 50 | 11 | 61 | 50 | 3 | 63 | 60 | 25 | 185 | 160 | 25 |
| 11 | Diet Root Beer | - | | | | - | | | - | | | - | | |
| 12 | Sasparilla | - | | | - | | | - | | | | - | | |
| 13 | Birch Beer | 490 | 480 | -70 | 490 | 560 | 13 | 523 | 510 | -47 | 1503 | 1550 | -47 |
| 14 | Root Beer | 551 | 530 | 31 | 641 | 610 | 16 | 586 | 570 | 68 | 1778 | 1710 | 68 |

**Tip!** You may want to also set dynamically calculated cells to grey so that you know you can't load data to that member.

**Tip!** Retain Numeric Formatting works with cell styles!

**Note!** Make sure you uncheck Use Excel Formatting on the Display tab. If this option is selected, Cell Styles are ignored.

12. Once you're finished playing with Styles (and before burning matching holes in your retinas due to horrendous color schemes), go to the *Styles* section on your Options and uncheck all the boxes on the Analytic Services *Style* section.

**Note!** Turning off Styles does not set your spreadsheet back to its pre-Essbase formatting. You may have to click *Refresh* or set Excel formatting to return to the desired state.

Smart View provides common styles that are used across connections. By default, "dirty" cells are cells where data has been changed by the user but not submitted to the cube. The background for any dirty cells will change to a light yellow:

Formatting and reporting options are practically endless with Smart View and our handy Office products!

---

**COMMUNICATION: ALAPAT TO ROSKE**

[2:39] ALAPAT: I was trying to write back in Klingon, but the auto-translator keeps switching back to English. I've been implementing OAC enough lately that I'm starting to think of the 'O' as the "One Ring to Rule Them All."

---

## SMART VIEW TIPS AND TRICKS

Now that I've mastered the majority of the Smart View Add-In menu items, let's take my skills to the next level of mastery in a short but important section.

### Speedy Refreshes

It is not enough for me to simply understand how to refresh and report data. I must understand *why* data refreshes the way it does. Why do some refreshes take longer than others?

Essbase refreshes are normally measured in seconds or sub-seconds. If my refreshes ever take more than thirty seconds, there are some things I can check:

- Retrieval size (number of members in your rows and columns)
- Use of attribute dimensions
- Use of dynamically calculated members
- Dense vs. sparse retrievals for BSO cubes

Let's begin by assuming that my desktop and network aren't older than dirt. If my hardware is more than a few years old, I should replace it, because doing so will definitely make things faster. Computers are easier to upgrade than people.

If my hardware is fairly recent, I'll begin by looking at how much data I'm retrieving. While 500 rows by 20 columns doesn't seem like much, that's over 10,000 cells of data I'm asking Essbase to return. While I can't exactly eliminate every other row on my report to save space ("Sorry about the missing numbers, boss, but Edward Roske told me that deleting even numbered rows on my reports would cut my retrieval time in half!"), I'll at least be aware of why my report is taking a long time.

The next thing to review is my use of members from attribute dimensions, dynamically calculated members, and dynamic time series members. As mentioned earlier, none of these members are pre-calculated. A refresh that is accessing stored members will almost always run more quickly than one that accesses dynamic members.

One of the most common mistakes people make is putting the top member from an attribute dimension on their report. Notice the Caffeinated member on this refresh:

| | A | B | C | D | E | F |
|---|---|---|---|---|---|---|
| 1 | | | Market | Product | Actual | Caffeinated |
| 2 | | Qtr1 | Qtr2 | Qtr3 | Qtr4 | Year |
| 3 | Sales | 95,820 | 101,679 | 105,215 | 98,141 | 400,855 |
| 4 | COGS | 42,877 | 45,362 | 47,343 | 43,754 | 179,336 |
| 5 | Margin | 52,943 | 56,317 | 57,872 | 54,387 | 221,519 |
| 6 | | | | | | |
| 7 | Marketing | 15,839 | 16,716 | 17,522 | 16,160 | 66,237 |
| 8 | Payroll | 12,168 | 12,243 | 12,168 | 12,168 | 48,747 |
| 9 | Misc | 233 | 251 | 270 | 259 | 1,013 |
| 10 | Total Expenses | 28,240 | 29,210 | 29,960 | 28,587 | 115,997 |
| 11 | | | | | | |
| 12 | Profit | 24,703 | 27,107 | 27,912 | 25,800 | 105,522 |

The presence of this member usually doesn't change the totals at all (I still have 105,522 in the bottom-right corner) but it takes a refresh that would be against stored information and makes it entirely dynamic. Why? Because I am telling Essbase to go grab all the products that are Caffeinated_True and add them together, and then grab all the products that are Caffeinated_False and add them together, and finally, add Caffeinated_False to Caffeinated_True to get total Caffeinated. Well, this is the same value as if I'd never asked for Caffeinated at all!

The solution is obvious: delete the Caffeinated member and my refresh will speed up by more than an order of magnitude. The more cynical among you might ask why Essbase isn't smart enough to notice that it's dynamically adding up every product when it could just take the stored Product total and be done with it. I don't have a good answer for that, so I'll pretend that I can't hear your question.

Density vs. sparsity for Essbase block storage cubes is a tricky subject because it really gets into how Essbase stores data behind the scenes and that's normally only of interest to an Essbase Administrator, a developer, or a highly paid (but deservedly so) consultant. Even though this is covered in Chapter 5, "Essbase Concepts Defined," I'm going review the subject just enough to understand how it affects retrieval times.

My base dimensions (i.e., not the attribute dimensions) fall into one of two types: dense and sparse. Dense dimensions are dimensions for which most combinations are loaded with data. Sparse dimensions are often missing values.

In Sample.Basic, the dense dimensions are Year, Measures, and Scenario. This is because when there's a value for one month (say, Sales) there tends to be a value for every month. If there's a value for Sales, there tends to be a value for COGS, Marketing, and so on. If there's a number for Actual, there tends to be a value for Budget. As such, Year, Measures, and Scenario are said to be dense dimensions.

The sparse dimensions for Sample.Basic are Product and Market. This is because not every product tends to be sold in every state. As I saw earlier, out of seven possible caffeinated drinks, Massachusetts only sold three of them. As such, Product and Market are said to be sparse dimensions.

Why does this matter to me? Well, a refresh consisting of dense dimensions (and only dense dimensions) in the rows and columns will tend to be much, much faster than a report with a sparse dimension in the rows or the columns.

When a report only has dense dimensions in the rows and columns, this is referred to as a dense retrieval. Here is an example of a dense retrieval against Sample.Basic:

| | A | B | C | D | E |
|---|---|---|---|---|---|
| 1 | | Product | Market | Scenario | |
| 2 | | Jan | Feb | Mar | Apr |
| 3 | Sales | 31,538.00 | 32,069.00 | 32,213.00 | 32,917.00 |
| 4 | COGS | 14,160.00 | 14,307.00 | 14,410.00 | 14,675.00 |
| 5 | Margin | 17,378.00 | 17,762.00 | 17,803.00 | 18,242.00 |
| 6 | Marketing | 5,223.00 | 5,289.00 | 5,327.00 | 5,421.00 |
| 7 | Payroll | 4,056.00 | 4,056.00 | 4,056.00 | 4,081.00 |
| 8 | Misc | 75.00 | 71.00 | 87.00 | 96.00 |
| 9 | Total Expenses | 9,354.00 | 9,416.00 | 9,470.00 | 9,598.00 |
| 10 | Profit | 8,024.00 | 8,346.00 | 8,333.00 | 8,644.00 |

It's a dense retrieval because Measures is in the rows, Year is in the columns, and both are dense dimensions. Notice that all the intersections tend to have values loaded to them. This is an example of a sparse retrieval against Sample.Basic:

| | A | B | C | D | E | F |
|---|---|---|---|---|---|---|
| 1 | | Jan | Sales | Actual | | |
| 2 | | New York | Massachusetts | Connecticut | Florida | New Hampshire |
| 3 | Cola | 678 | | 494 | 310 | 210 | 120 |
| 4 | Diet Cola | 120 | - | - | | 400 | - |
| 5 | Caffeine Free Cola | - | - | - | - | | 93 |
| 6 | Old Fashioned | 61 | | 126 | 180 | 190 | 90 |
| 7 | Diet Root Beer | - | - | | 260 | 360 | - |
| 8 | Sasparilla | - | - | - | - | - | - |
| 9 | Birch Beer | 490 | | 341 | - | - | 65 |
| 10 | Dark Cream | 483 | | 130 | 190 | 120 | 76 |
| 11 | Vanilla Cream | 180 | - | | 170 | 150 | - |
| 12 | Diet Cream | - | - | - | | 220 | - |
| 13 | Grape | 234 | | 80 | 123 | 80 | 45 |
| 14 | Orange | 219 | - | | - | - | - |
| 15 | Strawberry | 134 | | 80 | 94 | 81 | 43 |

This is a sparse retrieval because Product is in the rows, Market is in the columns, and both are sparse dimensions. Notice that a number of the values are missing. Though it doesn't have many more cells to refresh, this retrieval will take many times longer than the one above because of how Essbase refreshes data from sparse dimensions. Simply put, for sparse retrievals, Essbase refreshes a lot of data into memory on the server side that you'll never see or use.

While I might not have access to change dense and sparse settings, I can be aware that sparse retrievals will take much longer than dense retrievals.

### Excel Formula Retention

I skipped one member option in an earlier section of the chapter. Let's revisit this helpful feature now – formula retention when zooming. I can build Excel formulas into my analyses and retain those formulas while zooming in and out (with a few constraints).

1. Set up the following worksheet:

| | A | B | C | D |
|---|---|---|---|---|
| 1 | | Sales | East | Actual |
| 2 | | Qtr1 | Qtr2 | |
| 3 | Product | | 20621 | 22449 |

I want to add a subtotal for Qtr1 and Qtr2 to see how I have fared for the first half of the year. This subtotal does not exist in Essbase so I need to add it in Excel.

2. In *D3* add an Excel formula to perform this subtotal:

| | A | B | C | D |
|---|---|---|---|---|
| 1 | | Sales | East | Actual |
| 2 | | Qtr1 | Qtr2 | |
| 3 | Product | | 20621 | 22449 =SUM(B3:C3) |

3. Click *Refresh*.

The formula is retained.

4.  Now before you start zooming, select *Options* from the Smart View ribbon. Under *Member Options*, check the box to *Preserve Formulas and Comments in ad hoc operations* and also *Formula Fill*:

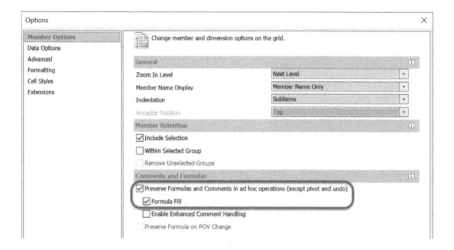

5.  Click *OK*.
6.  Zoom on *Product* and notice the formula fills as you zoom:

|  | A | B | C | D |
|---|---|---|---|---|
| 1 |  | Sales | East | Actual |
| 2 |  | Qtr1 | Qtr2 |  |
| 3 | Colas | $  6,292 | $  7,230 | $  13,522 |
| 4 | Root Beer | $  5,726 | $  5,902 | $  11,628 |
| 5 | Cream Soda | $  4,868 | $  5,327 | $  10,195 |
| 6 | Fruit Soda | $  3,735 | $  3,990 | $  7,725 |
| 7 | Diet Drinks | $  1,884 | $  2,096 | $  3,980 |
| 8 | Product | $  20,621 | $  22,449 | $  43,070 |

This works great up until I decide to pivot.

7.  Select *East* and click *Pivot* from the Essbase ribbon. You should be prompted with the following window:

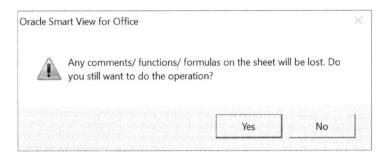

8.  Click *Yes* and note the formula is removed.

### #NumericZero vs. Zero

I want to highlight one additional selection under Data Options that is important if I am writing data back to Essbase. Under *Options >> Data Options*, I can set the Replacement options:

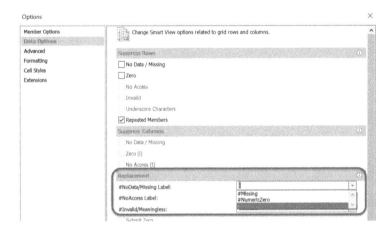

When I refresh data from Essbase, I choose how I want missing data to be displayed. It can be any text value I choose (e.g., "-") or the default value #Missing, but this may cause issues for the Excel formulas. To address this issue, some users may even choose "0." This works fine for reporting but if I need to submit data back to Essbase and I've used "0" as the replacement option, I will be writing a lot of zeroes back to the Essbase cube, increasing the cube size unnecessarily. A better alternative is to choose the #NumericZero which will display a "0" so Excel formulas work but "zero data" will not be submitted back to the cube. The only way to submit zeros back to Essbase is to explicitly check *Submit Zero* (though in most cases, leave this unchecked):

## Member Information

At any point in time I can find out more information about a member. What is the member name or alias? Is this member dynamically calculated or stored? What is the consolidation tag?

1. To find out all there is to know about a member (and then some), select the member in the spreadsheet.
2. Click *Member Information* from the Essbase ribbon:

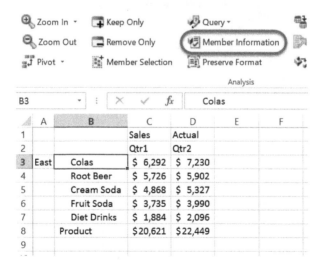

The Member Information window will display:

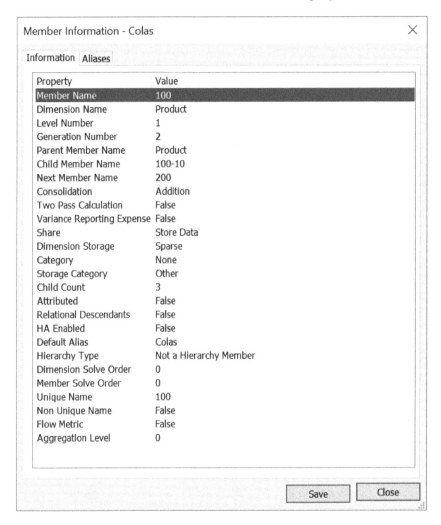

3. Click *Save* if you would like to save this information into a separate Excel spreadsheet:

| | A | B |
|---|---|---|
| 1 | Information | |
| 2 | | |
| 3 | Property | Value |
| 4 | Member Name | 100 |
| 5 | Dimension Name | Product |
| 6 | Level Number | 1 |
| 7 | Generation Number | 2 |
| 8 | Parent Member Name | Product |
| 9 | Child Member Name | 100-10 |
| 10 | Next Member Name | 200 |
| 11 | Consolidation | Addition |
| 12 | Two Pass Calculation | False |
| 13 | Variance Reporting Expense | False |
| 14 | Share | Store Data |
| 15 | Dimension Storage | Sparse |
| 16 | Category | None |
| 17 | Storage Category | Other |
| 18 | Child Count | 3 |
| 19 | Attributed | False |
| 20 | Relational Descendants | False |

## MDX Queries

For the more technically inclined users who want to the option to write an MDX query directly to Essbase, Smart View provides this capability!

1. From the Essbase ribbon, simply click *Query >> Execute MDX*:

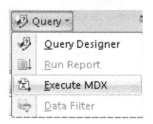

2.  Enter in some valid MDX syntax and click *Execute*:

Execute Free Form MDX Query                                                    ✕

Enter a valid MDX statement. Successful execution of MDX statement will overwrite currently selected worksheet.

|                                                                              |

|   Help                                              Execute        Cancel    |

For more detailed information on MDX, check out *Look Smarter Than You are with Essbase 11.1.2: An Administrator's Guide.*

### Change the Connection for Multi-Grid Report

To change a connection for a multi-grid report, I'll select the range of cells for which I want to change the connection. Using the Excel Name Manager, I'll delete the associated name range:

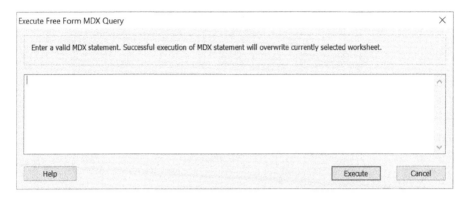

| | | | C | D |
|---|---|---|---|---|
| | 94E2_BAD1B66A85D7_1 | | ⋮ ✕ ✓ | |
| | EssbaseCluster_Sample_B. | | | |
| | EssbaseCluster_Sample_B. | | ket | Scenario |
| 2 | | Measures | | |
| 3 | Qtr1 | 24703 | | |
| 4 | Qtr2 | 27107 | | |
| 5 | Qtr3 | 27912 | | |
| 6 | Qtr4 | 25800 | | |
| 7 | Year | 10552 | | |
| 8 | | | | |
| 9 | | Product | Market | Scenario |
| 10 | | Measures | | |
| 11 | Qtr1 | 24703 | | |
| 12 | Qtr2 | 27107 | | |
| 13 | Qtr3 | 27912 | | |
| 14 | Qtr4 | 25800 | | |
| 15 | Year | 10552 | | |

In the Smart View panel, I'll right-click on the desired source and select *Ad hoc Analysis.*

### Options - Advanced

Let's review the remaining Options in Smart View. The Advanced section under Smart View Options contains a number of administrative settings for Smart View. The Advanced Options are global operations that apply to the entire workbook and any worksheets and workbooks going forward.

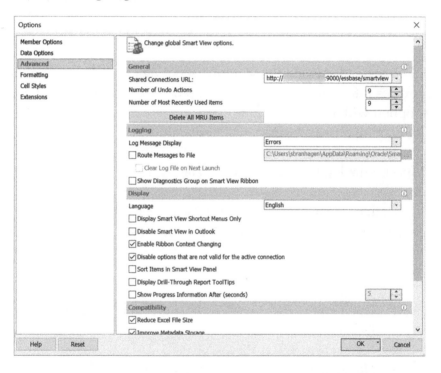

I've likely already set the first setting, the Shared Connections URL. I set the *Number of Undo* (and Redo) actions permitted from 0 to 100. I set the number of *Most Recently Used Items* from 0-15. This number of my most recently used connections will display in the Smart View home panel. If I'd like to clear my Most Recently Used connections list, I'll click *Delete All MRU Items.*

I can define the level of logging for Smart View actions to display and record. Log levels include Information, Warnings, Errors, and None. Information level will track all messages including errors and warnings.

Because a large amount of information is tracked, performance could be negatively impacted and this setting is usually set for troubleshooting. "Warnings" will track warnings and error messages. "Errors" will track error messages only and this is the setting that is typically recommended for Smart View logging.

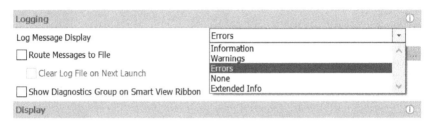

Extended Info exists for troubleshooting and debugging efforts. It provides information level messages plus all of the server responses. This option will negatively impact performance and should only be set for debugging purposes for a small period of time.

To route log messages to a file, check the *Route Messages to File* and specify the log file location. *Clear Log File on Next Launch* will clear the log file when Excel is closed.

Under the Display section of *Advanced* options, I can choose the language that is used throughout Smart View (sort of like when Buzz Lightyear is switched to Spanish mode with the simple flip of a switch in *Toy Story 3*).

1. Open a new Excel workbook and connect to *Sample.Basic* in Essbase Cloud.
2. Navigate to Smart View *Options*.
3. Navigate to *Advanced >> Display*.

4. Select *Spanish* as the language:

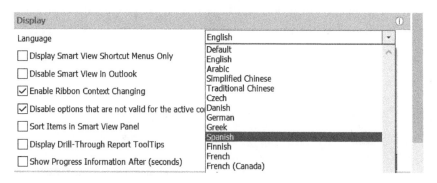

5. When prompted, click *OK*. In order for the language setting to take place, you must restart Excel:

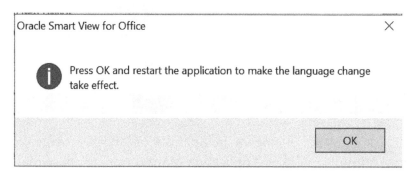

6. Close and reopen Excel. Be amazed at your new Spanish speaking Smart View ribbon:

7.  Open a recently used query from Sample.Basic. Note that the
    Essbase members and data still displays according to the
    Essbase outline:

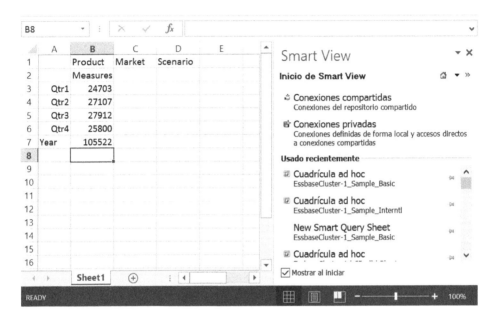

To view the members in Spanish or another language, the
Essbase Administrator (or Application Manager or Database Manager)
should build an alternate alias to house the additional descriptions. Then
I'd simply select the *Change Alias* option to choose that Alias table.

8. Click on *Opciones* (Options). Select *Advanzado* (Advanced) and change the language back to *Ingles* (English):

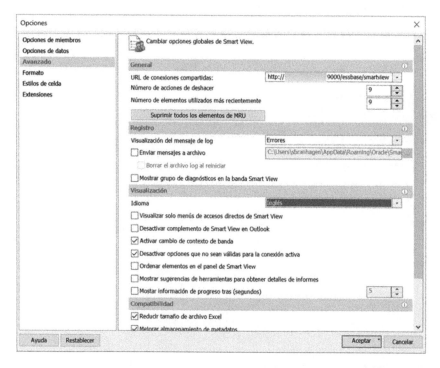

9. Click *Aceptar*. Close and reopen Excel and you are back to plain ol' English.

The default setting in Smart View is to see both Excel and Smart View options in my right-click short cut menus (which results in a pretty long menu selection):

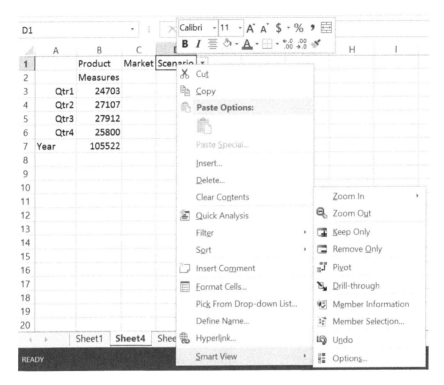

10. To just view Smart View short cut menus, check *Display Smart View Short Cut Menus Only*:

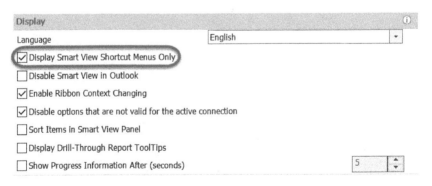

**Note!**

Did you know that Smart View right-click menus are context sensitive?

11. Right-click on a Member and view the available actions:

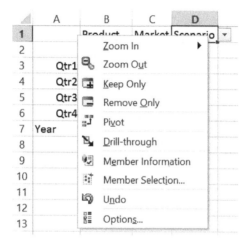

12. Right-click on a data point and view the available actions:

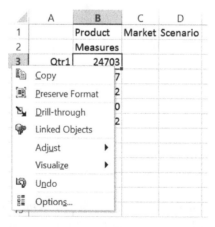

If *Enable Ribbon Context Changing* is checked, the active data provider ribbon (e.g., Essbase) will display for the new connection. If this setting is unchecked, the Essbase ribbon opens but the view remains on the Smart View ribbon.

*Disable options that are not valid for the active connection* is there to keep users sane. I keep this option checked so that I am not banging my head against the wall trying to figure out why a button isn't working the way I want. Some features in Smart View are data source-specific.

As of Smart View version 11.1.2.5.620, I can sort items in the Smart View panel using the *Sort Items in Smart View Panel* option. This will sort items in the panel numerically, then alphabetically first by category, then by items within the category.

I'll check the *Show Progress Information After (seconds)* option if I want to specify the amount of time the Smart View Progress status bar appears after an operation begins. Once checked, I'll specify the amount of seconds in the drop-down to the right of the down.

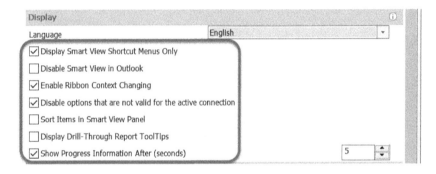

The last round of settings under the Compatibility section, *Reduce Excel File Size* and *Improve Metadata Storage*, should always be checked:

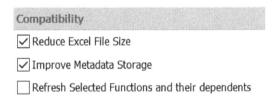

*Refresh Selected Functions and their dependents* is a setting I will consider if I have worksheets using functions like HsGetValue.

The last setting under the Mode section will turn off double-clicking for Zoom actions if unchecked:

### Options - Extensions

The Extensions section under Options lists the extensions that are installed to use Smart View for other Oracle products. The settings here also support power packs and extensions designed to do special tasks like Grid Formatter, Member Search, Substitution Variable manager, MDXScript Library, and more.

In this section, I choose how to handle the extensions. Do I want to enable or disable a particular extension? Do I want to check for an update? Do I want to enable logging for extension installation?

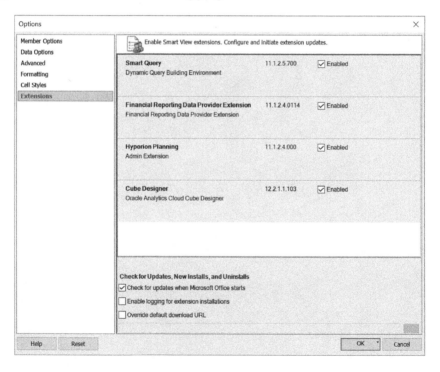

Extension options are global (they will apply to all worksheets).

**LOG ENTRY FOR EDUCATOR MISSION SPECIALIST OPAL ALAPAT**
*SOL 23, Entry 2*

Mission Smart View complete.

# CHAPTER 10: EXPLORE DATA IN DATA VISUALIZATION

---

**LOG ENTRY FOR VISUALIZATION PILOT WAYNE VAN SLUYS**
*SOL 24, Entry 1*

I have the final mission. Everyone else has breezed through their missions. Will data visualization be the same?

Just for reference, because it is a fairly new concept, data visualization is the visualization of data in graphical formats. I know…it's complicated. For thousands and thousands of years, analysts and users stared at rows and columns of numbers. It is almost incomprehensible that a better and faster way might be to highlight data trends and patterns in a visual perspective.

No doubt I have the hardest mission. Edward's rescue rests on my shoulders. I hope OAC can carry us through.

---

**COMMUNICATION: ROSKE TO VAN SLUYS**

[8:01] ROSKE: Wayne, no pressure or anything, but you are the final link, the last step, the ultimate challenge in this journey to save me. Don't mess it up, will ya?

---

## DATA VISUALIZATION DEFINED

Data visualization is a "hot topic," the next step in today's ongoing evolution of BI. Data visualizations help people understand data using visual representations. There are three key requirements for a good data visualization tool:

1) Anyone can use it
2) It can use any data (data in spreadsheets, apps, or cubes)
3) It has a rich, easy-to-use visual experience

Oracle introduced a new feature called Data Visualization (DV) to meet those requirements, and this feature is present in multiple products. Data Visualization Cloud (DVCS) is a single Cloud offering that focuses entirely on the Data Visualization feature. When OAC was released, they included DVCS in both Standard and Enterprise editions.

DV is also available in other Oracle BI options like Business Intelligence Cloud (BICS) and Data Visualization Desktop (DVD). DVD is another toolset that comes bundled with both OAC Standard and Enterprise editions, and it offers an on-premises client tool that has additional, more advanced features beyond DVCS.

DV allows users to upload and blend data files and then visualize the data in a multitude of graphical presentations. Users can then share insights and "tell a story" using Story Teller mode.

Just think... Exploring data in a visual context. No more death by PowerPoint! Keep discussions interactive and present! DV is fully mobile supported and requires approximately 50% fewer clicks to create visual presentations (when compared to competitor tools and OAC Analyses and Dashboards that are included in the OAC Enterprise Edition).

### Data Visualizations vs. Reporting vs. Ad Hoc

Data Visualization supports ad hoc analysis and visual exploration of data sources. For DV, think user driven data blending, simple aggregations, click-the-button type queries, and easy to create charting for data sources. Have you ever created a massive Excel spreadsheet model or Microsoft Access database to combine and consolidate data for analysis? OAC can replace all of those error-prone nightmares with a best practice solution. If all I need are simple mappings and aggregations, I can import Excel files directly into DV and then perform explorations and visualizations with DV. Or if I have more complex calculation requirements and want to be able analyze in both Excel and over the web, I can import data into an OAC cube and use DV or Smart View for ad hoc and visualization exploration activities.

I would not use DV as my enterprise reporting solution, where nicely formatted printable reports are needed (I would use tools like

Enterprise Performance Management Reporting Cloud Service). I would also not use DV for enterprise dashboards with controls and radio buttons to provide guided analysis for end users (I would use OAC Enterprise Edition dashboarding features).

### Comparing Oracle's BI Solutions

It can be confusing trying to understand all of Oracle's BI options, so here is my best effort to translate the available options:

- **Oracle Analytics Cloud (OAC)**
  - Go forward business analytics solution that offers multiple configuration and pricing options
  - OAC Standard Edition includes Essbase Cloud, DV Cloud, and DVD
  - OAC Enterprise Edition includes Essbase Cloud, DV Cloud, DVD, and BI Cloud
  - This is the "all-in-one" best practice business analytics offering
- **Business Intelligence Cloud (or BI Cloud)**
  - First BI Cloud solution released
  - On-premises solution with no advanced data modeling or Essbase connection support
  - OBIEE "lite" in the Cloud
  - Comes with Oracle Database Cloud Service instance to support data
  - Includes Analyses (more structured queries that can be saved) and Dashboards (enterprise dashboarding capabilities) features in addition to DV capabilities
- **Data Visualization Cloud Service (DVCS or DV Cloud)**
  - Provides user access to powerful data visualization capabilities for uploaded files
  - Line of business solution (think of business users uploading Excel Files)
- **Oracle Business Intelligence Enterprise Edition (OBIEE)**
  - Full end-to-end BI solution on-premises solution with support for Essbase, Planning, and HFM sources

## DV USER INTERFACES

To access the web interface, enter the Data Visualization OAC URL provided in my Oracle emails. Upon logging in, I'll be greeted by an introduction screen, highlighting OAC DV key features.

The home page has four main sections: Home, Data Sources, Console (for Service Administrators), and Academy:

- **Home** - navigate and search for existing content, along with options to create new content
- **Data Sources** - navigate and search for existing data sources, along with options to create new data sources, connections, and data flows; for Enterprise Edition, create and manage models
- **Console** - manage DV settings
- **Academy** - learn more through Oracle's documentation and video libraries

### DV Home

This is the new and improved DV Cloud Home web interface:

I can also access the "Classic Home" DV web interface. To do this, select *Open Classic Home* from the Home left panel:

This interface shows the same content in a slightly different display (more like Windows Explorer).

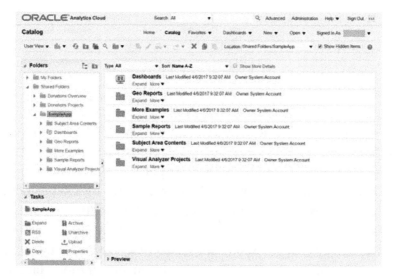

For most of this mission, I will use the "non-classic" DV interface.

I'll cover the remaining cards, Data Sources, Console, and Academy in more detail in the remainder of this chapter.

## DV DATA SOURCES

In the *Data Sources* card, I can immediately see a list of previously set up data sources, connections, and data flows for data exploration:

On the left pane, data sources are filtered by type. Data source types that I might see include Subject Areas (these are models created with OAC Enterprise Edition), Oracle Applications, Databases, and Files (uploaded data files from users). I can also filter by Connections and Data Flows. Connections is a list of connections to various data sources that have been created (e.g., Essbase, Oracle Database). From Connections, I can create a data source for use in a project. Data Flows are a way to create a new data file/data set from one or more data sources (with the exception of Essbase). A Data Flow can be opened to edit or run to refresh the data file that has been created by the flow. More on all of this in just a bit. Some data source types, like Subject Areas, are only available in OAC Enterprise Edition.

When I create data visualizations, I group them by "project." Some source types can be combined with other data sources into a single DV project. One exception is Essbase Cloud cubes; only one cube per DV Project can be chosen in the current version.

In the bottom of the left pane, there are options for creating new Data Sources, Connections, and Data Flows. I can either add them from here or I can add them from within a project.

**Note!** If you are reading and following along, you should be able to use the Data Visualization Desktop, the desktop alternative to the DV web interface.

## DATA PREP

DV is designed for the business user, so what type of file do you think it will accept? Ding, ding, ding! If you answered Excel, you are right! At the time that this book was authored, DV Cloud only accepts file types with an .xlsx extension. Other sources will be added in upcoming releases.

I can upload one or more files with my "numbers" or measures. Like in the relational world, numerical data is considered to be the "facts":

| | A | B | C | D | E | F | G | H | I | J | K | L |
|---|---|---|---|---|---|---|---|---|---|---|---|---|
| | | | | | | Sub | Customer Age | Customer | Customer | Sales | | Number |
| 1 | Year | Quarter | Month | Date | Category | Category | Group | Gender | Country | Territory | Revenue | Of Orders |
| 2 | 2015 | 2015-4 | 2015-11 | 11/1/2015 | Books & At All | | Age 24 or less | M | USA | CA | 9283.646 | 93 |
| 3 | 2015 | 2015-4 | 2015-11 | 11/1/2015 | Books & At All | | Age 24 or less | F | USA | CA | 94275.87 | 943 |
| 4 | 2015 | 2015-4 | 2015-11 | 11/1/2015 | Books & At All | | Age 25-31 | M | USA | CA | 37189.4 | 372 |
| 5 | 2015 | 2015-4 | 2015-11 | 11/1/2015 | Books & At All | | Age 25-31 | F | USA | CA | 232737.5 | 2328 |
| 6 | 2015 | 2015-4 | 2015-11 | 11/1/2015 | Books & At All | | Age 32-39 | M | USA | CA | 246407.8 | 2465 |
| 7 | 2015 | 2015-4 | 2015-11 | 11/1/2015 | Books & At All | | Age 32-39 | F | USA | CA | 17643.21 | 177 |
| 8 | 2015 | 2015-4 | 2015-11 | 11/1/2015 | Books & At All | | Age 40-49 | M | USA | CA | 63113.76 | 632 |
| 9 | 2015 | 2015-4 | 2015-11 | 11/1/2015 | Books & At All | | Age 40-49 | F | USA | CA | 94269.19 | 943 |
| 10 | 2015 | 2015-4 | 2015-11 | 11/1/2015 | Books & At All | | Age 50-59 | M | USA | CA | 109837.1 | 1099 |

**Note!** The term "fact" comes from relational database table design. Fact tables are the tables that would contain the numbers. An example fact table might have fields for

Product, Month, Entity, Number of Orders, and Revenue. Number of Orders and Revenue are the "facts" in this table.

The other columns are considered to be "attributes" of the facts:

| | A | B | C | D | E | F | G | H | I | J | K | L |
|---|---|---|---|---|---|---|---|---|---|---|---|---|
| | | | | | | Sub | Customer Age | Customer | Customer | Sales | | Number |
| 1 | Year | Quarter | Month | Date | Category | Category | Group | Gender | Country | Territory | Revenue | Of Orders |
| 2 | 2015 | 2015-4 | 2015-11 | 11/1/2015 | Books & A | All | Age 24 or less | M | USA | CA | 9283.646 | 93 |
| 3 | 2015 | 2015-4 | 2015-11 | 11/1/2015 | Books & A | All | Age 24 or less | F | USA | CA | 94275.87 | 943 |
| 4 | 2015 | 2015-4 | 2015-11 | 11/1/2015 | Books & A | All | Age 25-31 | M | USA | CA | 37189.4 | 372 |
| 5 | 2015 | 2015-4 | 2015-11 | 11/1/2015 | Books & A | All | Age 25-31 | F | USA | CA | 232737.5 | 2328 |
| 6 | 2015 | 2015-4 | 2015-11 | 11/1/2015 | Books & A | All | Age 32-39 | M | USA | CA | 246407.8 | 2465 |
| 7 | 2015 | 2015-4 | 2015-11 | 11/1/2015 | Books & A | All | Age 32-39 | F | USA | CA | 17643.21 | 177 |
| 8 | 2015 | 2015-4 | 2015-11 | 11/1/2015 | Books & A | All | Age 40-49 | M | USA | CA | 63113.76 | 632 |
| 9 | 2015 | 2015-4 | 2015-11 | 11/1/2015 | Books & A | All | Age 40-49 | F | USA | CA | 94269.19 | 943 |
| 10 | 2015 | 2015-4 | 2015-11 | 11/1/2015 | Books & A | All | Age 50-59 | M | USA | CA | 109837.1 | 1099 |

There isn't a concept of hierarchies in DV, only attributes. So the different generations or levels in typical hierarchies are simply attributes in DV. Parent-child formats in files are not supported in DV (yet). In the example below, Year, Quarter, Month, Date, Category, and Sub Category are all attributes of the data:

| | A | B | C | D | E | F | G |
|---|---|---|---|---|---|---|---|
| | | | | | | Sub | |
| 1 | Year | Quarter | Month | Date | Category | Category | Customer Age Group |
| 2 | 2015 | 2015-4 | 2015-11 | 11/1/2015 | Books & Audible | All | Age 24 or less |
| 3 | 2015 | 2015-4 | 2015-11 | 11/1/2015 | Books & Audible | A | Age 24 or less |
| 4 | 2015 | 2015-4 | 2015-11 | 1/1/2015 | Books & Audible | A | Age 25-31 |
| 5 | 2015 | 2015-4 | 2015-11 | 1/1/2015 | Books & Audible | All | Age 25-31 |
| 6 | 2015 | 2015-4 | 2015-11 | 11/ 015 | Books & Audible | All | ge 32-39 |
| 7 | 2015 | 2015-4 | 2015-11 | 11/1/2015 | Books & Audible | All | 32-39 |

As I upload multiple sources, I'll identify whether or not the source file extends the dimensions or extends the measures. More on this later when I get to the Blending Data section.

I will likely have to prepare the data before uploading into DV. Try to follow these rules when getting data ready for DV and external sources:

- File type must be .xlsx
- Files can have a maximum size of 50MB
- Avoid null values in attribute columns

- Delete aggregate rows (e.g., delete the Total Products column)
- Data must be "clean" data when uploaded
- Be mindful of any measures defined across the columns. What this refers to is if there are multiple data columns, instead of a single column of data.
  - o If measures go across the columns of a data file, be familiar with the names (e.g., account numbers or descriptions) because the column name can't be changed after the upload
- If I am uploading data files from multiple sources, it is best if the data across files match exactly
  - o For example, if I have one source that has a State column as "TX" and another source has the State column as "Texas", this data will not automatically match or join in DV
  - o I can wrangle the data in DV (more on this shortly) but the more in sync the data values are, the easier the experience is for users
- I can perform transformations "on-the-fly" (e.g., I can transform Jan to January after the file has been uploaded); however, keep in mind that DV is not an ETL solution

**Note!**

The way data is treated in DV is very different than how it's treated in Essbase Cloud. Although "unstructured" templates can be used in Essbase Cloud (which allow for more flexibility), data essentially has to be loaded to the Essbase cube in a structured format that conforms to the cube's dimensionality. DV solutions don't require prebuilt cubes and dimensions, and, therefore, allow for very flexible data sources. The concept behind DV is to take data from anywhere, merge it if multiple sources are used, and build quick analyses off of it. This is why transformations, "wrangling," "blending," and other cool data merging features are available, which I will cover later.

The first file that I will work with is the "KoolKart Sales.xlsx" file. I've used this file already earlier in this chapter, and it's also used in Chapter 4, "Unstructured Spreadsheet to Essbase Cube." It displays 6 months of KoolKart sales data with attributes like product category, customer age, and gender. This file will help me understand the demographics and buying patterns of KoolKart customers:

| | A | B | C | D | E | F | G | H | I |
|---|---|---|---|---|---|---|---|---|---|
| 1 | Year | Quarter | Month | Date | Category | Sub Category | Customer Age Group | Customer Gender | Customer Country |
| 2 | 2015 | 2015-4 | 2015-11 | 11/1/2015 | Books & Audible | All | Age 24 or less | M | USA |
| 3 | 2015 | 2015-4 | 2015-11 | 11/1/2015 | Books & Audible | All | Age 24 or less | F | USA |
| 4 | 2015 | 2015-4 | 2015-11 | 11/1/2015 | Books & Audible | All | Age 25-31 | M | USA |
| 5 | 2015 | 2015-4 | 2015-11 | 11/1/2015 | Books & Audible | All | Age 25-31 | F | USA |
| 6 | 2015 | 2015-4 | 2015-11 | 11/1/2015 | Books & Audible | All | Age 32-39 | M | USA |
| 7 | 2015 | 2015-4 | 2015-11 | 11/1/2015 | Books & Audible | All | Age 32-39 | F | USA |
| 8 | 2015 | 2015-4 | 2015-11 | 11/1/2015 | Books & Audible | All | Age 40-49 | M | USA |
| 9 | 2015 | 2015-4 | 2015-11 | 11/1/2015 | Books & Audible | All | Age 40-49 | F | USA |
| 10 | 2015 | 2015-4 | 2015-11 | 11/1/2015 | Books & Audible | All | Age 50-59 | M | USA |
| 11 | 2015 | 2015-4 | 2015-11 | 11/1/2015 | Books & Audible | All | Age 50-59 | F | USA |
| 12 | 2015 | 2015-4 | 2015-11 | 11/1/2015 | Books & Audible | All | Age 60 or above | M | USA |
| 13 | 2015 | 2015-4 | 2015-11 | 11/1/2015 | Books & Audible | All | Age 60 or above | F | USA |

The other file that I will work with is "DaaS Social Feeds-KoolKart.xlsx." This file is marketing-focused and contains 6 months of data. This data set originates from social media pages or posts that have "indicator words" associated with the business. For instance, it captures customers who may have tweeted something negative or positive about KoolKart. This file will help me understand the feelings of KoolKart customers on social media and when they were posted. It includes the total number of lines the indicator word was mentioned in and whether it was mentioned in a positive tone, neutral tone, or negative tone. It is broken down by date and product category:

| | A | B | C | D | E | F | G |
|---|---|---|---|---|---|---|---|
| 1 | Mentions Category | Date | Indicators | Total Number of Snippets | Percent Positive Tone | Percent Neutral Tone | Percent Negative Tone |
| 2 | Books , Audible | 11/1/2015 | Humor | 487 | 55.03 | 5.34 | 39.63 |
| 3 | Books , Audible | 11/1/2015 | Damaged | 376 | 55.05 | 5.32 | 39.63 |
| 4 | Books , Audible | 11/1/2015 | Recall | 529 | 54.82 | 5.29 | 39.89 |
| 5 | Books , Audible | 11/2/2015 | MEDIA: Viewing | 180 | 42.22 | 3.33 | 54.44 |
| 6 | Books , Audible | 11/2/2015 | Great Product | 243 | 41.98 | 3.29 | 54.73 |
| 7 | Books , Audible | 11/2/2015 | Sales & Coupons | 214 | 42.06 | 3.27 | 54.67 |

So I have two different files from two different sources. My genius plan is to combine the two together to see how social feeds can shed light on my sales data. Is that even possible? This is a perfect use case where DV technologies shine.

## CREATE A DATA FLOW

A Data Flow is similar to an Extract Transform and Load (ETL) process used in data warehouse systems, but way simpler. It's captured in a user interface that business users can create and follow. A Data Flow allows Power Users to combine data from a number of different sources and create a new data set for use in Data Visualization projects. Because I need to merge the two source files and take care of some transformations (did you see how different the product categories are listed?), I'll utilize a feature called Data Flows to accomplish this.

### Data Flows and Data Sets

The Data Flow that I will create will merge the KoolKart Sales data with the KoolKart Social Media data and produce one new data set (also referred to as a file). The final Data Flow will look like the example below:

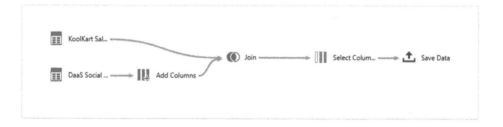

 **Note!** I must have a DV Content Author role to perform, create, and manage Data Flows and Projects.

1. In the DV web interface, select *Data Sources*:

2. In the left panel navigate to *Create >> Data Flow*:

The Data Flow work area opens and a window appears, prompting to add a data source.

3. Within the Add Data Source window, click the *Create New Data Source* button:

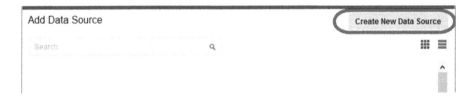

4. Click the *File* button:

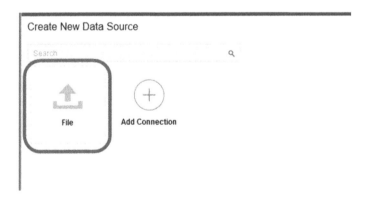

5. Navigate to the location of the two KoolKart files.

**Note!**     Email info@interrel.com for a copy of the OAC workshop files.

6.  First select "KoolKart Sales Data.xlsx" and click *Open*:

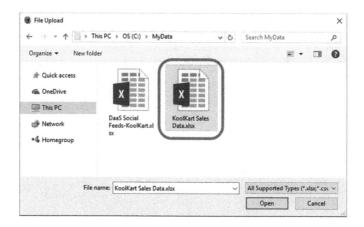

The data file to be uploaded is displayed:

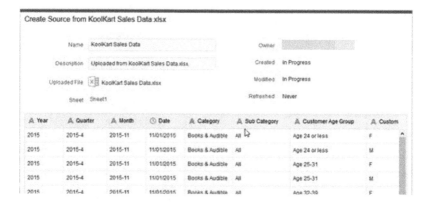

I now need to tag the attributes (which includes dimensions or attributes) and measures columns (the numbers). Data Flows read the file and do their best to guess at the attribute and measure columns, but it's best to review each column and confirm that it is correct (or change it if it isn't).

**Note!** As you hover over a column header, a gear icon appears. This indicates that an action can be done on the highlighted column.

7.  Scroll to the right to navigate to the *Revenue* column.
8.  Select the *Gear* icon for the *Revenue* column to confirm that it is tagged with:
    a.  Treat As: *Measure*
    b.  Aggregation: *Sum*

9.  Review the *Number of Orders* column properties:
    a.  Treat As: *Attribute*
    b.  Data Type: *Integer*

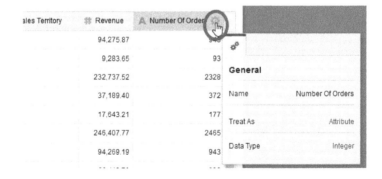

Notice with the *Number of Orders* column that DV hasn't seemed to have guessed very well. It set *Number of Orders* to an Attribute.

10. Fix that by tagging it as a *Measure* with aggregation set to *Sum*. When you tag the column as Measure, it should automatically set its aggregation to Sum:

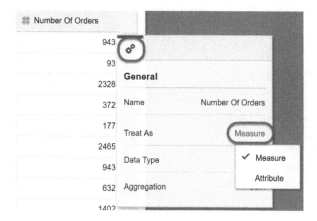

11. Once the column definitions have been updated, click the *OK* button in the lower left corner of the window:

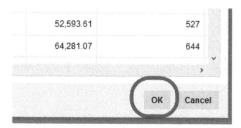

The Data Flow work area now shows an icon representing the KoolKart Sales Data.

The left panel shows the columns within the data, and the panel below the work area allows me to switch between *Step Details* (the current view) and *Preview*:

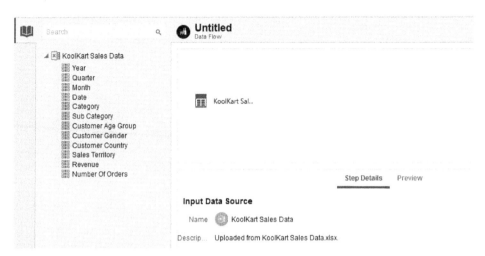

Preview mode will show the columns and rows of data for the selected step:

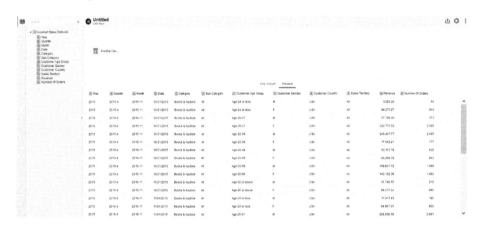

Now it's time to add the Social Media data file.

12. Right-click on the the icon for *KoolKart Sales* and select *Add Step*:

13. From the *Add Step* window select *Add Data*:

14. Using the same steps listed before, create a new data source for the file "DaaS Social Feeds-KoolKart.xlsx."

15. Review the columns within the Social Feeds data. Scroll to the right and change the *Total Number of Snippets* from *Attribute* to *Measure*, which should set *Aggregation Type* to *Sum*.

16. The last three columns contain the tone of the sentiment in the post. For these three columns, show their *Aggregation Type* as an *Average* rather than summing them up.

17. Change the Aggregation from *Sum* to *Average* for all three:

| Percent Positive Tone | Percent Neutral Tone | Percent Negative Tone |
|---|---|---|
| 55.05 | | 39.63 |
| 55.03 | | 39.63 |
| 54.82 | **General** | 39.89 |
| 41.98 | Name          Percent Positive Tone | 54.73 |
| 42.22 | | 54.44 |
| 42.06 | Treat As          Measure | 54.67 |
| 53.62 | Data Type          Double | 40.58 |
| 54.8 | Aggregation          Average | 40.32 |
| 55.56 | | 38.89 |

18. Click *OK* when all edits are done.

The Data Flow work area now shows a new icon representing the Social Media data. The Preview mode for each of the data sources shows the columns of the data source and a sample of the rows of data. I need to join these two sources together on date and product category. In looking at the two sources I see a problem. I might have to wrangle some data!

### Data Wrangling and Calculated Columns

Data wrangling is the process of manually mapping data from its original format to another that can be read easier. For my KoolKart data sets, I see an area where I will need to apply the DV wrangling functionality.

19. Click on *KoolKart Sales* and then *Preview*.

I see that the Sales data has a "&" symbol between the product categories:

|  | KoolKart Sal... |
|  | DaaS Social ... |

|  |  |  |  | Step Details | Preview |  |  |  |  |
|---|---|---|---|---|---|---|---|---|---|
| Year | Quarter | Month | Date | Category | Sub Category | Customer Age Group | Customer Gender | Customer Country | Sales Terr |
| 2015 | 2015-4 | 2015-11 | 11/01/2015 | Books & Audible | All | Age 24 or less | M | USA | All |
| 2015 | 2015-4 | 2015-11 | 11/01/2015 | Books & Audible | All | Age 24 or less | F | USA | All |
| 2015 | 2015-4 | 2015-11 | 11/01/2015 | Books & Audible | All | Age 25-31 | M | USA | All |
| 2015 | 2015-4 | 2015-11 | 11/01/2015 | | All | Age 25-31 | F | USA | All |

20. Click on *DaaS Social Feeds - KoolKart* and then *Preview*.

I see that the Social Media data has a comma between the product categories:

|  | DaaS Social |
|--|--|

|  |  |  | Step Details | Preview |  |  |  |
|---|---|---|---|---|---|---|---|
| Mentions Category | Date | Indicators | Total Number of Snippets | Percent Positive Tone | Percent Neutral Tone | Percent Negative Ton |
| Books , Audible | 11/01/2015 | Humor | 487 | 55.03 | 5.34 | 39.63 |
| Books , Audible | 11/01/2015 | Damaged | 376 | 55.05 | 5.32 | 39.63 |
| Books , Audible | 11/01/2015 | Recall | 529 | 54.82 | 5.29 | 39.89 |

One way to resolve this issue is to create a new column in the Social Media data to replace the comma with a "&" symbol. To do this, I will create a calculated column to address the product category naming difference.

To add a calculated column,
21. Select the Social Media data icon:

22. Right-click and select *Add Step.*

23. Select *Add Columns:*

The Step Details area shows a list of created columns, a formula editor in the center, and a list with available functions in the right portion of the screen:

24. Under the String functions, there is a REPLACE function. Expand *String* using the arrow icon ▸, then double-click on the the *Replace* function to add it to the formula editor:

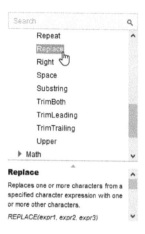

The formula editor now shows the REPLACE formula with the potential parameters that need to be filled in. There are three parameters within the parentheses. The first expression is the column I want to start with, the second expression is the string I want to replace, and the third is the string I want use instead:

25. Put the cursor over the first *expression* parameter. It should replace it with a blank:

26. From the Available Columns list on the left menu, select and drag the *Mentions Category* column over to the formula and place it over the cursor in the formula:

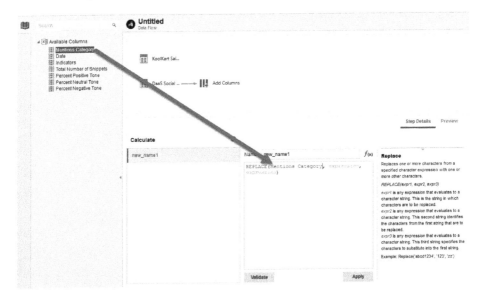

27. Set the final syntax of the REPLACE formula to read:

```
REPLACE(Mentions Category, ',' , '&')
```

28. Rename this column to *Category Mentions*.
29. Click the *Validate* button at the bottom of the formula editor:

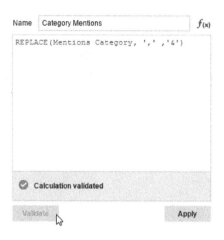

30. Click the *Apply* button.

Now that the attribute values match between the two data sets for product category, I need to join the data sets together.

31. Select the *KoolKart Sales Data* icon. Then, while pressing the Control Key (Ctrl), right-click *Add Columns* icon next to the Social Media icon (so that both files are selected), select *Join*:

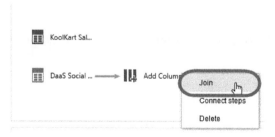

The Data Flow should now look like the image below:

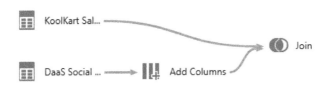

Within the Step Details panel, the Join definition is shown. DV was smart enough to join on the date column, but I also want to join on the category column:

32. In the *Match columns* area, click the + icon to add another join:

33. In the new row under *Input 1,* select *Category.*

34. Under *Input 2,* select the newly added column *Category Mentions:*

The data set is getting a bit confusing and I do not need all of these columns so I will remove the columns highlighted below:

35. Right-click and select *Add Step* to add another step to the Data Flow.

36. Choose *Select Columns* from the menu:

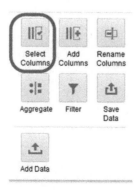

The Select Columns Step Details shows a list of *Available* columns on the left and *Selected* columns on the right:

37. On the right in the list of *Selected* columns, while holding Ctrl, select *Mentions Category*, *Date_1* and *Category Mentions*:

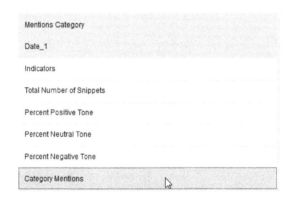

38. At the top of the *Selected* list, click the option *Remove selected*:

The Step Details for Selected Columns should look like the below:

| | Step Details | Preview | |
|---|---|---|---|

**Select Columns**

| Search | Add all | Selected(17/20) | Remove all |
|---|---|---|---|
| Mentions Category | | Year | |
| Date_1 | | Quarter | |
| Category Mentions | | Month | |

It looks like I have a good Data Set; let's complete the final step to save the data as a new data source.

### Save a Data Set

To save a Data Set,

39. Right-click and select *Add Step* to add another step to the Data Flow.
40. Select the *Save Data* icon:

41. Within the Step Details, provide a name for the new data source:

**Save a Data Flow**

In the future, I may get more data so I will want to save this data flow so that I can rerun it at a later time.

To save the Data Flow for future use,

42. In the upper right hand side of the web browser, select the

*Save*  and then *Save*:

43. Save it as "Kool Kart Flow" then click *OK*:

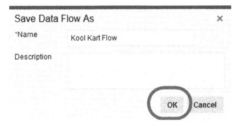

Now it's time to run the Data Flow and create the new Data Set.

44. Click the *Play* icon in the same toolbar:

A return message will appear in the header area, indicating the Data Flow has completed:

### Review Data Flow Output

Now let's go see our new data file that was created from the Data Flow.

45. Go back to the main home page.
46. Select the *Data Sources* icon.
47. In the left menu under *Display*, select *Files*.
48. If you have a lot of data files, use the *Search* dialog to limit the view and search for "Kool Kart":

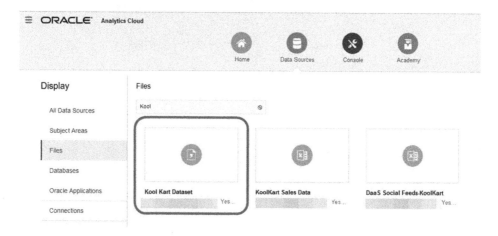

49. In the *Kool Kart Dataset* area, select the three small vertical blue dots ⋮ .

A context sensitive menu displays for the Kool Kart Data Set. I have the following available actions for data files imported into DV or created via data flows:

- **Create project** - create new DV projects based on this data file
- **Create analysis** - create new analyses (if licensing OAC Enterprise Edition) based on the data file
- **Edit** - edit the data file
- **Inspect** - inspect the data file (which means review the properties of the columns within the data file)
- **Reload data** - upload updated data (assumes the same file format definition)

- **Download CSV** - download the file in CSV format
- **Delete** - delete the data file

50. Select *Inspect*:

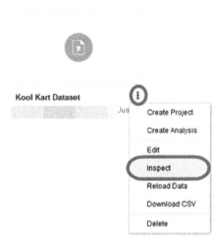

The data source properties screen will open, listing the columns and their properties:

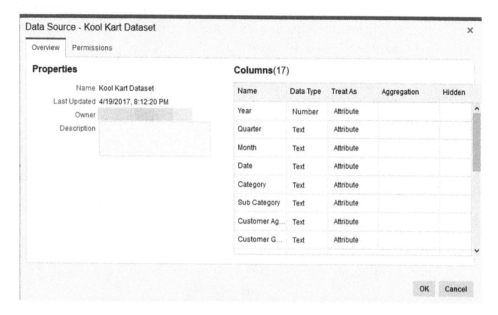

As I scroll down, I see that the columns I set to a *Measure* in the initial upload are now set to *Attribute*. This happens when DV attempts to make a first pass at what the file attributes should be. In this case, we'll need to override DV's assumptions:

Time to do a bit of clean up! I can update some of the data file properties directly from this dialog box.

51. Update the *Treat as* and *Aggregation* properties for the necessary columns (e.g., make sure to set all of the numerical columns to *Measure* and the Percent columns have an aggregation of *Average*):

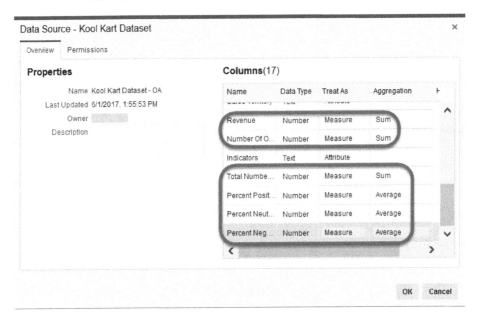

52. Click *OK*. You may get a confirmation message – if so, select *Yes* to confirm the update of the data set.

What if somehow the Date column's data type was not set to Date? If I need to change the Data Type for a column, I would *Edit* the file. I definitely want to make sure dates are assigned properly so that I can leverage date-specific features, such as Trend Line and Forecast. To change data types, I need to use the *Edit* action for the file.

To edit a file (one that is uploaded or one that is created from a data flow),

53. Select the data file and from the Menu, select *Edit*:

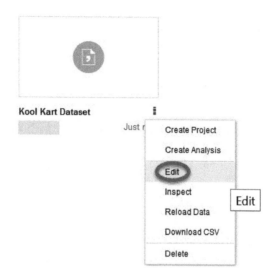

The Edit screen will open.

54. Hover over the *Date* column and select the *Action* icon.

55. If necessary, change the data type from *Text* to *Date*:

| Edit Kool Kart Dataset | | | | | | | |
|---|---|---|---|---|---|---|---|

| Name | Kool Kart Dataset | Owner | |
|---|---|---|---|
| Description | | Created | 1 days ago |
| | | Modified | Just now |
| | | Refreshed | 1 days ago |

| A Year | A Quarter | A Month | A Date ⚙ | A Category | A Sub Category | A Customer Ag |
|---|---|---|---|---|---|---|
| 2015 | 2015-4 | 2015-11 | 2015-11-01 | ⚙ | | Age 24 or less |
| 2015 | 2015-4 | 2015-11 | 2015-11-01 | | | Age 24 or less |
| 2015 | 2015-4 | 2015-11 | 2015-11-01 | **General** | | Age 24 or less |
| 2015 | 2015-4 | 2015-11 | 2015-11-01 | Name | Date | Age 24 or less |
| 2015 | 2015-4 | 2015-11 | 2015-11-01 | Treat As | Attribute | Age 24 or less |
| 2015 | 2015-4 | 2015-11 | 2015-11-01 | | | Age 24 or less |
| 2015 | 2015-4 | 2015-11 | 2015-11-01 | Data Type | Text | Age 25-31 |
| 2015 | 2015-4 | 2015-11 | 2015-11-01 | Books & Audible  All | Double | |
| 2015 | 2015-4 | 2015-11 | 2015-11-01 | Books & Audible  All | Integer | |
| 2015 | 2015-4 | 2015-11 | 2015-11-01 | Books & Audible  All | DateTime | |
| 2015 | 2015-4 | 2015-11 | 2015-11-01 | Books & Audible  All | Date | |
| 2015 | 2015-4 | 2015-11 | 2015-11-01 | Books & Audible  All | Time | |
| 2015 | 2015-4 | 2015-11 | 2015-11-01 | Books & Audible  All | Text | |

56. Click *OK* to save the changes.

Now I'm ready to start working with data visualizations and explore my new data file.

---

**COMMUNICATION: VAN SLUYS TO ROSKE**

[8:01] VAN SLUYS: I haven't messed it up so far (or they haven't figured it out yet). Don't worry. I got this, my facial haired friend.

# CREATE A DV PROJECT

To create data visualizations I need to create a Data Visualization Project (DV project). A DV project is a collection of related visualizations based on one or more blended data sources.

1. In the Data Sources screen, select the "Kool Kart Dataset" and from the menu select *Create Project*:

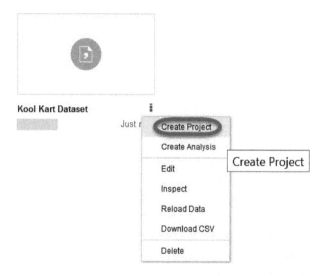

An alternate way to create a DV Project is from the home page in the left menu under *Create >> Project*. I can then select the "Kool Kart Dataset" in the *Add Data Source* screen.

The DV Project window displays:

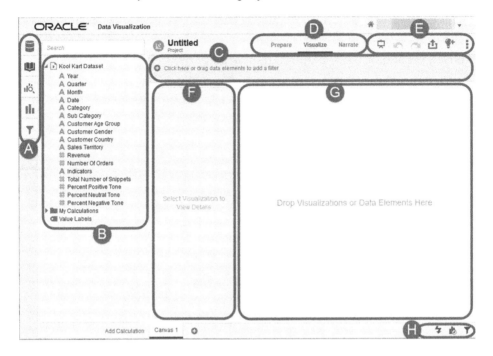

A. **Left navigation bar** - links to Data Sources, Data Elements, Analytics, Visualizations, and Filter Controls (more on this navigation bar in just a bit)

B. **Context sensitive content pane** - if Data Sources is selected, the Data Sources are listed with the option to add others; if Data Elements is selected, all data elements will display; if Visualizations is selected, a list of available visualizations will appear; if Analytics is selected, the various advanced analytics will appear

C. **Filter section for the canvas** - data elements can be dragged to this area to filter the visualizations in the project

D. The various parts of the Project

o **Prepare** allows for the data source to be examined, edited, and various calculated fields added

o **Visualize** is the primary work area for Data Visualization

o **Narrate** is where insights can be added

E. **Main Data Visualization menu bar** - contains Presentation Mode, Undo Last Edit, Redo Last Edit, Share Project, Add Insight, properties, and more

F. **Explore panel** - context sensitive to the visualization being worked with; provides drop zones for attributes and measures related to the visualization type

G. **Main canvas area** - for building visualizations; can contain one or more visualizations

H. **Canvas controls** - contains auto Apply Data (refresh mode), show/hide Explore Panel, show/hide Filters

The tabs listed along the left side of the DV interface allow me to toggle between different tasks as I go through the exploration process:

- **Data Sources** - lists data sources for the Project; from this tab, I can *Inspect, Reload Data, Download* the source as CSV, *Remove* the source from the Project (but not delete), *Delete* a data source, *Add a Data Source*, or view a *Source Diagram* where I can review and define matches or joins for multiple data sources:

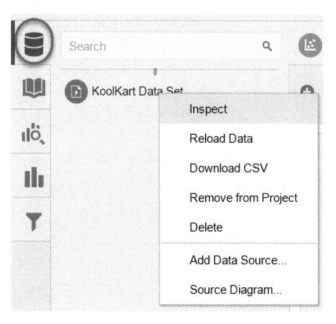

- **Data Elements** - lists the data elements from all data sources; I can select one or more data elements or columns and drag into my Canvas area:

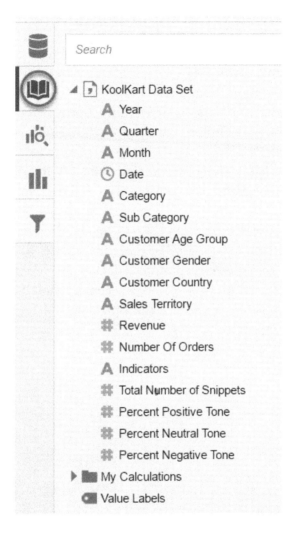

- **Analytics** - lists available analytic highlights that can be added to visualizations like trend lines or outlier highlights:

- **Visualizations** - lists the types of visualizations that can be added to the Canvas:

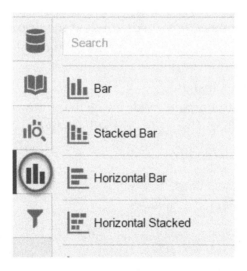

- **Filter Controls** - lists the available filter controls for the query

I'll be going through all of these tabs throughout my mission to save Edward.

## PREPARE PROJECTS

Prepare mode allows me to make changes to the data source from within the project. Prepare mode opens to the Inspect Data Source view. The benefit of Prepare is that I do not have to close the project to edit my Data Source; I can do it right from within Prepare:

### Using Smart Insights

DV Cloud has a cool new feature called Smart Insights that can help get me jumpstarted in my data exploration. Smart Insights provides the following benefits:

- Provides an at-a-glance assessment of the data
- Allows analysts to quickly understand the information the data contains
- Shows how measures are distributed in various attributes
- Provides a starting point for further data analysis

To use Smart Insights,
2. Switch to Prepare mode by clicking the word *Prepare* in the top toolbar. The work area will change to *Data View* (note the ⊞ is highlighted):

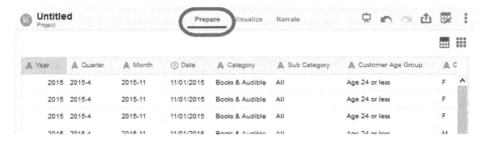

The Data View of Prepare mode allows for the data source to be edited. Calculated columns can also be added.

Depending on the data type of the column selected, the options for calculations change, as shown in image below:

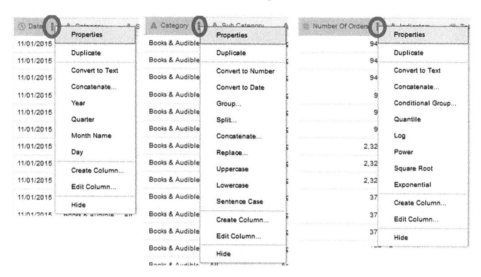

The Visual View of Prepare mode is referred to as Smart Insights. This is accessed by using the Visual icon ▦ in the upper right hand corner. This view allows me to see how the data is distributed across the values of each attribute:

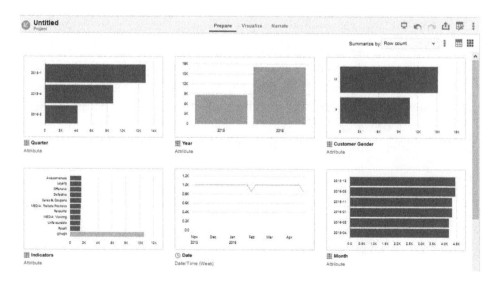

The Visual View can be changed to display the attributes by any of the measures in the data source by changing the *Summarize by* setting:

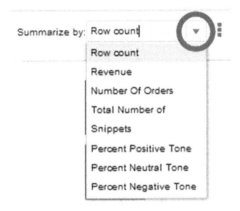

The style of the visualizations align to the type of data in the attribute:

- **Non-numeric or Text** - horizontal bar chart
- **Date and Time** - line chart
- **Numeric** - vertical bar chart

I can choose whether or not I want to show null rows in an attribute. The "include others" option is useful when the data has many different values in an attribute. The number of values on an axis (also referred to as "binning") is limited. Binning is a way to group a number of values into a smaller number of "bins." For example, if I have data about a group of people, I might want to arrange their ages into a smaller number of age intervals:

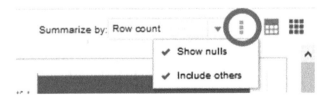

The binning of values on the X and Y axes follow these basic rules:

- Number of bars depends on data distribution
- Normally ten bars are shown and all other data is displayed in a bar called Other
- If 20% or more of the data falls into Other, the system will break that data into the number of bars needed

In reviewing the data, row count does not provide much insight. When I switch the *Summarize by* to Revenue, I start to see some interesting patterns in the data. Quickly I can see that Electronics & Computers have the highest total Revenue:

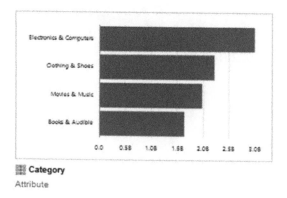

**Category**
Attribute

However, when I look at Revenue by Date, I can see that there is a dip in Revenue in Feb 2016:

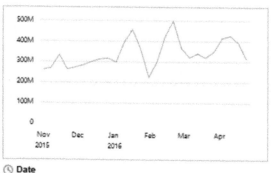

**Date**
Date/Time (Week)

When I switch to Number of Orders I see that the Number of Orders is high for Movies & Music and low for Electronics & Computers:

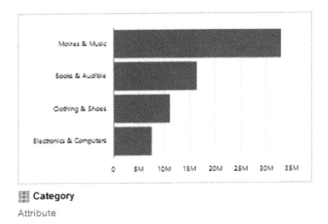

**Category**
Attribute

I see in the Date visualization that the Number of Orders drop considerably in Feb. 2016:

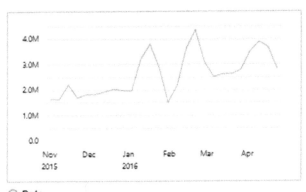

**Date**
Date/Time (Week)

When I switch to Percent Positive Tone, I see in the Category visualization that the Electronics & Computers Category is low:

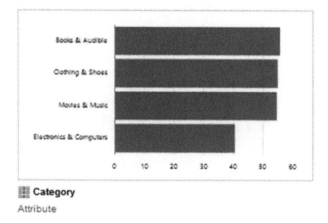

**⊞ Category**
Attribute

When I switch to Percent Negative Tone, I see in the Category visualization that the Electronics & Computers Category is high:

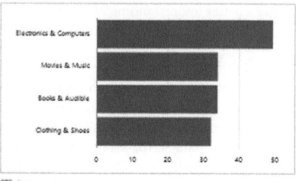

**⊞ Category**
Attribute

The Month visualization shows that Percent Negative Tone is highest in 2016-02 and 2016-03:

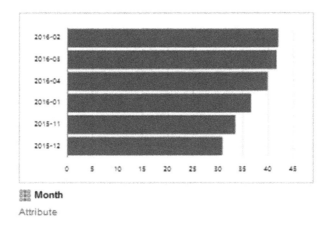

**Month**

Attribute

These Smart Insights are great but they only show one dimension against one measure. Smart Insights give me a place to start exploring the data more efficiently. I will be able to add more than one dimension in DV Cloud to get a better understanding of my data.

## VISUALIZE PROJECTS

Visualize mode allows me to explore my data using a rich library of graphical views. Data Visualization leverages the concept of "Visual Grammar," which is the use of color, shape, size, and location to explore and display data. Visualize mode is the primary work area within a Data Visualization Project. Here, I will create charts and graphs to analyze my data and, as I find patterns that I would like to share with others or use in a presentation, I am able to save them off as Insights. These Insights are then used to help tell a story about my data.

### Create a Visualization

Creating visualizations is actually really easy and intuitive. But when I am writing down the detailed steps and trying to translate easy "click and drag" movements, it can seem like a complicated series of detailed steps. Once you have the basics down, you will be exploring in your sleep. Are you ready?

3.  Within the project, switch to *Visualize* mode:

To create a visualization,

4.  From the Kool Kart Dataset, hold down the control key and select Month and Revenue.

5.  Drag to the area of the canvas that reads *Drop Visualizations or Data Elements Here:*

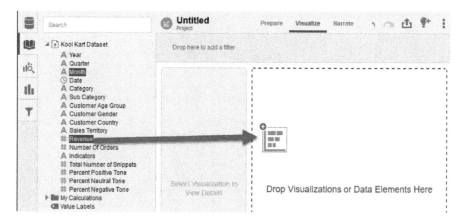

Data Visualization will automatically select the best visualization (although this can be changed at any point):

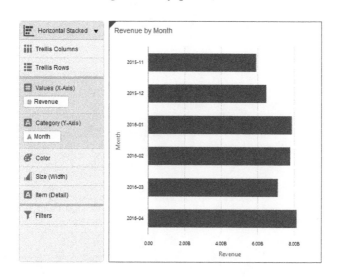

There are a number of ways to add data elements into visualizations:

- Drop data elements into the blank canvas
- Drop data elements in the blank space between two visualizations
- Drop a data element above another data element

One of the Smart Insights showed that Revenue dipped around Feb 2016. I would like to see if I can see which Product Category might be having a problem.

6. Drag *Category* to the Color drop zone:

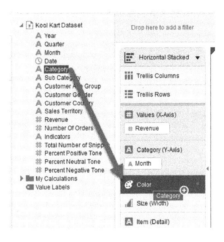

This should result in the following data visualization:

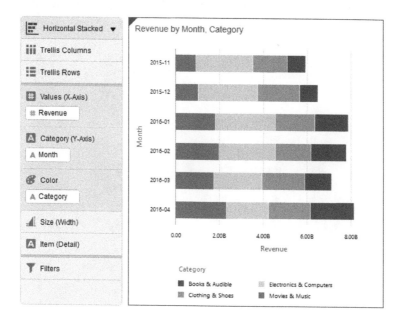

This type of visualization makes it hard to see a trend so I will switch to a different one.

7.  Select the down arrow next to *Horizontal Stacked*. When I select the Horizontal Stacked label, I get a menu of different visualizations to select from:

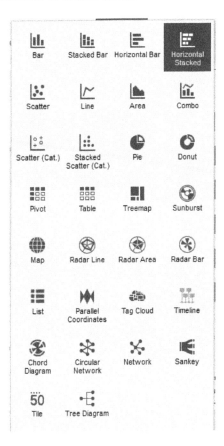

8.  Select *Line*.

Switching to Line graph, I can see that while Books and Audible had a bad Feb 2016, Electronics and Computers appears to be trending downward:

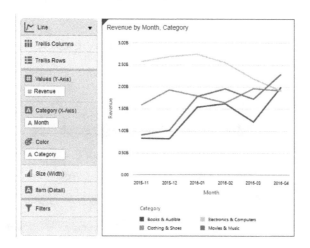

I would like to do a bit more investigation into the revenue before I dive further into the monthly activity. I am interested in Kool Kart Revenue by Sales Territory.

9. Select *Sales Territory* and *Revenue* using Control Key and selecting then drag on to the canvas above the trend chart.
10. A heavy blue line should appear indicating you are inserting above the trend chart:

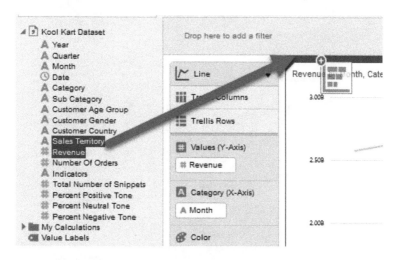

**Note!**  You can move the new section by clicking and dragging to the top, bottom, left or right of the existing sections.

The Horizontal Stacked bar chart is the recommended best visualization for the elements selected:

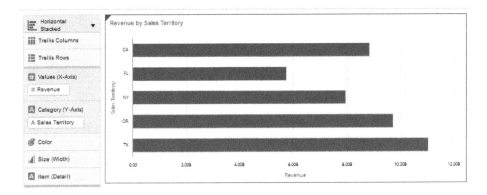

However, I think that geographic data is better viewed on a Map.

11. In the visualization Properties panel, click on Horizontal Stacked to open menu to change visualization and select *Map*:

I think you can agree that that geographic data is better viewed on a Map:

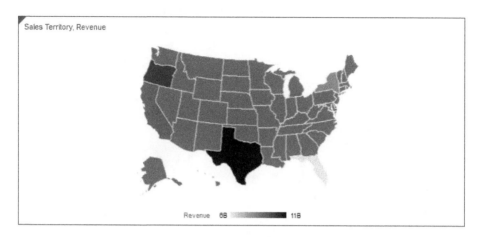

I am also interested in Revenue broken out by Age Group. The two types of charts that best display this type of information are Pie and Donut. The difference is that the Donut chart also displays the total Revenue.

12. Click the ▬▬▬ icon to switch to the *Visualization Menu*:

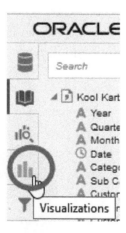

13. Select the *Donut* chart and drag to the canvas so that the thick blue placement line is just left of the Sales Territory Revenue Map (and does not span down along The Sale by Month, Category Chart):

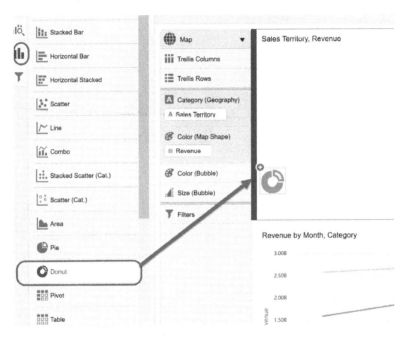

14. Switch back to the Data Elements panel and drag *Revenue* to the Values section and *Customer Age Group* to the Color section:

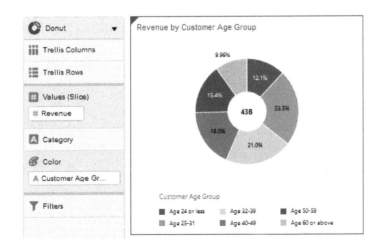

My Project is coming together nicely (your project may look a little different depending on where you dragged and dropped the new visualizations):

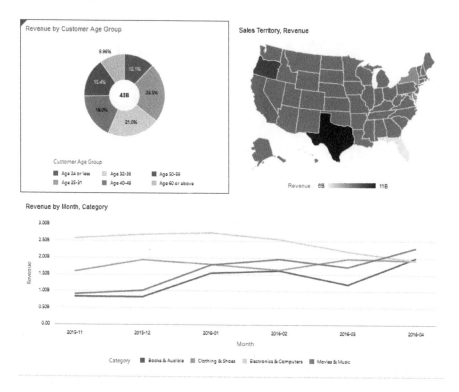

## NARRATE PROJECTS WITH INSIGHTS

As I build my visualizations, I may want to capture a visualization in the DV Project with what Data Visualization calls an Insight. An Insight will capture a snapshot of the current canvas and save it within the project. I can add commentary about the visualization that will be saved with the insight. A DV project may have multiple insights. In my Excel brain, this is like saving a worksheet within a workbook.

Insights can be updated as needed before I am ready to share them with others. I can Include insights in stories (more on stories in just a bit), or just keep them for myself.

My Project has everything I want on it and I would like to capture it for a presentation of my findings:

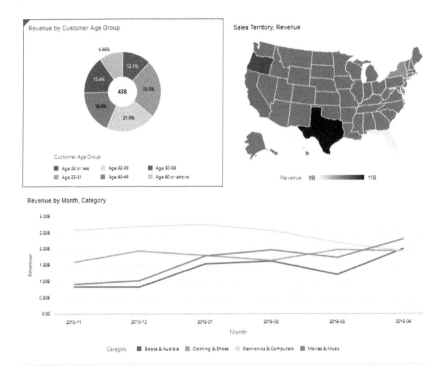

## Create an Insight

To create an Insight,

15. Select the *Insight* icon in the top menu bar:

The Insight is created:

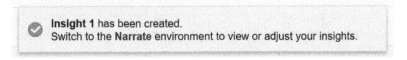

**Insight 1** has been created.
Switch to the **Narrate** environment to view or adjust your insights.

16. Click *Narrate* to switch to Narrate mode:

The Insight is saved to the project with a generic name "Insight#." I can rename this to something more meaningful and add a description as well. The Insight will maintain its own filters, whereas in Visualize mode the filters are shared across all visualizations within the project. The visualization within the Insight can be changed, just like in Visualize mode.

The default display of the Narrate mode has the Explore pane turned off, the Story Navigator pane open, and a new icon in the lower right menu:

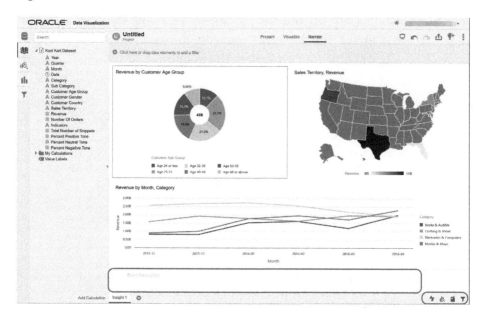

## Present a Story

I normally spend hours (and hours) pasting graphs from Excel into PowerPoint (and then repasting as the data changes). Data Visualization provides a way to "tell a story" with its Story Teller feature.

17. Click the *Story Navigator* icon in the lower right corner

This opens and closes the Story Navigator Note area within the Insight:

18. Right-click on the *Insight* tab to view the context sensitive menu for the Insight. You can Rename, Include in Story, Clear, Duplicate, or Delete the insight:

19. When the mouse is hovered over the right side of the Note area, an Action button will appear:

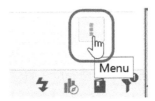

The Story Navigator Menu allows for the Text to be edited, flagged to be included in the Story when Presentation Mode is displayed, and removed:

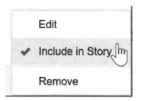

20. Add a note to the insight: "Clothing & Shoes and Electronics & Computers are the main contributors to sales yet do not appear to be trending up as with Movies& Music and Books & Audible despite our social media campaign. Sales appear strong in age groups 25-31 and 32-39 and Texas."

21. In the upper right hand side of the web browser, click to *Save* the project and give it a meaningful name:

## ADVANCED VISUALIZATIONS

DV Cloud provides several ways to update, change, and add visualizations. So far I've used the Explore Panel, which is the main properties screen for the visualization that is displayed:

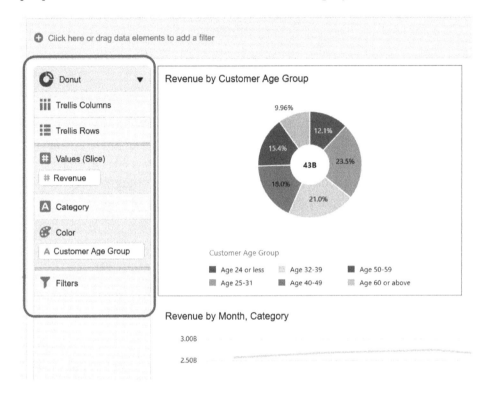

I can also update the visualization via icons within the chart or graph:

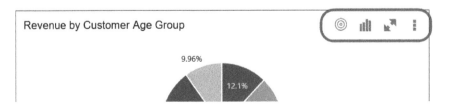

22. Mouse over a visualization (hover the mouse over one of the charts) and click on the *Show Assignments* (bullseye) icon ◎
.

By now I'm getting pretty good at this...

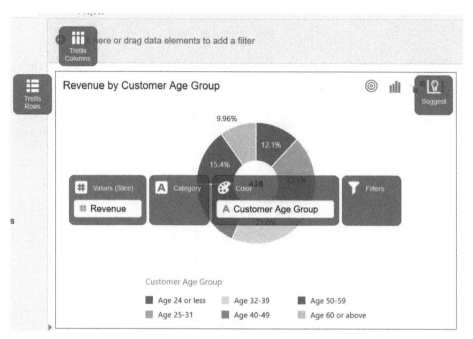

### Adding a Canvas

I can add additional canvases to my DV project. This allows me to keep my original work and expand into additional areas. The ability to add another canvas to the project allows for greater flexibility and allows for the reuse of created calculations and added data sources.

23. Navigate back to Visualize mode.
24. To add another canvas to the project, select the + icon at the bottom left corner of the Project panel:

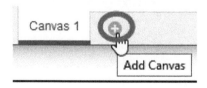

With this canvas I would like to explore the social media activity to see if there may be some indicators to help explain the shift in revenue for Clothing & Shoes and Electronics & Computers. Revenue by Month on the previous canvas is not giving me a complete picture – I need more detail.

25. Select Date and Revenue from the Data Elements panel, right-click and select *Create Best Visualization*:

This chart shows the daily activity of Revenue and I can quickly see that there is big drop in Feb 2016:

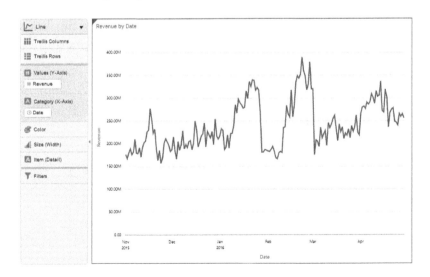

Since I'm interested in Clothing & Shoes and Electronics & Computers, I will filter the canvas.

### Filters

I can create filters in the visualizations at the Project level or at the visualization level. Filters will reduce the amount of data shown (good for performance) and focus on just what I need to see. I may have multiple filters defined and can drag and drop to rearrange them.

I can apply filters of various types including Range, List, Date, and Expression (expression filters are Boolean filters that I create to filter the data).

To add a filter,

26. Select *Category* from Data Elements and drag to *Filter* area:

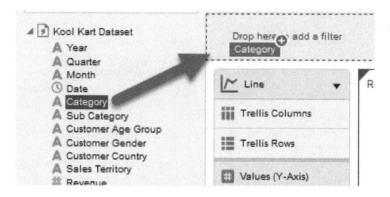

27. In the Category filter, select *Clothing & Shoes* and *Electronics & Computers*:

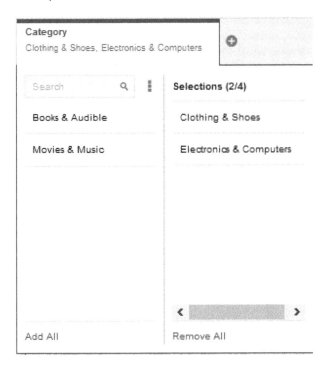

**Note!**  To remove a selection, click it again in the *Selections* pane and it will return to the unselected list.

Now I would like to see the Clothing & Shoes and Electronics & Computers separated out.

28. Drag *Category* from Data Elements to Trellis Columns:

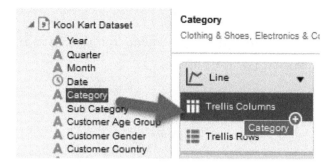

The canavas now shows two different charts within the one visualization:

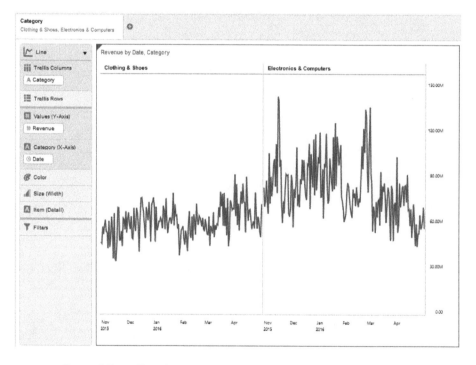

## Copy Visualizations

It can be very helpful and efficient to copy and paste visualizations within a canvas.

To copy a visualization,

29. Click on the properties menu for the visualization. Then select to *Copy Visualization*:

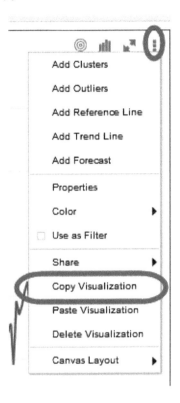

30. Right-click in the space above the Revenue by Date chart and select *Paste Visualization*:

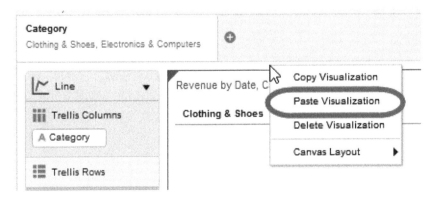

I will use this second chart to view the social media data, but first I need to create a calculated data element:

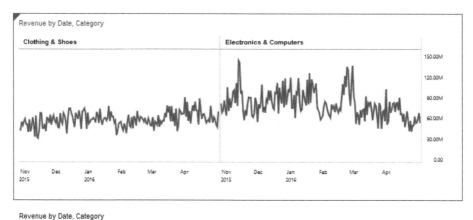

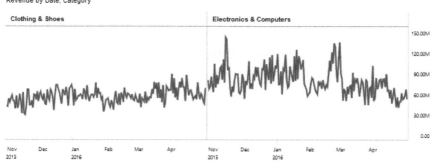

## Calculated Data Elements

Calculated data elements can be added into my DV project and visualizations. Right-clicking on *My Calculations* shows the *Add Calculation...* dialog to create a new calculated data element:

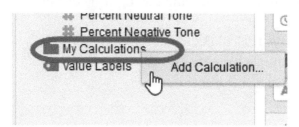

I can then manually build in a calculation expression or use the functions to help create the formula:

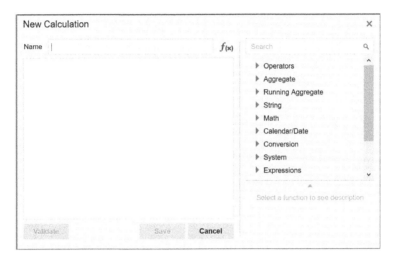

The calculated element will be stored under My Calculations in the left navigation pane and can be added to visualizations:

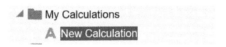

Due to the exponential nature of spikes in activity volume on social media, activity volumes are usually compared on logarithmic scales (an advanced math algorithm for those of you who might not remember calculus class). Log scales help "smooth" the data, addressing issues of skewness in data towards large values; i.e., cases in which one or a few points are much larger than the bulk of the data. Let's add a calculated column for measuring the log scale of snippets volume.

To create a calculated column,

31. Right-click on *My Calculations* and select *Add Calculation*.

32. Name the new calculation *Activity(log scale)*, use the search feature above the functions to find the LOG function and double-click on it to add to the formula editor:

33. Select *Total Number of Snippets* from the Data Elements and drag it into the formula:

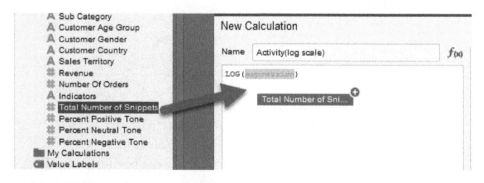

34. Click the *Validate* button in lower left corner to check the syntax of the new calculation:

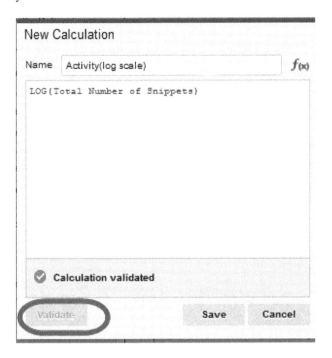

35. Click *Save*:

36. Select the bottom visualization by clicking on it.
37. From the Data Elements panel, select *Activity(log scale)* and drag it on top of the Revenue in the Values (Y-Axis) property. The Revenue element should show a red border and red X in upper corner; this indicates that the element is replacing the current element:

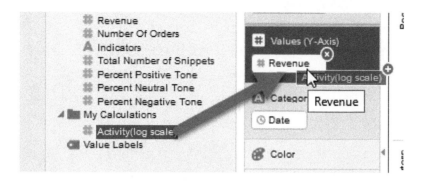

My bottom chart now shows the Social Media snippets related to Clothing & Shoes and Electronics & Computers and the activity seems to correlate to the overall revenue for both Clothing & Shoes and Electronics & Computers:

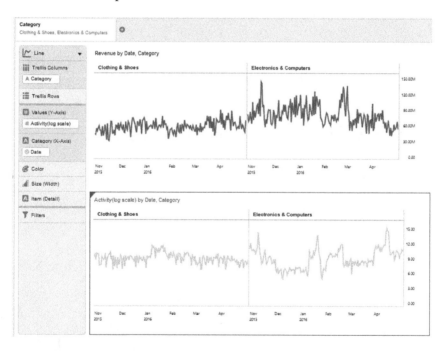

The log scale allows a large range to be displayed without small values being compressed down into bottom of the graph. In the charts below using the Total Number of Snippets I cannot see the activity pattern on days where there is not a lot of posts because the days with a lot of activity skews the chart:

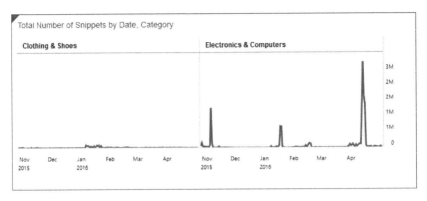

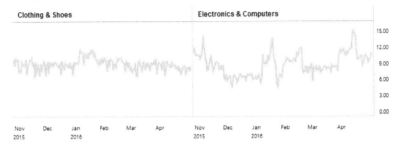

38. Select the *Insight* icon in the top menu bar:

39. Once the insight is created, click *Narrate* to switch to Narrate mode.

40. Click the *Story Navigator* icon in the lower right corner (if the story navigator is not already open):

This opens and closes the Story Navigator Note area within the Insight.

41. Enter a description to the to the insight: "Social Media Snippets related to Clothing & Shoes and Electronics & Computers seems to correlate to the overall revenue for Clothing & Shoes and Electronics & Computers."

**More Visualizations**

I am curious to see how social media tone is trending in comparison to Revenue and Social Media Activity.

42. Toggle back to *Visualize* mode.

43. Copy the bottom visualization and paste it beneath the other two visuals, as shown below:

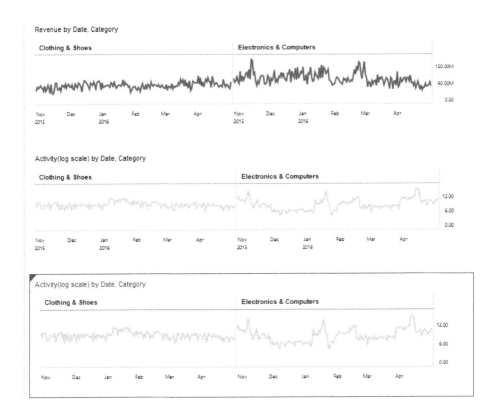

44. Select *Percent Positive Tone, Percent Neutral Tone and Percent Negative Tone* and *drag* to the Values (Y-Axis) and replace Activity(log scale):

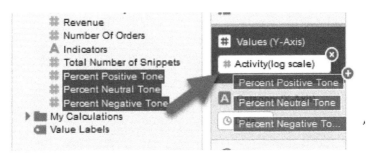

The bottom chart now shows the trend of tonality of the social media sentiment:

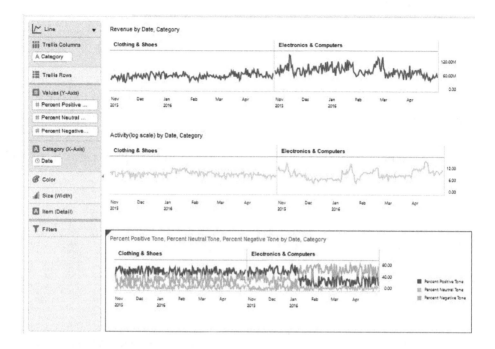

I need to change the chart type for the bottom chart to make it easier to read. I think the Area chart does a good job at displaying this type of data.

45. Change the Line chart to *Area* chart:

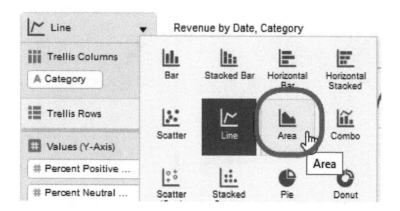

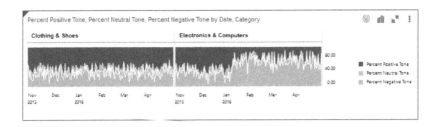

This is better but I think seeing it a bit larger will help me see the data better.

46. Click the *Maximize Visualization* icon in the upper right corner of the visualization:

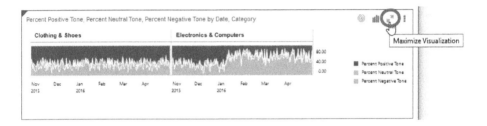

Interesting, as I hover my mouse over the maxized visualization I can see that there is an increase in Negative Sentiment towards Electronics & Computers starting in the 2nd week of January:

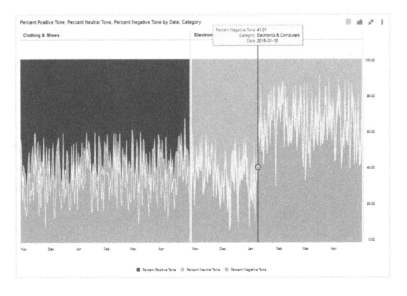

This deserves further investigation; but first I need to return the visualization to its original size.

47. Click the *Close Maximized Visualization* icon:

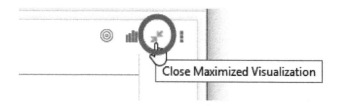

48. Select *Indicators* and *Total Number of Snippets*.
49. Right-click and select *Pick Visualization...*:

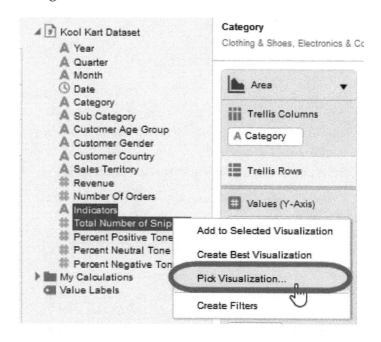

50. Select *Tag Cloud*.

This is also interesting, but I want to focus on Computers & Electronics after mid January:

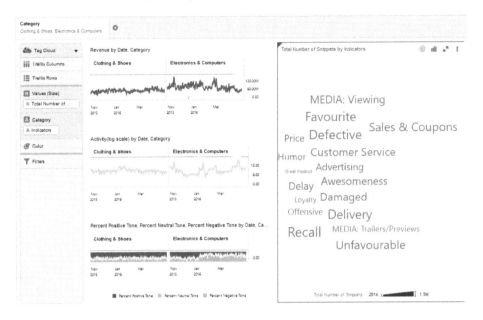

51. Change the *Category* filter to only *Computers & Electronics* by clicking on *Category Filter*.

52. Select *Clothing & Shoes* and it will unselect it:

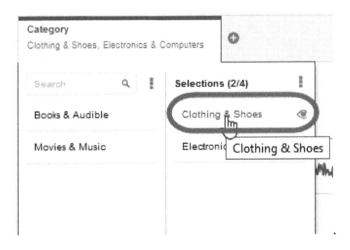

53. Drag *Date* to Filter and set Start Date to *Jan 09, 2016* and End Date to *Apr 29, 2016*. Click anywhere outside of the filter window to close filter:

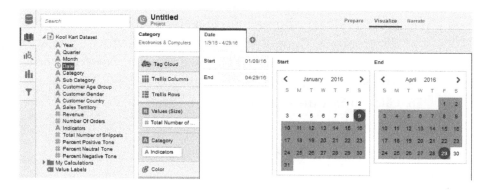

I would like to investigate which of the Indicators have a high Negative Sentiment.

54. With the Tag Cloud graph selected, select *Percent Negative Tone* and drag to *Color* property of the *Tag Cloud*:

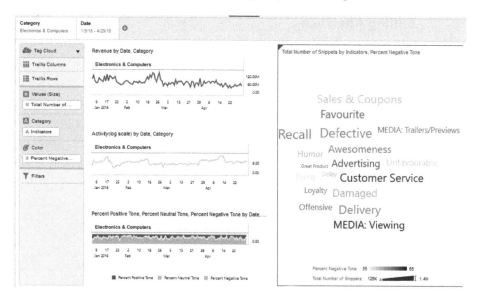

In looking at the size of the tag, I see that indicator words like "Defective" and "Recall" are frequently mentioned and by looking at the darker color I can see that "Customer Service" and "MEDIA: Viewing"

seem to be contrbuting to the bulk of negative sentiment. This is a good time to add another insight.

55. Using the steps covered above, add an Insight with a note: "Social Media shows high negative sentiment related to Electronics & Computers starting in mid-January. Negative comments are in the area of Customer Service, Recall, MEDIA: Viewing, and Defective."

56. Click to *Save* the project:

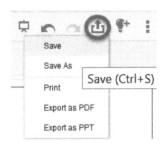

### Adding Analytics

DV has a variety of built in analytics that work with different visualizations. These analytics can be accessed via the side menu by dragging them into the canvas:

They also can be activated via the properties of a selected visualization:

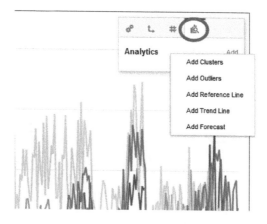

Or by right-clicking within a visualization:

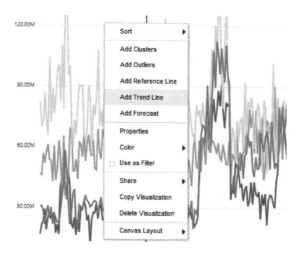

I would like to see how Revenue by Product has tracked and what a 30 day forecast might look like.

57. Add a new canvas to the project:

58. Reset the filters to display all product categories and all dates.

59. Using the Line visualization, create a simple visualization showing Revenue by Date and display color by Category:

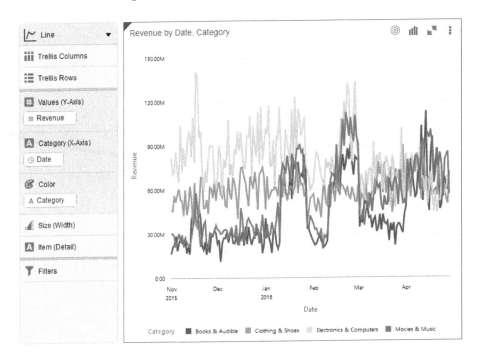

Let's add a trend line to see how the Revenue is trending.

60. Right-click anywhere in the visualization and select *Properties*.

61. Click on the *Analytics* icon:

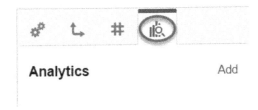

62. Click *Add* then from the menu select *Add Trend Line*:

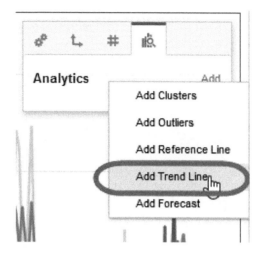

The visualization will change:

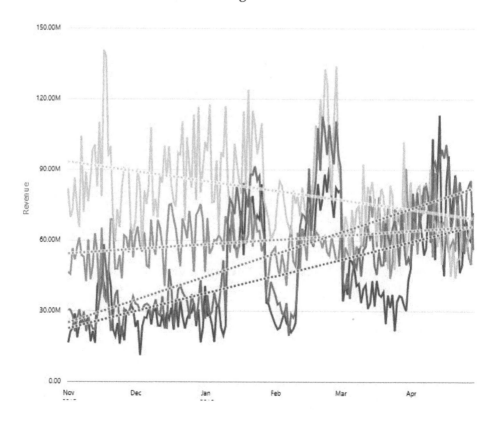

This visualization is a bit muddy and difficult to interpret.

63. Move *Category* from Color to *Trellis Rows*:

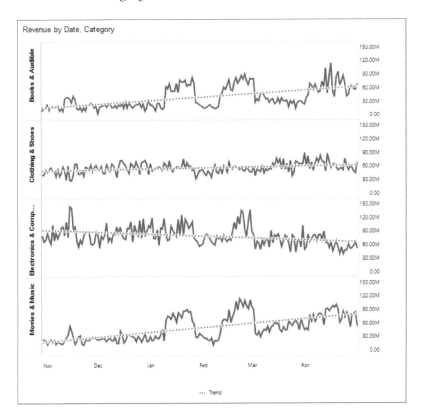

This trend line is helpful to see overall how the revenue has been trending, but there is one more analytic function that I would like to use. Since I have used Date on the X-Axis I can use the Forecast function.

64. Right-click anywhere in the visualization and select *Properties*.
65. Click on the *Analytics* icon to navigate to the Analytics section.

66. Click *Add* then from the menu select *Add Forecast* and set the Periods to 30:

The visualization will update. Now this is interesting. I can see that the 30 day forecast for Clothing & Shoes, while trending slightly up, looks to pretty flat:

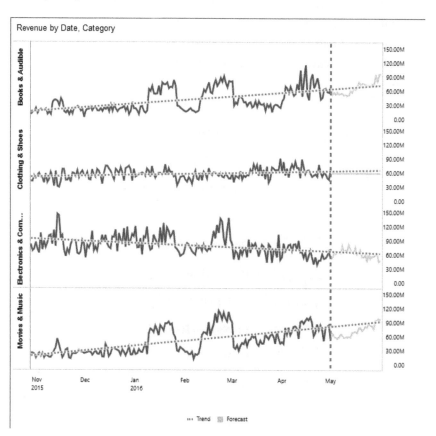

### Explore

At any time I can click the *Explore* icon to toggle on and off the visualization definition pane:

The idea is that once my visualizations are set, I am ready to explore!

### Synchronize Visualizations

By default, *Synchronize Visualizations* is turned on. This is part of the Brushing concept within DV. Brushing allows for selecting a data value in one visualization and seeing related data highlighted in other visualizations on the same canvas. If I click on an element in one visualization, it will automatically update and sync with other visualizations. I can see how the change will apply in other visualizations. I can turn this off if desired (if I want a change to apply to a single visualization and not the entire Project):

## Other Ways to Add Data Elements to Visualizations

So far I've done a lot of clicking and dragging, which is great, but there are other ways to add data elements to a visualization. I can control-click (hold Ctrl and click) to select multiple data elements and then right-click to select *Add to Selected Visualization, Create Best Visualization,* or *Pick Visualization...*:

## Clear Canvas

At any point, I can clear the canvas of the visualization that I am working on and start over within the project. If I have a visualization that I want to save, I can add an insight. Once the insight is added, I can clear my canvas and start with a new exploration.

To clear the canvas,

67. To start over or "clear the canvas,, select the ⋮ icon in the upper right hand corner (or right-click in the visualization).

68. Select *Clear Canvas:*

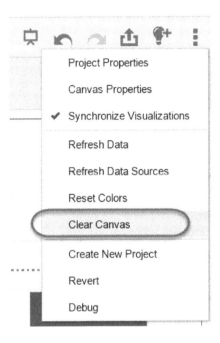

I can start a new visualization within the DV project.

## BLEND DATA

Blending data is the joining of two or more files or sources for data exploration. I can blend data in DV Cloud a number of different ways. I've already shown one of the ways when I created a Data Flow. I can also blend data from within a project.

My current exploration has shed light on a bunch of issues, but I would like to further analyze this data by Regional and Territorial Managers:

|   | A | B | C |
|---|---|---|---|
| 1 | Regional Manager | Territory Manager | Territory |
| 2 | Cliff | Sam | CA |
| 3 | Cliff | Diane | OR |
| 4 | Norm | Rebecca | NY |
| 5 | Woody | Carla | TX |
| 6 | Woody | Frasier | FL |

### Add a Data Source to a DV Project

In order to do this, I need to blend another data source into this project. My VP of Sales, Ron G., has provided me a spreadsheet with the latest listing of Regional and Territory Managers, "Territory Manager Assignments.xlsx." I will store it in a local folder for easy retrieval.

To add a new data source to a project,
69. Right-click on *Kool Kart Dataset*.
70. Select *Add Data Source…*:

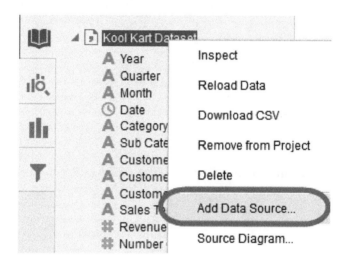

71. Select *Create New Data Source*.
72. Select *File*.
73. Navigate to where the "Territory Manager Assignments.xlsx" file is stored.
74. Select the file and click *Open*.

The file will open in Prepare mode of the Project:

| A Regional Manager | A Territory Manager | A Territory |
|---|---|---|
| Cliff | Diane | OR |
| Cliff | Sam | CA |
| Norm | Rebecca | NY |
| Woody | Carla | TX |
| Woody | Frasier | FL |

75. Click *Add* to add the file to the Project:

| | | |
|---|---|---|
| Name | Territory Manager Assignments | Owner |
| Description | Uploaded from Territory Manager Assignm | Created   In Progress |
| Uploaded File | Territory Manager Assignments.xlsx | Modified   In Progress |
| Sheet | Sheet1 | Refreshed   Never |

76. At the bottom of the screen, switch the view to *Source Diagram*:

77. The source diagram shows the two data sources with a zero in the link between. *Click* on the link:

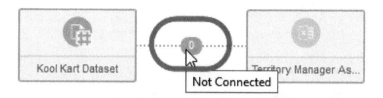

The Connect Sources dialog will open, displaying the connection between them. Since there is no connection I will add one.

78. Click *Add Another Match*:

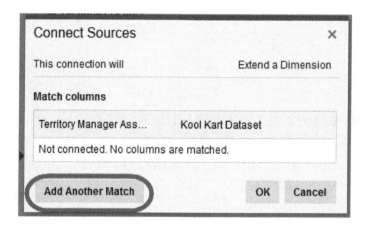

79. Click *Select Column* under Territory Manager Assignment and select *Territory* from the list of data elements:

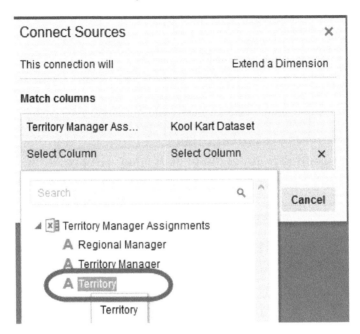

80. Select Sales Territory from the Kool Kart Dataset list and then click *OK* to save the connection:

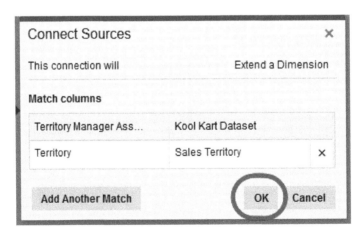

Now my data sources are joined together:

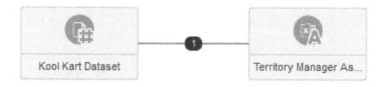

In the Data Elements panel I now see the Territory Manager Assignments file:

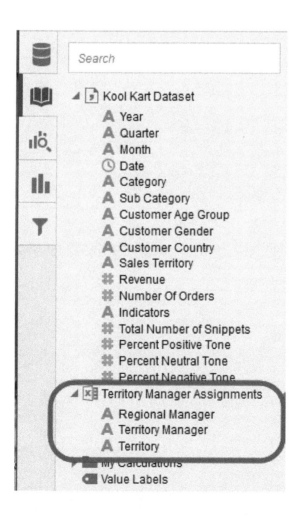

**Create Visualization with Blended Data**

To blend data,

81. Switch over to *Visualize* mode.

82. Add another canvas to the project by selecting the + icon at the bottom left corner of the Project panel:

83. Select the *Visualizations* icon in the left side menu and double-click *Pivot*:

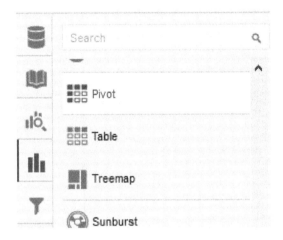

84. Switch back to the Data Elements tab on the left side menu by selecting .

The canvas will set up with the appropriate drop zones for the Measures and Attributes:

85. Drag *Territory Manager* to Rows and *Revenue* and *Number of Orders* to Values:

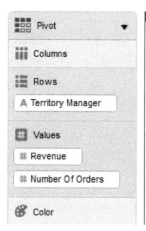

Revenue, Number Of Orders by Territory Manager

|         | Revenue           | Number Of Orders |
|---------|-------------------|------------------|
| Carla   | 11,032,601,606.88 | 84,913,629       |
| Diane   | 9,708,689,413.53  | 74,722,467       |
| Frasier | 5,736,952,835.43  | 44,154,015       |
| Rebecca | 7,943,473,155.51  | 61,136,805       |
| Sam     | 8,826,081,285.30  | 67,928,301       |

86. Drag *Category* below Territory Manager in Rows:

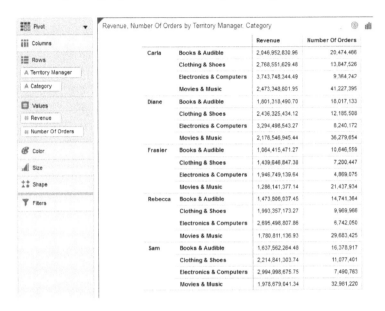

| | | | Revenue | Number Of Orders |
|---|---|---|---|---|
| | Carla | Books & Audible | 2,046,952,830.96 | 20,474,466 |
| | | Clothing & Shoes | 2,768,551,629.48 | 13,847,526 |
| | | Electronics & Computers | 3,743,748,344.49 | 9,364,747 |
| | | Movies & Music | 2,473,348,801.95 | 41,227,395 |
| | Diane | Books & Audible | 1,801,318,490.70 | 18,017,133 |
| | | Clothing & Shoes | 2,436,325,434.12 | 12,185,508 |
| | | Electronics & Computers | 3,294,498,543.27 | 8,240,172 |
| | | Movies & Music | 2,176,546,945.44 | 36,279,654 |
| | Frasier | Books & Audible | 1,064,415,471.27 | 10,646,559 |
| | | Clothing & Shoes | 1,439,646,847.38 | 7,200,447 |
| | | Electronics & Computers | 1,946,749,139.64 | 4,869,075 |
| | | Movies & Music | 1,286,141,377.14 | 21,437,934 |
| | Rebecca | Books & Audible | 1,473,806,037.45 | 14,741,364 |
| | | Clothing & Shoes | 1,993,357,173.27 | 9,969,966 |
| | | Electronics & Computers | 2,695,498,807.86 | 6,742,050 |
| | | Movies & Music | 1,780,811,136.93 | 29,683,425 |
| | Sam | Books & Audible | 1,637,562,264.48 | 16,378,917 |
| | | Clothing & Shoes | 2,214,841,303.74 | 11,077,401 |
| | | Electronics & Computers | 2,994,998,675.75 | 7,490,783 |
| | | Movies & Music | 1,978,679,041.34 | 32,981,220 |

87. Select the Visualizations  tab on the left side menu.

88. Drag the *Sankey* option to the main canvas area:

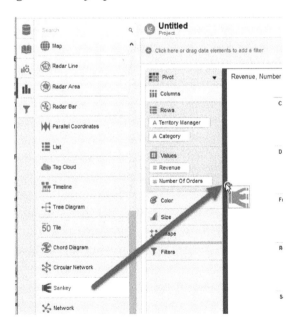

89. Toggle back to the Data Elements ![] tab on the left side menu.

90. Drag *Territory Manager* to *Category*.

91. Drag *Category* beneath *Territory Manager*.

92. Drag *Revenue* to *Color*.

93. Drag *Number of Orders* to *Size*:

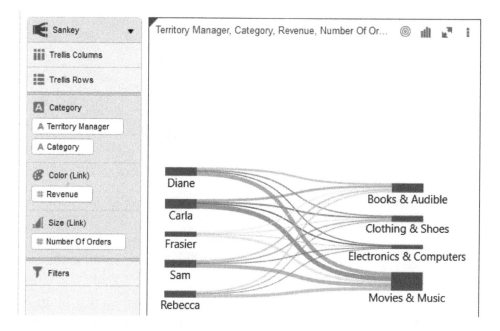

The Sankey chart allows me to see a variety of measures within one visualization. I can quickly see that Carla and Diane have more Orders based on the size of the bar above their name. I can also see that Music & Movies make up more Orders than the other categories.

By using Color and Size on the Sankey chart I am able to quickly see that Diane and Carla had more Movies & Music Orders  but higher Revenue with Electronics & Computers:

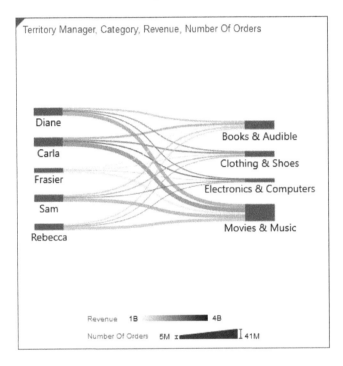

Data Visualization has a powerful feature named Brushing. As mentioned before, Brushing allows for selecting a data value in one visualization and seeing related data highlighted in other visualizations on the same canvas.

To use Brushing,

94. Select *Carla* in the Sankey chart (note how the row with Carla is highlighted in the Pivot):

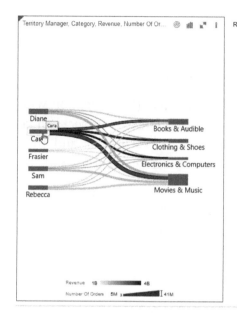

95. Select *Music &Movies* in the Sankey chart, note how the rows with Music &Movies are highlighted in the Pivot:

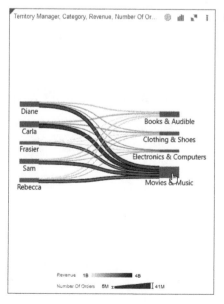

96.  Add an Insight and a note in the Story Navigator Note area: "Diane and Carla appear to be out performing others. Need to look into sales performance with Frasier, Sam, and Rebecca."

97. Save the Project.

## SHARING DATA VISUALIZATIONS

Sometimes there is a need to share a created visualization with someone who may not have access to the technology. A Project can be shared by clicking the *Save Project* icon in the menu bar and then selecting to either print or export the project. I'm going to export my project as a PDF:

I can also share individual visualizations within a Project as well.

### Export Visualizations

After first selecting to export, a second menu will open, allowing for selection of what to include in the Export.

I can select only Canvas pages or Story pages; all pages, current page, a range of pages or none:

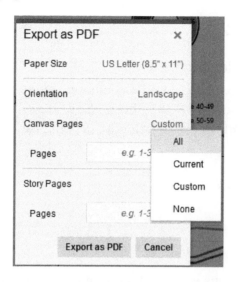

An individual visualization can also be shared by clicking the Actions icon in the upper right corner of the visualization. Notice that this sharing feature has an additional Data option:

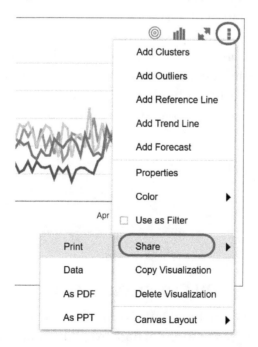

**Note!** Content shared as PPT will export in .PPTX format and the canvas or visualization will be embedded as a static image.

### Present Visualizations

I can also switch to Presentation Mode, which is a more streamlined presentation of the visualizations. I can't edit the visualizations while in presentation mode, but I can easily toggle in and out of this mode.

98. Click the *Presentation Mode* icon:

All extraneous working menus and icons are hidden and a clean user interface is presented.

99. Click the *Presentation Mode* icon again to get out of Presentation Mode.

I can set a project to be view-only for all users by changing the parameter "reportMode=presentation" in the project URL. I can then share that URL directly with other DV Cloud users by e-mail or instant message. The screen shot below shows the default version, which is not view-only:

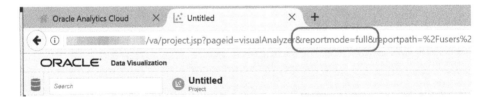

## DV Cloud and Essbase

So I've shown how DV Cloud can create some pretty cool presentations and explorations of data from files that I upload. I can also use DV Cloud to connect directly to Essbase Cloud cubes in my OAC instance. I can do this via a couple of routes. I can navigate to Data Sources and select the desired Essbase cube (considered a Database), or I can create a new project and select the desired Essbase cube at that point. I will create a connection to my Essbase Cloud instance. Once the connection is created, I can then add different Essbase cubes as different Databases within Data Sources.

To complete my mission to save Edward, I need to create some visualizations for The Beverage Company and Sample.Basic. Gone are the days of just showing plain ol' numbers!

The overall steps to connect an Essbase Cloud cube to DV are:

1) Create a connection to the Essbase Cloud instance (one time step)
2) Create a Data Source with a type of Database for each Essbase Cloud cube
3) Create a DV project and select a single Essbase Database Data Source

### Create an Essbase Connection

To create a connection to the Essbase Cloud instance,

1. From the DV home page, select the *Data Sources* card.
2. Select *Connection* under *Create:*

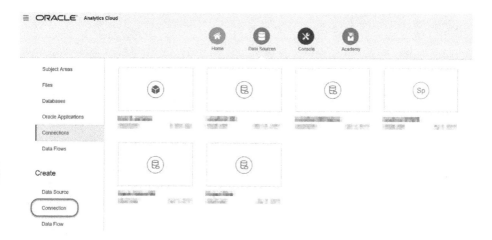

3.  Select *Oracle Essbase (Beta)*:

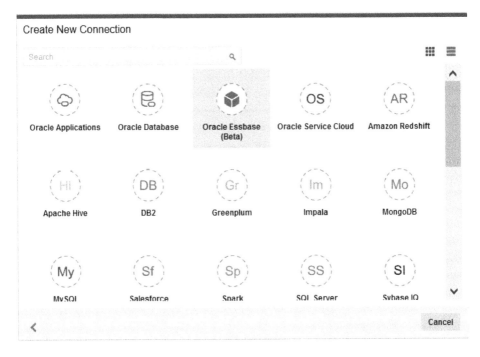

4.  Enter the name for the Essbase Cloud instance connection (I'm going to call mine "EssCS").
5.  Fill out the required login credentials for Essbase Cloud. For the DSN field, use the URL for OAC but point to port 1423 instead.

6.  Change to the authentication option to *Require users to enter their own username and password*:

Add a New Connection

Oracle Essbase Database (Beta)

*New Connection Name   EssCS

*DSN   http://████████:1423

*Username   ████████

*Password   ████████

*Authentication   ◯ Always use this username and password
◉ Require users to enter their own username and password

‹                                                    Save    Cancel

7.  Click *Save*.

I only need one connection for each Essbase Cloud instance. Note that I cannot create DV Projects using an Essbase Cloud connection. I can only *Edit* or *Delete* Essbase connections:

EssCS ████          Localhost DB
cloud.user          2 days a⌐   Edit
                                Delete
                                Create New Data Source

### Create an Essbase Cube Data Source

I've created a connection to Essbase Cloud but I haven't actually created a Data Source (which is required to query data in DV Projects). I'll create individual Data Sources for each Essbase Cloud cube.

To connect to an Essbase cube in my OAC instance,

8.   From the DV Home interface, select *Data Sources.*

9.   Select *Data Source* under *Create:*

10. Choose the Essbase connection for the Essbase Cloud instance (I choose EssCS):

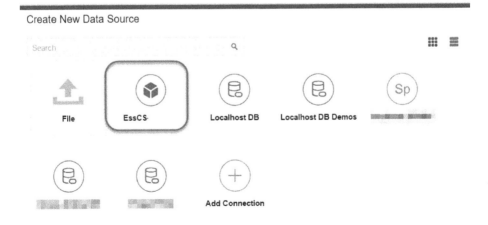

11. Select *Sample.Basic* from the list of available Essbase Cloud cubes:

KoolExp.KoolExp       KoolKart.Sales       Sample.Basic       Sample_Dynamic....

12. Click *OK*.

The cube now becomes a Data Source (with a type of Database) that I can use in one or more DV Projects.

### Create a DV Project with Essbase Cloud Cube Data Source

To create a project with an Essbase Cloud data source,

13. Navigate back over to the DV home page.
14. Click *Project* under *Create*:

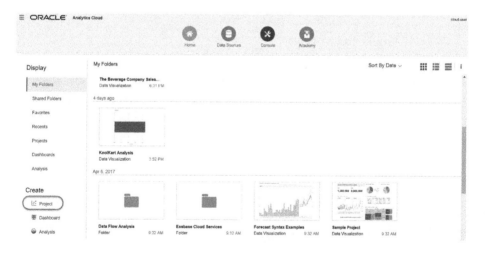

15. In the *Add Data Source* dialogue, select the *Data Sets* tab.

16. Select the Sample.Basic Data Source:

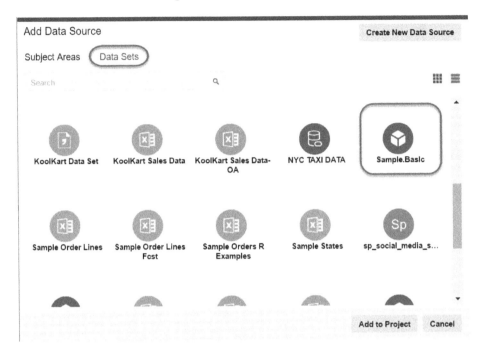

17. Click *Add to Project.*

Sample.Basic is added as a Data Source for the new project. Remember I can only have one Essbase cube data source in a DV Project:

18. To view the details behind the Essbase cube, right-click on Sample.Basic and select *Inspect:*

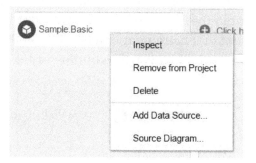

19. The Data Source Name, Connection Type, Connection Name, and Cube Name are displayed:

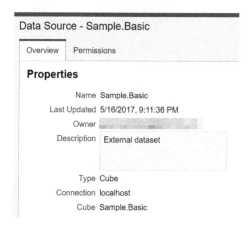

20. Click *Cancel.*

I'm ready to explore and analyze!

### Visualize

Let's explore how the Essbase cube has been added into DV Cloud.

21. Now that Sample.Basic has been added as a data source to the project, click the Data Elements 📖 icon (if not already there).

By default, an Essbase Cloud cube data source will list the facts (usually the Measures/Accounts dimension, the one tagged as Accounts) as the first element in the data source columns. I also know this because it's the only element that has a pound symbol (#) in the name. Then the rest of the dimensions will be listed in outline order. In Sample.Basic I have just a few accounts:

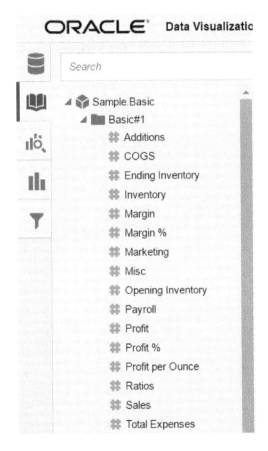

Just by looking at the way the other dimensions are structured, I can see that they've been brought into DV Cloud in generational format:

TBC named the generations Months and Quarter back in the cube definition in Essbase Cloud for Sample.Basic, and as you can see below, those assigned generation names are brought across into DV Cloud:

### Dimensions

| Name |
| --- |
| Year |
| Measures |
| Product |
| Market |
| Scenario |
| Caffeinated |
| Ounces |
| Pkg Type |
| Population |
| Intro Date |

Storage Type: Dense

Dimension Type: Time

Generations

| Number | Name |
| --- | --- |
| 1 | History |
| 2 | Quarter |
| 3 | Months |

This is also true for the Product and Market dimensions:

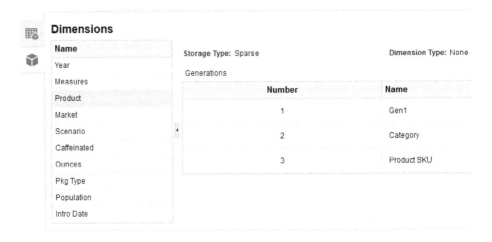

The User Defined Attributes (UDAs) for Market are also brought over as columns:

Attribute dimensions are available for analysis as well:

22. Select *Sales* from Basic#1, *Quarter* from the Year dimension, and *Product SKU* from the Product dimension. Hold Ctrl and left click to select all three columns at the same time.

23. Drag the columns into the Canvas area:

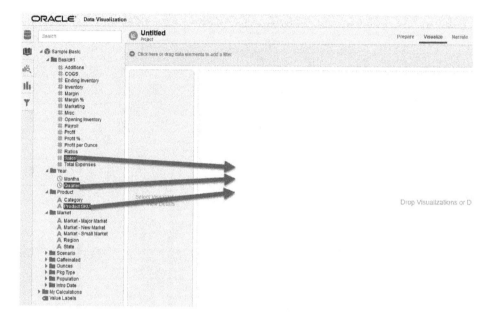

The data is displayed in a line chart visualization by default:

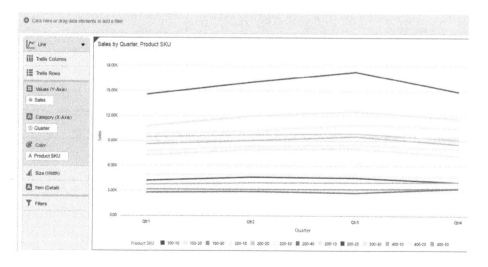

24. Click the *Change Visualization* icon (hover mouse over the image to see the icon description):

25. Select the Bar chart:

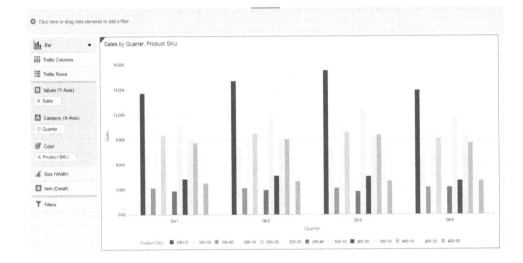

26. Drag *Region* from the Market dimension into the Trellis Columns section:

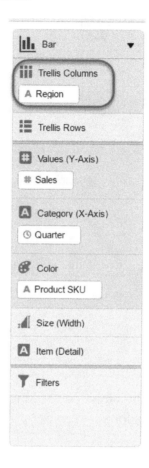

I now begin to see interesting patterns in the data. The East is doing very well while South sales are significantly less. What is going on in the South?

### Add a Filter

Using my newly acquired filtering skills, I'll add a filter to this data. As mentioned before, these filters will apply to the entire canvas and any insights that I create.

27. Drag *Region* to the Filter section of the Canvas:

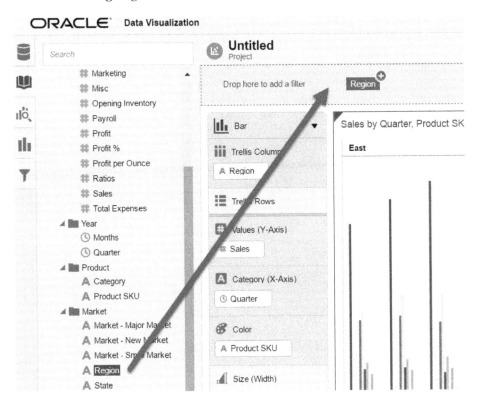

28. Select *South* (the worst performing region) and *East* (the best performing region).

The visualization is now filtered for East and South only.

29. Drag *Quarter* from Category to *Trellis Rows*.

30. This is becoming challenging to read in bar mode. Change the visualization type to *Pie*:

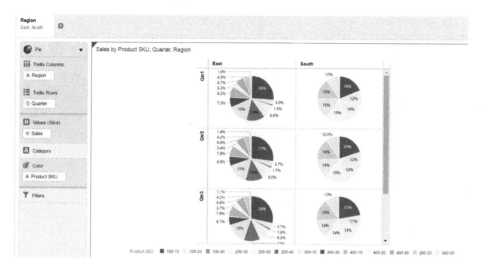

My visualizations are looking great! Before I go too much farther, I should probably save my project.

31. Click the *Share Project* icon in the upper right hand corner above the canvas. Select *Save:*

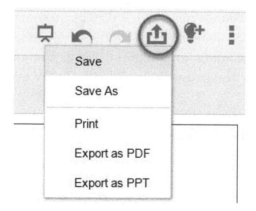

32. Name the DV Project and optionally add a description. I saved my project as "The Beverage Company Sales Analysis":

33. Click *OK*.

**Add an Insight**

I have a web meeting set up with TBC to show these analyses to them. I'd like to add some narrative to these visualizations and create a story for our upcoming presentation. I will use my awesome new Insights and Story Navigator skills to do this in DV Cloud.

To add an Insight,

34. Click the *Add Insight* icon:

The Insight is saved to the project with a generic name "Insight#." I can rename this to something more meaningful and add a description as well.

35. Click *Narrate*:

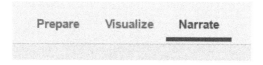

36. At the bottom, right-click on the "Insight 1" tab and select *Rename*:

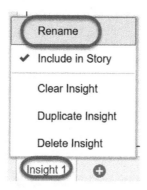

37. Name the insight "Sales Comparison East (Best) vs. South (Worst)" and click the check button:

38. Click the *Story Navigator* icon  in the bottom right hand corner.

39. Enter a description or comment on the visualization:

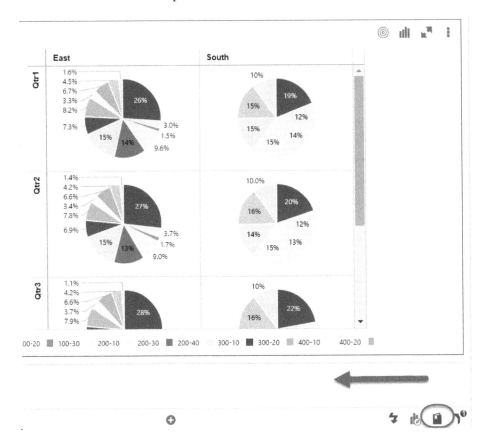

40. Select *Visualize* to navigate back to the working Canvas.

41. Delete *Quarter* from the Trellis Rows section:

42. Change the visualization to *Treemap*:

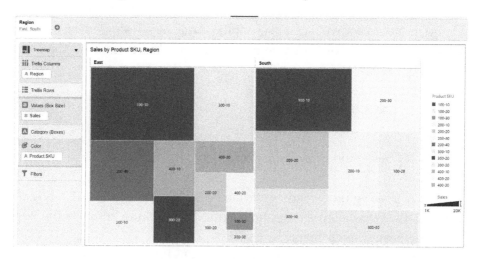

43. Click the *Add Insight* icon:

44. Click *Narrate*:

45. Right-click on the "Insight 2" tab and select *Rename.*
46. Name the insight "No Sales in South for…"
47. Click the *Story Navigator* icon 🔖.
48. Enter a description for the insight: "No Sales in South for Products 200-40 and 400-10. After speaking with the regional manager, product launch for these products has been delayed due to XYZ.":

No Sales in South for Products 200-40 and 400-10. After speaking with the regional manager, product launch for these products has been delayed due to XYZ.|

Comparison East (Best) vs. South (Worst)   No Sales in South for ...   ➕

### Present an Essbase Story

Now that I've made quick work of visualizations using Essbase Cloud as a data source, I can present the data! As I discussed earlier, DV Cloud has some cool "story telling" features. I'll now show them off using my Essbase cube source.

To use Story Navigator,

49. Select the *Presentation Mode* icon:

A presentation-ready interface displays within DV. I navigate through the two insights that I have added by clicking between the dots at the bottom of my screen:

So while I can export visualizations to PowerPoint and PDF and print them, why not just use the Presentation Mode to share insights with others?

This method will always have the latest data flowing through:

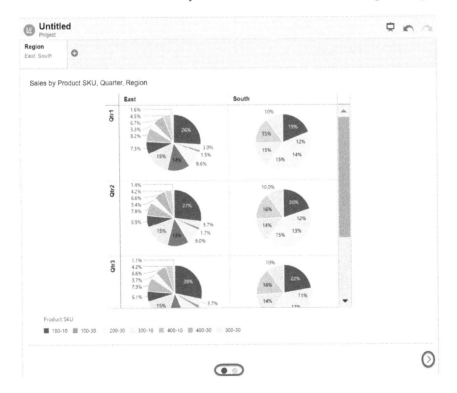

50. Select the *Presentation Mode* icon again to toggle back to Prepare/Visualize/Narrate mode.

### Add a Calculation

I can also add additional calculations to my OAC Essbase cube source just like I did for an uploaded file. The steps are the same. These calculations will only exist in the DV Cloud project where it is created. For example, I'm going to create a metric that calculates the total number of projects in Sample.Basic.

To add a calculated column to a DV project for an Essbase source,

51. Add a new canvas to the project.

52. Right-click on My Calculations and select *Add Calculation*:

The Calculation Editor will display. I can type the syntax for the calculation directly into the open space or I can search the available functions:

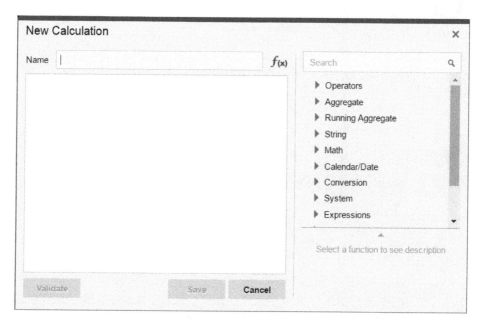

53. Type the name "Payroll % of Total Expenses" into the Name field.

54. Drag *Payroll* from the data elements expression editor:

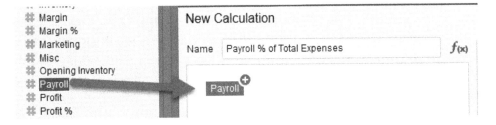

At the time this was written, the syntax could not be directly keyed into the expression editor. It must either be drag and dropped, as shown above, or selected within a function, as shown below:

**Note!**

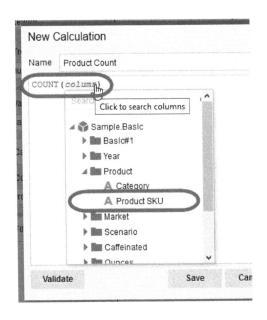

55. Type in the division symbol "/" or expand the Operator from the right side of the menu and select from the list:

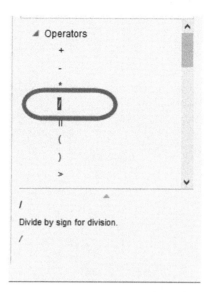

56. Drag *Total Expenses* from the data elements expression editor so that the syntax reads: Payroll/Total Expenses:

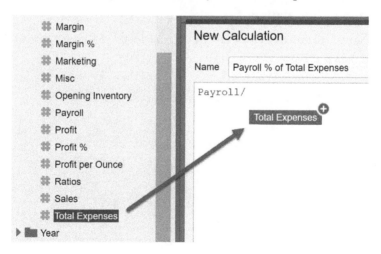

57. Click *Validate* to ensure the syntax is valid:

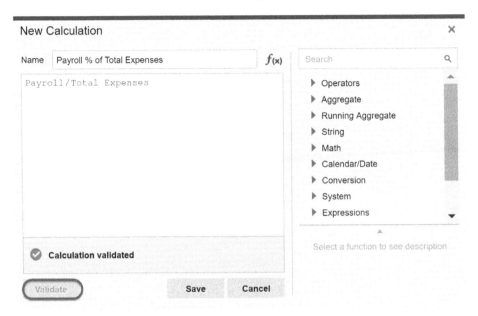

58. Click *Save* and the calculated column is created.

### Use a Calculation

Now I'll put my calculation into action. I'd like to see the Payroll % of Total Expenses for each state.

59. Switch to *Visualizations* menu >> select *Table* >> drag onto the canvas:

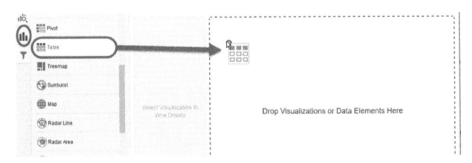

60. Switch back to the Data Elements view.

61. Drag *State, Total Expenses, Payroll,* and *Payroll % of Total Expenses* to Rows in the Table Explore panel:

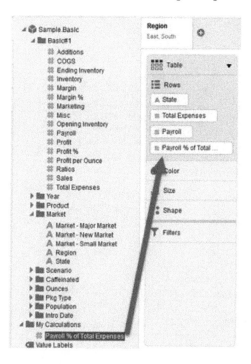

It makes more sense to have the "Payroll % of Total Expenses" column formatted as a percent. This is a quick and easy property change.

62. Right-click the visualization and select *Properties*:

63. Move to the *Values* tab, expand *Payroll % of Total Expenses*, and change the Number Format to *Percent*:

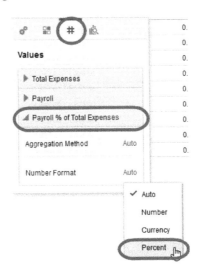

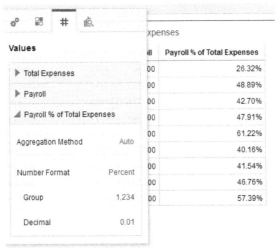

Now I can see my Total Expense, Payroll, and Payroll % of Total Expense for each state in the East and South (remember I still have a filter on, which I will remove shortly):

State, Total Expenses, Payroll, Payroll % of Total Expenses

| State | Total Expenses | Payroll | Payroll % of Total Expenses |
|---|---|---|---|
| New York | 8,914.00 | 2,346.00 | 26.32% |
| Massachusetts | 3,412.00 | 1,668.00 | 48.89% |
| Florida | 5,564.00 | 2,376.00 | 42.70% |
| Connecticut | 4,083.00 | 1,956.00 | 47.91% |
| New Hampshire | 3,337.00 | 2,043.00 | 61.22% |
| Texas | 4,041.00 | 1,623.00 | 40.16% |
| Oklahoma | 4,333.00 | 1,800.00 | 41.54% |
| Louisiana | 3,625.00 | 1,695.00 | 46.76% |
| New Mexico | 3,659.00 | 2,100.00 | 57.39% |

This is good information, but it would be easier to see which states are doing better than others by sorting from highest value to lowest.

64. Click the *Sort* icon next to Payroll % of Total Expenses and select *High to Low*:

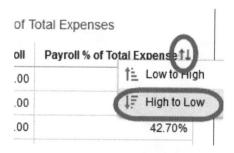

That's better! But a table showing the states does not make it easy to see if there is a pattern in certain parts of the country. A map view would help.

65. Switch to the *Visualizations* menu >> select *Map* >> drag onto
    the canvas:

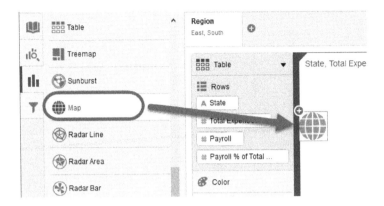

66. Switch back to the *Data Elements* 📖 view.
67. Select *State* beneath Market and drag to the Category area on
    the Map Explore Panel:

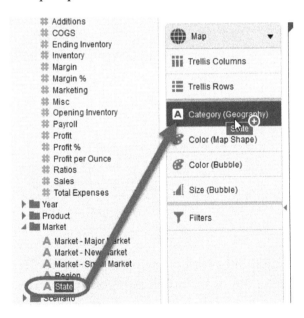

68. Select *Payroll % of Total Expense* and drag to the Color area on the Map Explore Panel:

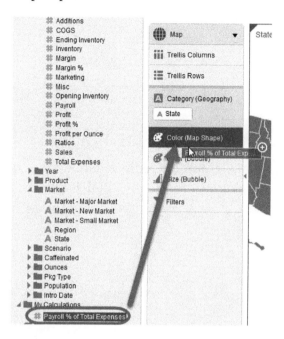

Now my visualization is nice and easy to interpret:

69. The canvas is still filtered to the East and South regions. To see all of the states, click on the menu for the Region Filter and select *Disable*:

I now have a graphical representation of which parts of the country have a higher Payroll % of Total Expenses, along with the numbers in a table:

DV Cloud and Essbase together are a good pair of tools for analysts who are looking for trends and data patterns. I can quickly create charts and graphs with Essbase data.

### Things to Know about DV and Essbase

In these early releases of OAC, it is important to note a few things about Essbase Cloud cube sources, DV Cloud, and available functionality:

- The dimension tagged as Accounts "flattens" out to be the Measures fact "table"; meaning, this will be a flat list of accounts (with no sense of hierarchy)
- DV Cloud brings in generational columns for all other dimensions (no parent-child support or "value" hierarchy support)
- A single Essbase Cloud cube per DV Cloud project is allowed
- It's not possible to join any other data source or file into a DV project that already uses an Essbase Cloud cube
- One can view only member names (no aliases)
- DV Cloud does not allow "drillable" actions nor hierarchies
- UDAs are brought in as columns that can be visualized
- Attribute dimensions are brought in as columns that can be visualized
- I can add calculated columns

## ASSIGN SECURITY

Assigning and managing security for DV is similar to the other Oracle Cloud products. I create users in My Services and provision roles. The DV pre-defined user level roles include DV Content Author and DV Consumer. Once a user has been provisioned for DV in My Services, I can then assign object-specific access for catalog objects (folders, projects, data sources, etc.). For more details on creating users in My Services, please review Chapter 3, "Launch Into the Cloud".

### Users, Roles, and Application Roles

DV Cloud application roles determine what users can see and do after they log into one of the DV solutions. OAC supports pre-defined application roles and user-defined application roles:

- **BI Service Administrator** - application role that allows users to administer Oracle Analytics Cloud and delegate privileges to others using the Console. This role also inherits membership of the other application roles. This role is the main Administrator role for BI Cloud (in Enterprise Edition) and DV features; it does not apply to Essbase Cloud.

- **DV Content Author** - application role that allows users to create visualization projects, load data for data visualizations, and explore data visualizations
- **DV Consumer** - application role that allows users to explore data visualizations

DV application roles are assigned in the DV Cloud Console. I select the *Console* card:

Under *Console* from the DV header, I can view tabs for *Users, Roles,* and *Application Roles*:

I see the provisioned DV users listed under the Users tab. I can modify users, prompt users to change their password, manage their application roles, and remove users.

Under the Roles tab, I can create and manage custom roles for my users (this is sort of like a security group):

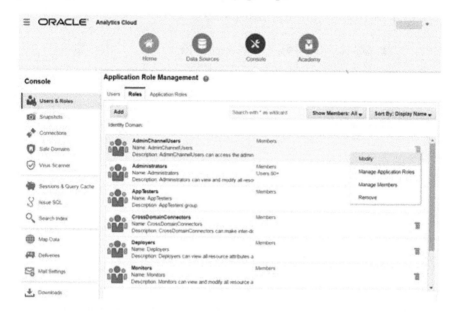

The Application Roles tab is where I assign the OAC Application Roles (in the case of DV, DV Content Author, or DV Consumer):

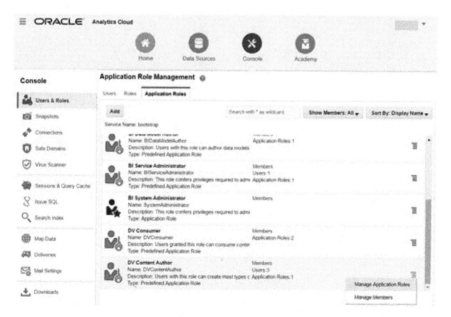

I click the ⬛ icon and see two options: *Manage Application Roles* and *Manage Members.* Under Manage Application Roles, I can add or remove other roles to the Application Role:

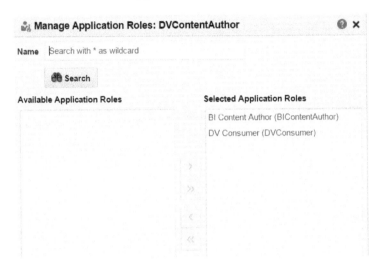

Under Manage Members, I can add or remove users to and from the Application Role:

## Assign Object Permissions

The final step in the security process is to assign object-specific access.

To assign artifact access,

1. Log into the DV Cloud URL.
2. Under Home, click the link to *Open Classic Home:*

From the Classic Home view, under Recent, I see my recent Projects (and other analyses and dashboards if I have OAC Enterprise Edition). I can also select *Catalog* and navigate the folder structure to search for a project.

3. For a project, select *More.*
4. From the drop-down, choose *Permissions:*

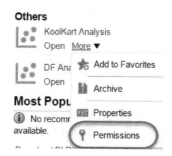

I can edit, add, and remove permissions for the artifact in the Permissions dialogue:

5.  Click the + icon to add access for a new user.
6.  Select *Search* to see a list of users.

I can search for users, roles, and application roles and assign access. Once the user/role/application role is selected, I can assign the type of security:

- Full Control
- Modify
- Open
- Traverse
- No Access
- Custom

Most of these roles are self-explanatory. Traverse is the tricky role and is really applicable for OAC Enterprise Dashboards. For example, I can grant users the Traverse permission for the Sales folder in the shared folder area. Users who have Traverse for this folder can access items embedded in dashboards stored in this folder. Also, they can access embedded items in dashboards stored in sub-folders, such as the /<shared folder area>/Sales/Guest folder.

However, users can't access (view, expand, or browse) the folder and sub-folders from the Catalog in the Classic Home interface.

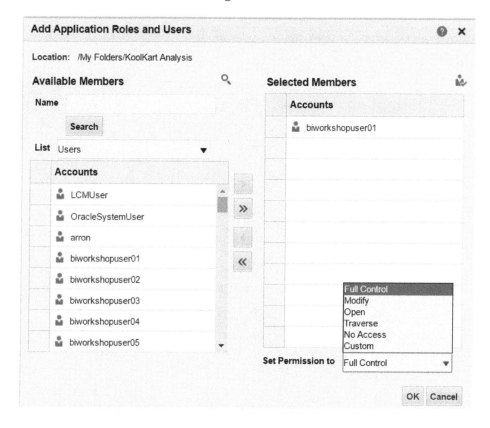

7. Select a user and assign them *Open* access.
8. Click *OK*.

Now that I've completed the security for the DV part of the mission, am I done? Not quite. I need to review a few administrative tasks for DV that will help make the mission a sustainable success.

## MANAGE DATA SOURCES

Let's take a moment and review a number of tasks related to managing data sets and sources.

From the OAC home page, navigate to *Data Sources* from the main OAC header:

1.  Click the *Option* icon on any Data Source to view the available tasks:

 The options available will depend on the data source type selected.

**Note!**

### Inspect

As mentioned before, the *Inspect* action allows me to view information about the uploaded file, including who uploaded it and the last time it was loaded. I can update the description, any attribute or measure assignments for columns, and aggregation tags for measures. I can also assign permissions for data sets from the *Inspect* menu option (which I covered in the Security section by clicking the *Permissions* tab).

### Reload Data

I can also reload data as new data comes in. Let's do that for a flat file data source.

1. If not already there, navigate to *Data Sources* from the main DV Cloud home page:

2. On the left pane, filter by type *Files*:

3. Click the *Option* icon on any of the Data Sources listed and select *Reload Data*:

4.  Select the file and click *Upload*. A message will be displayed with the number of records loaded:

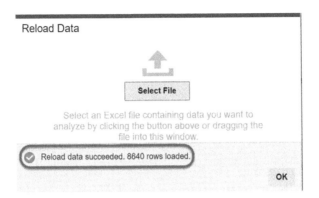

## Delete and Download

I can delete a data source at any time or re-download it to Excel.

1.  If not already there, navigate to *Data Sources* from the main DV Cloud  home page:

2.  Click the *Option* icon and select *Download CSV* or *Delete* (depending on what you would like to do with the data source):

## MANAGE VISUALIZATIONS

The best place to manage visualizations is in the Classic Home Catalog section. Here I can manage folders (Expand, Delete, Copy, Rename, Create Shortcuts, Define Properties, and Assign Permissions) and DV Projects:

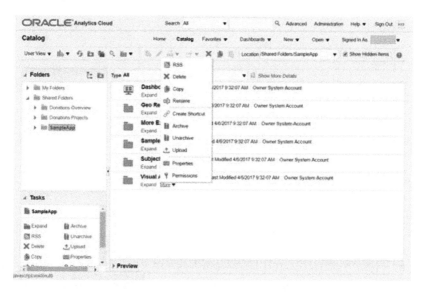

I can Open or Edit DV projects, Delete, Copy, Rename, Add to Favorites, Create Shortcut, define Properties, and assign Permissions.

## DV CLOUD CONSOLE

OAC Service Administrators can manage DV Cloud in the Console. There must always be at least one user who is a Service Administrator.

Here is the Console:

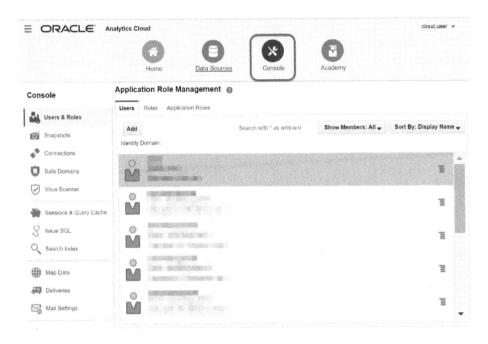

I've already covered *Users and Roles* in the Security section. Other administration activities that can be performed here include: managing snapshots, sessions, index settings, and more.

### Snapshots

While Oracle does backup my Cloud instance, I may want to take snapshots periodically. A snapshot captures the current state of the DV Cloud environment at a single point in time. The snapshot contains the data model, catalog content (like analyses, dashboards, filters, etc.), and application roles and security assignments. Snapshots may be downloaded from and uploaded to DV Cloud. I'll use this feature if I purchase multiple environments and want to migrate content between them.

To create a new snapshot,

1.  Navigate to *Console* from the main DV Cloud home page:

2.  Click on *Snapshots*:

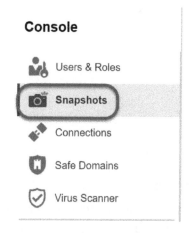

3.  Click on *New Snapshot*:

4.  Enter a description and click *OK*:

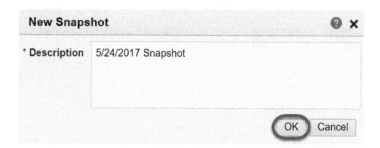

Once a snapshot is taken, I can *Restore, Download, Delete, or Edit* the snapshot through the action menu next to the snapshot:

 Up to 10 snapshots may be stored online.

**Note!**

## Manage Sessions

To view and manage active sessions (who has logged in and for how long) in DV Cloud, jump to *Sessions & Query Cache* from the Console. I can view all sessions or filter sessions for a specific user using the Filter option:

*Manage Sessions* is mostly for troubleshooting, especially when dealing with analyses and queries against a database. I can see how long a query takes to run. If there is an error, I can get more information by looking at the log for that session.

## DV CLOUD ACADEMY

I couldn't possibly cover all of the how to's and detailed steps for Data Visualization and Data Visualization Cloud Services here.

To continue my learning experience, do not miss the Academy area which will provide documentation, videos, tutorials, and more on all things Oracle Analytics Cloud:

```
LOG ENTRY FOR VISUALIZATION PILOT WAYNE VAN SLUYS
SOL 30


      Mission Data Visualization complete. Man, that
was  way  easier  than  I  thought.  Of  course,  I  didn't
mess it up. Edward, here we come!
```

# EPILOGUE

**Meanwhile, back on earth...**

"Crap," Danielle said. "We still haven't communicated out to anyone that Edward and the project are alive beyond i.n.t.e.r.R.e.l. and JWE? You've got to be kidding me."

Director Chang glared across the room and said, "You know you could really work on your language, Danielle." He refrained from commenting on her seemingly small vocabulary or habitual expressions.

"You don't have to face those darn i.n.t.e.r.R.e.l. supporters like Mike Janik and Bill Mowle. We should have told them when we first knew the project was alive. Now we have to share this Earth-shattering news to the world along with the update that the Ranger crew successfully completed their Oracle Analytics Cloud Standard Edition mission."

This was going to be rough and Danielle knew it. Not only did she have to deliver the biggest mea culpa in i.n.t.e.r.R.e.l.'s history, but every second would be remembered forever (well, maybe for fifteen minutes). She was confident that none of the concern showed in her voice as she leaned into the computer microphone on i.n.t.e.r.R.e.l.'s regularly-scheduled, free webcast.

"Thank you all for attending today. We have an important announcement to make. We have viewed recent Oracle EPM Cloud logs and have confirmed that Consultant Edward Roske and the Vision implementation are, currently, alive. In fact, he has successfully implemented Oracle PBCS in just a few sols."

"Now the crew of the Ranger is on their way back to try and rescue Edward. They've completed their Oracle Analytics Cloud Standard Edition portion of the mission and are one step closer to retrieval after being catapulted around the Earth. If everything goes according to plan, we'll have Edward rescued once we complete the OAC Enterprise Edition mission (coming soon)."

After one full second of utter silence, the webcast chat session exploded with questions.

---

**COMMUNICATION: ROSKE TO MCMULLEN**

Hi Commander. After working with each other for over 12 years at i.n.t.e.r.R.e.l., I think I know you pretty well (except that I didn't know about your '90s hip hop obsession). I'm guessing you still blame yourself for my situation but please don't. You were faced with an impossible scenario and had to make a decision (even worse than the budget we had back on that one client where they were shooting for 80% higher than the prior quarter actuals).

And it's all going to be OK (I think). You guys have completed the Oracle Analytics Cloud Standard Edition Mission. You solved Juggling Wolverine Enterprise's problems, building Essbase cubes in the Cloud for TBC and KoolKart, analyzing data in Excel with Smart View, and visualizing data with "Data Viz." And now you are currently being hurtled through space to rescue me in the Cloud.

To finally reach me, you'll have to complete the Oracle Analytics Enterprise Edition mission. With all that has happened, what else could possibly go wrong?

Stay cloudy, my friend.

# INDEX